A Hands-on Introduction to

BIG DATA ANALYTICS

T0323437

A Hands-on Introduction to

BIG DATA ANALYTICS

Funmi Obembe and Ofer Engel

§ Sage

1 Oliver's Yard
55 City Road
London EC1Y 1SP

2455 Teller Road
Thousand Oaks
California 91320

Unit No 323-333, Third Floor, F-Block
International Trade Tower, Nehru Place
New Delhi 110 019

8 Marina View Suite 43-053
Asia Square Tower 1
Singapore 018960

Senior commissioning editor: Ruth Stitt
Assistant editor: Charlotte Hegley
Assistant editor, digital: Benedict Hegarty
Production editor: Nicola Marshall
Proofreader: Richard Walshe
Indexer: C&M Digitals
Marketing manager: Lucia Sweet
Cover design: Francis Kenney
Typeset by: C&M Digitals (P) Ltd, Chennai, India
Printed in the UK

Library of Congress Control Number: 2023941596

British Library Cataloguing in Publication data

A catalogue record for this book is available from the British Library

ISBN 978-1-5296-0009-4
ISBN 978-1-5296-0008-7 (pbk)

TABLE OF CONTENTS

DEDICATION

Dedicated to my sons – Oluwatoni & Inioluwa

– Funmi Obembe

Dedicated to Sam Jama

– Ofer Engel

DETAILED TABLE OF CONTENTS

LIST OF CASES

ABOUT THE AUTHORS

Funmi Obembe is Head of Technology at the University of Northampton, UK where she leads on the strategic development and operational management of the subject area which covers Computing, Engineering and Games programmes. Prior to going into full time academia, she worked in the technology industry/health informatics sector for many years as a data professional. Funmi is passionate about bringing together in teaching and research both theoretical aspects of technology and their practical applications. Her main research areas are in technology enhanced learning, open data/big data analytics, knowledge management and machine learning algorithms for knowledge representations.

Ofer Engel is a data scientist and educator at the University of Groningen. His main interest lies at the intersection between causal inference in the social sciences and applied philosophy. He studied networks in organisations and has worked as an investigator for a number of European funded projects on responsible research and innovation.

ACKNOWLEDGEMENT

I am extremely grateful for the support of my family throughout the process of writing this book. My husband, Demola, has always been one of my greatest cheerleaders, and I am immensely grateful for that. I am also thankful to my sons, brothers, parents, and friends, whose support has been relentless. I want to express my gratitude to the anonymous reviewers who provided comprehensive and useful feedback on all the chapters of the book. A big thank you to the team at Sage as well. Finally, this acknowledgment would not be complete without expressing my appreciation to my past and current students at De Montfort University and the University of Northampton. You make knowledge sharing a joy always.

Funmi Obembe

PREFACE

Recent decades have witnessed a rapid development of technologies, infrastructures, techniques, and processes enabling big data. These have all proven to be great enablers of big data analytics. In 2006, Clive Robert Humby, a British mathematician and entrepreneur, suggested that 'Data is the new oil', a precious resource whose value can be extracted through a process of refinement to fuel the world's economies. Over the years, this metaphor has proven itself time and time again. Universities are increasingly delivering modules and programmes on big data analytics across their faculties. This has been driven to a large extent by the demand for and shortage of data professionals in the industry.

The emergence of big data analytics has brought about radical changes in various sectors, such as healthcare, finance, and retail, and with it we see a growth in the demand for data professionals. Universities and private companies are investing to help society meet this demand, launching new programmes and courses designed to upskill data professionals and a wide range of related fields such as the 'Internet of Things', data science, artificial intelligence, causal inference, econometrics, and big data analytics.

But the rise of data analytics hasn't fuelled just businesses. The collection of data, its interpretation and the application of new methods have a real and lasting effect on people like you and me: our lives, our health, our relationships, and our careers. The impact on people's lives is not always of their choosing, and the sense that people are losing control has raised debates about the ethical consequences of data. The realization that numerical analysis can have ethical and even political consequences is not new, but in recent decades this realization has moved from the margins of critical cultural studies into the mainstream of numerical analysis, an urgent issue discussed throughout this book.

A wide range of textbooks today seek to cover these topics, especially in data science and machine learning. However, most textbooks are written at a high level of abstraction, rarely preparing readers to address real business problems. Employers must therefore resort to a costly onboarding process to prepare new hires for the job. In contrast, our textbook moves part of this process to higher education. Our focus is to bring readers to a level where they can hit the ground running as data professionals in this area. To achieve this, we combine theoretical foundations with an emphasis on applying big data analytics, illustrated with real-life use cases, examples, and exercises, using real-life data (e.g., from open data portals). The book uses open-source technologies (such as Anaconda Navigator and Jupyter), so readers can use the book without purchasing proprietary software.

This book focuses on tools of the trade and their implications, the actual architecture and design of distributed computing. For example, we discuss the management of large datasets, the specific skills required for developing data models and algorithms that process data, and the interplay between on-premises data analytics platforms and cloud computing services.

Since Python is one of the most popular languages in use among data professionals, we use many examples written in Python and the Python variant of Apache known as Spark (i.e., PySpark).

A second distinguishing feature of this textbook is its approach to data ethics. Instead of viewing ethics as an add-on encapsulated in a dedicated chapter, we interweave ethical principles and their applications throughout the text to cultivate an attitude of 'ethics by design' rather than 'ethics as an afterthought'. This is done by including a feature where a relevant case study or ethics-related issue is discussed in each chapter. One such case study is the UK's National Health Service (NHS) care data scheme, which was a programme that was designed to improve the safety and care of NHS patients by linking patient information across all health providers for a complete picture. The aim was to use these linked datasets for research purposes, hoping to improve health performance. However, despite its laudable objectives, the NHS data initiative proved to be very controversial, with some of the criticism centred around a lack of patient awareness of the programme and how to opt out. Since then, more importance has been given to transparency and accountability regarding personal data. Other examples that highlight the need for ethics by design include cases with algorithmic bias, such as that highlighted in the UK 2020 A-level results, where, due to the Covid-19 pandemic, grades were generated based on an algorithm. The bias highlighted in the algorithm, in this case, was that the grades generated by the algorithm appeared to favour those from independent/private schools while penalizing students from disadvantaged backgrounds.

THE STRUCTURE OF THE BOOK

The book is structured into 12 chapters. Chapter 1 introduces big data analytics and discusses its enablers and challenges. It also explores the key concept of ethics by design in big data analytics. Chapter 2 covers basic big data analytics concepts, such as data gathering and wrangling. The big data technologies to be used in the text are also discussed in this chapter. Chapter 3 then introduces Apache Spark, a unified analytics engine used for large-scale data processing, which is used extensively in this book. Chapter 4 builds on the previous chapter and focuses on big data storage, particularly the Hadoop Distributed File System (HDFS) and NoSQL (which stands for 'Not Only SQL') technologies. In Chapter 5, the use of cloud computing for big data analytics is presented and discussed. This is increasingly becoming the preferred way of handling big data analytics for organizations, so data professionals must be conversant with the ideas. Real-world examples and the more common architectures and security issues are discussed in this chapter. This also includes an introduction to the three main service models of cloud computing – Infrastructure as a Service (IaaS), Platform as a Service (PaaS) and Software as a Service (SaaS) – and the advantages of cloud computing for big data. Chapter 6 looks at how big data analytics is used to draw out insights. This includes insights drawn through exploratory, descriptive, diagnostic, predictive, and prescriptive analytics across various sectors. Chapter 7 covers graph analytics and its use of various algorithms to explore the relationships between entities. Chapter 8 is devoted to the important topic of big data analytics and machine learning. Machine learning algorithms are a subset of artificial intelligence crucial in solving many big data analytics problems. This chapter covers the more common machine learning algorithms used for big data analytics, including algorithms that fall under the categories of supervised, semi-supervised, and unsupervised. Chapter 9 introduces natural language processing (NLP), which falls under machine learning and provides methods to help analyse the contents of natural textual data and large amounts of unstructured data, and is increasingly becoming more important in big data analytics. This chapter introduces this important aspect of big data analytics and then covers aspects of NLP such as sentiment analysis, topic modelling, and tokenization using NLP libraries. Chapter 10 focuses on real-time big data analytics, which involves processing and drawing insights from data as the data is received (streamed). This chapter covers both the theoretical aspects of real-time big data analytics and also focus on hands-on applications. As we approach the end of the book in Chapter 11, big data visualization is covered. Visualization goes hand in hand with data analytics; this is particularly true with regard to big data. Visualization is important in drawing out insights from data. This chapter uses various visualization libraries and visualization-based data discovery tools to produce various visualizations. Techniques such as what type of visualization to use in various scenarios and how to interpret the results are also covered. This chapter summarizes some earlier visualization approaches as various analytics techniques were treated. These include using libraries such as matplotlib, gmplot, and PixieDust. Having covered various important aspects of big data analytics in the preceding chapters, the book ends with Chapter 12 by revisiting what has been achieved in the field and looking forward to future possibilities. Challenges that are yet to be resolved are also highlighted. These challenges include moving away from black-box machine learning models with the emergence and progress in explainable AI.

PEDAGOGICAL FEATURES

The following features have been included in each chapter to support learning. These are represented with icons throughout the book.

- Chapter objectives
- Ethics by design feature
- Industry insights feature
- References and annotated further reading
- Test your knowledge

ONLINE RESOURCES

This textbook is accompanied by online resources to aid teaching and support learning. To access these resources, visit: https://study.sagepub.com/obembe.

A *Teaching Guide* providing practical guidance, support, and additional materials for each chapter.

PowerPoint slides that can be downloaded and adapted to suit individual teaching needs.

1

INTRODUCTION TO BIG DATA ANALYTICS

CHAPTER CONTENTS

CHAPTER OBJECTIVES

In this chapter:

- You will define concepts related to big data and their features.
- You will learn about the enablers of big data analytics and their role in various sectors.
- You will explore the challenges of big data analytics.
- You will learn about ethics by design and its application to big data analytics.

1.1 WHAT ARE BIG DATA AND BIG DATA ANALYTICS?

We live in a digitalized world, where data is generated in unprecedented amounts everywhere you turn. Simple, innocuous devices like the smartphone you carry around with you constantly generate all sorts of data, such as location data and health data from apps and wearable devices used to track various activities such as sleep patterns, physical activities, and other behavioural patterns. As far back as 2013, *Computer World* described the massive levels of data generated by smartphones (Poelker, 2013); 6 billion smartphones were already in use back then, each one generating about 60 gigabytes (GB) of data per year, translating to an annual total of 335 exabytes. This amount increased substantially in subsequent years – this is truly big data.

Considering the deluge of data generated by smartphones and other sources, we must recognize that this is not just about data for data's sake but that this data has real consequences for us. First, the availability of the data confers power on those who have it. They can observe, analyse, and act based on this data. Researchers, companies, and public actors can observe people and get them to participate in massive experiments without asking for their explicit consent and without participants being aware of what is happening. From all this data, actionable insights can be drawn out; this is where big data analytics truly comes into its own.

In health settings, the insights could lead to better health outcomes, and for organizations generally, it could give a competitive advantage. An example of insights that can be drawn using big data analytics is seen in a great TED talk in which Malte Spitz (2012) described his attempt to acquire a copy of all the data his mobile phone company collected about him over six months. Initially, the company declined his request, but after he threatened to take them to court, they complied. Using this data, he could visualize his network, compiling an image showing where he was at every point over the course of six months: when and where he caught the train every day, when and where he made phone calls, etc. In his talk, Malte reflected on the implications of having one company with access to this level of information for every individual in society. Such a company could observe what everyone in society is doing, who is speaking to whom and with what frequency. They could observe what people are doing and intervene and provide different service conditions to different population segments to test and optimize their provision. This is a problem not only because of the risk of malicious actors. Actors find themselves with data that is only sometimes accompanied by clear guidelines about how it should be used to prevent harm. There is a requirement for uniform and comprehensive legal and normative framework that addresses various data issues. Otherwise this leaves researchers with the task of resolving dilemmas or dealing with unintended consequences. We will discuss these types of issues further in the sections below.

Another source of big data is social media. Over the last two decades, there has been an enormous rise in the use of social media across the entire globe. The top seven social media platforms in the world alone each have over a billion users, and the amount of user-generated content across all the social media platforms is enormous; almost 50% of the world's population is said to be active daily on social media (just under 4 billion users!), and all these activities are generating incredible amounts of data. The insights drawn from the big data generated by social media should not be underestimated; over the years, it has made possible some very insightful discoveries and insights. Recent examples include a host of research carried out during the Covid-19 pandemic on the use of social media and the insights that can be drawn from it using big data analytics. At the end of this chapter, we include some interesting articles in the further reading section.

Although it is often associated with online activity, big data is not limited to life online. Physically situated industries and retailers collect fine-grained data about their customers, competitors, suppliers, and employees (Zuboff, 2019). Devices are developed and technologies refined to monitor and control people's offline behaviour, nudging them in various ways and enrolling them in randomized experiments as part of their business processes. Another data source that generates data in the physical world is based on the Internet of Things (IoT). The IoT refers to devices that are connected to the internet: wearable fitness apps, voice assistants such as Cortana and Alexa, smart TVs, smart watches, video games, domestic devices connected across smart homes, but also drones, electric eyes, hearing aids, temperature gauges, and even wristwatches all generate extremely large amounts of data. With the pace at which devices are connected to the internet in one form or another, there might come a time in the not-so-distant future when most devices will be part of the IoT (especially in the global North). There are already billions of devices connected to the IoT, and it is forecasted that by 2025 these will generate a total of 79.4 zettabytes (ZB) of data (statista, 2020). Big data analytics makes it possible to explore, investigate, and perform descriptive, predictive, and prescriptive analytics on the data to draw out actionable insights from it.

Another data source is the data collected, stored, and processed by governments. This practice, and the 'deluge of data' that ensued, allowed public servants to recognize emerging patterns in what was thought to be random processes. All this led to the rise of statistical and probability theory in Europe in the mid-seventeenth century (Hacking, 1990). Since the computerization of public records in the late 20th century, even more data has become digitized, systematized, and standardized. Vital statistics records (such as birth and death), health records, and tax and school records can now be combined, allowing researchers to address fundamental debates around public policies and their consequences (Farber, 2015).

If you sell goods and services to private consumers, you are in the retail sector, a part of the economy revolutionized by big data analytics. Plenty of organizations in this sector use big data analytics in innovative ways to produce insights which support decision-making, ultimately helping them meet their strategic goals: increasing their workers' productivity, using limited resources more efficiently, and keeping their customers happy and coming back for more. Organizations such as Amazon and Netflix use recommendation engines fuelled by customer-generated data to inform their customers of specific and relevant personalized offers. Another technique increasingly used by retailers is sentiment analysis, which extracts subjective moods, opinions, emotions, and attitudes from free-flowing text. This is a subfield of natural language processing (NLP) that uses machine learning and NLP techniques. These techniques are used by organizations in the sector to make evidence-based decisions on improving customer satisfaction and ultimately meeting the goal of sustained competitive advantage. Retail giants like Walmart also use big data to rapidly draw out insights; these in turn help to resolve issues as they occur, almost in real time (Marr, 2016).

Big data analytics has upended the health sector, empowering doctors to detect diseases/anomalies using predictive analytics and prompting the rise of prescriptive analytics. For example, in response to the Covid-19 pandemic, big data analytics has been used to understand the virus better, develop vaccines at an unprecedented pace, and monitor travel and the spread of the virus. These have all had a tremendous impact on public health. Many other examples can be seen in healthcare and across various sectors, and we discuss some of these in subsequent chapters throughout this book.

The above are just a small selection of examples illustrating the breadth and depth of big data analytics, touching every area of socio-economic life. In subsequent sections, we go into more detail on these.

Big data can be structured, semi-structured, or unstructured:

- *Structured data* is associated with specific information about the nature of the data itself and its properties, information known as 'metadata'. Metadata is a detailed description of the properties of the data, the type of variables involved (which could be numeric, character, date, time, etc.), the different relationships between data items, and the overarching data model. Examples include data in relational databases and spreadsheets.
- *Unstructured data* consists of data items that are generally not linked to one another through pre-defined metadata or a data model. Examples include photographs, videos, and social media data. Estimates suggest that 70–80% of all data in organizations falls into this category.
- *Semi-structured data* is a cross between the structured and unstructured data. It is a type of structured data but lacks a rigid pre-defined data model. Examples include XML and JSON files.

These different types of data types are depicted in Figure 1.1. Historically, most digitized data has been completely unstructured. This presented a challenge for storage, retrieval, and analysis, but today it is possible to store and process all forms of big data, though the method of analysis still depends on the type of data one wishes to explore.

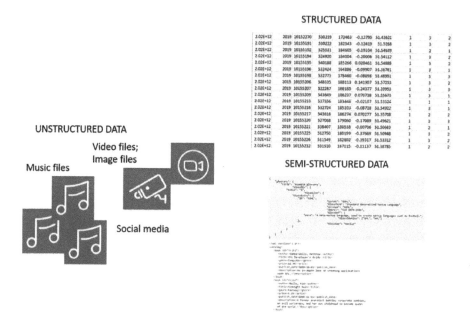

Figure 1.1   A variety of data types – structured, semi-structured, and unstructured

So, what exactly is big data? And what is big data analytics? There are numerous definitions of big data, which, taken together, provide an indication of what big data means. One famous definition for big data reads 'Big data is high volume, high velocity, and/or high variety information assets that require new forms of processing to enable enhanced decision making, insight discovery and process optimization' (Gartner Glossary, n.d.; Sicular, 2013). 'High volume' can be taken to refer to data sizes beyond the capabilities of traditional systems (terabytes, petabytes, exabytes, etc.). Another famous definition was made public by the open-source software initiative Apache Hadoop, defining big data as 'Datasets which could not be captured, managed and processed by general computers within an acceptable scope' (Chen et al.,).

These definitions point to the three Vs of big data – volume, velocity, and variety – which we will elaborate on below. But they also highlight the rise of forms of information processing that are more innovative and cost-effective. Not only can big data be collected and stored, but it ushers a new generation of technologies to process, mine, and analyse the data, extracting insights and informing decision-making by individuals, organizations, companies, and governments. It is not enough to have vast amounts of data generated and stored; the data needs to be used to generate insights and discover patterns, trends, and associations. Out of these patterns, it is then possible to make predictions and inform decisions.

Back in 2018, the total amount of data in the world was estimated to be 33 ZB. Within the short space of just 2 years, the estimate had grown by 79% to 59 ZB and by 2025 it is predicted to rise by almost 200%. These quantities are unprecedented (Vopson, 2021). One of the reasons for this growth is the rise of enabling technologies for storage (the Hadoop Distributed File System (HDFS) came to the rescue here) and growing processing performance (Hadoop MapReduce and then Apache Spark, which can handle both batch processing and streaming data). This book introduces some of those technologies, how to use them and indeed how to perform big data analytics.

A great example of how having big data can enable drawing out insights that would be missed with smaller amounts of data can be seen in the TED talk by Kenneth Cukier called 'Big data is better data' (Cukier, 2014). Cukier starts this talk by stating that America's favourite pie is apple pie and that this is known because of data (e.g., by analysing data from supermarket sales). Initially supermarkets in America sold only large 30 cm pies and by far the most popular among them was the apple pie. But when supermarkets started selling smaller 11 cm pies, the sale of the apple pie fell to fourth or fifth place. What happened? With the large pie a whole family had to agree on which pie to buy (since it had to be shared) and it turned out that apple pie was most people's second favourite pie, so people compromised and went for the common second favourite. However, once the smaller individual pies were available every member of the family could have their actual favourite pie. The pies are an analogy to the very fine resolution of big data. In this new paradigm, people no longer need to compromise. Instead, very specific needs and expectations can be identified and catered to.

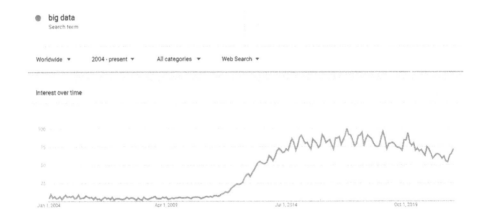

Figure 1.2 Big data over time: search trends (Google Trends graph)

The term 'big data' first emerged in the early 1990s but really began to gain widespread traction in the early to mid-2000s. The growing popularity is reflected in the Google Trends graph shown in Figure 1.2.[1] At first, the term was used to denote the increasing size of data: the number of observations and the number of variables. But the term then evolved to refer to some of the unique attributes of such data, also known as the Vs of big data. The three attributes first identified in the popular literature were volume, velocity, and variety. These were commonly known as the three Vs of big data, but the number of properties increased to four, then five. Others have gone so far as to define seven or even 10 Vs of big data. In this book we stick with the most common properties, the following five Vs:

- *Volume* – how much memory is required to represent the data (e.g., in terabytes or petabytes). Statistically speaking, large volumes of data allow us to identify events that are very rare but of great social or economic importance. For example, they allow us to identify rare events and anomalies. A larger sample size and more accurate methods of collecting and recording data can help mitigate the impact of random sampling bias, enhancing the statistical power of tests and enabling researchers to detect smaller effects and avoid both false negatives and false positives. However, it's important to remember that statistical significance alone doesn't guarantee practical significance, and results may still lack real-world importance even with a larger sample size. Additionally, large volumes of data do not preclude the possibility of systematic bias, but more about that below.
- *Velocity* – the speed at which the data is generated, (e.g., real-time, batch, streams). Velocity also means that data collection is constant, and devices are permanently on. This property of big data has two advantages. First, data that spans several years allows researchers to 'travel back in time', as it were, and identify participants' behaviour that preceded a certain time of interest (Budak & Watts, 2015). New indicators can be developed to produce estimates of ongoing socio-economic activity in real time in a way that was impossible before. In this way, resources could be mobilized to where they are most needed just in time, improving the efficiency of larger systems.
- *Variety* – various types and forms of data, (e.g., structured, unstructured, semi-structured), but also a variety of contexts in which data has been collected that allows researchers to qualify their theories and find mechanisms that operate in very different ways at different locations or points in time. A case in point is a famous study on social mobility in the United States that used the tax records from 40 million people across the country and found surprisingly large discrepancies in intergenerational mobility, depending on geographic locations (Chetty et al., 2014). In other words, although people in older generations could climb the socio-economic ladder, their children failed to do so. This kind of insight has important practical consequences for public policy, but it would not be possible without the heterogeneity of data sources originating from a vast range of systems which can be combined, linked, and processed locally.
- *Veracity* – refers to the accuracy and trustworthiness of data. Here we can distinguish between different dimensions of veracity. The first is reliability, which refers to the likelihood of obtaining similar data if we collect it by independent processes. The second is validity, which refers to the likelihood of the data representing whatever it is we want it to represent. A third dimension

refers to the completeness of the data. It is often the case that when collecting data, we end up with gaps in the data due to errors or omissions. Sometimes it is possible to try and predict the values of the missing data, a process called imputation. But this is not always viable nor always accurate. Data that is unreliable, invalid, or incomplete can yield insights that are less valuable than otherwise. Data veracity depends on the source of the data, the process of eliciting it, and the way it is stored. There have been examples where data has been stored carelessly, leading to avoidable Covid-19 deaths in the UK (Kelion, 2020).

- *Value* – this can be extracted from data in three ways. First, data is valuable to the extent that it allows users to identify recurring patterns and emergent trends, such as identifying trends in customer behaviour, identifying segments in the population that are likely to behave in a certain manner, and recognizing anomalies as they occur. A second way to extract value is to predict outcomes. For example, big data analytics can be used to predict customer churn, lifetime value, or the likelihood of a customer making a purchase. The third and perhaps the most challenging way to extract value is to help end-users decide the range of interventions they can make and what would be the likeliest consequences of those interventions. Note that there is a subtle but crucial difference between making predictions regarding observed data and determining the likely consequences of making interventions. The first depends on identifying correlations in data, whereas the second depends on making causal associations, which is a much stronger claim and a more difficult one to make.

Thus big data is more than just a large amount of data (volume) but is also about the various forms of data (variety). It also includes data at rest and streaming data (velocity), the uncertainty of data (veracity), and, crucially, the insights and worth that data brings (value).

1.2 BIG DATA ANALYTICS ENABLERS

In this section, we briefly explore some of the factors that have led to the explosion in big data and big data analytics. This list is not exhaustive but aims to cover some of the more popular factors.

- *Reduced storage costs*. Data storage has truly come a long way. The cost of data storage has significantly fallen over the years. Back in 1980 when IBM developed the first gigabyte hard drive, it is said to have cost US$81,000, which is over US$250,000 in present-day terms. Today you can buy a 1GB drive for less than $5. In terms of physical size too, the actual devices have greatly reduced in size. These have contributed tremendously to the rise of big data and big data analytics.

- *Commodity hardware compatibility.* This was another enabler which allowed relatively inexpensive off-the-shelf hardware to be used for data storage and processing, as against expensive specialist hardware. This was an important factor particularly in the early days of big data when the focus was on processing batch data at rest using Hadoop MapReduce (a big data software framework). Nowadays NoSQL databases and big data frameworks such as Apache Spark are being more widely adopted as replacements for MapReduce, and things are beginning to change in this space in terms of the use of high-end machines and the like.

- *The open-source community.* The open-source economy has seen collaborations that have resulted in innovative technologies, frameworks and tools being developed, maintained, and improved in rapid time frames. The open-source economy and culture has also led to an ever-widening landscape in terms of the technologies and frameworks being developed for use in this space. Some of these technologies and frameworks include the following (among many others):

  o *Apache Hadoop* is an open-source software framework used for distributed storage and processing of big datasets using the MapReduce programming model.
  o *Apache Spark* is a powerful open-source processing engine built around speed, ease of use, and sophisticated analytics.
  o *Apache Kafka* is an open-source stream processing platform.
  o *Apache Hive* is a data warehouse software project built on top of Apache Hadoop for providing data summarization, query, and analysis.
  o *Apache Pig* is a high-level platform for creating programs that run on Apache Hadoop.
  o *Apache HBase* is an open-source, non-relational, distributed database modelled after Google's Bigtable and is written in Java.
  o *Apache Oozie* is a server-based workflow scheduling system to manage Hadoop jobs.
  o *Apache Flume* is a distributed, reliable, and available service for efficiently collecting, aggregating, and moving large amounts of streaming data into the HDFS.
  o *Apache Sqoop* is a tool designed for efficiently transferring bulk data between Apache Hadoop and structured data stores such as relational databases.
  o *Apache Mahout* is a project of the Apache Software Foundation to produce free implementations of distributed or otherwise scalable machine learning algorithms focused primarily in the areas of collaborative filtering, clustering, and classification.
  o *MongoDB* is a free and open-source cross-platform document-oriented database program.

- *Increased computation power.* Computation power refers to the ability of a computer to perform calculations and is measured in terms of the number of operations that the computer can perform per second. The higher this number, the more powerful the computer is. Historically, computers had limited computation power, making it practically impossible to carry out analytics on vast amounts of data. However, today, the increase in and enhancement of computation power has been one of the important enablers of big data and big data analytics.

As mentioned at the start of this section, the factors that have been briefly discussed are a subset of the various enablers that have brought about the advancement and innovations that we see in the world of big data and big data analytics today. This advancement has also cut across different sectors, disciplines, and geographical locations and in the next section we touch on this.

1.3 BIG DATA ANALYTICS IN VARIOUS SECTORS

1.3.1 Business

Businesses are constantly searching for new ways to generate value for their customers and create sustainable competitive advantage for their shareholders. Of those innovations that were brought about by data science, perhaps the single most important was the two-sided marketplace, a business model that allows two distinct groups of customers to interact with one another through an intermediary. The intermediary, which is typically a platform or marketplace, provides value to both groups of customers by mixing and matching customers with one another while optimizing their interactions. Scores of businesses using this model emerged, using data to provide clearing houses for both sides of the marketplace. It has become a staple exercise for students in business schools all over the world, to compare platforms such as Airbnb and Uber, with traditional business models such as taxi companies and hotel chains. Two sided markets come in different shapes and forms. Examples include:

- Search engines such as Google, Bing, and Yahoo identify hierarchical structures of relevance in the web, and present them to end-users as search results.
- Communication platforms such as WhatsApp and WeChat allow individuals and business to communicate via text messaging, voice, and video.
- Social media platform such as Facebook and LinkedIn allow users to share and exchange information through virtual communities and networks.
- Matching platforms such as Tinder or TaskRabbit bring individuals end-users into contact for physical interaction and exchange.
- Content and review platforms such as YouTube, TripAdvisor, and Yelp allow people to post content and review services.

- Booking aggregators such as booking.com, Expedia and Agoda allow end-users to create customized packages of services by mixing and matching service providers
- Retail platforms such as Amazon, Etsy, eBay, and Alibaba that provide end-users access to products.
- Payment platforms such as Ali Pay, PayPal, and Visa provide users and businesses with financial transaction services.
- Crowdsourcing and crowdfunding platforms such as Kickstarter provide a way for people to raise funding for various causes.
- Development platforms such as app stores and gaming consoles allow gamers and developers to interact.
- Sharing economy platforms enable capacity-constrained assets such as properties, cars, and bicycles to be shared, either through a peer-to-peer sharing scheme, as in the case of Uber and Airbnb, or through the sharing of platform owner-provided assets, as in the case of Zipcar and a public bicycle hiring schemes.

Often these platforms suffer net losses for many years, yet financial markets value them very highly because of the belief that they have immense network effects that almost isolate them from competition. Once they obtain a certain critical mass, they are likened to a flywheel. This is a mechanical structure that captures rotational energy, but in the business world pundits use the term to refer to a business that enjoys a reinforcing feedback loop, a digital platform that becomes more attractive as it draws in more users, which makes it even more attractive and so on. It is precisely the size of a company such as Facebook that makes it immune to competition: with over a billion people using the platform every day, advertisers would be hard pressed to find a platform with an equivalent reach. Looking more closely, however, one might discern different types of network effects. The first type are primary network effects whereby a service becomes more valuable the more people are using it. Primary network effects operate in certain platforms such as LinkedIn, where you can find more job opportunities because there are more users on the platform, attracting even more users. But primary network effects are less relevant for search engines such as Google, where the users incur value from the relevance of the search results, and not from the number of other people using the platform. For such platforms there is no primary network effect, so if users find a competitor search engine that is better than Google, they may easily switch to it. Economic theory tells us that emerging companies offering a superior value proposition to Google's would eventually outcompete Google. In contrast, consider a company such as Facebook, whose value proposition depends (in part) on the volume of its customer base. Such a company would be a lot harder to dislodge, because even if a new entrant developed superior services, they would need first to convert everyone to their platform before they could outcompete the incumbent, at least in theory. That precisely is the main advantage of primary network effects, but it is important to remember that not all platforms have them.

Thus not all platforms are on the same footing. Social media platform users who want to contact one another benefit from primary network effects. In contrast, platforms associated with the sharing economy have billions of dollars, but unlike search engines, their users are not predominantly subject to primary network effects. Instead, we are now dealing with so-called secondary network effects. So, for example, passengers using Uber, Lyft, and Didi do not benefit from other passengers' usage, at least not directly. Instead, they benefit from the existence of a large number of available drivers in their vicinity. In turn, the drivers themselves do not necessarily benefit from there being a large pool of drivers, but from the availability of a very large customer base. Passengers and drivers are two sides of a network, benefiting from a large pool of stakeholders on the other side. Once the two-sided network reaches a critical mass, the matching quality can be secured and a complex array of feedback mechanisms kicks in, and the network expands with more passengers and more drivers. The platform grows at a negligible cost to the platform provider, its size shielding the provider from competitors that have not reached the critical mass required to dethrone it.

But in order to deliver high-quality matching, platform providers rely on data analytics not only to analyse markets and predict their dynamics, but also to intervene and literally design them. Market design involves attention to detail. It conceptualizes the market as a complex network of interacting parts and processes, in which theories and abstract conceptual models are of little use. Market designers need therefore to transform their top-down mindset of theoretical economics to the nitty-gritty, bottom-up mindset of data engineering.

1.3.2 Finance

Data scientists, data engineers, and data analysts have a range of roles to play in financial institutions, making finance one of the sectors most heavily invested in data technologies. Examples of the types of data typically used by financial institutions are time-bound data such as tick data, economic data, transactional, and geospatial data. Collecting, sorting, and analysing large volumes of time series in parallel is the key to evaluating and managing financial risk, fraud, and compliance. As in other sectors, the main challenge is how best to leverage the massive volumes of data generated by financial institutions into insights that can inform decision-making. Traditionally, data is often stored in silos, rigid structures written in legacy software, combined with a complex array of regulations that hinder efficient integration, coordination, oversight, and control of existing processes.

Some of the important roles of big data analytics in the financial industry are the following:

- *Mitigating the risks from so-called flash crashes*. A flash crash is a sudden, rapid decline in the price of a security or market index. Flash crashes are often characterized by high volatility and a lack of liquidity. They can be caused by a variety of factors, such as algorithmic trading, in which computer programs are used to automatically trade securities. Algorithmic trading can sometimes lead to flash crashes if a feedback mechanism is triggered, leading algorithms to imitate one another and reinforce their buying or selling decisions. Other causes could be market panic, when investors sell securities in a frenzy without considering the securities' underlying value, or liquidity problems, when traders believe that it would become difficult to buy or sell securities at a fair price. Flash crashes can have a significant impact on the financial markets, leading to unexpected losses of large sums of money, and a general loss of confidence in the markets. But big data analytics can be used to mitigate the risk of flash crashes by identifying patterns in market data that may indicate a potential flash crash. Once these patterns are identified, they can be used to develop trading strategies that can help to reduce losses in the event of a flash crash.

- *Regulatory compliance and data governance.* Because of the volume, speed, and sensitivity of their data, financial institutions face what appear to be competing drivers between efficiency, speed, and, ultimately, profit on the one hand, and regulatory compliance, data privacy, and security on the other.
- *Data integration and exchange.* The ability to combine data from various sources and transform it into a required form is an important but, in many cases, non-trivial requirement in the financial industry, particularly when considering the proliferation of data in the sector.
- *Cybersecurity risks.* Financial institutions are particularly vulnerable to these, and measures need to be carefully put in place to mitigate against cybersecurity attacks and other malicious attacks such as hackings and ransomware episodes.
- *Sophisticated customer management.* Financial services such as banks, credit agencies, and insurers used to rely on personal information, public records, inquiries and records of one's loans and lines of credit. More recently, devices, websites, and mobile banking apps have begun to provide more personalized information. Profiles on social media, location trackers, and loyalty cards provide even more granularity: certain words used, or even facial expressions or accents, could be studied to assess creditworthiness. On the plus side, more data could reduce risk and make financial services less costly to the consumer. The fact that financial services use data to assess risk is not new, nor is the opaqueness as to how exactly they use this kind of data. Supporters say that by better knowing their customers, insurers can nudge people to adopt healthier habits. Banks can provide protection to customers against fraud, and people outside the financial system can gain access to finance in exchange for an agreed level of monitoring. But customers may be wary if they feel they do not have total control over their online information, or if they worry that their data is used for purposes other than those advertised. In addition, algorithms are opaque and can lead to wrong decisions. If customers are wrongly classified, they can find themselves stuck without an ability to escape or understand why.

1.3.3 Healthcare

One of the distinguishing features of big data analytics is its relevance across almost every facet of life, and we have already seen several examples of this. Healthcare is one area where big data analytics has been embraced and in which many breakthroughs have been seen, yet even so, it is said that the surface has barely been scratched when it comes to the potential of big data analytics. One of the most prominent areas in healthcare in which big data analytics has been widely used is the diagnosis and management of diseases. Examples of this can be seen in risk stratification, where various datasets are used to predict and identify high-risk patients so that interventions can be put in place early to avoid the worst health outcomes. The impact that big data analytics can have in the health sector is increasingly being recognized by governments across the world. The UK government recently published a policy document titled *Data Saves Lives: Reshaping Health and Social Care with Data* (Department of Health and Social Care, 2022), demonstrating the importance of data in combating the Covid-19 pandemic. The document reaffirms the UK government's commitment to the advancement of the use of data in the health and social care sectors, ensuring health professionals have access to the data that they need and empowering researchers with the data needed to develop innovative models of care.

1.4 BIG DATA ANALYTICS CHALLENGES

In this section we discuss the challenges that exist because of big data analytics. We first consider general challenges, and then focus on ethical challenges.

1.4.1 General challenges

As seen in earlier sections, the emergence of big data analytics has given rise to a range of benefits. However, there are also several challenges that have arisen specifically in big data and big data analytics, including the following:

- *Processing large amounts of data*. The initial framework that was used to tackle this was Hadoop MapReduce, which is implemented in Java and was infamous for being difficult to program. Hadoop MapReduce and other alternatives that have since surfaced will be explored in subsequent sections.
- *Limited supply of specialists and knowledge*. A lot has been done and continues to be done to bridge this skills gap so that demand does not continue to outstrip the availability professionals with the right skillsets. This book has been written to contribute towards addressing this challenge.
- *Scalability*. This was particularly a challenge in the early days of big data and big data analytics, when the ability to scale up data projects was more limited. However, the advent of distributed systems (compared to traditional systems), cloud computing with its 'unlimited' scalability, and the varied technologies that are now available in the big data landscape continue to help address this challenge.
- *Heterogeneity of data*. The very nature of big data, as seen in the earlier discussion on the various Vs, means that the data is often heterogeneous.

Challenges thus tend to arise around data integration and analysis. In a bid to combat this, various algorithms have been implemented to handle data cleansing, integration, and processing of heterogeneous big data. These all have their pros and cons, and as such they continue to be refined and new algorithms are still being developed.

- *Security, privacy, and data protection.* The amount of data that is stored and processed and what can be gleaned from it if it gets into the wrong hands or is used in the wrong way makes the issue of security and data protection a crucial one. There are many examples of data breaches leading to disastrous consequences. For example, a data breach in the adult streaming website CAM4 took place in March 2020, resulting in the exposure of 10 billion records and many millions of users. This leaked data included sensitive information such as full names, email addresses, sexual orientation, chat transcripts, password hashes and payment logs among others (Tunggal, 2023). The need to protect security, privacy, and data protection has spawned the growth of a large research community. Over the years governments have also tried to put laws and policies in place to ensure that data is protected, including the Data Protection Act in the UK and General Data Protection Regulation (GDPR) in Europe.

- *Big data governance.* Data governance is all about the processes and procedures that organizations put in place for the management, utilization, and protection of their data. There are additional complications introduced by the peculiarities of big data, such as the volumes of data involved. These are in addition to the other challenges that we have previously discussed such as those of security, privacy, and scalability.

- *Data provenance.* To make use of data, we must have a reliable way to know how it came about. But the ease with which data can be copied, transformed, communicated, and combined on the web means that it can be very difficult to determine the data-generating process with great precision. The term 'data provenance' is often used to refer to the process of tracing and recording the origins of data and its movement between different nodes in the network. A system to assure a reliable data provenance must be kept in place, to secure the veracity of the data, and hence the relevance of the insights we obtain from it.

1.4.2 Ethical challenges

With big data come a host of ethical issues. Big data analytics by its very nature means that large amounts of data are being stored, processed, and analysed for different purposes. This immediately raises a whole host of questions: What data is being stored? Who owns the data? Who has access to the data, and should they? Has permission been given by the data owner for storage? Has permission been given by the data owner for the particular use? Is the usage legal? Are there privacy concerns? Are there security concerns? How was the data collected? Is the usage fair or could there be potential bias issues?

Ethical challenges are not new. However, with the advance of big data the potential for abuse has increased, and directly correlating with that is the need for responsible usage. Ethical issues can be subjective, so there is a need for frameworks and policies to guide what can be done and what must not be done in this area. We will focus on a few main areas that significantly highlight some of the ethical challenges when it comes to big data:

- *Privacy*. The term 'privacy' refers to the idea of data subjects who own their data and have a right to determine how it is used. In the context of big data, privacy relates to issues of collection, access, use, and legal right to data. For instance, in the health sector, only authorized users should have access to patients' personal data, and in the UK for instance this is supported by policies and the law. When we look at the wider society in terms of privacy, we start to explore issues such as patient privacy and public health – which should be prioritized? Which is more important: customers' privacy or the generation of insights for competitive advantage for businesses? How would we judge what actions might infringe on the rights of data subjects? Who will decide and how will the decisions be enforced?
- *Security*. Precisely because of its value, there are those who would like to have access to data they do not own. Once they obtain this access, rogue actors may use it for their own purposes, or may even seek to destroy the data altogether. But such a security breach may infringe a data subject's privacy or compromise business confidentiality. New forms of attacks against systems accompany the evolution of big data technologies. In the early days, big data was stored predominantly in on-premises data centres and the priority was to ensure that there was a strong security perimeter guarding a secure internal network and any external links. However, with the rise in cloud computing the issue of security is even more important, as the data is no longer hosted on-premises, and in many cases it is even processed remotely. Chapter 5 discusses these issues in the context of cloud computing. Why is security an ethical issue? Organizations that store and process data have a responsibility to ensure that the data is secure and if this responsibility is neglected then that is clearly wrong and the consequences in terms of fines, reputational damage, and the like can be very costly for such organizations.
- *Bias*. Big data analytics can easily lead to biased insights and decision-making. Bias in collected data means that whatever insights are drawn using the data would give rise to flawed conclusions that could result in discrimination and other negative consequences. Also bias in algorithms will also result in defective outcomes. For example, in US healthcare it was found that algorithms that had been developed to predict which patients needed extra medical care were biased towards white patients. In the further reading section we have included links to a couple of interesting articles on bias in big data analytics.
- *Trust and transparency*. When any ethical challenge surfaces it tends to result in a lack of trust, which in the long run can be quite detrimental. For instance, NHS care.data was a national programme aimed at extracting data from GP

surgeries into a central database. The idea was that having that amount of data available in a central database would provide opportunities to generate benefits to the whole of society in terms of public health, better healthcare provision and management. However, it all fell apart due to a lack of public trust which was in part fuelled by various factors such as the perceived lack of transparency over how the data would be accessed and used and a lack of adequate consultation. Even though substantial amounts of money had been spent on the project and it would potentially have provided great advantages at a national level, it eventually had to be scrapped due to these trust and transparency challenges. An even more topical example is the NHS Covid-19 tracing app, where it was found that due to a possible low level of trust in the NHS and government there were more negative comments and lower adoption rates among the black, Asian, and minority ethnic communities. Transparency issues also arise in the use of models in machine learning and deep learning algorithms, where the models are basically black boxes and as such predictions or results obtained using these models are not easily explained or understandable to humans. This raises ethical issues particularly when decisions that affect lives are being made based on the results from these models. Research in the field of explainable artificial intelligence (AI) could potentially make a great difference when it comes to transparency of models and algorithms.

1.5 ETHICS BY DESIGN

When it comes to ethical challenges in big data and big data analytics, one approach that is gaining traction in the analytics and development world is *ethics by design*. With this approach ethics is not an afterthought or bolted on at the end of a project. On the contrary, it is all about embedding ethics into the very design of the project, building it into the requirement specifications and data collection process, data storage, data processing, and how the analytics is carried out. This ensures that at each stage the right questions are being asked and the solutions being taken onboard consider as a priority the ethical issues and challenges that arise. Throughout this book we interweave the principles of ethics by design. Our objective is to show how ethics is an organic part of technology, a principle flowing naturally from our common hope for a more sustainable, responsible future. Some of the principles behind ethics by design can be seen in frameworks including (but not limited to) the following:

- The data ethics canvas developed by the Open Data Institute (n.d.), which aims to address data ethics in three stages: the data stewarding stage, where data is collected, maintained, and shared; the information extraction stage; and the decision stage.
- The UK government data ethics framework (Central Digital and Data Office, 2020), which guides the appropriate and responsible use of data in the public sector, focusing on transparency, accountability, and fairness.

● The European Commission guidelines for ethics by design, particularly for AI, which can be adapted for big data and big data analytics (European Commission, 2021).

In addition, professional bodies have come up with their own ethical frameworks. One such body is the Institute of Electrical and Electronics Engineers (IEEE), which is the world's largest technical professional organization dedicated to advancing technology for the benefit of humanity. The IEEE has recommended the following guidelines:

● Ethics in design (IEEE P7000)
● Transparency (IEEE P7001)
● Data privacy (IEEE P7002)
● Algorithmic bias (IEEE P7003)

This book embeds ethics as part and parcel of the various technologies explored, discussed, and reflected upon. Our aim as data professionals is to ensure that the consideration of ethical issues and embedding of best practices when it comes to ethics become second nature.

SUMMARY

In this chapter we introduced big data and big data analytics. We also discussed some of the factors that enabled their emergence, outlined use cases for big data analytics in three representative sectors, and explored the challenges facing big data analytics. We concluded by focusing on ethical challenges and the concept of ethics by design.

TEST YOUR KNOWLEDGE

1 What is big data?
2 What is big data analytics?
3 Give three enablers of big data.
4 Give three examples of the use of big data analytics in two sectors.
5 What are the five Vs of big data?
6 What do you understand by the phrase 'ethics by design'?

FURTHER READING (OPTIONAL)

Alsunaidi, S. J., Almuhaideb, A. M., Ibrahim, N. M., Shaikh, F. S., Alqudaihi, K. S., Alhaidari, F. A., Khan, I. U., Aslam, N. and Alshahrani, M. S. (2021) Applications of big data analytics to control COVID-19 pandemic. *Sensors*, 21(7), 2282. https://doi.org/10.3390/s21072282
Chew, A. M. K. and Gunasekeran, D. V. (2021) Social media big data: The good, the bad, and the ugly (un)truths. *Frontiers Big Data*, 4, 623794. doi:10.3389/fdata.2021.623794

Crawford, K. (2013) The hidden biases in big data. *Harvard Business Review*, 1 April. Retrieved from https://hbr.org/2013/04/the-hidden-biases-in-big-data

Dowthwaite, L., Fischer, J., Perez Vallejos, E., Portillo, V., Nichele, E., Goulden, M. and McAuley, D. (2021) Public adoption of and trust in the NHS COVID-19 contact tracing app in the United Kingdom: Quantitative online survey study. *Journal of Medical Internet Research*, 23(9), e29085. https://doi.org/10.2196/29085

Ghani, N. A., Hamid, S., Hashem, I. A. T. and Ahmed, E. (2019) Social media big data analytics: A survey. *Computers in Human Behavior*, 101, 417–28. https://doi.org/10.1016/j.chb.2018.08.039

Haleem, A., Javaid, M., Khan, I. H. and Vaishya, R. (2020) Significant applications of big data in COVID-19 pandemic. *Indian Journal of Orthopaedics*, 54(4), 526–8. https://doi.org/10.1007/s43465-020-00129-z

Milaninia, N. (2021) Biases in machine learning models and big data analytics: The international criminal and humanitarian law implications. *International Review of the Red Cross*. IRRC No. 913. Retrieved from https://international-review.icrc.org/articles/biases-machine-learning-big-data-analytics-ihl-implications-913

Ristevski, B. and Chen, M. (2018) Big data analytics in medicine and healthcare. *Journal of Integrative Bioinformatics*, 15(3), 20170030. https://doi.org/10.1515/jib-2017-0030

NOTE

1   Google Trends is a tool for comparing the popularity of search terms and trends over different regions and periods; see https://trends.google.com/

REFERENCES

Budak, C. and Watts, D. (2015) Dissecting the spirit of Gezi: Influence vs. selection in the Occupy Gezi Movement. *Sociological Science*, 370–97. doi:10.15195/v2.a18

Central Digital and Data Office (2020) Data ethics framework. Retrieved from https://www.gov.uk/government/publications/data-ethics-framework/data-ethics-framework

Chen, M., Mao, S. and Liu, Y. (2014) Big data: A survey. *Mobile Networks and Applications*, 19(2), 171–209.

Chetty, R., Hendren, N., Kline, P. and Saez, E. (2014) Where is the land of opportunity? The Geography of intergenerational mobility in the United States. *Quarterly Journal of Economics*, 129(4), 1553–623. doi:10.1093/qje/qju022

Cukier, K. (2014) Big data is better data. Retrieved from https://www.ted.com/talks/kenneth_cukier_big_data_is_better_data

Department of Health and Social Care (2022) *Data Saves Lives: Reshaping Health and Social Care with Data*. Retrieved from https://www.gov.uk/government/publications/data-saves-lives-reshaping-health-and-social-care-with-data

European Commission (2021) *Ethics by Design and Ethics of Use Approaches*. Retrieved from https://ec.europa.eu/info/funding-tenders/opportunities/docs/2021-2027/horizon/guidance/ethics-by-design-and-ethics-of-use-approaches-for-artificial-intelligence_he_en.pdf

Farber, H. S. (2015) Why you can't find a taxi in the rain and other labor supply lessons from cab drivers. *Quarterly Journal of Economics,* 130(4). doi:10.1093/qje/qjv026

Gartner Glossary (n.d.) Information technology: Big data. Retrieved from https://www.gartner.com/en/information-technology/glossary/big-data

Hacking, I. (1990) *The Taming of Chance.* Cambridge: Cambridge University Press.

Kelion, L. (2020) Excel: Why using Microsoft's tool caused Covid-19 results to be lost. Retrieved from BBC: https://www.bbc.co.uk/news/technology-54423988

Marr, B. (2016) *Big Data in Practice: How 45 Successful Companies Used Big Data Analytics to Deliver Extraordinary Results.* Chichester: John Wiley & Sons.

Open Data Institute (n.d.) *What is the Data Ethics Canvas?* Retrieved from https://theodi.org/article/the-data-ethics-canvas-2021/

Poelker, C. (2013) Smartphones, big data, storage and you. *Computer World,* 12 June. Retrieved from https://www.computerworld.com/article/2473730/smartphones--big-data--storage-and-you.html

Sicular, S. (2013) Gartner's big data definition consists of three parts, not to be confused with three 'V's. *Forbes,* 27 March. Retrieved from https://www.forbes.com/sites/gartnergroup/2013/03/27/gartners-big-data-definition-consists-of-three-parts-not-to-be-confused-with-three-vs/

Spitz, M. (2012) Your phone company is watching. Retrieved from https://www.ted.com/talks/malte_spitz_your_phone_company_is_watching

statista (2020) Data volume of internet of things (IoT) connections worldwide in 2019 and 2025. Retrieved from https://www.statista.com/statistics/1017863/worldwide-iot-connected-devices-data-size/

Tunggal, A. T. (2023) The 70 biggest data breaches of all time. Retrieved from https://www.upguard.com/blog/biggest-data-breaches

Vopson, M. M. (2021) The world's data explained: How much we're producing and where it's all stored. Retrieved from https://theconversation.com/the-worlds-data-explained-how-much-were-producing-and-where-its-all-stored-159964

Zuboff, S., & Schwandt, K. (2019) *The Age of Surveillance Capitalism: The Fight for a Human Future at the New Frontier of Power.* London: Profile Books.

2

BIG DATA
TECHNOLOGIES

CHAPTER CONTENTS

CHAPTER OBJECTIVES

In this chapter:

- You will learn about the big data technology landscape.
- You will be introduced to data storage and some of the technologies commonly used to store big data.
- You will be introduced to data acquisition, data wrangling and piping, and some of the most popular technologies used in this space.
- You will revisit data analytics and explore some of the technologies used for big data analytics.
- You will be introduced to data visualization and some of the technologies used for it.
- Finally, the technologies used later in the book will be highlighted and the rationale behind the choices outlined.

2.1 THE BIG DATA TECHNOLOGY LANDSCAPE

This chapter discusses some of the technologies that handle the storage and processing of big data, where processing consists of data mining, wrangling, analytics, and visualization. Figure 2.1 depicts this process from end to end.

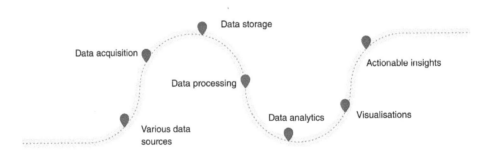

Figure 2.1 Foundations of a big data analytics system

The emergence of big data technologies can be traced back to the first data storage technologies starting from punch cards, vacuum tubes for random access memory, magnetic disk storage, flash drives, and solid state drives. Those early technologies have now evolved into the modern data silos, data lakes and cloud data storages (Foote, 2017). The first milestone can be traced to the beginning of the 2000s, when software engineers Doug Cutting and Mike Cafarella founded Apache Nutch, an extensible and scalable open-source web crawler. The project soon ran into significant challenges, when its founders realized that that their architecture could not scale to cover the vast number of pages on the web. They had their breakthrough after reading two seminal white papers, published by Google. The first paper (Ghemawat et al., 2003) described the architecture used by Google for storing data, crawling the web, and indexing pages. The second white paper (Dean & Ghemawat,

2004) described the MapReduce data-processing model, a framework for processing big datasets on distributed clusters (clusters are discussed in a subsequent section). From this work, a collection of open-source software utilities emerged that is now known as Apache Hadoop and MapReduce. The origin of the name 'Hadoop' is interesting: Doug Cutting was inspired by his son's toy elephant, which is why the icon representing Hadoop is an elephant. The two white papers are interesting resources which we encourage you to read!

Apache Hadoop is defined on its official webpage as follows: 'Apache Hadoop software library is a framework that allows for the distributed processing of large datasets across clusters of computers using simple programming models' (Apache Hadoop, n.d.). It is made up of three main components:

- Hadoop Distributed File System (HDFS), which is the storage unit;
- Hadoop MapReduce, which is the processing unit;
- Hadoop YARN, which is the resource management unit.

Let us go into some more detail on each of these.

2.1.1 Hadoop Distributed File System

A key component of the Apache Hadoop framework, HDFS is a distributed file system designed to store and process large datasets across multiple machines. It provides fault tolerance and high throughput for handling large-scale data-processing tasks and is optimized for storing and processing data in a batch-oriented manner. Being a distributed storage unit, HDFS provides key advantages over non-distributed storage systems:

- *Fault tolerance and automatic recovery*. These ensure reliability by replicating data across multiple nodes. As HDFS is distributed it is implemented with several servers (large implementations can have thousands) so if one server fails, the system is able to detect this and automatically recover by working with the servers that are still live.
- *Scalability*. HDFS scales horizontally to handle petabytes of data by distributing files across multiple machines. Since it is made up of several servers, scaling up is a straightforward affair, since servers can be flexibly added to the cluster on demand. A Hadoop cluster is the collection of nodes (another word for computers, machines, or servers) that make up the HDFS implementation. In contrast, non-distributed systems such as massively parallel processing (MPP) database systems make it extremely expensive to scale up.
- *Data locality*. HDFS co-locates data with computation, improving performance by reducing network traffic.
- *High throughput*. HDFS is optimized for sequential data access rather than random access, enabling high throughput for big data workloads.
- *Low-cost deployment hardware*. Composed of a cluster of low-cost hardware nodes, deployment using HDFS is relatively cost-effective.

A simplified architecture of the HDFS is depicted in Figure 2.2. The architecture consists of the following components:

- *Name node.* The master node manages the file system namespace and metadata, keeping track of where data is stored in the cluster.
- *Data node.* The worker nodes are responsible for storing and retrieving data upon request from the clients or other components.
- *Block.* HDFS stores files as blocks, typically 128 MB in size. Blocks are replicated across multiple data nodes for fault tolerance.
- *Secondary name node.* This server assists the name node by periodically checkpointing the file system metadata to improve system reliability.

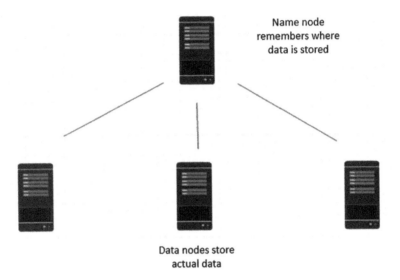

Name node
remembers where
data is stored

Data nodes store
actual data

Figure 2.2   Simplified HDFS architecture

Some large HDFS implementations consist of many thousands of nodes. The name node is the master/control node, controlling how data is distributed across the data nodes and managing the file system's metadata. Metadata is itself data that provides information about your dataset, for example it could have details such as the author's name, the date the dataset was created, and when it was last modified. The name node normally has a backup node which helps make it more failsafe, so that if something goes wrong with the name node the backup node can take over. The data nodes physically store the data and replicate it across other nodes. Data nodes also send block reports to the name node. Figure 2.3 depicts the process of block storage.

When a file is loaded into HDFS for storage it is broken down into blocks. These individual blocks are then stored in data nodes. Every Hadoop instance has a pre-defined block size (in the example in Figure 2.3, the default is 128 MB). The loaded file is split into as many evenly sized blocks as possible, the final block only using up the remaining space, so in the

Figure 2.3 HDFS block storage

example in Figure 2.3 the file of size 513 MB is split into four evenly sized blocks of the default size of 128 MB and the final block just uses 1 MB (i.e., 513 = 128 + 128 + 128 + 128 + 1). Each of the blocks has its own metadata which contains a header with a version, type information and checksums for the stored block. The checksums are important as they are used to check that the files have not been corrupted during uploading/transmission. Once the file is split into the relevant blocks, these blocks are distributed among data nodes in the cluster. This makes possible shared and distributed parallel processing of data (Figure 2.4 illustrates this with the example from Figure 2.3)

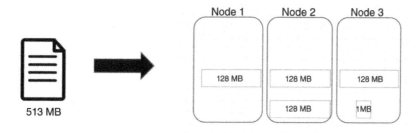

Figure 2.4 Distribution of HDFS blocks to data nodes

After the blocks are distributed to data nodes, the blocks are then replicated. Each HDFS system has a pre-defined replication factor. For example, if the replication factor is 3 (a common replication number), every block would be replicated across data nodes three times. The main objectives of block replications are fault tolerance and data locality. Regarding fault tolerance, if a block has been replicated across several nodes and one of those nodes fails, the system could use other copies residing on other nodes which are still alive and running. Similarly, data locality moves the processing task to the closest node, thereby obtaining performance gains.

To sum up, when a file is written to HDFS, it gets split into blocks. The name node controller then determines which data nodes the blocks should be written to, and the data nodes then replicate the blocks. You can think of the name node as the conductor in an orchestra who knows when each musician should come in, whether or not they are able to come in at certain points and so on. The data nodes are like the musicians, they are the actual workers who are playing the instruments based on instructions they receive from the conductor. If a data node fails, the name node knows because all the data nodes periodically send the name node what is called a 'heartbeat' and every tenth heartbeat is called a 'block report'. The name node in turn then builds metadata from the block reports it receives from the data nodes. If the name node does not receive heartbeats from any particular data node, the name node knows that that particular data node is lost and it checks the metadata it holds to find the affected data, and then sends a message to another data node that is live to replicate the data that was held on the lost data node. This process makes HDFS incredibly failsafe. If a data node is lost, HDFS can still carry on. However, if the name node fails (without a backup) then HDFS also fails.

It is easy to underestimate the importance of having the right data storage platform, whether that is in terms of it being able to adequately handle the data volumes that need to be stored in it or in terms of how it handles failure and its ability to recover automatically and swiftly. Unfortunately, the value of having appropriate storage facilities is often underestimated – until things go wrong. An example of when things went wrong is the incident within Public Health England (PHE) in 2021 during the Covid-19 pandemic when a bad decision was made to store Covid-19 test results in Microsoft Excel (Kelion, 2020). The PHE developers then further compounded the problem by picking the old Excel format (XLS) which can only handle 65,536 rows of data (as against 1,048,576 rows that the latter version of Excel can handle – however, using this newer version might just have delayed the emergence of the problem). In this case this choice of wrong storage platform meant that figures were grossly underreported, and the issue was not immediately spotted.

2.1.2 Other data storage technologies

In addition to HDFS, numerous other storage technologies are used for big data. In this section we briefly discuss some of the most popular ones, categorizing them based on the type of data models that they hold; the list is not exhaustive and, as seen earlier, it is constantly increasing as new technologies are added to the landscape. Traditional relational databases scale vertically, which can be quite expensive and finite. Big data storage technologies, on the other hand, scale horizontally – additional nodes are just added to the cluster and hence they can scale infinitely. They are also generally schemaless and can handle unstructured data, something traditional relational database systems cannot do. Essential properties when choosing the right technology for a particular big data storage architecture also include factors such as scalability, high performance, availability, consistency, and security. There are several different ways we could categorize the data storage technologies, for instance according to whether they fall under NoSQL, NewSQL and/or distributed, in-memory, or object-based storage databases. However, for our purposes we have categorized them based on the data models that they hold.

Key-value

The key–value store data model is one of the most popular big NoSQL database types; it is simple and has extremely fast performance. Like all NoSQL databases, it is highly scalable and thus very flexible. Listed below are some of the more popular big data storage technologies that fall under this category.

- Scalaris
- BerkeleyDB
- Amazon DynamoDB
- Aerospike (in-memory)
- Redis (in-memory)
- Voldemort
- KAI
- MemcacheDB
- Memcached
- Couchbase
- Riak
- CockroachDB

Column-oriented

These are database management systems in which data tables are stored by column rather than by row as in traditional relational database systems. Again, as in key-value models, scalability is horizontal and infinite. Examples of these include:

- Bigtable
- HBase
- Hypertable
- Apache Cassandra
- Kudu

Document

Document databases are NoSQL databases that are non-relational database systems and are used to both store and query semi-structured data such as JSON and XML files. Examples of these include:

- MongoDB
- Terrastore (in-memory)
- Rocket U2
- Qizx
- RethinkDB
- OrientDB
- SimpleDB

- Couchbase Server
- CouchDB

Graph

Graph databases use graph structures (edges, nodes, and relationships) to store data. Examples of these include:

- HyperGraphDB
- InfiniteGraph
- Neo4j
- AllegroGraph
- SciDB

Massively parallel processing

MPP databases are used for storage and processing data which are split among different nodes so that the processing is carried out by multiple processors. Examples of these include:

- Greenplum
- PostgreSQL
- MariaDB (column store)

Data warehouses

These include:

- Snowflake
- Google BigQuery
- Amazon Redshift
- Azure Synapse

On-premises or cloud storage

An important aspect of big data storage is the choice between on-premises and cloud storage. This is discussed in detail in Chapter 5, including factors such as the pros and cons of both in terms of size, costs, security, high availability, and data movement rates.

2.1.3 Hadoop MapReduce

Hadoop MapReduce is the processing unit of Apache Hadoop. MapReduce allows big data to be processed across multiple nodes in a scalable and parallel manner.

MapReduce, as suggested by its name, is made up of two main functions, a map function and a reduce function, and there is also a sort/shuffle/merge phase where data is shuffled and sorted. The map function takes as its input parameter key–value pairs and outputs intermediary key–value pairs as follows:

```
[(u'1609', 1),

 (u'the', 1),

 (u'sonnets', 1),

 (u'by', 1),

 (u'william', 1),

 (u'shakespeare', 1),

 (u'1', 1),

 (u'from', 1),

 (u'fairest', 1),

 (u'creatures', 1)]
```

If MapReduce was being used to work out the number of occurrences for each word in the file, the output from the map function would be passed into the reduce function which would aggregate the values and output the aggregated value as follows:

```
[('shakespeare', 255),

 ('1', 13),

 ('fairest', 39),

 ('creatures', 27),

 ('we', 3201),

 ('increase,', 9),

 ('thereby', 21),

 ('beauty's', 30),

 ('rose', 44),

 ('never', 959)]
```

2.1.4 Hadoop YARN and other resource negotiators

Hadoop YARN is a resource management unit; the YARN stands for 'Yet Another Resource Negotiator'. It was not introduced into Hadoop until 2012, before which Hadoop had a job tracker which managed resources but caused a bottleneck in the system. With the introduction of YARN, the resource manager layer was separated from the processing layer. Other resource management and workflow tools include Kubernetes (K8), Mesos, Oozie, Azkaban, Ambari, and Zookeeper.

2.1.5 The Impact of the open-source community

The role of the open-source community in the advancement and proliferation of big data technologies cannot be overemphasized. Earlier on in Doug Cutting and Mike Cafarella's quest to come up with a solution that could handle the volumes of data that they were trying to process they came to that realization and, working with Yahoo! in 2008, Hadoop was released to the Apache Software Foundation as an open-source project. The Apache Software Foundation has revolutionized community-led development; it is said that through the foundation over $22 billion of software products have been made freely available to the public. Having Apache Hadoop (and a host of other products) available as open source means that the products are constantly being updated and enhanced, knowledge is shared, and this has accelerated to a great degree the speed at which innovations have come about.

The emergence of big data technologies has been truly explosive, and such technologies are continually being developed. Matt Turck, a partner at early-stage venture capital firm FirstMark, based in New York, has been blogging (Turck, 2020) on the big data landscape each year since 2012. One particularly interesting aspect of this blog is an infographic produced each year depicting the current landscape, which illustrates the incredible growth that has taken place. To see how rapidly the big data landscape has changed and the increase in the number of big data technologies from 2012, do visit the blog site. The infographics illustrate beautifully the exponential growth that has occurred in the sector.

2.3 BIG DATA ACQUISITION, WRANGLING, PIPELINES, AND ASSOCIATED TECHNOLOGIES

Closely associated with extract, transform, and load (ETL) technologies are technologies used to acquire data from a range of sources, transform it into a compatible structure, and load it, often into data storage systems downstream the value chain. Also note that so-called 'reverse ETL' is often associated with a similar operation but in reverse: data is copied from a central data warehouse and transferred into operational systems for analysis and decision-making, including (but not limited to) SaaS tools used for growth, marketing, sales, and support. When it comes to big data analytics the acquisition of data, wrangling, and data pipelines are fundamental processes that determine whether or not effective big data analytics resulting in actionable insights from the data can happen. In this section we discuss these important topics in relation to big data and big data technologies.

2.3.1 Big data acquisition

Data acquisition is all about how data is sourced, where it is sourced from, and how it is loaded for storage and subsequently processed. As has previously been discussed, data comes from a variety of sources, including handheld devices such as smartphones, data generated from social media such as tweets, data generated by transactions such as credit card payments, logs, data from open data portals and other organizational transactions. Open data portals are increasingly becoming more important when it comes to the provision of data that insights can be drawn from. These insights can potentially affect government policies and citizen engagement. There are currently many thousands of open data portals across the globe and many governments and organizations (both private and public) provide various datasets through them. Listed below is a very small selection of open data portals:

- www.data.gov
- www.data.gov.uk
- https://data.police.uk/
- https://data.europa.eu
- https://data.worldbank.org
- opendata.paris.fr
- www.data.gouv.fr
- www.dati.piemonte.it
- www.dati.gov.it
- www.data.overheid.nl
- https://nigeria.opendataforafrica.org/
- https://opendata.nhsbsa.net/
- https://www.pagasa.dost.gov.ph
- https://data.ballarat.vic.gov.au
- https://opendata.vallourec.com
- https://data.tg.ch
- https://data.orleans-metropole.fr
- https://opendata-martinique.edf.fr
- https://epn-agglo.opendatasoft.com
- https://aix-en-provence.opendatasoft.com
- https://nihr.opendatasoft.com
- https://prc-digitalwallonia.opendatasoft.com
- https://inai.opendatasoft.com
- https://sports-sgsocialgouv.opendatasoft.com
- https://data.idelis.fr
- https://www.opendata56.fr

When the data that is generated from these sources starts to exhibit the properties of big data (recall the fives Vs discussed in Chapter 1: volume, velocity, variety, veracity, and value) the processes used for the data acquisition have to be tailored to handle such big data. Regular data acquisition proceeds in line with the following steps:

- Determine what problem you are trying to solve.
- Determine what datasets you need to solve the problem.
- Determine the sources of the data.
- Determine the characteristics of the data in each source. For example, is it data at rest or real-time data? What sort of volumes are involved?

- Consider relevant ethical issues. For example, do you have a legal right to the data?
- Determine the appropriate technologies and/or tools for the data acquisition.

There are numerous big data acquisition technologies, and which one you use is determined to a large extent by the type of data that is being acquired, how it is to be stored, wrangled, and processed. Each of these processes needs to be seen as part of a whole process and not handled or approached in isolation from the other stages. The following are some of the common big data acquisition technologies:

- Apache Kafka – for the acquisition of real-time streaming data
- Apache Flume – for the acquisition of unstructured and semi-structured data.
- Sqoop – for the acquisition of structured data
- Pulsar – for the acquisition of real-time streaming data
- Apache Spark – covers the acquisition of all data forms (i.e., unstructured, semi-structured and structured data).

2.3.2 Big data wrangling

Data wrangling (also known as data munging) is the next step after data acquisition and is all about cleansing and transforming the acquired raw data into unified formats ready for processing and analytics. Data pre-processing is an extremely important step in the journey from raw data to actionable insights for big data analytics. It is said that for your average project, data preparation takes up 60–80% of the time, which underscores how important it is. Data wrangling, if well done, is the step that ensures that the analytics is done on reliable and accurate data. Some common data wrangling tools include open-source software such as Apache Spark, Python, R, and Pandas. This also includes applications like Talend, OpenRefine, and DataWrangler.

2.3.3 Big data pipelines

In this context, by 'big data pipeline' we mean the set of tools and operations that can be set up to automatically cover the end-to-end processes of going from a data's source to the target system (i.e., the system architecture). Examples of common big data pipelines include the following:

- Streaming big data pipelines – these handle streaming (real-time) data. Some of the technologies used in this pipeline include Apache Spark, Apache Storm, and Apache Kafka.
- All-purpose big data pipelines – these are pipelines that handle general datasets (e.g., batch data, streaming data). They tend to be designed to handle one or the other.
- Lambda big data pipelines – these tend to be designed to handle both batch and streaming data.

Big data pipelines can handle the various forms of data (i.e., unstructured, semi-structured and structured) and care must be taken in their design to ensure that they are optimized to handle the volumes and varieties of data that would pass through the various components of the pipeline.

2.4 DATA ANALYTICS AND ASSOCIATED TECHNOLOGIES

In this section the most common types of data analytics are discussed. Data analytics starts with data, and big data analytics helps us to make the most of data. Across all sectors, this includes being able to perform analytics on data that results in the drawing out of actionable insights. One possible consequence of big data analytics for organizations is competitive advantage from having or developing certain factors that allow them to produce goods or services better or more cheaply than their rivals. It also drives innovations which help improve productivity, reduce costs, and help disciplines to make rapid progress.

2.4.1 Descriptive analytics

Here data is used to understand what happened in the past; for example, it is often used to monitor important metrics, such as key performance indicators. Figure 2.5 shows the distribution of GCSE candidates by area in England in 2015/16 and 2016/17; we return to this example in Chapter 6.

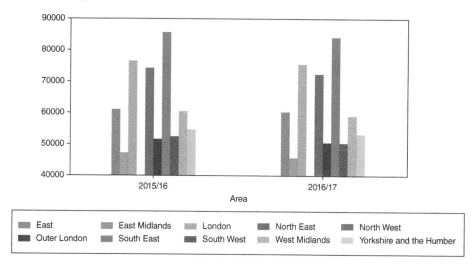

Figure 2.5 Distribution of GCSE candidates by area (2015/16 and 2016/17)

2.4.2 Diagnostic analytics

Diagnostic analytics helps us understand why something happened in the past by analysing trends and patterns. This follows on from descriptive analytics and starts to go into greater depth than simply describing what has happened.

Trigger warning – this page contains references to suicide which some individuals may find distressing.

2.4.3 Predictive analytics

Here data is used to predict what is most likely to happen in the future. An example of predictive analytics in the health sector is the development of a model to predict the likelihood that a patient will self-harm or attempt suicide. Such a model will be based on several data parameters such as the patient's emotional state, past and current risk behaviour and motivation levels. See Figure 2.6 for a subset of a concept map that depicts the factors that contribute to the likelihood of suicide.

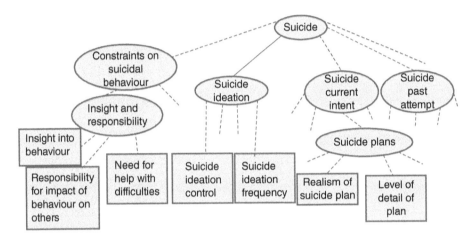

Figure 2.6 Subset of suicide concept map

Data is used here to come up with recommendations that can be taken to influence or affect outcomes. An example here is risk stratification which is used to identify high-risk patients early on which makes it possible to implement interventions to change outcomes and empowers doctors to give proactive care to their patients based on the available data (Arden & GEM, 2023).

2.4.4 Storytelling With data: data visualization

There is a popular adage which says, 'A picture is worth a thousand words' – nowhere is this more applicable than when it comes to big data analytics. There are various visualization tools used for big data, including libraries and technologies. The following are some of the more popular ones:

- Google Charts
- Tableau

- Microsoft Power BI
- Plotly
- QlikView
- Datawrapper
- D3.js
- PixieDust

Visualizations are part and parcel of all the analytics that we do and can be an extremely powerful tool in turning analytics into stories and enabling information and highlights to be understood almost immediately. Figure 2.7 shows various kinds of visualization. Chapter 11 provides a more detailed discussion.

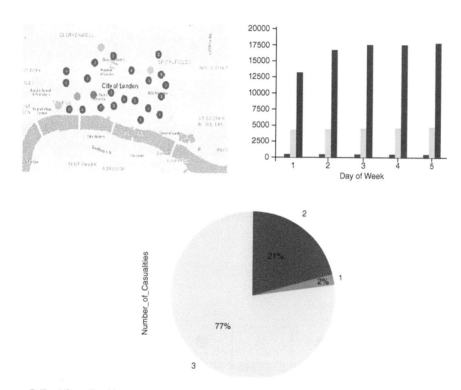

Figure 2.7   Visualizations

2.5 BIG DATA TECHNOLOGIES USED IN THIS BOOK

Having had a general look at big data technologies, we now focus on the main technologies that are used in this book. This section also includes step-by-step instructions for downloading and installing them. The main programming environment that is used in this book is the Jupyter development environment, and we start by focusing on what it is, how to use it, and how to install it. We then look at another free environment which can be used for data processing and visualization, the Google Colaboratory (Colab). For those who would rather pay a small premium for ready-made environments that do not need any installation or configuration there are several commercial alternatives available, including Databricks, Hortonworks, and CloudxLab.

Following on from the development environments, the discussion then moves on to the technologies that we can run in these environments, technologies, and libraries, such as Apache Spark, Python, and PixieDust.

2.5.1 Environments

Jupyter Notebook and the more recent JupyterLab are interactive development environments that support over 40 programming languages including Python, Julia, R, and Scala. Jupyter is an extremely powerful development environment that allows developers to acquire, transform, process, and draw out insights from data. It supports visualizations, interactive dashboards and heavy churning and processing of data. It is because of the flexibility and versatility that it offers that is has been chosen as one of the main development environments for this book.

Jupyter can be installed in various ways; for our purposes we recommend installing it via Anaconda. Anaconda is said to be the world's most popular data science platform, and the Anaconda individual edition offers students, researchers, and solo practitioners access to easily installed open-source data science technologies, Jupyter Notebook and JupyterLab among them. To install Anaconda, first download the Anaconda individual edition from https://www.anaconda.com/, it is the free download available under 'Individuals' on the website, then install the executable file; depending on your system it might take a little while to install. Once the installation is done, Anaconda is now ready to run.

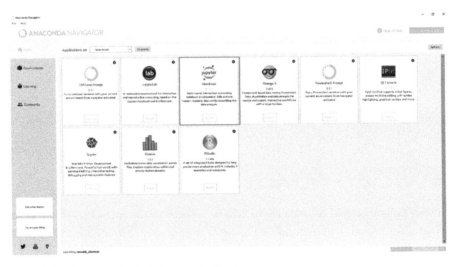

Figure 2.8   A screenshot of Anaconda Navigator

To launch Jupyter, click on launch on the box highlighted in Figure 2.8. This will open up the Jupyter Notebook in a web browser as seen in Figure 2.9, where the box highlighted shows the programming languages that have been installed on this instance of Jupyter.

Figure 2.9 A screenshot of Anaconda Navigator

Another free development environment is the Google Colaboratory. Colab allows a developer to write and execute code in their browser without needing to do any installation or configuration. Colab does this by providing a hosted Jupyter Notebook service. It also provides free access to graphical processing units and tensor processing units, which are otherwise very expensive to buy. Graphical processing units are specialized processors which initially were developed for fast graphical rendering. Their ability to process data concurrently at great speeds has made them useful for machine learning and big data analytics. Tensor processing units are also specialized processors and are tailored for accelerating machine learning workloads. To use Colab, you just need to sign up for it using a Google mail account at https://colab.research.google.com/. No installation is needed, although some configuration needs to be done by running some lines of code. Information on this can be found on the Colab website.

As already mentioned, one of the technologies that we will use in these environments is Apache Spark (in its Python variant, PySpark). To install this in the environment provided by Anaconda, some additional steps need to be carried out:

Step 1. Download Apache Spark from https://spark.apache.org/downloads.html. There are different releases. Choose the latest release, download, and install. Move the file to a subdirectory in your home directory.

Step 2. Next install pip and PySpark. Install pip from https://pip.pypa.io/en/stable/ installation/ to help install PySpark. After installing pip, run `$ pip install pyspark` to install PySpark.

Alternatively, refer to https://sparkbyexamples.com/pyspark/install-pyspark-in-anaconda -jupyter-notebook/ for step-by-step installation instructions to install PySpark in Anaconda and Jupyter Notebook.

2.5.2 Using Jupyter Notebook: a simple example

In this section, we go through an end-to-end hands-on example covering data acquisition, data visualization, and the drawing out of insights from the acquired data. The idea at this point is not to dwell on specific syntax and details but rather to give you a feel of how the Jupyter development environment can be used for the various stages of big data analytics. The example uses data from an open data portal. Work through the following steps:

Step 1. Open a new Jupyter Notebook, click on 'new' and choose 'Python 3'. A browser window will open that will look something like Figure 2.10.

Figure 2.10   Opening your Jupyter Notebook

Step 2. Install PixieDust in your environment and import the required libraries, typing in and executing the following code:

```
pip install pixiedust

import requests

import pixiedust
```

Step 3. Go to the police open data portal (https://data.police.uk/).
Step 4. From the open data portal application programming interface (API) documentation, determine the data that you are interested in and the code you need to pull it. For this example, we are pulling street-level crime from a specific latitude and longitude in January 2020.

```
# Street-level crimes

# Using the Latitude and Longitude from a specific location

# Jan 2020

street_crime_2020=requests.get("https://data.police.uk/api/crimes-street/
all-crime?lat=52.6298&lng=-1.1396&date=2020-01")
```

Step 5. We use PixieDust to visualize the acquired data:

```
display(street_crime_2020.json())
```

The output is shown in Figure 2.11.

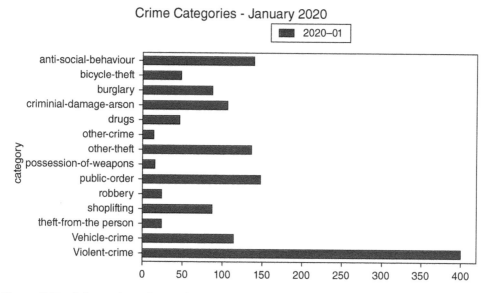

Figure 2.11   Crime categories part I, January 2020

Step 6. For comparison purposes, we pull the street crime data for the same location but now for January 2021:

```
display(street_crime_2021.json())
```

The output is shown in Figure 2.12.

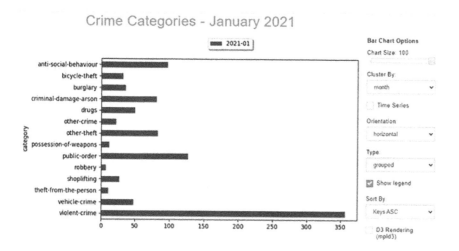

Figure 2.12   Crime categories part I, January 2021

Step 7. Next we combine the data from January 2020 and January 2021:

```
# Let's combine the results

combined_results = street_crime_2020.json() + street_crime_2021.json())
```

Step 8: We visualize and compare the two datasets (now combined):

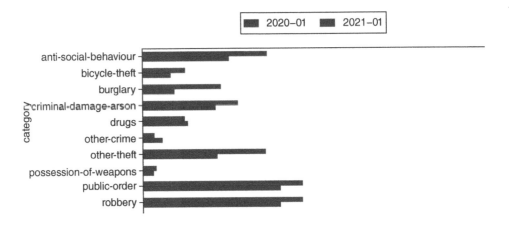

```
display(combined_results)
```

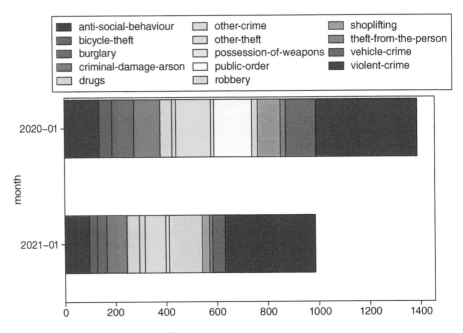

Figure 2.13 Visualizing the results

With this very simple example, what insights can you draw from the datasets? If you think about external factors such as the timing of the lockdowns during these periods, does it change the insights you identify?

Exercise. By reading through the API documentation on the police open data portal, can you pull the available data for stop and searches in any city of your choice in the month of your choice and draw out insights on stop and searches in that city, particularly in terms of age ranges and gender? Try this yourself and then have a look at one approach to the problem in Chapter 6.

2.6 ETHICS BY DESIGN

To map out the ethical issues in a systematic manner, we introduce a framework that covers the main issues that can arise in the context of big data analytics. Various frameworks have been developed over the years to help incorporate ethics by design into every step of the analysis process. Considering the vast amounts of data that are handled and the potential impact a mistake can have on people's lives, special care is required to implement ethics by design.

One of the ethics frameworks that has been specifically designed for data projects is the Open Data Institute's (ODI) data ethics canvas (Open Data Institute, n.d.). The framework addresses 15 issues by raising questions for those inhabiting different roles, such as the project managers and developers. These questions are designed to sensitize stakeholders to various aspects of the project, such as its key data assets, possible sources of bias in data collection, data handling and sharing procedures, and aligning the purpose of the data with processes. Additionally, there are questions on openness and transparency and their consequences, whether positive or negative.

Another useful framework was published by the UK government(Central Digital and Data Office, 2020). Although this framework was developed for use in government and the wider public sector, it has been a guiding document for data projects in other sectors. The structure of the framework is divided into three main principles, those principles highlighting the practical measures that must be considered: transparency, accountability, and fairness. Under each of these, there are five specific actions to serve as guides:

1   Define and understand public benefit and user need.
2   Involve diverse expertise.
3   Comply with the law.
4   Review the quality and limitations of the data.
5   Evaluate and consider wider policy implication.

It can clearly be seen that there are areas of overlap between the ODI data ethics canvas and the government data ethics framework; this is to be expected as their general aim is the same.

Having considered the above framework and other data ethics frameworks and theories, we have identified six primary areas that we believe are paramount when working with data. Before embarking on any big data analytics project, these six areas need to be explored in the context of each project. This is an iterative process: as progress is made with the project, it is necessary to keep reviewing them, to help ensure that data ethics by design is indeed taking place. The six areas are as follows:

- *Transparency.* In this context, transparency refers to the ability to clearly understand and interpret the processes, algorithms, and methodologies involving big data. This includes openness and clarity in data collection, transformation, analysis, and decision-making processes. Transparency plays a crucial role in building trust and mitigating potential biases or ethical concerns. It allows stakeholders to comprehend how data is used, how insights are derived, and how decisions are made based on those insights. Transparent data analytics enables effective communication, enables reproducibility and auditability of results, and facilitates the identification and mitigation of potential errors or biases, thus enhancing the reliability and integrity of the analytical outcomes.
- *Accountability.* Accountability refers to the responsibility and answerability of individuals, organizations, and systems involved in collecting, managing, and utilizing large volumes of data. It encompasses the ethical, legal, and regulatory obligations associated with data handling, privacy, and security. In the realm of big data, accountability plays a crucial role in ensuring transparency, fairness, and trustworthiness. It involves taking ownership of data practices, including data collection, storage, processing, and sharing, and being accountable for the impact and consequences of those actions. Accountability helps establish clear lines of responsibility, promotes adherence to ethical standards and legal requirements, and enables individuals and organizations to be held liable for any misuse or mishandling of data. By fostering accountability in big data analytics, stakeholders can build trust, mitigate risks, and protect privacy concerns in data-driven processes and decision-making.
- *Fairness.* The equitable treatment and unbiased outcomes in the collection, analysis, and utilization of data, fairness aims to ensure that individuals or groups are not subjected to discrimination or unjust treatment based on their personal attributes, such as race, gender, age, or socio-economic status. Securing this principle involves mitigating biases and prejudices that can arise from the algorithms, models, or data used in decision-making processes. It strives to prevent the reinforcing of existing inequalities or the creation of new ones. By promoting fairness, big data initiatives can contribute to a more inclusive and just society, where decisions and opportunities are distributed fairly and without discrimination. Fairness in big data is crucial for building trust, upholding ethical standards, and ensuring that the benefits of data-driven systems are accessible to all individuals and communities, regardless of their background or characteristics.
- *Autonomy.* Autonomy in big data refers to the ability of individuals or entities to exercise control and make informed choices, without being influenced by data collection or processing. The principle of autonomy is wary of practices that are designed to guide people's beliefs and choices and to 'nudge' them into acting in certain ways that are in the interests of another party. Autonomy also emphasizes the

importance of respecting individuals' rights and preferences in the context of data-driven processes. To meet the goal of autonomy, individuals should have clear and transparent information about data practices, and they should be asked for informed consent and allowed to exercise their rights.

- *Responsibility*. Closely related to the principle of accountability, responsibility refers to the ethical and moral obligations of individuals, organizations, and institutions involved in the collection, management, and utilization of large-scale data. This principle recognizes the potential impacts and consequences of data practices on individuals, society, and the environment. Responsible data handling entails ensuring data privacy and security, adhering to legal and regulatory requirements, and avoiding harm or discrimination. It also encompasses being accountable for the accuracy, integrity, and reliability of data, as well as the transparency of data processes. Responsible use of big data requires considering the broader societal implications and striving to promote the common good. By embracing responsibility in big data, stakeholders can foster trust, protect privacy, mitigate risks, and harness the power of data in a way that aligns with ethical principles and social values.
- *Privacy*. This principle acknowledges individuals' rights to control their personal information in the context of large-scale data collection, storage, and analysis. It involves safeguarding sensitive data from unauthorized access, use, or disclosure. This principle is derived from the principle of autonomy because it recognizes individuals' rights to maintain their autonomy, anonymity, and confidentiality while participating in data-driven processes. This includes the injunction to obtain informed consent for data collection and ensuring that data is collected and used only for specified purposes. Privacy also involves implementing robust security measures to prevent data breaches and unauthorized access to personal information. Protecting privacy in big data is crucial for preserving individuals' rights, maintaining trust in data-driven systems, and mitigating the potential risks of surveillance, identity theft, or discriminatory practices.

We refer to this framework (shown in Figure 2.14) as the TAFARP data ethics framework. Throughout this book we use the framework to both highlight cases where its use could have prevented problems and to ensure that we are carrying out and promoting ethics by design.

2.7 INDUSTRY INSIGHTS

Our industry insight for this section based on the data analytics stage focuses on Spotify's patent for personality tracking technology. Spotify is a digital music platform that provides users access to millions of songs. It also provides content creators with a platform to distribute their content and mobilize an audience. Spotify is said to have over 400 million active users and is one of the largest digital music services in the world. In terms of using data for competitive advantage, Spotify has excelled at innovating over the years, expanding its customer base and the increasing the attractiveness of its service. In October 2020 Spotify was

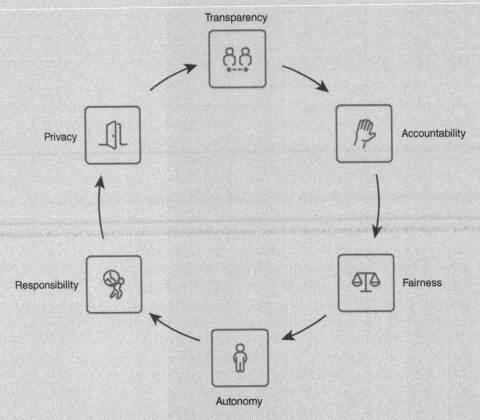

Figure 2.14   TAFARP data ethics by design framework

granted a patent for personality tracking technology (Stassen, 2021). Based on the affect detected in their speech, Spotify can try to predict a user's emotional state and adjust its recommendations appropriately. This is an example of how big data analytics opens up the possibility of incredibly innovative processes. As always, as responsible data professionals, ethics needs to be at the forefront of all we do, and this raises several questions. Using our TAFARP data ethics by design framework (Figure 2.14), questions of transparency, privacy, and autonomy arise. Does Spotify have the consent of its users to analyse their speech for this purpose? If so, was the process of obtaining this authorization clear to users, and was the purpose for which it would be used spelt out to them? Can the same method be used for example in the health sector, where children or adults with disability have their affect analysed in this manner?

Another industry insight is seen in the use of big data for customer retention analytics. This covers all types of analytics: descriptive, diagnostic, predictive, and prescriptive. It is concerned with using all these types of analytics to reduce customer churn. Organizations that have been able to do this particularly well include Netflix, which has a strong customer retention rate, maintained over the years by making effective use of big data. The vast volumes of data collected from its millions of customers are analysed and used to implement recommendation engines which give the customers personalized recommendations (Kapoor, 2021).

SUMMARY

In this chapter, the big data technology landscape has been discussed, including data acquisition, data storage, data wrangling, data piping, data analytics, and data visualization. The relevance of each of these categories was covered and their contribution to big data analytics discussed. The most popular technologies that fall under each of these categories were also listed. The technologies to be used in the rest of the book were highlighted and the rationale behind these choices outlined. The technologies covered in this chapter included both open-source and non-open-source technologies such as Hadoop, Apache Spark, and HDFS. We also introduced the TAFARP data ethics by design framework.

TEST YOUR KNOWLEDGE

1   What are the three main components of Apache Hadoop?
2   What is data wrangling?
3   State one primary difference between traditional databases and HDFS.
4   HDFS is easily scalable: true or false?
5   When a file is loaded into HDFS for storage, the file is broken down into blocks: true or false?
6   A block's metadata contains checksums for the stored block: true or false?
7   The data node manages the file system's metadata and controls how data is distributed across data nodes: true or false?
8   The name node sends block reports to the data node: true or false?
9   After uploaded files split into block, there is block replication: true or false?
10 The objectives of block replication are fault tolerance and data locality: true or false?
11 If a data node fails, HDFS fails: true or false?
12 Data that gets loaded into HDFS goes through the name node: true or false?
13 Name three ethical issues that arise because of big data storage.
14 In designing and implementing a big data architecture, what are the four most important things to bear in mind?

FURTHER READING (OPTIONAL)

Chang, F., Dean, J., Ghemawat, S., Hsieh, W. C. and Wallach, D. A. (2006) Bigtable: A distributed storage system for structured data. Retrieved from https://static. googleusercontent.com/media/research.google.com/en//archive/bigtable-osdi06.pdf
Siddiqa, A., Karim, A. and Gani, A. (2017). Big data storage technologies: A survey. *Frontiers of Information*, 18, 1040–1070. https://doi.org/10.1631/FITEE.1500441
The Open Data Barometer site, an interesting site with a global measure on how governments are using and publishing open data for accountability, innovation, and social impact: https://opendatabarometer.org/

REFERENCES

Apache Hadoop (n.d.) *Apache Hadoop.* Retrieved from https://hadoop.apache.org/

Arden & GEM (2023) NHS and healthcare risk stratification. Retrieved from https://www.ardengemcsu.nhs.uk/services/business-intelligence/risk-stratification/

Central Digital and Data Office (2020) Data Ethics Framework. Retrieved from Government efficiency, transparency and accountability: https://www.gov.uk/government/publications/data-ethics-framework

Dean, J. and Ghemawat, S. (2004) MapReduce: Simplified data processing on large clusters. *OSDI '04: Sixth Symposium on Operating System Design and Implementation* (pp. 137–50). San Francisco, CA: Google Research. Retrieved from https://research.google/pubs/pub62/

Foote, K. D. (2017) A brief history of data storage. Retrieved from https://www.dataversity.net/brief-history-data-storage

Ghemawat, S., Gobioff, H. and Leung, S. T. (2003) The Google file system. *SOSP'03.* New York: ACM. Retrieved from https://static.googleusercontent.com/media/research.google.com/en//archive/gfs-sosp2003.pdf

Kapoor, V. (2021) How Netflix uses big data for consumer satisfaction. Retrieved from https://www.econtribune.com/post/how-netflix-uses-big-data-for-customer-satisfaction

Kelion, L. (2020) Excel: Why using Microsoft's tool caused Covid-19 results to be lost. Retrieved from https://www.bbc.co.uk/news/technology-54423988

Open Data Institute (n.d.) Toolkits for the public and private sectors. Retrieved from https://theodi.org/service/tools-resources/

Stassen, M. (2021) Spotify's latest invention monitors your speech, determines your emotional state... and suggests music based on it. Retrieved from https://www.musicbusinessworldwide.com/spotifys-latest-invention-will-determine-your-emotional-state-from-your-speech-and-suggest-music-based-on-it/

Turck, M. (2020). Resilience and vibrancy: The 2020 data & AI landscape. Retrieved from https://mattturck.com/data2020/

3

APACHE SPARK

CHAPTER CONTENTS

CHAPTER OBJECTIVES

In this chapter:

- You will learn about Apache Spark and how to use it for big data analytics.
- You will be introduced to the Apache Spark Core for data loading, processing, and analytics.
- You will also be introduced to the built-in modules in Apache Spark which provide libraries for data processing and analytics.

3.1 INTRODUCTION

Apache Spark is an open-source, distributed computing system based on a unified analytics engine for large-scale data processing. Spark provides a unified analytics platform, an interface for programming clusters with implicit data parallelism and fault tolerance. Originally developed at Berkeley's AMPLab at the University of California, the Spark codebase was later donated to the Apache Software Foundation, which has maintained it ever since. Spark has its architectural foundation in the resilient distributed dataset (RDD), a read-only data depository distributed over a cluster of machines which enables fault-tolerant distributed processing. The RDD is the fundamental data structure in Spark, allowing data to be stored in memory and processed in parallel across multiple nodes in a cluster. Spark leverages memory-based caching to perform operations on data residing in memory, which significantly improves processing speed and efficiency. It also supports a wide range of analytics capabilities, including SQL queries, graph processing, machine learning, and streaming data processing, all within a single framework. Spark automatically partitions data across the cluster, enabling parallel processing and efficient utilization of resources for data-intensive tasks.

The main aim of this chapter is to provide a high-level introduction to Apache Spark and its use for data analytics. In addition to the Apache Core, the chapter explores several built-in modules:

- *Spark Streaming*. A unified engine for two types of data processing: batch processing and streaming processing. It provides a high-level programming interface (API), allowing third parties to read data from various sources, process it using Spark's powerful libraries, and write the results back to various sinks. Like the other libraries, Spark Streaming is built on top of Spark Core, providing a unified API for both batch and streaming processing. This makes it easy to switch between batch and streaming processing without having to learn a new API.
- *Apache Spark MLlib*. This is the machine learning library which provides various machine learning algorithms such as logistic regression, decision trees, and topic modelling.

- *Apache GraphFrames.* This is a graph processing library, which is used to process graphical data such as data in the form of social networks and tree structures.
- *Apache Spark SQL.* This the module that Apache Spark provides for working with structured data.

Figure 3.1 depicts the elements of Apache Spark, namely the Spark Core and the additional libraries. Each of these is discussed in the subsequent sections. More details and illustrations with more complex use cases are provided in later chapters.

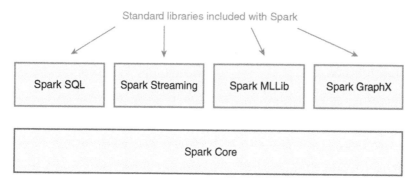

Figure 3.1   Apache Spark Core and its modules

3.2 APACHE SPARK

Apache Spark is an open-source computing framework for big data processing and analysis, one of the most widely used frameworks for large, distributed data processing. Apache Spark was originally initiated as a research project by Matei Zaharia at UC Berkeley's AMPLab in 2009 as part of his PhD; it was then open-sourced in the following year. Today it is being developed by hundreds of developers from many organizations who are part of the open-source community. The inspiration for Apache Spark came from the limitations of the MapReduce programming model, which we explored in the previous chapter. In particular, it was necessary to address MapReduce's limited ability to support interactive queries and machine learning analytics. Prior to Apache Spark, MapReduce was the main programming model used for processing big data. But MapReduce was more suited to handling batch data, which is collected over time and then processed all at once. It was much more limited when it comes to streaming data, which is processed as it is generated. Whereas batch data processing is typically used for tasks that require a lot of processing power, such as machine learning and data mining, streaming data processing is typically used for tasks that require real-time analysis, such as fraud detection and anomaly detection (see Table 3.1).

Table 3.1 Comparing batch to streaming data

Feature	Batch data	Streaming data
Data collection	Data is collected over time.	Data is collected as it is generated.
Data processing	Data is processed all at once.	Data is processed in real time.
Typical use cases	Machine learning, data mining	Fraud detection, anomaly detection

Prior to the rise of Apache Spark, the main alternative to MapReduce was Hadoop, an open-source software framework used to store and process large amounts of data across a cluster of computers. Hadoop is still a popular choice for big data processing because it is scalable, fault-tolerant, and has been around for a while. However, to use it for certain tasks such as machine learning, additional resources are needed, such as Apache Mahout. The advantage of Apache Spark is that it provides a self-contained framework for a wide range of data processing. In addition to providing a processing framework for big data, Apache Spark also has other benefits:

- It processes memory quickly.
- It is relatively accessible to new learners.
- It provides built-in modules/libraries for sophisticated analytics.
- It has a general-purpose interface.
- It is scalable and fault-tolerant.

Compared to MapReduce, there are additional advantages which can contribute to the choice to use Apache Spark:

- Hadoop MapReduce is implemented in Java and is not always user-friendly or easy to learn.
- Spark is written in Scala but provides programming interfaces in Java, R, Python, and Scala. In this book we use the Python interface which is known as PySpark.
- While Hadoop MapReduce is suited for batch processing, Spark can be used for both real-time processing and batch processing.
- Spark provides a unified framework with built-in modules and additional functionality such as its machine learning library MLlib.
- When it comes to data-processing speeds, for in-memory processing Apache Spark is up to 100 times faster for data in RAM than MapReduce and up to 10 times faster for data in storage.

3.2.1 Resilient distributed dataset

Apache Spark Core contains foundational services such as memory management, storage connections, task scheduling, and resilient distributed datasets. RDDs are the fundamental data structure of Apache Spark, one that is used for a wide variety of big data-processing tasks. Their features include:

- *Immutability.* RDDs are immutable, which means that they cannot be changed once they are created. This makes them ideal for parallel processing, as multiple tasks can work on the same RDD without interfering with each other. As we shall see below, transformations create new RDDs (they do not alter the existing RDDs).
- *Distribution.* RDDs are distributed, which means that they are stored across multiple nodes in a cluster. This allows Spark to scale to handle large amounts of data.
- *Resilience.* RDDs are resilient, which means that they can be recovered from failures. If a node in the cluster fails, the RDDs that were stored on that node can be re-created from the other nodes in the cluster.
- *Ease of use.* RDDs are easy to use and can be integrated with other popular big data tools.
- *Flexibility.* RDDs can be used for a wide variety of data-processing tasks.
- *Partitions.* RDDs represent data in memory divided into partitions in multiple nodes (recall from Chapter 2 that nodes are individual machines in the cluster). A single RDD has one or more partitions distributed across multiple nodes, and each partition is processed on a single node (though a single node can handle multiple partitions).

We distinguish between two types of operations:

- *Transformations* are operations that create new RDDs from existing RDDs. They do not evaluate the RDDs immediately, but rather create a graph of transformations that can be evaluated later. This is called lazy evaluation.
- *Actions* are operations that evaluate RDDs and return a value, causing Spark to execute the computation.

Examples of transformations include:

- `map`. The `map` operation takes an RDD and applies a function to each element in the RDD.
- `reduce`. The `reduce` operation takes an RDD and combines all the elements in the RDD using a function.
- `filter`. The `filter` operation takes an RDD and returns a new RDD that contains only the elements that satisfy a predicate.
- `join`. The `join` operation takes two RDDs and returns a new RDD that contains all the pairs of elements that have matching keys.

Examples of actions include:

- `count`. The `count` action counts the number of elements in an RDD.
- `collect`. The `collect` action collects all the elements in an RDD into a local collection.
- `saveAsTextFile`. The `saveAsTextFile` action saves the contents of an RDD to a text file.

Complex data-processing pipelines use transformations and actions, pipelines that can be used to process large amounts of data efficiently. Another important feature of RDDs is their so-called 'lineage'. In general, lineage refers to the ability to track the origin of each element in an RDD. This is important for several reasons, including:

- *Debugging*. Lineage can be used to debug data-processing pipelines by tracking down the source of errors.
- *Explainability*. Lineage can be used to explain how data was processed, which can be helpful for auditing and compliance purposes.
- *Resilience*. Lineage can be used to recover from failures by re-creating RDDs. Because of their immutability, if a node in the cluster fails, the RDDs that were stored on that node can be re-created from the other nodes in the cluster.

A lineage is represented by a data structure known as a directed acyclic graph (DAG). A DAG consists of a set of nodes, each of which represents an RDD, and a set of edges, each of which represents a transformation that was applied to a 'parent' RDD in order to get the 'child' RDD. Each time a child RDD is created, it holds metadata that describes the transformation that created it from its parents. Thus, each RDD can be traced all the way back to its source.

Using Apache Core and RDDs, let us now carry out some hands-on data analytics. We will be using the Jupyter development environment for most of our processing and analytics (refer to Chapter 2, if you need to, for installation/access instructions). For this initial example we will use RDDs to explore a file that contains a dataset of all of William Shakespeare's sonnets. We are particularly interested in the number of occurrences of each word across all his sonnets and we would like to arrange them according to frequency of use. This simple example will enable us to explore Spark Core, RDDs, and various operations on RDDs (both transformations and actions). We would encourage you to work along with the example. The file with the full dump of Shakespeare sonnets can be downloaded from the Project Gutenberg website at https://www.gutenberg.org/ebooks/1041. Alternatively, you can also use any other file of your choosing for the same exercise.

The entry point to Spark Core is the SparkContext. The SparkContext is the heart of a Spark application. So, after setting up the configurations for the environment we are using, we define the SparkContext and then we are ready to start programming, create our RDDs and begin our processing and analysis.

```
from pyspark import SparkContext, SparkConf

conf = SparkConf().setAppName("appName")

sc = SparkContext(conf=conf)
```

So, start by uploading the Shakespeare file to your storage folder. Then open a new Jupyter Python 3 notebook (see Figure 3.2).

Then run the scripts to configure the environment for PySpark and define the SparkContext (see Figure 3.3). Note that configurations are different in various environments.

Figure 3.2   Jupyter Notebook

```
os.environ["SPARK_HOME"] = "/usr/spark2.4.3"
os.environ["PYLIB"] = os.environ["SPARK_HOME"] + "/python/lib"
os.environ["PYSPARK_PYTHON"] = "/usr/local/anaconda/bin/python"
os.environ["PYSPARK_DRIVER_PYTHON"] = "/usr/local/anaconda/bin/python"


# import and define spark context
from pyspark import SparkContext, SparkConf
conf = SparkConf().setAppName("appName")
sc = SparkContext(conf=conf)
```

Figure 3.3   Configuration and SparkContext

Now that the environment is configured and the SparkContext defined, we can load the file into an RDD. To do this we will use the textFile operation. textFile is a transformation that takes the contents of a file and creates an RDD with them (Figure 3.4).

```
# Create a RDD using the shakespeare file
# Remember to replace 'path' with your path and location to the file

spRDD = sc.textFile("hdfs:///path/shakespeare.txt")
```

Figure 3.4   Creating an RDD from the Shakespeare text file

RDDs are associated with lazy evaluation. This means that they do not get instantiated until an action is called. So even though we have created a new RDD spRDD, it will not be instantiated until we call our first action on it. It is good practice to test that your RDD has been created without any problems by calling an action on it as soon as possible, otherwise you can write hundreds of lines of code before calling an action and then find out that somewhere along the line you have a failure and debugging then becomes a lot more complicated. So, let's go ahead and call a couple of actions on spRDD.

```
# Return the first item in the RDD

spRDD.first()

Output:
'1609'

# Return the first 15 items in the RDD

spRDD.take(15)

Output:

['1609',
 '',
 'THE SONNETS',
 '',
 'by William Shakespeare',
 '',
 '',
 '',
 '                  1',
 '  From fairest creatures we desire increase,',
 "  That thereby beauty's rose might never die,",
 '  But as the riper should by time decease,',
 '  His tender heir might bear his memory:',
 '  But thou contracted to thine own bright eyes,',
 "  Feed'st thy light's flame with self-substantial fuel,"]
```

Figure 3.5 Calling actions on spRDD

The first of the actions in Figure 3.5, first returns the first item in the RDD, while the second, take(15), returns the first 15 items in the RDD. We see that, as mentioned earlier, actions result in data being returned. In Figure 3.6 we see part of the contents of the file; comparing this to the results from the actions (see Figure 3.5), we see that the correct data is returned.

```
1609

THE SONNETS

by William Shakespeare

                    1

    From fairest creatures we desire increase,
    That thereby beauty's rose might never die,
    But as the riper should by time decease,
    His tender heir might bear his memory:
    But thou contracted to thine own bright eyes,
    Feed'st thy light's flame with self-substantial fuel,
    Making a famine where abundance lies,
    Thy self thy foe, to thy sweet self too cruel:
    Thou that art now the world's fresh ornament,
    And only herald to the gaudy spring,
    Within thine own bud buriest thy content,
    And tender churl mak'st waste in niggarding:
        Pity the world, or else this glutton be,
        To eat the world's due, by the grave and thee.


                    2

    When forty winters shall besiege thy brow,
    And dig deep trenches in thy beauty's field,
    Thy youth's proud livery so gazed on now,
    Will be a tattered weed of small worth held:
    Then being asked, where all thy beauty lies,
    Where all the treasure of thy lusty days;
    To say within thine own deep sunken eyes,
    Were an all-eating shame, and thriftless praise.
    How much more praise deserved thy beauty's use,
    If thou couldst answer 'This fair child of mine
    Shall sum my count, and make my old excuse'
    Proving his beauty by succession thine.
        This were to be new made when thou art old,
        And see thy blood warm when thou feel'st it cold.


                    3

    Look in thy glass and tell the face thou viewest,
    Now is the time that face should form another,
    Whose fresh repair if now thou not renewest …
```

Figure 3.6 Partial view of Shakespeare sonnet file

If there had been an error in our code, perhaps a syntax error or the location of the file was incorrectly entered, we would now get an error message that would point to the issue. Figure 3.7 shows an example of an error message that is returned when the wrong file path is entered. Such an error message can help point to the source of the problem, which is useful for debugging. If you do run into problems, carefully look through the returned error message.

```
Py4JJavaError: An error occurred while calling o52.partitions.
: org.apache.hadoop.mapred.InvalidInputException: Input path does not exist
: hdfs:/path/shakespearexxx.txt
        at org.apache.hadoop.mapred.FileInputFormat.
singleThreadedListStatus(FileInputFormat.java:287)
```

Figure 3.7   Error message

Having created a new RDD, and run some actions on it, let us now look at some transformations and how these can help go further with our data exploration.

A concept that you might have come across in the past is that of lambda (anonymous) functions. These come in handy when it comes to transformations on RDDs, so we cover them briefly before going into the actual transformation on the Shakespeare spRDD. A lambda function is like other functions in that it takes in inputs and processes them based on defined rules and returns an output. However, it differs from other functions in that the function does not have a name (hence the term anonymous function).

So, for example in the function lambda x: x+1, x is the input and x + 1 the function applied to the input, the result of which is the value it produces. So, if x = [0,2,4,5], the function will return [1,3,5,6].

Let us now return to the Shakespeare file and perform some transformations on it. Remember that our aim here is to find out how many occurrences of each word Shakespeare used in his sonnets and the most frequently occurring words.

The first transformation that we use (see Figure 3.8) is the map transformation. This returns a new RDD (remember RDDs are immutable, so the original RDD cannot be modified) by applying a function to each element of the original RDD, spRDD. It then returns a new RDD made up of a list of lists comprising the lines in the file. Again, recalling that RDDs have lazy evaluation, we have run a couple of actions as soon as possible, to ensure that the new RDD has been created without any issues. So, spRDD_Map.first() returns the first item in *spRDD* because this was created with map (which returns a list of lists); the first item is a list ['1609']. If you compare this to the result from spRDD in Figure 3.5 when the action

```
# Using the map transformation to create a new RDD,
# where the split() function splits each item in the original RDD into a list
(all contained in a list)

spRDD_Map = spRDD.filter(lambda line: len(line) > 0).map(lambda line: line.
split())

# Running some actions on spRDD2
# Return the first item in the RDD

spRDD_Map.first()

Output:
['1609']

spRDD_Map.take(10)

Output:
[['1609'],
 ['THE', 'SONNETS'],
 ['by', 'William', 'Shakespeare'],
 ['1'],
 ['From', 'fairest', 'creatures', 'we', 'desire', 'increase,'],
 ['That', 'thereby', "beauty's", 'rose', 'might', 'never', 'die,'],
 ['But', 'as', 'the', 'riper', 'should', 'by', 'time', 'decease,'],
 ['His', 'tender', 'heir', 'might', 'bear', 'his', 'memory:'],
 ['But', 'thou', 'contracted', 'to', 'thine', 'own', 'bright', 'eyes,'],
 ["Feed'st", 'thy', "light's", 'flame', 'with', 'self-substantial', 'fuel,']]
```

Figure 3.8 Map transformation

first() was run it simply returned the first item in the file '1609' and not a list like map returns.

So, still bearing in mind our end goal of exploring the Shakespeare file to determine the occurrences of words, let us go on to our next transformation.

The next transformation is flatMap. This is similar to map but returns a flattened list (not a list of lists). So, when we look at the data returned by take(10) applied to the new flattened RDD, spRDD_FlatMap, in Figure 3.9, we see that a single list is returned and the action first() returns the first value in that list.

```
# Using the flatMap transformation to create a new flattened RDD (a single list
of all the words in the file)

spRDD_FlatMap = spRDD.filter(lambda line: len(line) > 0).flatMap(lambda line:
line.split())

# Return the first item in the RDD

spRDD_FlatMap.first()

Output:
['1609']

# Return the first 10 items in the RDD

spRDD_FlatMap.take(10)

Output:
['1609',
 'THE',
 'SONNETS',
 'by',
 'William',
 'Shakespeare',
 '1',
 'From',
 'fairest',
 'creatures']
```

Figure 3.9 `flatMap` **transformation**

Next, we will take `spRDD_FlatMap` and from it create a new RDD in the form of a key–value pair. To create the key–value pair, as seen in Figure 3.10, a number of operations are carried out. For every item in `spRDD_FlatMap`, the code filters out where the item has a length greater than zero (i.e., it is not blank) and then maps each of these items and returns the word in lower case along with a '1' besides it. This creates a key–value pair, where the word is the key and the '1' the value. We see how these key–value pairs look from the data returned by the actions in Figure 3.10. There are lots of actions that can be run on RDDs; if, for instance, you are particularly interested in seeing the items in the RDD returned in descending order, then you would run the `top` action as seen in Figure 3.11.

With the key–value pairs in hand we can now use the reduceByKey transformation (Figure 3.12). This runs on a dataset of key–value pairs (k, v) and performs a summary function for each value associated with a key. So, in our case, it runs on the entire dataset of key–value pairs (remember that has each word with a '1' as the value) and does a summation for each word in the dataset. So if, for instance, the word *sunset* is found in the dataset, for every occurrence of the key (word) *sunset*, it sums up the values (i.e., all the 1s) resulting in a final key–value pair with *sunset* occurring once in the new RDD countsbyword, but the value next to it would be the number of times *sunset* occurs in the original file.

```
# Creating a key-value pair RDD from the flattened RDD

kvpairs = spRDD_FlatMap.filter(lambda word: len(word) > 0).map(lambda word:
(word.lower(),1))

# Return the first item in the RDD

kvpairs.first()

Output:
('1609', 1)

# Return the first 10 items in the RDD

kvpairs.take(10)

Output:
[('1609', 1),
 ('the', 1),
 ('sonnets', 1),
 ('by', 1),
 ('william', 1),
 ('shakespeare', 1),
 ('1', 1),
 ('from', 1),
 ('fairest', 1),
 ('creatures', 1)]
```

Figure 3.10   Key-value pair

```
# Return the top 10 items (sorted in descending order) in the RDD

kvpairs.top(10)

Output:
[('}', 1),
 ('}', 1),
 ("zwagger'd", 1),
 ('zounds,', 1),
 ('zounds,', 1),
 ('zounds,', 1),
 ('zounds,', 1),
 ('zounds,', 1),
 ('zounds,', 1),
 ('zounds,', 1)]
```

Figure 3.11 Top action

Let's use one last transformation to put the occurrences of the words in descending order, so we can see the most frequently occurring words. The keyBy transformation creates a tuple consisting of a key and a value as seen in Figure 3.13, and when we run a top(10) action on this, we see the 10 most frequently occurring words in Shakespeare's sonnets. If you look through the code that we have used to get this result you will see that in just a few simple lines of code, we are able to draw this insight from the dump of all Shakespeare's sonnets. We can thus begin to appreciate the power of Apache Spark and big data analytics. As we progress in the book we will look at more complicated examples, but hopefully this gives you a feel for what is possible. Note that there are different ways to achieve our objectives, and we encourage you to explore using various transformations and actions yourself. Finally, just before we leave this example, let us add a simple visualization to depict the 10 most frequently occurring words (Figure 3.14).

RDDs are lower-level APIs and are particularly useful for analysis of unstructured data (like the file with the Shakespeare sonnets that we have just explored). They are good for low-level control on datasets and low-level transformations and actions.

3.2.2 DataFrames and Apache Spark SQL

Apache Spark SQL is a module in Spark that provides a programming interface for working with structured and semi-structured data using DataFrames. DataFrames are a distributed collection of data organized into named columns, like a table in a relational database. In a similar manner to RDDs, DataFrames are immutable distributed collections of data. Unlike

```
# Use reduceByKey transformation to sum up/ return number of occurrences of
each word

countsbyword = kvpairs.reduceByKey(lambda v1, v2: v1 + v2)

# Return the first item in the RDD

countsbyword.first()

Output:
('shakespeare', 255)

# Return the first 10 items in the RDD

countsbyword.take(10)

Output:
[('shakespeare', 255),
 ('1', 13),
 ('fairest', 39),
 ('creatures', 27),
 ('we', 3201),
 ('increase,', 9),
 ('thereby', 21),
 ("beauty's", 30),
 ('rose', 44),
 ('never', 959)]
```

Figure 3.12 reduceByKey **transformation**

RDDs, DataFrames are designed for processing both structured data and semi-structured data. Like RDDs, they have lazy evaluation (so remember it is good practice to call an action on them as soon as possible!) and they are distributed. DataFrames in Spark SQL offer a higher level of abstraction than RDDs, making it easier to perform structured data-processing tasks and seamlessly integrating with RDDs. As RDDs can be converted to DataFrames and vice versa, this enables interoperability between the two data structures.

Spark SQL is a programming module for structured data processing. It is a library for structured data. Spark SQL enables the integration of SQL queries with Spark programs, allowing structured data to be queried directly, which in turn makes it easy to run SQL queries alongside complex analytical algorithms. While the Spark Core uses RDDs, Spark SQL uses Schema RDDs to work on schemas, tables, and records (structured data), also

```
# Use the keyBy transformation to create a new RDD with the value as key

countsbywordKeyed = countsbyword.keyBy(lambda x:x[1])

# Return the first item in the RDD

countsbywordKeyed.first()

Output:
(255, ('shakespeare', 255))

# Return the top 10 items (sorted in descending order) in the RDD

countsbywordKeyed.top(10)

Output:
[(27484, ('the', 27484)),
 (25991, ('and', 25991)),
 (19540, ('i', 19540)),
 (18656, ('to', 18656)),
 (17952, ('of', 17952)),
 (14365, ('a', 14365)),
 (12455, ('my', 12455)),
 (10660, ('in', 10660)),
 (10597, ('you', 10597)),
 (10473, ('that', 10473))]
```

Figure 3.13   keyBy **transformation**

known as DataFrames. The key features of DataFrames in Apache Spark SQL include the following:

- *Schema and type inference.* DataFrames have a schema, which defines the structure of the data, including column names and data types. The schema enables efficient query execution and optimization. Additionally, DataFrames can infer the schema automatically from the data.
- *High-level APIs.* Spark SQL provides a set of high-level APIs for data manipulation and query operations on DataFrames, such as filtering, grouping, aggregations, joins, and window functions. These APIs simplify complex data-processing tasks.

```
# import relevant libraries needed for visualisation

import matplotlib.pyplot as plt
%matplotlib inline

# Put the top 10 words in a new variable using the map transformation and the
take() action

top10words = topWordCountsFull.map(lambda x:x[1]).take(10)

top10words

Output:
[('the', 27484),
 ('and', 25991),
 ('i', 19540),
 ('to', 18656),
 ('of', 17952),
 ('a', 14365),
 ('my', 12455),
 ('in', 10660),
 ('you', 10597),
 ('that', 10473)]

xValue = []
yValue = []

for tup in top10words:
        xValue.append(tup[0])
        yValue.append(tup[1])

#plot the data
topN = list(range(1,11))
plt.xlabel('Word')
plt.ylabel('Count')
plt.title('Chart of Ten Top Reocurring Words')
plt.bar(topN, yValue)
plt.xticks()
plt.xticks(topN, xValue)
```

(Continued)

Figure 3.14   (Continued)
Output:

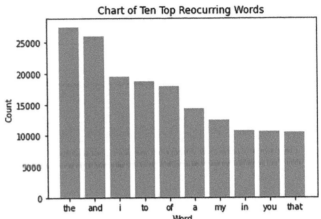

Figure 3.14   Visualization of the 10 most frequently occurring words

- *Catalyst optimizer.* DataFrames benefit from the Catalyst optimizer in Spark SQL, which optimizes query plans based on the DataFrame operations and the available statistics. This optimization improves the overall performance of data-processing tasks.
- *Data sources and formats.* DataFrames support a wide range of data sources and formats, including Parquet, Avro, JSON, CSV, and JDBC. They provide seamless integration with external data sources and enable efficient data ingestion and extraction.

There are numerous sources for Spark SQL, including:

- Parquet files (a columnar storage format)
- JSON documents (consisting of attribute–value pairs and array data types)
- HIVE tables (Hive is a data warehouse structure built on top of Hadoop)
- Text files
- Cassandra database (open-source distributed NoSQL database management system)

In a similar manner to how SparkContext is the main entry point for an application using the Spark Core API, SQLContext is the main entry points for Spark SQL:

```
from pyspark import SparkConf, SparkContext

from pyspark.sql import SQLContext

sc= SparkContext()

sqlContext = SQLContext(sc)
```

For DataFrames the main entry point is SparkSession. It provides the entry point for interaction with Spark DataFrames, and is available in PySpark as *spark*. SparkSession is used to create DataFrames, register DataFrames, and execute SQL queries.

There are various ways to create DataFrames. One way is to use an existing RDD using SparkSession's `createDataFrame()` method. Alternatively they can be created from various sources such as a JSON file, a text file, Parquet file or ORC file, a table in Hive, or an external database.

Let us do some hands-on exploration using DataFrames and Spark SQL, like we did with RDDs. For this quick exercise we will use a file downloaded from an open data portal, the Department for Transport road safety data (Department for Transport, 2022). We recommend downloading your own file from the open data portal, which will give you the flexibility to choose parameters that are of interest to you.

As before, open a new Jupyter Python 3 notebook. Then run the configuration scripts and define the SparkSession and the SQLContext. Once this is done, we are ready to create the DataFrame. In Figure 3.15, we can see that the command to create the DataFrame from the text file includes options that allow us to provide additional information, such as whether or not the text file has a header row, any delimiters and whether or not the schema should be inferred. A dataset's schema gives information about the columns in the dataset and their formats – for example, whether a column is made up of integers or strings. With the option set to true for `inferSchema`, based on the value in each column of the dataset the system works out what each column's data-

```
#create a DataFrame directly from Accidents2019 csv file (remember to change
the path to the location where you have the file you are uploading)

accidents_2019DF = spark.read.option("header", "true").option("delimiter",
",")\
.option("inferSchema", "true").csv("path/Accidents2019.csv")

accidents_2019DF
```

```
Output:

DataFrame[accident_index: string, accident_year: int, accident_reference:
string, location_easting_osgr: string, location_northing_osgr: string,
longitude: string, latitude: string, police_force: int, accident_severity:
int, number_of_vehicles: int, number_of_casualties: int, date: string, day_
of_week: int, time: string, local_authority_district: int, local_authority_
ons_district: string, local_authority_highway: string, first_road_class: int,
first_road_number: int, road_type: int, speed_limit: int, junction_detail:
int, junction_control: int, second_road_class: int, second_road_number:
int, pedestrian_crossing_human_control: int, pedestrian_crossing_physical_
facilities: int, light_conditions: int, weather_conditions: int, road_surface_
conditions: int, special_conditions_at_site: int, carriageway_hazards: int,
urban_or_rural_area: int, did_police_officer_attend_scene_of_accident: int,
trunk_road_flag: int, lsoa_of_accident_location: string]
```

Figure 3.15 Creating the DataFrame directly from the text file

```
accidents_2019DF.printSchema()
```

```
Output:
root
 |-- accident_index: string (nullable = true)
 |-- accident_year: integer (nullable = true)
 |-- accident_reference: string (nullable = true)
 |-- location_easting_osgr: string (nullable = true)
 |-- location_northing_osgr: string (nullable = true)
 |-- longitude: string (nullable = true)
 |-- latitude: string (nullable = true)
 |-- police_force: integer (nullable = true)
 |-- accident_severity: integer (nullable = true)
 |-- number_of_vehicles: integer (nullable = true)
 |-- number_of_casualties: integer (nullable = true)
 |-- date: string (nullable = true)
 |-- day_of_week: integer (nullable = true)
 |-- time: string (nullable = true)
 |-- local_authority_district: integer (nullable = true)
 |-- local_authority_ons_district: string (nullable = true)
 |-- local_authority_highway: string (nullable = true)
 |-- first_road_class: integer (nullable = true)
 |-- first_road_number: integer (nullable = true)
 |-- road_type: integer (nullable = true)
 |-- speed_limit: integer (nullable = true)
 |-- junction_detail: integer (nullable = true)
 |-- junction_control: integer (nullable = true)
 |-- second_road_class: integer (nullable = true)
 |-- second_road_number: integer (nullable = true)
 |-- pedestrian_crossing_human_control: integer (nullable = true)
 |-- pedestrian_crossing_physical_facilities: integer (nullable = true)
 |-- light_conditions: integer (nullable = true)
 |-- weather_conditions: integer (nullable = true)
 |-- road_surface_conditions: integer (nullable = true)
 |-- special_conditions_at_site: integer (nullable = true)
 |-- carriageway_hazards: integer (nullable = true)
 |-- urban_or_rural_area: integer (nullable = true)
 |-- did_police_officer_attend_scene_of_accident: integer (nullable = true)
 |-- trunk_road_flag: integer (nullable = true)
 |-- lsoa_of_accident_location: string (nullable = true)
```

Figure 3.16   Printing the schema of the DataFrame

```
sqlContext.registerDataFrameAsTable(accidents_2019DF, "tbAccidents_2019")
```

Figure 3.17 Registering the DataFrame as a table

type should be. It is also possible to manually specify what the schema should be. The `printSchema()` function can be used to check the schema of the newly created DataFrame as in Figure 3.16.

To run SQL queries against a DataFrame, it needs to be registered as a table. Once this is done, SQL queries can be executed against the registered table (see Figure 3.17). Having registered table `tbAccidents_2019`, we can run SQL queries on it. Some examples can be seen in Figures 3.18–3.21. Finally, we add a visualization plotting accident severity against speed limit, which immediately tells us that the majority of the accidents

```
sqlContext.sql("select * from tbAccidents_2019").take(2)
```

```
Output:

[Row(accident_index='2.01901E+12', accident_year=2019, accident_
reference='10128300', location_easting_osgr='528218', location_northing_
osgr='180407', longitude='-0.153842', latitude='51.508057', police_force=1,
accident_severity=3, number_of_vehicles=2, number_of_casualties=3,
date='18/02/2019', day_of_week=2, time='17:50', local_authority_district=1,
local_authority_ons_district='E09000033', local_authority_highway='E09000033',
first_road_class=3, first_road_number=4202, road_type=1, speed_limit=30,
junction_detail=1, junction_control=2, second_road_class=3, second_road_
number=4202, pedestrian_crossing_human_control=0, pedestrian_crossing_
physical_facilities=5, light_conditions=1, weather_conditions=1, road_
surface_conditions=1, special_conditions_at_site=0, carriageway_hazards=0,
urban_or_rural_area=1, did_police_officer_attend_scene_of_accident=3, trunk_
road_flag=2, lsoa_of_accident_location='E01004762'),

 Row(accident_index='2.01901E+12', accident_year=2019, accident_
reference='10152270', location_easting_osgr='530219', location_northing_
osgr='172463', longitude='-0.127949', latitude='51.436208', police_force=1,
accident_severity=3, number_of_vehicles=2, number_of_casualties=1,
date='15/01/2019', day_of_week=3, time='21:45', local_authority_district=9,
local_authority_ons_district='E09000022', local_authority_highway='E09000022',
first_road_class=3, first_road_number=23, road_type=2, speed_limit=30,
junction_detail=0, junction_control=-1, second_road_class=-1, second_
road_number=-1, pedestrian_crossing_human_control=9, pedestrian_crossing_
physical_facilities=9, light_conditions=4, weather_conditions=1, road_
surface_conditions=1, special_conditions_at_site=0, carriageway_hazards=0,
urban_or_rural_area=1, did_police_officer_attend_scene_of_accident=3, trunk_
road_flag=2, lsoa_of_accident_location='E01003117')]
```

Figure 3.18 SQL query to select all the data from the table and return two of the rows

```
# Casualties per day of week
sqlContext.sql("select Day_of_Week, Number_of_Casualties, count(*) as Count
from tbAccidents_2019 group \
by Day_of_Week, Number_of_Casualties").show()
```

Output:

```
+-----------+--------------------+-----+
|Day_of_Week|Number_of_Casualties|Count|
+-----------+--------------------+-----+
|          4|                  10|    1|
|          6|                   1|15245|
|          3|                   1|14278|
|          7|                   4|  296|
|          2|                   2| 2177|
|          1|                   7|   17|
|          2|                   3|  626|
|          7|                   1|11866|
|          4|                   7|   10|
|          1|                   2| 2009|
|          1|                   9|    1|
|          5|                   7|    9|
|          5|                   6|   19|
|          6|                   8|    3|
|          1|                   1| 9837|
|          6|                   5|   92|
|          4|                   9|    3|
|          1|                   3|  644|
|          6|                  13|    2|
|          6|                  12|    1|
+-----------+--------------------+-----+
only showing top 20 rows
```

Figure 3.19   SQL query to return the total number of casualties by day of the week

that happened in 2019 were at 30 miles per hour and were fortunately minor ones (see Figure 3.22).

3.3 APACHE SPARK GRAPHFRAMES

Apache Spark GraphFrames is a package for Apache Spark which provides DataFrame-based graphs. It provides APIs for graph processing in Scala, Python, and Java. GraphFrames represent graphs: vertices (e.g., users) and edges (e.g., relationships between users). GraphFrames are based on DataFrames, while the GraphX is based on RDDs, GraphX extends the Spark RDD to produce a new abstraction, the resilient distributed graph (RDG). GraphFrames and

GraphX are both used for graph processing in Apache Spark. However, they enable different levels of processing, GraphX is lower-level and enables fine-grained control over graph computations while GraphFrames is more high-level and user-friendly than GraphX. We will focus here on GraphFrames. To help understand this package and its use we will start with a brief introduction to graphs.

```
# Return distinct list of Speed Limits

sqlContext.sql("SELECT distinct Speed_Limit FROM tbAccidents_2019").show()
```

Output:

```
+-----------+
|Speed_Limit|
+-----------+
|         -1|
|         20|
|         40|
|         50|
|         70|
|         60|
|         30|
+-----------+
```

Figure 3.20   SQL query to return the distinct list of speed limits

A graph is a set of vertices connected to each other via edges. There are different types of graphs including:

- Directed, where the edges are all directed from one vertex to another
- Undirected, where the edges have no defined direction or are bidirectional
- Cyclic, which contain at least one graph cycle
- Acyclic/tree, which contain no graph cycle (see Figure 3.23)
- Weighted, which have weights assigned to their edges or vertices
- Unweighted, in which all edges/vertices have no weights.

GraphFrames are great for any datasets that fall into the categories above, such as social networks and graphical datasets. GraphFrames are based on the property graph model

```
sqlContext.sql("SELECT Date, \
                       COUNT(*) \
                       FROM tbAccidents_2019 \
                       GROUP BY Date \
                       ORDER BY Date").show()
```

Output:

```
+----------+--------+
|      Date|count(1)|
+----------+--------+
|01/01/2019|     231|
|01/02/2019|     318|
|01/03/2019|     305|
|01/04/2019|     312|
|01/05/2019|     309|
|01/06/2019|     320|
|01/07/2019|     329|
|01/08/2019|     351|
|01/09/2019|     268|
|01/10/2019|     372|
|01/11/2019|     417|
|01/12/2019|     251|
|02/01/2019|     193|
|02/02/2019|     294|
|02/03/2019|     286|
|02/04/2019|     350|
|02/05/2019|     342|
|02/06/2019|     243|
|02/07/2019|     327|
|02/08/2019|     351|
+----------+--------+
only showing top 20 rows
```

Figure 3.21 SQL query to return a count of the number of accidents recorded for each day

G = (V, E) where each vertex V is represented as an (id, attribute/data) pair and each edge E as an (src, dst, attribute/data) tuple.

GraphFrames come with a number of standard graph algorithms built in, including:

- Breadth-first search
- Connected components

```
import matplotlib.pyplot as plt
import pandas as pd


Panda_Accident_Type = Accident_type.toPandas()


%matplotlib inline


plot_Outcome=Panda_Accident_Type.pivot(index='Speed_limit', columns='Accident_
Severity', values='count') \
                        .plot(kind='bar', figsize=(10,5))
plot_Outcome.set_title("Speed Limit vs Accident Severity",color="b")
plot_Outcome.set_ylim(0,58000)
plot_Outcome.set_xlabel("Speed Limit",color="b")
plt.legend(loc='center left', bbox_to_anchor=(1, 0.5));
```

Output:

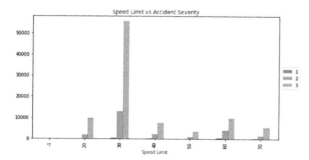

Figure 3.22 Visualization of accident severity (1, critical; 2, major; 3, minor) against speed limit

- Strongly connected components
- Label propagation algorithm
- PageRank
- Shortest paths
- Triangle count

Using a Jupyter Python notebook, we will take a high-level look at the use of GraphFrames. As with previous examples, start by running the relevant configuration and define the SQLContext. Additionally, we also need to import the GraphFrames library (see Figure 3.24).

So, to create a GraphFrame we need a DataFrame that represents the vertices V and a second DataFrame that represents the edges E between the vertices in the data. Figure 3.25 shows a simple

Trigger warning – the following page contains references to suicide which some individuals may find distressing.

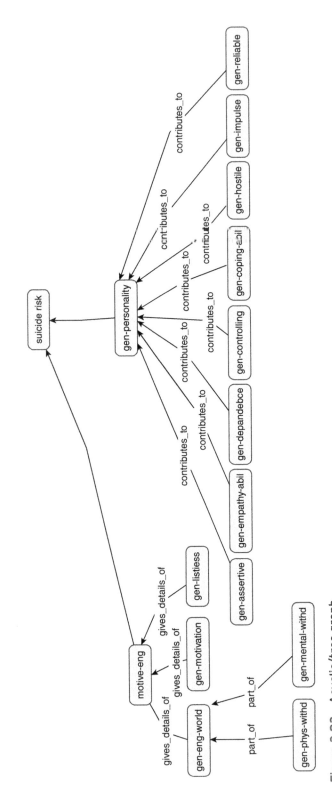

Figure 3.23 Acyclic/tree graph

```
From graphframes import *
```

Figure 3.24 Importing GraphFrames library

```
# Create a Vertex DataFrame with unique ID column "id"

v = spark.createDataFrame([
  ("a", "Alice", 34),
  ("b", "Bob", 36),
  ("c", "Charlie", 30),
], ["id", "name", "age"])


v.show()
```

Output:

```
+---+-------+---+
| id|   name|age|
+---+-------+---+
|  a|  Alice| 34|
|  b|    Bob| 36|
|  c|Charlie| 30|
+---+-------+---+
```

```
# Create an Edge DataFrame
e = spark.createDataFrame([
  ("a", "b", "friend"),
  ("b", "c", "follow"),
  ("c", "b", "follow"),
], ["src", "dst", "relationship"])


e.show()
```

Output:

```
+---+---+------------+
|src|dst|relationship|
+---+---+------------+
|  a|  b|      friend|
|  b|  c|      follow|
|  c|  b|      follow|
+---+---+------------+
```

Figure 3.25 Create vertex and edge DataFrames to create GraphFrames

```
# Create GraphFrame from the Vertex and Edge DataFrames
g = GraphFrame(v, e)
g
```

```
Output:
GraphFrame(v:[id: string, name: string ... 1 more field], e:[src: string, dst:
string ... 1 more field])
```

Figure 3.26 Create GraphFrame

example where we manually create a vertex made up of a unique id column, names, and ages of some people. The vertex DataFrame needs to always have a unique id column. We then create the edge DataFrame which is made up of the vertex ids where there is a connection between people. From these DataFrames we then create the GraphFrame (see Figure 3.26).

Even though this is a very simple example, we can still carry out some explorations on it. In Figure 3.27, we return the indegrees, outdegrees, and degrees of the GraphFrame, respectively representing the number of edges going into a vertex, the number of edges coming out of a vertex, and a count of both the edges going in and those coming out. For our simple example, we can easily do this manually. However, when we are dealing with a dataset with thousands of edges and vertices we start to appreciate this functionality more. We can run additional queries (as in Figure 3.28) and run more complex algorithms; these are discussed in detail in Chapter 7.

Typical use cases for GraphFrames include page ranking, analytics on web pages, social networks, and mobile phone systems.

3.4 APACHE SPARK MLLIB

Apache Spark MLlib is Apache Spark's machine learning library (Apache Spark, n.d.). It contains many machine learning algorithms and utilities. The aspects of machine learning using MLlib that we focus on are shown in Figure 3.29. This figure leaves out an additional type of machine learning known as reinforcement learning.

The algorithms provided by MLlib include:

- Classification: logistic regression, naive Bayes, and so on
- Regression: generalized linear regression, survival regression, and so on
- Decision trees, random forests, and gradient-boosted trees
- Recommendation: alternating least squares (ALS)
- Clustering: *K*-means, Gaussian mixtures (GMMs), and so on
- Topic modelling: latent Dirichlet allocation (LDA)
- Frequent item sets, association rules, and sequential pattern mining

As with other libraries we will now go through a hands-on example. The example we will use falls under supervised learning (linear regression), Figure 3.30 illustrates the general journey for supervised learning.

```
# Query: Get in-degree of each vertex.
g.inDegrees.show()
```

Output:

```
+---+--------+
| id|inDegree|
+---+--------+
|  c|       1|
|  b|       2|
+---+--------+
```

```
# Query: Get out-degree of each vertex.
g.outDegrees.show()
```

Output:

```
+---+------+
| id|degree|
+---+------+
|  c|     2|
|  b|     3|
|  a|     1|
+---+------+
```

```
# Query: Get degree of each vertex.
g.degrees.show()
```

Output:

```
+---+---------+
| id|outDegree|
+---+---------+
|  c|        1|
|  b|        1|
|  a|        1|
+---+---------+
```

Figure 3.27 Indegrees, outdegrees, and total degrees

The initial steps are to import into the development environment all the relevant librar-ies, followed by the data, which are then pre-processed, followed by all the other steps depicted in Figure 3.30 right up to using the model to make predictions and its subsequent evaluation. As you will see in later chapters where machine learning using big data is

```
# Query: Count the number of "follow" connections in the graph.

g.edges.filter("relationship = 'follow'").count()

# Find the youngest user's age in the graph.
# This queries the vertex DataFrame.

g.vertices.groupBy().min("age").show()
```

Output:

```
+--------+
|min(age)|
+--------+
|      30|
+--------+
```

Figure 3.28   Additional queries

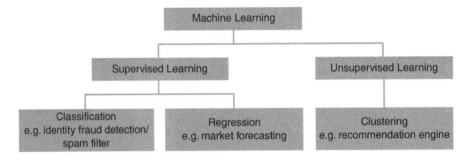

Figure 3.29   Machine learning

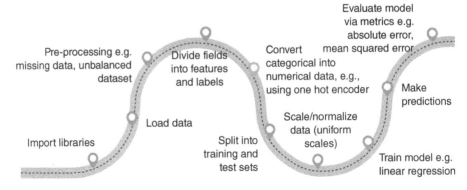

Figure 3.30   Supervised learning journey

```
from pyspark.mllib.regression import LabeledPoint
from pyspark.ml.regression import LinearRegression
```

Figure 3.31 Configuration script, defining of SparkSession, and importing of relevant tables

```
# load the data

data=spark.read.csv(path/clean_loan_stats_3c.csv', header=True,
inferSchema=True)


data.printSchema()

Output:
root
 |-- id: string (nullable = true)
 |-- member_id: string (nullable = true)
 |-- loan_amnt: integer (nullable = true)
 |-- funded_amnt: integer (nullable = true)
 |-- funded_amnt_inv: integer (nullable = true)
 |-- term: string (nullable = true)
 |-- int_rate: string (nullable = true)
 |-- installment: double (nullable = true)
 |-- grade: string (nullable = true)
 |-- sub_grade: string (nullable = true)
 |-- emp_title: string (nullable = true)
 |-- emp_length: string (nullable = true)
 |-- home_ownership: string (nullable = true)
 |-- annual_inc: double (nullable = true)
 |-- verification_status: string (nullable = true)
 |-- issue_d: string (nullable = true)
 |-- loan_status: string (nullable = true)
 |-- pymnt_plan: string (nullable = true)
```

Figure 3.32 Loading loan dataset and printing out the schema

covered, the evaluation stage is crucial to the whole process as it helps to ensure that the model works, and the results obtained from it are accurate. For safety-critical use cases, the outcomes can be catastrophic if this step is skipped or not done well.

As with other examples, open a new Jupyter Python notebook, run the configuration scripts, define the SparkSession, and import the relevant libraries (see Figure 3.31 for importing of the LabeledPoint and LinearRegression libraries). Now download Wendy Kan's lending club loan data from this book's online resources (Figure 3.32).

The schema shows that the dataset has fields such as id, member_id, funded_amnt, int_rate (interest rate), and instalment. All of these are features that could influence the loan amount given to a person. So, our aim is to train a model that we can use to predict the loan amount that a person might be given based on various features. So, datasets are generally made up of features, in addition to which some datasets include a special feature known as the label. If we are trying to predict a feature which is present in the dataset based on other features in the dataset, the feature we are trying to predict is known as a label. In this case we say that our data is labelled because we have the loan_amnt (loan amount) field in the dataset. If, however, the feature we are trying to predict is not present in our dataset then we say the data is not labelled.

To really simplify this example, we will use domain expertise and a correlation func tion to choose a few features to use to train our predictive model. So instead of trying to guess which features to choose for our simple model, we use a combination of domain knowledge and correlation checks. Figure 3.33 depicts correlation checks

```
from pyspark.ml.stat import Correlation

data_ml.stat.corr("annual_inc","loan_amnt")
0.3919615305715742


data_ml.stat.corr("last_pymnt_amnt","loan_amnt")
0.4243182145422379



data_ml.stat.corr("installment","loan_amnt")
0.9478973044210571


data.stat.corr("total_pymnt","loan_amnt")
0.8930317733309153
```

Figure 3.33 Using correlation to choose features to use

between individual features and the label. Alternatively, we could run correlation checks against all the features and the label; this would return a correlation matrix showing the correlations of every single feature and the label, which could then be used to select the features with the strongest correlations to use in training the model while still being mindful of guarding against multicollinearity.

Correlations can hence be used as an aid in feature selection, to select the most relevant features. When training your model, to reduce computational cost you might want to reduce input variables as much as possible, and correlation can help with this. The type of feature selection method used is determined to a large extent by the type of input and output variables (i.e., numerical or categorical). One type of correlation is the Pearson correlation

```
# select needed columns


data_ml=data.selectExpr("installment", "annual_inc","total_rec_late_
fee","last_pymnt_amnt","delinq_amnt","loan_amnt")


data_ml
```

Output:
Data frame[installment: double, annual_inc: double, total_rcc_late_fee:double,
last_pymnt_amnt: double,delinq_amnt: int, loan_amnt: int]

```
data_ml.printSchema()
```

Output:
root
 |-- installment: double (nullable = true)
 |-- annual_inc: double (nullable = true)
 |-- total_rec_late_fee: double (nullable = true)
 |-- last_pymnt_amnt: double (nullable = true)
 |-- delinq_amnt: integer (nullable = true)
 |-- loan_amnt: integer (nullable = true)


```
data_ml.show()
```

Output:

```
+-----------+----------+------------------+---------------+-----------+---------+
|installment|annual_inc|total_rec_late_fee|last_pymnt_amnt|delinq_amnt|loan_amnt|
+-----------+----------+------------------+---------------+-----------+---------+
|     321.08|   58000.0|               0.0|         321.08|          0|    10400|
|     336.64|   78000.0|               0.0|       12017.81|          0|    15000|
|     326.53|   69000.0|               0.0|        9338.58|          0|     9600|
|      260.2|   50000.0|               0.0|           17.7|          0|     7650|
|     319.08|  125000.0|               0.0|         319.08|          0|    12800|
|     516.36|   63800.0|               0.0|       17813.19|          0|    21425|
|     578.22|   75000.0|               0.0|       10888.01|          0|    17000|
|     800.71|   72000.0|               0.0|         800.71|          0|    23325|
|      83.03|   89000.0|               0.0|        2294.26|          0|     2500|
|     468.17|   60000.0|               0.0|           50.0|          0|    12975|
|     172.98|   26000.0|               0.0|           43.4|          0|     5250|
|      351.4|  109777.0|               0.0|        4935.54|          0|    16000|
|      332.1|   90000.0|               0.0|          332.1|          0|    10000|
|     581.95|   55000.0|               0.0|         581.95|          0|    21075|
|      70.31|   37000.0|               0.0|        1255.43|          0|     2000|
|     194.99|  120000.0|               0.0|          578.3|          0|     6000|
|       97.5|   60000.0|               0.0|        1117.63|          0|     3000|
|      69.33|   32200.0|               0.0|        1897.69|          0|     2000|
|     140.61|   50000.0|              15.0|         1606.9|          0|     4000|
|      601.7|   67000.0|               0.0|       24652.44|          0|    28000|
+-----------+----------+------------------+---------------+-----------+---------+
only showing top 20 rows
```

Figure 3.34   Selection of needed features to create new DataFrame

coefficient, which is a measure of linear correlation between two sets of data. However, it can only determine linear correlation and returns values between –1 and +1. The results can be interpreted as follows:

- +1: perfect positive correlation (as one value increases the other increases too).
- –1: perfect negative correlation (as one value increases the other decreases).
- Between ±0.5 and ±1: strong correlation.
- Between ±0.3 and ±0.49: moderate correlation.
- Below ±0.29: low correlation.
- 0: no correlation.

So, with the simple examples depicted in Figure 3.33, features with some correlation to the label are selected and used to create a new DataFrame (see Figure 3.34)

```
# create features array (all fields except last field)

feature_columns = data_ml.columns[:-1]

feature_columns

Output:
['installment',
 'annual_inc',
 'total_rec_late_fee',
 'last_pymnt_amnt',
 'delinq_amnt']

from pyspark.ml.feature import VectorAssembler

#creating a features array by passing a list of features to the
#VectorAssembler class

assembler=VectorAssembler(inputCols=feature_columns,outputCol="features")
```

Figure 3.35 `VectorAssembler` function

To train our linear regression model to predict the loan amount based on the selected features, we need to transform the features into a form that can be used to train the module. To do this we use the `VectorAssembler` function to merge the features (columns) into a vector column.

In Figure 3.35, the input columns passed into the `VectorAssembler` function are all the previously selected features in the DataFrame except for the label (this is removed in the first

```
# use assembler to create the features column

data2 = assembler.transform(data_ml)

data2.show()
```

Output:

```
+----------+----------+-----------------+---------------+-----------+--------+--------------------+
|installment|annual_inc|total_rec_late_fee|last_pymnt_amnt|delinq_amnt|loan_amnt|            features|
+----------+----------+-----------------+---------------+-----------+--------+--------------------+
|    321.08|   58000.0|              0.0|         321.08|          0|    1040|[321.08,58000.0,0...|
|    336.64|   78000.0|              0.0|       12017.81|          0|    1500|[336.64,78000.0,0...|
|    326.53|   69000.0|              0.0|        9338.58|          0|     960|[326.53,69000.0,0...|
|     260.2|   50000.0|              0.0|           17.7|          0|     765|[260.2,50000.0,0....|
|    319.08|  125000.0|              0.0|         319.08|          0|    1280|[319.08,125000.0,...|
|    516.36|   63800.0|              0.0|       17813.19|          0|    2142|[516.36,63800.0,0...|
|    578.22|   75000.0|              0.0|       10888.01|          0|    1700|[578.22,75000.0,0...|
|    800.71|   72000.0|              0.0|         800.71|          0|    2332|[800.71,72000.0,0...|
|     83.03|   89000.0|              0.0|        2294.26|          0|     250|[83.03,89000.0,0....|
|    468.17|   60000.0|              0.0|           50.0|          0|    1297|[468.17,60000.0,0...|
|    172.98|   26000.0|              0.0|           43.4|          0|     525|[172.98,26000.0,0...|
|     351.4|  109777.0|              0.0|        4935.54|          0|    1600|[351.4,109777.0,0...|
|     332.1|   90000.0|              0.0|          332.1|          0|    1000|[332.1,90000.0,0....|
|    581.95|   55000.0|              0.0|         581.95|          0|    2107|[581.95,55000.0,0...|
|     70.31|   37000.0|              0.0|        1255.43|          0|     200|[70.31,37000.0,0....|
|    194.99|  120000.0|              0.0|          578.3|          0|     680|[194.99,120000.0,...|
|      97.5|   60000.0|              0.0|        1117.63|          0|     300|[97.5,60000.0,0.0...|
|     69.33|   32200.0|              0.0|        1897.69|          0|     200|[69.33,32200.0,0....|
|    140.61|   50000.0|             15.0|         1606.9|          0|     400|[140.61,50000.0,1...|
|     601.7|   67000.0|              0.0|       24652.44|          0|    2800|[601.7,67000.0,0....|
+----------+----------+-----------------+---------------+-----------+--------+--------------------+
only showing top 20 rows
```

Figure 3.36 New DataFrame with compound features column

line of code). The output column for the `VectorAssembler` function is defined in the code as 'features' – you can use any name of your choice, but it is good practice always to use meaningful parameter names.

The `VectorAssembler` function is then used to create the compound features column (see Figure 3.36).

Next, as depicted in the supervised learning journey in Figure 3.30, the dataset is split into training and test data. The linear regression algorithm is used to implement the model which is trained with the training data, and predictions are then made with the test data (see Figure 3.37). In Figure 3.38, we see the actual loan amounts together with the loan amounts predicted using our model.

From the supervised learning journey, the last step has to do with evaluating our model, and there are various algorithms we can use, including the mean absolute error (MAE), which

```
#split data into training and testing data
 train, test = data2.randomSplit([0.7,0.3])


# Linear Regression algorithm and specify features columns name and the labels
column name

algorithm = LinearRegression(featuresCol="features", labelCol="loan_amnt")


# Training the model using fit method
LRModel = algorithm.fit(train)


# make predictions using the model
prodictions = LRModel.transform(test)


# DataFrame that contains the original columns, the features column and the
prediction column generated by the model
predictions


Output:
DataFrame[installment: double, annual_inc: double, total_rec_late_fee: double,
last_pymnt_amnt: double, delinq_amnt: int, loan_amnt: int, features: vector,
prediction: double]
```

Figure 3.37   **Using training data to fit the model and test data for predictions**

is the average of the absolute difference between the original values and the predicted values, the root mean square error (RMSE), which takes the difference between each observed and predicted value and divides the sum of all these values by the number of observations. We can also check the classification accuracy (percentage of correct predictions for the test data). In subsequent chapters these are explored in more depth and used in various exercises.

3.5 APACHE SPARK STREAMING

The final Apache Spark module to be considered at a high level in this chapter is Apache Spark Streaming. This is used for processing real-time data from various sources and is a key extension to the Spark Core API. A scalable and fault-tolerant real-time streaming processing engine built on top of Apache Spark, this module allows for processing and analysing live data streams in real time, enabling near-instantaneous insights and actions. Spark Streaming leverages the micro-batch processing model, where data is ingested in small batches and processed using Spark's powerful batch processing capabilities. It supports various data

loan_amnt	features	prediction
1200	[40.43,47000.0,20259.0,957.54,0.0]	1649.404674366386
1500	[52.0,25000.0,64576.0,1239.21,0.0]	2094.8762109698096
1475	[54.97,35000.0,39036.0,530.34,0.0]	2083.2974677739244
2100	[68.75,36000.0,15925.0,68.38,0.0]	2427.5815540242456
2000	[69.33,39000.0,6611.0,206.22,0.0]	2445.0517724515457
1800	[72.34,30000.0,31119.0,72.34,0.0]	2561.2209408605627
2400	[82.39,65000.0,48734.0,1343.85,0.0]	3062.5049669324353
2500	[83.51,115000.0,12885.0,1170.33,0.0]	3065.6060459382575
2500	[87.89,40000.0,42620.0,623.27,0.0]	3129.0005306261396
3000	[96.09,62000.0,329014.0,96.09,2.0]	4001.5306542884573
3000	[102.99,42000.0,45246.0,1075.54,0.0]	3649.4081175174356
3600	[117.0,42000.0,196686.0,70.66,0.0]	4262.238896915335
3375	[119.14,10000.0,2742.0,119.08,0.0]	3952.542547054381
3800	[126.2,140000.0,17286.0,1328.95,0.0]	4443.167456824725
3525	[127.19,20000.0,55333.0,21.24,0.0]	4298.523914408616
3600	[129.9,55000.0,28152.0,2080.82,0.0]	4566.049660413012
4000	[138.65,35000.0,3628.0,138.28,0.0]	4588.392567640164
4200	[140.29,47098.8,43874.0,140.29,2.0]	4854.1443557080975

Figure 3.38   Actual loan amounts versus predicted loan amounts

sources for streaming input, including Kafka, Flume, HDFS, and TCP sockets, making it ver-satile and adaptable to different streaming scenarios. It also exposes high-level APIs that enable developers to express complex stream processing operations easily, such as windowed aggregations, event time processing, and stateful computations which rely on historic infor-mation and current input to determine outputs. Finally, it can integrate seamlessly with other Spark components, allowing users to combine streaming with batch processing, machine learning, and SQL-based analytics within a single unified platform.

The design goals for Spark Streaming include the following:

- Low latency
- One-time-only event processing
- Scalability
- Integration with Spark Core API

In the same way that SparkContext is the entry point for Spark Core and SQLContext is the entry point for Spark SQL, the entry point for Spark Streaming is StreamingContext. StreamingContext represents a connection to a Spark cluster using an existing SparkContext, specifying the time interval in seconds for the streaming of data into batches; this argument is called the `batchDuration`. StreamingContext is also used to create discretized streams (DStreams) from the input sources. DStreams are basic abstractions provided by Spark Streaming; they are a continuous sequence of RDDs created from a continuous stream of data. Each RDD represents a time window.

DStreams can be created either from streaming data sources (e.g., X, formerly known as Twitter) or from transformations on other DStreams. They support two operations: transformations (lazy evaluation applies) and output operations.

```
$ nc - lk 99992
one one
how
world
cat cat dog
testing testing testing
computing is fun!
one one one
```

Figure 3.39 Command prompt with port 99992 opened and used to stream words

We will use a simple hands-on example to illustrate this, using the command prompt and a Jupyter Notebook. Using the command prompt, open a port and manually enter data into it (this is to mimic real-time data); see Figure 3.39. In later exercises we will use real-time datasets such as tweets.

In the Jupyter Notebook the relevant configurations need to be set and the StreamingContext defined. Additional code is then written to watch the port that has been opened in the console and read the data streaming through it; a number of transformations are then used to count the occurrence of the words streaming through and DStreams are used to output this values every 10 seconds (`batchDuration` was set to 10 seconds when the StreamingContext was defined; see second line of code in Figure 3.40).

3.6 ETHICS BY DESIGN

It can seem as though data breaches are constantly in the news. In 2021 it emerged that 533 million people's Facebook accounts had been exposed to hackers (Holmes, 2021) and LinkedIn users' information was for sale on the dark web (Jowitt, 2021). People are becoming increasingly aware of the amount of personal information that is held about them and expect companies to protect it. Data ethics is simply all about the ethical use of data by organizations, which among other things includes thinking about the way in which they treat the information they hold on their customers. Assume for a moment that you are a business

```
from pyspark.streaming import StreamingContext
ssc = StreamingContext(sc, 10)

lines = ssc.socketTextStream('localhost', 9992)

counts = lines.flatMap(lambda line: line.split(" ")).map(lambda x: (x,1)) \
.reduceByKey(lambda a,b: a+b)


counts

counts.pprint()

Output:
-------------------------------------------
Time: 2023-06-24 19:49:00
-------------------------------------------


-------------------------------------------
Time: 2023-06-24 19:49:10
-------------------------------------------
('cat', 2)
('one', 2)
('world', 1)
('how', 1)
('dog', 1)


-------------------------------------------
Time: 2023-06-24 19:49:20
-------------------------------------------
('testing', 3)


-------------------------------------------
Time: 2023-06-24 19:49:30
-------------------------------------------
('one', 3)
('computing', 1)
('fun!', 1)
('is', 1)


-------------------------------------------
Time: 2023-06-24 19:49:40
-------------------------------------------
```

Figure 3.40   Spark Streaming: simple example

owner; you need to be thinking about the data you handle. Do you keep it safe, and let your customers know what data your firm holds? Do you hold more data than you need? If you buy customer lists for marketing purposes, are you confident in the way in which that information was collected?

Here are five reasons why businesses need to think about the way in which they gather and use data and customer information:

Revenue. Put simply, ensuring you use data ethically protects your bottom line. Failing to ensure that customer data is safe leaves your company open to legal action and financial penalties. Research by digital transformation firm Fenergo found that 198 fines were imposed in 2020, 141% up on the previous year, with penalties totalling $10.4 billion. In March 2021, travel booking site Booking.com was fined £475,000 for being too slow to report a breach in which credit card information was stolen.

Trust. We know that public trust in companies using data appropriately is lower than trust levels generally. After the Cambridge Analytica scandal, 32% of Facebook users stopped using the site as often as before. That rose to 38% the following year. A study by KPMG found that 97% of consumers rated data privacy as important to them when choosing who they do business with. If your customers are considering it important, then it is something that businesses should be taking very seriously. Organizations that explicitly make clear that protecting the privacy of their consumers is a primary goal are more likely to build trust in them and their brand.

Building customer loyalty. When your customers know that you are keeping their private information safe, you benefit from a loyal fan base, and word of mouth is the best recommendation. It could also become a selling point for doing business with your company. The key is transparency and ensuring that customers know what data you hold and how you use it. Consumers expect more from brands they buy from.

Reputation. More than ever, people expect full transparency, control, and choice over how their data is shared and used by companies. Unethical data usage, security breaches, and leaks lead to bad press and affect your company's reputation, which in turn can hit the bottom line. For example, the Cambridge Analytics scandal knocked $36 billion off Facebook's stock value 24 hours after the story was published by the *Guardian* and the *New York Times*.

Being a trailblazer. Many organizations consider data ethics a 'good to have' rather than an imperative, but the direction of travel indicated by the UK government shows that the legislation of ethical conventions is likely. Those businesses which get on board now, audit their data, interrogate how it is used and communicate this transparently with customers will be the ones who gain a reputation for being good to buy from and do business with. Firms that explain clearly how they process data and security practice, outline what they collect data for, and quickly disclose details of breaches if things do go wrong will be the ones who earn trust.

As a data professional these issues should not be ignored or underestimated and the best approach to take is always to tackle each project and task with a mindset informed by the frameworks described in Chapter 2. Use the TAFARP framework (see Figure 2.14, p. 44) as a checklist or filter to reflect on issues of concern. So, for example, when using the Apache MLlib library to train a model and predict loan amounts, users might apply the framework to interrogate their plans and designs. Here are a few examples of possible considerations.

- Under *fairness*, a designer would reflect on the extent to which the training data are a fair representation of the population of interest. Does the training data include a fair representation of minorities, for example, and how would one go about confirming this? If there is any inherent bias in the data, this would transfer over to our model and then further make predictions that could discriminate against a specific sector of society. An example of a situation where something similar happened was with Amazon, which inadvertently ended up with a sexist AI recruiting tool (Dastin, 2018). The tool showed bias against women because most of the data that the model was trained on were from men (a reflection of a male-dominant tech environment). Another similar example was in the case of a study that discovered that millions of black people had been affected by racial bias in US hospitals which had been using a decision-making support software, implemented based on data which by nature of its source was biased. The source and nature of datasets cannot be overemphasized; if your data is garbage, then the saying *garbage in, garbage out* will apply to whatever model you design with it.
- Under *privacy*, a customer should have the option to opt out of certain services or features. Data fields such as personally identifiable information, which is data that can uniquely identify a patient, should be kept private and protected. An example of where this went wrong was seen in the case of the store Target, which was carrying out some innovative and very effective big data analytics using its customer data and was able to predict what items individual customers were likely to eventually buy and then target them with vouchers, offers and so on for these items. In this instance Target had analysed the historic data of customers who signed up to their baby registries and had been able to draw out patterns. For example, women on the baby registry began purchasing significant quantities of unscented lotion and vitamin supplements, both of which are commonly preferred by pregnant women (Hill, 2012). So, based on this they sent out coupons for baby items to identified customers, one of whom was a teenage girl whose father did not know she was pregnant until after she started receiving these coupons. If during the design of the model and for its proposed use privacy had been thoroughly considered, the outcomes might have been different.
- Under *autonomy*, another interesting aspect to explore involves the potential conflict between utilizing individuals' data and respecting their autonomy in

deciding whether to opt in or opt out. One sector where this is sometimes seen is in the health sector where there is the argument about whether a patient's privacy or the public health is more important and whether overwriting any individual patient's rights should be allowed. This was a topical issue during the Covid-19 pandemic, particularly with regard to the proposed Covid-19 app and then more recently when it came to the UK's government initial plan to force NHS staff to either receive the Covid-19 vaccination or lose their jobs. It is important that before embarking on any project or task we explore the issues that arise under this and all the other areas of the design by ethics framework.

Throughout the book we will continue to bring in data by ethics in context, because it is extremely important and because we know that it starts with a change in the way we think about design and development in general. We hope that by the time you complete this book your default approach will always be to consider ethical issues first and throughout your project.

3.7 INDUSTRY INSIGHTS

Apache Spark is widely used across industry, and this includes organizations of various sizes and in different sectors. Larger organizations that use Apache Spark include Amazon, eBay, Yahoo, and Netflix. In this section we discuss its use in two different sectors. The first is the entertainment industry, in the form of Netflix. For their big data analytics and storage platforms Netflix originally used Pig and Hive before making the decision to migrate to Spark, one reason being that they found Pig difficult to use. In the further reading section, there are links to two recordings where they discuss their migration to Spark and their use of Spark Streaming for near-real-time recommendations.

The second is the health sector, where again there are many ways in which Apache Spark is used. Here we focus on NHS Digital's Data Access Environment (DAE). The DAE (NHS, n.d.) is an environment that is built on Apache Spark to provide a collaborative analytics platform. This environment provides many advantages, including keeping patient data safe. Whereas in the past they would have given access to datasets by physically transferring the data, now they provide access to the environment at appropriate access levels. The DAE also reduces the burden of trying to sort out the right infrastructure for those who want to carry out big data analytics or run data science algorithms on vast amounts of data; the cloud set-up is scalable and so if more resources are needed it will scale up to provide enough performance for the query or algorithm. In also providing this Apache Spark-based data learning environment they are able to give access to other researchers and collaborate with others more easily. They are also now able to draw out insights from the data that they could not previously do because the data is in one place and the computing power needed is also available.

SUMMARY

This chapter introduced Apache Spark, distinguishing between its core and each of its modules. For each of the modules we also carried out some simple hands-on exercises. The chapter ended with a discussion on ethics by design, and the application of our data ethics framework to some case studies. The final section we covered was the use of Apache Spark in industry, by focusing on examples from two organizations, the first from the entertainment industry and the second from the health sector.

TEST YOUR KNOWLEDGE

1   What is Apache Spark?

2   What are the modules (libraries) provided by Apache Spark?

3   What are some of the elements that are key when considering ethics by design?

4   What does lazy evaluation mean with regard to RDDs? What is the one thing you should do after creating an RDD to help with troubleshooting?

5   The term big data can refer to:

   a   Structured data only

   b   Unstructured data only

   c   Semi-structured data only

   d   All of the above

   e   Structured data and unstructured data only

6   Which of the following tend to create large datasets?

   a   Internet of Things

   b   Search engines

   c   Social media sites

   d   All of the above

7   On your web browser, navigate to an open data portal of your choice and download a dataset on a topic that you are interested in. Then open a new Jupyter Python notebook and use PySpark to carry out analytics on the dataset using any of the libraries covered in this chapter and see what insights you can draw out. Can you find any external source to collaborate your findings?

FURTHER READING (OPTIONAL)

Databricks (2022) Day 1 Morning Keynote | Data + AI Summit 2022. Retrieved from https://databricks.com/session/migrating-to-apache-spark-at-netflix

matplotlib (n.d.) matplotlib.pyplot. Retrieved from https://matplotlib.org/3.5.3/api/_as_gen/matplotlib.pyplot.html

PyData (n.d.) Pandas API reference. Retrieved from https://pandas.pydata.org/docs/reference/index.html

Sharma, K. (2019). How to keep human bias out of AI. Retrieved from https://www.ted.com/talks/kriti_sharma_how_to_keep_human_bias_out_of_ai?language=en

Sharma, N. and Chow, E. (2018) Near real-time Netflix recommendations using Apache Spark. Retrieved from https://www.youtube.com/watch?v=IGfvVd-v3P8

Spark Apache. (n.d.) Spark overview. Retrieved from https://spark.apache.org/docs/latest/

Wallace, M. (2014) The ethics of collecting data. Retrieved from https://www.ted.com/talks/marie_wallace_the_ethics_of_collecting_data

REFERENCES

Apache Spark (n.d.) MLlib: RDD-based API. Retrieved from https://spark.apache.org/docs/latest/mllib-guide.html

Dastin, J. (2018) Amazon scraps secret AI recruiting tool that showed bias against women. Reuters. Retrieved from https://www.reuters.com/article/us-amazon-com-jobs-automation-insight/amazon-scraps-secret-ai-recruiting-tool-that-showed-bias-against-women-idUSKCN1MK08G

Department for Transport (2022) Road safety data. Retrieved from https://www.data.gov.uk/dataset/cb7ae6f0-4be6-4935-9277-47e5ce24a11f/road-safety-data

Hill, K. (2012) How Target figured out a teen girl was pregnant before her father did. Forbes. Retrieved from https://www.forbes.com/sites/kashmirhill/2012/02/16/how-target-figured-out-a-teen-girl-was-pregnant-before-her-father-did/

Holmes, A. (2021) 533 million Facebook users' phone numbers and personal data have been leaked online. Retrieved from https://www.businessinsider.com/stolen-data-of-533-million-facebook-users-leaked-online-2021-4?r=US&IR=T

Jowitt, T. (2021) Data on 700 million LinkedIn users for sale on dark web – report. Retrieved from https://www.silicon.co.uk/projects/software-vendors/700-million-linkedin-users-dark-web-404931

NHS (n.d.) Using Databricks in DAE. Retrieved from NHS Digital: https://digital.nhs.uk/services/data-access-environment-dae/user-guides/using-databricks-in-the-data-access-environment#top

4

BIG DATA STORAGE

CHAPTER CONTENTS

CHAPTER OBJECTIVES

In this chapter:

- You will learn about the limitations and challenges of the traditional data storage approaches for big data.
- You will be introduced to NoSQL databases, which are popular choices for data storage in the big data world.
- You will revisit HDFS, which was introduced in detail in Chapter 2.
- Finally, you will explore ethical challenges of big data storage and real-world examples from industry.

4.1 INTRODUCTION

Over the past decade, the exponential growth of data and the demand for scalable and flexible storage and processing solutions have spurred the rise of NoSQL databases and the Hadoop Distributed File System (HDFS). Traditional relational database management systems (RDMSs), while effective for structured data, faced limitations in handling the volume, variety, and velocity of big data. This led to the emergence of NoSQL databases, which offer a non-relational approach to data management, prioritizing scalability, performance, and flexibility. Concurrently, the need for distributed storage and processing of vast amounts of data led to the development of HDFS, a distributed file system specifically designed for big data workloads. In this context, organizations sought solutions that could efficiently store and process massive datasets, handle unstructured and semi-structured data, and enable parallel processing across clusters of commodity hardware. NoSQL databases and HDFS have become instrumental in empowering businesses to unlock the potential of big data, facilitating scalable and fault-tolerant storage and analysis of diverse data types.

While HDFS and NoSQL have some similarities in terms of distributed storage, their functionalities and use cases differ significantly: HDFS is a distributed file system designed specifically for handling large-scale data-processing tasks. It is part of the Apache Hadoop ecosystem and is optimized for storing and processing data in a batch-oriented manner. HDFS breaks down files into blocks and distributes them across a cluster of commodity hardware, ensuring fault tolerance and high throughput for big data workloads. HDFS is commonly used in conjunction with frameworks like Apache Spark and MapReduce for data processing and analytics. Among the advantages of HDFS over traditional relational databases are the following:

1 *Scalability*. HDFS is highly scalable and can handle massive datasets by distributing them across a cluster of commodity hardware. It allows for linear scaling as more nodes can be added to the cluster, accommodating the growing storage and processing needs of big data workloads.

2   *Fault tolerance.* HDFS provides built-in fault tolerance by replicating data blocks across multiple nodes in the cluster. In the event of a node failure, data can be seamlessly recovered from replicas, ensuring high availability and data reliability.

3   *Cost-effectiveness.* HDFS leverages inexpensive commodity hardware, which makes it a cost-effective solution for storing and processing large amounts of data. It eliminates the need for expensive storage area networks or enterprise-grade hardware typically associated with relational databases.

4   *Batch processing.* HDFS is optimized for batch processing workloads, where large datasets are processed in parallel across the cluster. It excels in scenarios that involve processing massive volumes of data in a distributed and fault-tolerant manner, such as data analytics, machine learning, and extract, transform, and load (ETL) operations.

On the other hand, NoSQL databases are a class of non-relational databases that provide flexible, scalable, and high-performance storage solutions. NoSQL databases are designed to handle unstructured, semi-structured, and structured data, making them suitable for handling diverse data types and accommodating rapidly changing data schemas. NoSQL databases are often used in real-time applications, web and mobile apps, and scenarios that require high scalability and horizontal data partitioning. Among the advantages of HDFS over traditional relational databases are the following:

1   *Flexibility and schemaless design.* NoSQL databases provide a flexible data model that allows for dynamic and schemaless data structures. They can handle unstructured, semi-structured, and rapidly changing data, making them suitable for agile and evolving applications where the data schema is not pre-defined or fixed.

2   *Scalability and performance.* NoSQL databases are designed to scale horizontally by distributing data across multiple nodes. They can handle high volumes of read and write operations and offer high throughput and low latency, making them well suited for applications that require fast and scalable data access, such as real-time analytics or high-traffic web applications.

3   *Distributed and fault-tolerant architecture.* NoSQL databases often employ distributed architectures that provide fault tolerance and high availability. Data is automatically replicated across nodes, ensuring data durability and availability even in the face of node failures.

4   *Support for unstructured data types by design.* NoSQL databases excel in handling diverse data types, including unstructured and semi-structured data such as JSON, XML, and binary blobs. They can store and process large volumes of complex data structures, enabling efficient handling of big data and accommodating the needs of modern data-driven applications.

Both HDFS and NoSQL databases can be utilized in cloud environments. Cloud computing platforms, such as Amazon Web Services (AWS) and Microsoft Azure, provide infrastructure and services for hosting and managing these technologies. Cloud storage services can be leveraged to store data in HDFS or NoSQL databases, allowing organizations to benefit from the scalability, elasticity, and cost-efficiency of cloud computing.

HDFS and NoSQL databases are both prominent technologies used in the context of big data storage and management. However, they serve different purposes and have distinct characteristics. Let us compare them:

- *Data model*. HDFS is a distributed file system designed for storing large volumes of data. It follows a file-based data model, where data is stored in files and organized into directories and subdirectories. HDFS provides a hierarchical structure and is suitable for batch processing and handling unstructured data. NoSQL databases offer various data models such as key–value, document, columnar, and graph. Each data model caters to specific use cases. NoSQL databases are designed to handle structured, semi-structured, and unstructured data, providing more flexibility in data organization and retrieval than traditional relational databases.

- *Achieving scalability*. HDFS is highly scalable and can handle petabytes or even exabytes of data by distributing it across multiple nodes in a cluster. It achieves scalability by employing a distributed architecture and data replication. NoSQL databases are also designed for scalability, allowing horizontal scaling by adding more servers or nodes to the database cluster. They are built to handle massive volumes of data and provide automatic sharding (this is a database partitioning technique used to improve scalability and performance) and replication mechanisms to ensure data distribution and availability.

- *Data-processing paradigm*. HDFS is primarily optimized for batch processing frameworks like Apache MapReduce and Apache Spark. It is designed for sequential read/write operations and is well suited for large-scale data-processing tasks. NoSQL databases can support various data-processing paradigms, including real-time streaming, interactive queries, and batch processing. They provide APIs and query languages that enable efficient data retrieval and manipulation for different use cases.

- *Data consistency and ACID transactions*. HDFS sacrifices strong consistency and atomicity, consistency, isolation, and durability (ACID) properties in favour of scalability and fault tolerance. It prioritizes data availability over strict consistency guarantees, making it suitable for use cases where eventual consistency is acceptable. NoSQL databases have varying levels of consistency models, ranging from strong consistency to eventual consistency. Some NoSQL databases provide ACID transactions, while others prioritize high availability and offer eventual consistency.

- *Use cases*. HDFS is commonly used in big data analytics and processing environments, where large-scale data storage and batch processing are required. It is well suited for applications like log analysis, data warehousing, and machine learning. NoSQL databases cater to a wide range of use cases, including real-time applications, content management systems, user profile management, IoT data storage, and more. They offer flexibility and scalability to handle diverse data types and workloads.

From the description above you can see that HDFS and NoSQL serve different purposes in the context of big data storage and management. HDFS excels in distributed file storage for large-scale batch processing, while NoSQL databases provide flexible data models, scalability, and support for various data-processing paradigms. The choice between HDFS and NoSQL depends on specific use case requirements, data access patterns, and the desired trade-offs between consistency, scalability, and data model flexibility. The choice of data storage architecture requires decision-makers to match between requirements and available technologies:

- Articulate your requirements in terms of storage capacity, type of storage, etc. What type of data will be stored and what type of analysis and processing power would be necessary?
- Know what the big data storage options are, so that you can decide which best meets your requirements.

At times decisions are made to adopt a technology because there is a lot of hype around about it or because it is said to be the latest technology around; that is the wrong way to make this decision and is likely to result in failure in the long run. Section 4.5 describes the key considerations for big data storage in greater detail.

4.2 TRADITIONAL DATA STORAGE APPROACHES

In the realm of data storage and management, two fundamental technologies have shaped the landscape for several decades: relational database management systems (RDBMSs) and file systems. These systems emerged at different times and serve distinct purposes in storing and organizing data. But the rise of new data types and especially unstructured and semi-structured data, together with the need for highly scalable and flexible data storage and processing, has made the limitations of traditional RDBMSs more noticeable. Newer technologies, including NoSQL databases, distributed file systems, and big data frameworks, have emerged to address these evolving data management requirements.

An example of an organization that experienced challenges with its big data storage approach is the US Census Bureau, which is responsible for conducting the US Census every 10 years. During the 2010 census, the Bureau faced challenges with its traditional on-premises data storage infrastructure which resulted in performance problems and processing delays. A report by the Congressional Research Service stated:

By then, the MITRE Corporation, which periodically advised the Bureau about its information technology (IT) programs for the 2010 census, had found that [field data collection automation] is in serious trouble. It is not clear the system will meet Census' operational needs and quality goals. The final cost is unpredictable. Immediate, significant changes are required to rescue the program. However, the risks are so large considering the available time that we recommend immediate development of contingency plans to revert to paper operations. (Williams, 2011)

Lessons were learnt and the Census Bureau has embarked on a modernization of its storage systems. More details on this can be found in a report on its website (Thieme, 2022). Another organization which had problems with its big data storage solution which contributed to a loss of competitive advantage is MySpace, perhaps the most popular social network in the early 2000s; this is discussed in Section 4.5. The rest of this section provides a brief overview of two well-known traditional data storage approaches.

4.2.1 Relational databases

Relational database management systems were pioneered in the 1970s, revolutionizing data management by introducing a structured and efficient way to store, organize, and retrieve data. The core concept of RDBMSs is based on the relational model, where data is organized in tables consisting of rows and columns, allowing for efficient data access, query optimization, and data integrity. RDBMSs excel in handling structured data, enforcing relationships, and ensuring data integrity with primary and foreign keys. They offer a powerful query language (SQL) for flexible data retrieval and transactional capabilities to maintain data consistency. RDBMSs have played a crucial role in applications that require structured data management, such as enterprise resource planning, financial systems, and customer relationship management.

Traditional RDBMSs, such as Oracle Database, Microsoft SQL Server, and MySQL, have been widely adopted across enterprises and organizations of all sizes for their reliability, stability, and adherence to ACID properties. These systems excel in handling structured data, enforcing relationships between tables through primary and foreign keys, and providing support for complex querying and transactional operations.

A database schema is a blueprint or structure of a database. It describes the tables, columns, and data types that are stored in the database. The schema is used to define the structure of the database and to ensure that data is stored in a consistent way. Schemas are typically written in a special language called a data definition language, a language used to create, alter, and drop tables, columns, and other database objects.

Tables are the fundamental structures in which data is stored. They are made up of rows (records) and columns (fields or attributes). Each row or record in the table corresponds to a unit of analysis. Tables usually have a primary key which uniquely identifies each row in the table; a simple example can be seen in Figure 4.1 where for the patient table, `PatientID` is the primary key because it uniquely identifies each row. Each patient is also associated with a ward and a `WardID`, but a ward can include many patients and since `WardID` cannot uniquely identify a patient, it cannot be a patient's primary key. It can, however, be the primary key of the ward table.

The presence of primary keys in the tables ensures the integrity of the data, prevents corruption and makes data retrieval more efficient. Relational databases also have foreign keys which establish relationships between tables. In the example in Figure 4.1, `WardID` is a foreign key in the patient table (and it is used to connect the patient table to the ward table). However, in the ward table, `WardID` is the primary key (because it uniquely identifies each row in that table). A foreign key in one table refers to the primary key in another table, thereby linking the tables together. Relationships in relational databases define the how tables are connected to each other. Other elements of relational databases include queries, which are used to retrieve specific data from tables based on specific criteria.

PatientID	Name	WardID
P1	Sarah Jones	1
P2	Peter Doe	2
P3	Dupe King	1
P4	Lisa Doe	1

Relationship

WardID	WardName
1	Maternity
2	Psychiatry
3	Admissions

Figure 4.1 Relational database tables

While RDBMSs have been widely adopted and used for decades, they also have limitations. Despite their strength in structured data management, RDBMSs face challenges in scaling, when handling massive volumes of data and trying to accommodate unstructured and semi-structured data types efficiently. Additionally, the rigid schema and complex normalization processes of RDBMSs can hinder agility in rapidly changing data environments. Another limitation is the cost of purchasing and maintaining an RDBMS. Finally, they have limited capacity to deal with real-time processing, so vast volumes of real-time data could be a serious challenge.

Nevertheless, traditional RDBMSs continue to play a vital role in many industries, providing a reliable and established foundation for structured data management. Their maturity, extensive ecosystem, and comprehensive tooling make them the default choice for applications that demand data consistency, ACID compliance, and complex querying capabilities.

4.2.2 File systems

Traditional file systems have played a pivotal role in data storage and management, providing a hierarchical structure for organizing files and directories on storage devices. These systems have a long history, evolving alongside the development of computing technologies. Emerging in the early days of computing, traditional file systems such as FAT (File Allocation Table), NTFS (New Technology File System), and ext4 (fourth extended file system) offered a simple and efficient method for storing and retrieving files. They provided a straightforward way to organize data into a hierarchical structure, enabling direct access to files and supporting essential file operations like creation, deletion, and modification.

The strengths of traditional file systems lie in their simplicity and ease of use. They have been the foundation of operating systems, allowing users to interact with files and folders in a familiar manner. Traditional file systems are efficient at handling small to medium-sized files and are well suited for applications that deal with unstructured or semi-structured data, such as documents, images, videos, and audio files. They also allow file management, renaming, and a granular access rights and system of file permissions.

However, traditional file systems face limitations when it comes to modern applications and the evolving needs of data management. One of the primary limitations is the lack of efficient organization and retrieval mechanisms for large-scale and unstructured data. Traditional file systems rely on a hierarchical structure, which becomes challenging to navigate and search as the number of files and directories increases.

Additionally, traditional file systems often lack built-in support for advanced metadata management, versioning, and access control, which are critical in collaborative environments or when dealing with sensitive data. Scalability is another concern, as traditional file systems may struggle to handle massive volumes of data efficiently or distribute the load across multiple storage devices or nodes.

As modern applications increasingly deal with big data, unstructured data, and distributed computing environments, the limitations of traditional file systems have become more pronounced. Newer storage technologies, such as distributed file systems like HDFS, object storage systems, and cloud-based storage solutions, have emerged to address these challenges. These technologies provide scalable and fault-tolerant storage, support parallel processing, and offer advanced features such as data replication, data locality optimization, and metadata management.

While traditional file systems have served as the foundational storage method for decades, they have limitations when it comes to modern applications and the demands of big data and distributed computing. Emerging storage technologies have been developed to overcome these limitations and provide more efficient and scalable solutions for managing and processing large volumes of data in diverse and dynamic environments.

4.3 BIG DATA STORAGE SOLUTIONS

Several big data storage solutions have emerged to address the unique challenges posed by handling massive volumes of data. Examples include the Hadoop Distributed File System, Apache Cassandra, Apache HBase, Amazon S3 (Simple Storage Service), and Apache Kafka. These are just a few examples of big data storage solutions, each with its own strengths and use cases. Depending on the specific requirements of an organization, other technologies such as Apache Spark, MongoDB, and Elasticsearch may also be utilized as part of a comprehensive big data storage and processing architecture. This section considers some of the popular big data storage solutions, namely NoSQL databases, distributed storage systems, and cloud storage for big data.

4.3.1 NoSQL databases

NoSQL databases are also known as 'not only SQL' databases (IBM, n.d.). These databases are part of the generation of databases that were designed and developed to address the unique challenges of big data, challenges such as scalability, performance, and cost-effectiveness. NoSQL databases do not require pre-set schemas and so can generally effectively store the different formats of big data (including unstructured data). Thus, the NoSQL database has been designed to deal with the characteristics of big data – specifically, it is designed to handle the volume, velocity, and variety of the data. Unlike the more traditional storage systems, NoSQL databases can handle structured, non-structured, and semi-structured data.

NoSQL databases use four main types of data models:

- Key–value
- Column-oriented
- Document
- Graph

In this subsection we consider some examples.

Column family databases – HBase

In column-oriented databases data tables are stored by column rather the more traditional row (seen in relational databases). Scalability is horizontal and hence works well for big data storage, and is to all intents and purposes infinite. Some examples of column-oriented databases include Bigtable, BigQuery, HBase, Snowflake, and Apache Cassandra. Figure 4.2 shows a simple example of a column-oriented data model.

Consider Apache HBase, for example. HBase is a Hadoop database and it is distributed, scalable, and a big data store. The HBase website claims that its goal is to host extremely large tables (billions of rows and millions of columns) on commodity hardware. Unlike traditional data storage solutions, this structure is scalable by design (Apache HBase Team, n.d.). There

Row-oriented

ID	Name	Age
1	Ade	37
2	John	18
3	Karen	42

Column-oriented

ID	Name
1	Ade
2	John
3	Karen

ID	Age
1	37
2	18
3	42

Figure 4.2 Column-oriented data model

are a few ways to access and manage an HBase database; we will use the HBase console. To launch the HBase shell type the following command in the console and then press enter:

```
hbase shell
```

To launch the HBase console type:

```
hbase(main):004:0>
```

Now let us create a table called 'Patients', with two columns, Name and WardID. Note that in the create statement, table names and column family are surrounded by single quotes.

```
create '<table name>','<column family>'
hbase(main):004:0> create 'Patients', 'Name', 'WardID'
```

To verify that it has been created you can run the list command to see the contents of the folder:

```
hbase(main):004:0> list
```

Let us add a row to the table using the put command:

```
hbase(main):004:0> put 'Patients', 'Jane Doe', '1'
```

Let us add a second row to the table:

```
hbase(main):004:0> put 'Patients', 'Peter King', '2'
```

To see the entire table, we use the `scan` command:

```
hbase(main):004:0> scan 'Patients'
```

To delete the table, we have to disable it first:

```
hbase(main):004:0> disable 'Patients'
```

Now that it is disabled we can drop the table:

```
hbase(main):004:0> drop   'Patients'
```

If you need help at any time or want more information on a command – simply type `help` for a list of the various commands and their usage:

```
hbase(main):004:0> help
```

Key-value databases - Amazon DynamoDB

Key–value databases are based on a simple architecture, where a value (the data) is associated with a key to identify its location. This database is organized and structured via keys, lending the database substantial performance relative to more traditional databases that are organized via indices that tend to slow down performance. Key–value databases scale out easily, making them ideal for big data storage. Figure 4.3 depicts a simple example of the contents of a key–value database.

Key		Value
University	⟶	De Montfort
City	⟶	Leicester
Country	⟶	UK

Figure 4.3 Key-value data model

Amazon DynamoDB (AWS, n.d.) is a fully managed NoSQL database service provided by AWS. It offers seamless scalability, automatic replication, and low-latency performance. DynamoDB supports key–value and document data models and provides flexible querying options, global secondary indexes, and on-demand capacity provisioning. As is the case with other NoSQL solutions, it is scalable by design, able to handle vast volumes of data. To use Amazon DynamoDB, users need to sign up to AWS, and acquire an AWS access key to program the DynamoDB. Access to this storage system can be achieved by running commands on the console, using the AWS CLI, the API, or the NoSQL workbench. The NoSQL workbench is a client-side GUI application that can be used for data modelling and data visualization. Details on how to use all the various platforms and systems to access DynamoDB can be found in the DynamoDB documentation.

To carry out some common DynamoDB tasks using the DynamoDB console, follow the instructions below:

Step 1. Open the AWS management console and in the search box start to type `DynamoDB`. You will then see under Services, 'DynamoDB Managed NoSQL Database'.

Step 2. To create a table, click on the 'DynamoDB Managed NoSQL Database' from step 1 and select 'Create Table'. This will open a page for the table details. Enter the required table name (e.g., `Patients`). Add a partition key name; this is used to spread data across partitions, so choose an attribute with values that will be evenly distributed.

Step 3. Enable DynamoDB autoscaling in the settings (if required). After completing all the configurations, click on 'Create Table'.

Step 4. To add data to the newly created table, click on 'Explore Items' and then select the table. Click on the attributes you want to add data to and enter the values, then click on 'create item'.

Step 5. To query the table, click on 'Explore Items' and then the table as before. Then click on 'Query'. There are various ways to query the table; one way is to type your search criteria in the box of the attribute you are interested in, then click on 'run'. Alternatively, you can click on the drop-down menu and select 'Begins with', for instance, and then enter the value you are interested in. Explore this functionality to get familiar with the various options.

Step 6. To delete an existing item (attribute), change the query drop-down list back to 'scan'. Select the check-box next to the item you want to delete. Then in the actions drop-down menu, pick 'Delete items'.

Step 7. To delete a table, in the console select the check-box next to the relevant table, and then select 'Delete'.

In terms of using Amazon DynamoDB and getting further hands-on experience with it, although AWS is a commercial service, there are special provisions for students to encourage its use by them and to give opportunities to upskill. For more information on this, see AWS (2022).

Among other examples of popular NoSQL data storage solutions are the following:

- *MongoDB*. MongoDB is a widely adopted document-oriented NoSQL database that provides high scalability, flexibility, and performance. It stores data in flexible JSON-like documents, allowing for dynamic schemas and easy horizontal scaling. MongoDB supports rich querying capabilities and offers features like automatic sharding, replication, and indexing for efficient data access and distribution.
- *Apache Cassandra*. Cassandra is a highly scalable and distributed NoSQL database known for its ability to handle massive amounts of data across multiple commodity servers or cloud instances. It is designed for high

availability and fault tolerance, with a decentralized architecture that ensures linear scalability. Cassandra is suitable for write-intensive workloads and provides consistency levels that can be tuned and optimized.

- *Redis.* Redis is an in-memory data structure store that can function both as a NoSQL database and a caching system. It is highly optimized for speed and performance, allowing for extremely fast read and write operations. Redis supports various data structures, including strings, lists, sets, and hashes, and offers advanced features like pub/sub messaging, data replication, and clustering.
- *Apache HBase.* HBase is a distributed and scalable NoSQL database that runs on top of Hadoop and HDFS. It provides real-time read/write access to large datasets, making it suitable for use cases requiring low-latency data retrieval. HBase follows a columnar data storage model and offers linear scalability and fault tolerance.
- *Couchbase.* Couchbase is a NoSQL database that combines the flexibility of a document-oriented database with the distributed scalability of a key–value store. It provides a JSON-based document model, supporting rich querying, indexing, and replication features. Couchbase is designed for high availability and offers automatic data partitioning and rebalancing.

Further solutions include document databases, systems that are used to store and query semi-structured data such as JSON and XML files. Other examples of these types of databases include terrastore (in-memory) and graph databases, designed to store data using graph structures (edges, nodes, and relationships). Examples include Neo4j, AllegroGraph and HyperGraphDB. The popular Neo4j is a graph database management system which provides graph algorithms that enable fast queries to be ran on complex graph datasets. In this book for big data graph analytics we use Apache GraphFrames (see Chapter 7). These are just a few examples of NoSQL data storage solutions, each with its own strengths, data models, and features. The choice of a specific NoSQL database depends on the requirements of the application, scalability needs, data access patterns, and other factors.

4.3.2 Distributed storage systems

Distributed file systems can store large volumes of unstructured data. They are well suited for the storage of big data for various reasons, including scalability; they are by design able to handle large amounts of data. Their distributed design allows them to distribute data across multiple nodes and to scale horizontally, which makes it easy to simply add additional nodes to increase the capacity of data that they can store as the data storage needs increase. They are also by design fault-tolerant, cost-effective, and high-performance. Examples of distributed storage systems include GFS, HDFS, Amazon S3, and Google Cloud Storage. In this chapter we focus on HDFS.

HDFS was discussed in detail in Chapter 2. In this section for the sake of completeness we introduce some HDFS commands. As mentioned in Chapter 2, HDFS is the storage platform for Hadoop and was designed for big data. It provides several advantages for big data storage; these include cost-effectiveness, good fault tolerance, and it scales by design easily.

HDFS being distributed provides key advantages over non-distributed storage systems. Among these benefits are the following:

- Good fault tolerance which makes it very reliable. As HDFS is distributed it is implemented with several servers (large implementations can have thousands) so if one server fails, the system is able to detect this and automatically recover by working with the servers that are still live. We illustrate this pictorially later in this section.
- HDFS scales easily by design. This is a major advantage of HDFS: as it is made up of several servers, if there is a need to scale up because data storage needs to increase, scaling up is straightforward and is merely a matter of adding additional servers to the cluster. A Hadoop cluster is the collection of nodes/computers/servers that make up the HDFS implementation. In contrast to this, in settings where non-distributed systems are used (e.g., massively parallel processing) if there is a need to scale up, it is an extremely expensive and non-trivial task to do so.
- Deployment is on low-cost hardware. Again, as the Hadoop cluster is made up of a cluster of low-cost hardware nodes, deployment using HDFS is very cost-effective.

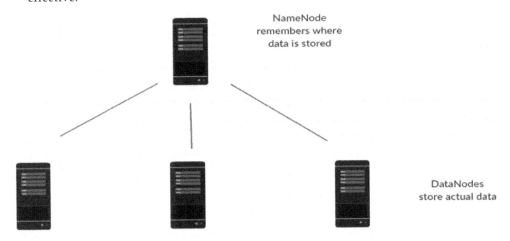

Figure 4.4 Simplified HDFS architecture

A simplified version of the HDFS architecture is depicted in Figure 4.4. The HDFS cluster is made up of a name node and data nodes; some large implementations have thousands of nodes in them. The name node is the master/control node and it both controls how data is distributed across the data nodes and manages the file system's metadata. Metadata is itself data that provides information about your dataset, for example it could have details such as the author's name, the date the dataset was created and when it was last modified. The name node normally has a backup node which helps make it more failsafe, so that if something goes wrong with the name node the backup node can take over. The data nodes physically store the data and replicate data across other nodes, as well as sending block reports to the name node. Figure 4.5 depicts the process of block storage.

Figure 4.5   HDFS block storage

When a file is loaded into HDFS for storage it is broken down into blocks. These individual blocks are then stored in data nodes. Every Hadoop instance has a pre-defined block size (in the example in Figure 4.5, the default is 128 MB). The loaded file is split into as many evenly sized blocks as possible, with the final block only using as much space as necessary; in the example in Figure 4.5, the file of size 513 MB is split into four evenly sized blocks of the default size of 128 MB and the final block just uses 1 MB (i.e., 513 = 128 + 128 + 128 + 128 + 1). Each of the blocks that files are split into have their own metadata which contains a header with a version, type information, and checksums for the stored block. The checksums are important as they are used to check that the files have not been corrupted during uploading/transmission. Once the file is split into the relevant blocks, these blocks are distributed among data nodes in the cluster. This makes possible share nothing where no resources are shared between nodes and distributed parallel processing of data (Figure 4.6 illustrates this with the example from Figure 4.5).

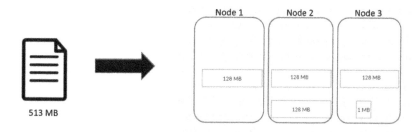

Figure 4.6   Distribution of HDFS blocks to data nodes

So, when a file is written to HDFS it gets split into blocks; the name node determines which data nodes the blocks should be written to, and the data nodes then replicate the blocks. You can think of the name node as like the conductor in an orchestra who knows when each musician should come in, whether or not they are able to come in at certain points and so on. The data nodes are like the musicians; they are the workers who are playing the instruments based on instructions they receive from the conductor. If a data node goes down the name node knows because all the data nodes periodically send the name node what is called a heartbeat, and every tenth heartbeat is called a block report. The name node in turn builds metadata from the block reports it receives from the data nodes. If the name node does not receive heartbeats from any particular data node, the name node knows that that particular data node is lost; it checks the metadata it holds to find the affected data, and then sends a message to another data node that is live to replicate the data that was held on the lost data node. This process makes HDFS incredibly failsafe. If a data node is lost, HDFS can still carry on. However, if the name node is down (without a backup) then HDFS is down. In a production system, it is not recommended to have a name node without a backup name node, as it is a critical component.

It is easy to underestimate the importance of having the right data storage platform, whether that is in terms of it being able to adequately handle the data volumes that need to be stored in it or of how it handles failure and its ability to recover automatically and swiftly. Unfortunately, often until things go wrong the value of having appropriate storage facilities is underestimated. An example of when things went wrong is the incident within Public Health England (PHE) in 2021 during the Covid-19 pandemic when a bad decision was made to store Covid-19 test results in Microsoft Excel (Kelion, 2020). The PHE developers then further compounded the problem by picking the old format of Excel (XLS) which can only handle about 65,000 rows of data (as against the 1 million plus rows that the latter version of excel can handle – however, using this newer version might just have delayed the emergence of the problem). In this case this choice of the wrong storage platform meant that figures were grossly underreported, and the issue was not immediately spotted.

There are several HDFS commands for carrying out various operations; some of them are listed below:

- `ls`: this command is used to list all files.
- `hadoop fs -copyFromLocal filename`: this command copies the file to HDFS.
- `hadoop fs -ls filename`: this lists the file and can be used to check that the transfer was successful.
- `hadoop fs -cat filename`: run this command to see the contents of the file in HDFS.
- `hadoop fs -put filename`: this is another command to upload a file into HDFS.
- `hadoop fs -rm filename`: run this command to delete the file from HDFS.
- `hdfs dfs -ls`: this command lists files/folders in HDFS.
- `hdfs dfs -touchz /test1.txt`: this command creates an empty file in HDFS (`touchz` lets you create a zero-length file, if you have the right permissions; it can be used to check whether an application has the right permissions to write to an area).
- `hdfs dfs -put *.*`: run this command to upload multiple files.

- `hdfs dfs -getmerge -nl /user/ mergedfile.txt`: this command concatenates all the files in the folder into a single file (`mergedfile.txt` in this example).
- `hdfs dfs -du -s -h /user`: this command shows disk usage in megabytes.

Cloud storage is another very important storage solution for big data. Cloud computing is covered in Chapter 5 but is mentioned here briefly for completeness. Among the cloud storage and service providers for big data are Amazon S3, Google Cloud Storage, and Azure Blob Storage.

4.4 STORAGE OPTIMIZATION AND DATA COMPRESSION

Storage optimization and data compression are about fully maximizing and utilizing available resources. They provide techniques to reduce storage requirements and improve performance. When it comes to big data, as mentioned several times already, vast amounts of data are involved, so returns from storage optimization have many advantages. It helps to reduce costs (as less storage is needed) and improves processing and performance. Among key techniques for optimizing storage space are the following:

- Compression
- Deduplication
- Data partitioning
- Columnar storage
- Tiered storage

Data compression gives great benefits when it comes to big data and impacts positively on performance and processing time. These should all be taken into account in the planning stage and when key considerations are being explored. Key considerations for big data storage are discussed in the next section.

4.5 KEY CONSIDERATIONS FOR BIG DATA STORAGE

Having considered big data storage, traditional storage approaches, and big data storage solutions such as distributed systems, NoSQL databases, and cloud storage for big data, we will now return to some of the questions raised at the beginning of this chapter. How should data storage solutions be chosen by organizations and for specific projects? What are the key considerations to follow in making these choices? Recall that we said earlier that the choice of which data storage architecture to go with depends to a large degree on your project or business requirements, and to make the right decision two things are key:

- The need to clearly articulate and understand well what your requirements are
- Knowing what the big data storage options are, so that you can choose which best meets your requirements.

It is essential that you clearly understand the requirements for the project at hand. For instance, what are your requirements in terms of storage? How about in terms of disk size? How many disks are needed per machine? What about the memory size? CPUs? What type of architecture is needed? Distributed? NoSQL? NewSQL? Where do you want this data to be stored? In the cloud? On the premises? Hybrid? What storage optimization technique would you put in place? What data compression techniques would you use? All of these and more need to be clearly understood and articulated. Do not go ahead and make decisions on what to adopt until this step is thoroughly done and complete. As mentioned earlier, at times decisions are made to adopt specific technologies based not on requirements but possibly on hype or perhaps because everyone else it is doing the same. This is a recipe for disaster in terms of your big data storage needs.

Understanding the available big data storage options is a key step in being able to choose which best suits your requirements. This chapter is part of the starting point for this. The area of big data storage can be complicated and as such should not be underestimated when planning. Scalability has been mentioned several times in this chapter and we mention it again here because it really is important. Whatever big data solution you design and develop should be future-proof and be able to expand as your data needs increase, and that expansion should be possible in a cost-effective manner, otherwise your choice might end up being a white elephant. See the further reading section for more articles on this.

It is also important to remember that once your big data storage system is set up, it is important to periodically review things to ensure that the system remains fit for purpose. Outdated or inadequate data storage systems can hold an organization back from being innovative and as effective as they otherwise would be. An example of a company that is said to have suffered such a fate is MySpace. MySpace (Britannica) is said to have been the most popular social network in the early 2000s. It expanded rapidly but was said to continue using a traditional centralized storage architecture which led to performance issues and challenges when it came to scaling up the system to match its growing needs; this unfortunately contributed to its losing competitive advantage to the likes of Facebook. It also had other data storage issues in 2019 when it lost 12 years' worth of uploaded content onto its site due to faulty server migration (Hern, 2019). Performance, fault tolerance, and having regular backups might all sound very straightforward, but if not done correctly it can have far-reaching detrimental effects.

4.6 ETHICS BY DESIGN

When it comes to data storage, and particularly big data storage, ethical issues are crucial. In this section, as with every chapter, we will use the TAFARP data ethics by design framework introduced in Chapter 2 (see Figure 2.14, p. 44) to discuss issues that pertain to ethics by design in light of data storage.

There are three main areas that must not be overlooked when choosing or designing big data storage facilities or infrastructure:

- Data security issues
- Data privacy issues
- Sustainable energy consumption

When it comes to data storage, the issue of data security, breaches, and leaks is probably more reported in the public domain than any other issue. A quick online search will return several data breaches and leaks that cut across different sectors. There are even websites that are dedicated to updating the public on data breaches and leaks. One such website is the Information Is Beautiful website (Beautiful, 2022) which has a visualization of the world's biggest data breaches and hacks ranging from large losses/breaches with millions of records involved, such as the 533 million records lost by Facebook in March 2021 due to a vulnerability patch in 2019 and the 250 million records exposed by Microsoft when customer support records were left online with no password protection in January 2020, to much smaller breaches/leaks with just a few records. The website is intriguing because the breaches/leaks have been set up in a word cloud format with years along the vertical axis. To get summarized information on any breach you just need to hover over the item, and for more detailed information, clicking on the relevant breach takes you to the webpage of the actual original story.

Using the TAFARP data ethics by design framework, let us consider how data by design might have helped to prevent one of these breaches. Deep Root Analytics, a data analytics firm, inadvertently kept online an insecure database that contained 198 million US voters' information (Walsh and AFP, 2017). The database held people's personal details such as name, date of birth, address, phone numbers, and voter's registration details. The database apparently did not have any security on it to bar unauthorized access and as such was basically accessible to anyone with internet access. How could ethics by design have helped prevent a situation like this? The main element of the TAFARP framework that would have made a marked difference in this case is privacy. As the database was being set up, questions around privacy such as whether the database is secure enough to ensure the privacy of individuals' data? should have been explored and relevant structures put in place as data by design was implemented. Questions around ensuring that only authorized personnel had access to the database should have been answered. Issues around transparency should also have been considered, such as whether consent has been given for this data to be held and whether data owners are clear on the purpose the data would be used for. All of these and other similar ethical concerns could have helped to prevent the breach that eventually happened. Sometimes when it comes to big data storage and other aspects of big data, people want to ignore ethical issues because it can in the short term seem like an additional hassle, but it can and does help prevent future problems. Governments are also increasingly enforcing legislation to ensure that important issues such as privacy and security are taken seriously by those who store and process data. Some of these measures include various state privacy acts in the USA, the General Data Protection Regulation (GDPR) in Europe, Brazil's General Law for the Protection of Personal Data, Zimbabwe's Cyber and Data Protection Act, and South Africa's Protection of Personal Information Act. In some countries the penalties for infringements can be quite steep. For instance, with the European GDPR there is a maximum fine of €20 million or 4% of annual global turnover (whichever is greater). Among the current highest GDPR fines are those imposed on Amazon (€746 million), WhatsApp (€225 million), and Google (€90 million).

Finally, when it comes to data storage, particularly in data centres, questions around sustainable energy consumption also need to be asked. We all have a responsibility to act ethically when it comes to the protection of our world. So, when it comes to big data storage, measures should be put in place to mitigate against detrimental environmental impacts. Designing and implementing systems that are energy-efficient should be prioritized (Bahga & Madisetti, 2016).

4.7 INDUSTRY INSIGHTS

Our industry insights for this chapter focuses on the impact of big data storage and big data analytics on the oil and gas industry. Over the last few years big data storage and analytics have revolutionized the oil and gas sector and several organizations have been doing some innovative work in this space. One of these companies is Tachyus, whose focus is on optimizing energy production for the oil and gas industry. To achieve this, it developed a data-driven platform to allow decisions to be made that maximize assets. The oil and gas industry also generates large volumes of data from sensors, pipelines, well sites, equipment, and so on. The platform Tachyus developed leverages this and stores data from all sorts of sources such as drilling logs, maintenance, records, and production data, and it then uses machine learning algorithms to make predictions which provide insights that help inform decisions (Evenson, Womak & Lin, 2020). This platform has, across 25,000 wells, helped to achieve an increase of up to 20% in the costs of production and a decrease of up to a 40% in injection costs. This is just one example of how big data storage and analytics support efficiency savings and the promotion of competitive advantage.

SUMMARY

In this chapter the limitations, and challenges of the traditional data storage approaches for big data have been discussed. Distributed databases with a particular focus on HDFS (which is a very popular layer for big data technology clusters) was revisited. NoSQL technologies, which are also popular choices for data storage in the big data world, were discussed and some hands-on exercises for Apache HBase and Amazon DynamoDB done. The role of ethics by design when it comes to big data storage has also been explored. The chapter concluded with an example of insights from the oil and gas industry and the impact of big data on the sector.

TEST YOUR KNOWLEDGE

1   State two advantages of using HDFS for big data storage.
2   State two advantages of using NoSQL technologies for big data storage.

3 Explain the importance of ethics by design when it comes to big data storage.

4 Sign up for AWS and use the Amazon DynamoDB console to create some tables, input data into them, and run some queries.

5 Repeat the previous task but instead of using the console, read the documentation and create tables, input data into the tables, and run queries on them programmatically.

FURTHER READING (OPTIONAL)

An early paper on the column-oriented data model:

Stonebraker, M. Abadi, D. J., Batkin, A., Chen, X., Cherniack, M., Ferreira, M., Lau, E., Lin, A., Madden, S., O'Neil, E., O'Neil, P., Rasin, A., Tran, N. and Zdonik, S. (2005) C-store: A column-oriented DBMS. In *Proceedings of the 31st International Conference on Very Large Data Bases (VLDB '05)*. VLDB Endowment, 553–564.

Blog by IBM that explains the difference between SQL and noSQL databases:

Anderson, B. and Nicholson, B. (2022) SQL vs. NoSQL databases: What's the difference? https://www.ibm.com/cloud/blog/sql-vs-nosql

Article on big data storage:

Simplilearn (2022) Introduction to big data storage. https://www.simplilearn.com/big-data-storage-article

Brief article on data storage optimization:

Applied Data Systems (2023) Data storage optimization: What is it and why does it matter? https://applieddatasystems.com/data-storage-optimization-what-is-it-and-why-does-it-matter/

Article on cloud data storage optimization:

Das, J. (2023) Data storage 101: Everything you need to know. https://blog.aspiresys.com/cloud/data-storage-optimization-101-everything-you-need-to-know/

REFERENCES

Apache HBase Team (n.d.) Apache HBase Reference Guide. Retrieved from https://hbase.apache.org/book.html

AWS (2022) AWS Educate. Retrieved from Start your Cloud Journey with AWS Educate Today: https://aws.amazon.com/education/awseducate/

AWS (n.d.) What Is Amazon DynamoDB? Retrieved from https://docs.aws.amazon.com/amazondynamodb/latest/developerguide/Introduction.html

Bahga, A. and Madisetti, V. (2016) *Big Data Science & Analytics: A Hands-On Approach.* VPT.

Britannica (n.d.) Myspace: Web site. Retrieved from https://www.britannica.com/topic/Myspace

Evenson, O., Womak, D. and Lin, S. (2020) How AI can pump new life into oilfields: Fueling oil and gas industry performance. Retrieved from IBM Expert Insights: https://www.ibm.com/downloads/cas/5BNKGNLE

Hern, A. (2019) Myspace loses all content uploaded before 2016. *Guardian*, 18 March. Retrieved from https://www.theguardian.com/technology/2019/mar/18/myspace-loses-all-content-uploaded-before-2016

Hu, F. (2016) *Big Data: Storage, Sharing, and Security.* Boca Raton, FL: CRC Press.

IBM (n.d.) What are NoSQL databases? Retrieved from https://www.ibm.com/topics/nosql-databases

Information Is Beautiful (2022) World's biggest data breaches & hacks. Retrieved from https://www.informationisbeautiful.net/visualizations/worlds-biggest-data-breaches-hacks/

Kelion, L. (2020) Excel: Why using Microsoft's tool caused Covid-19 results to be lost. *BBC News*, 5 October. Retrieved from BBC: https://www.bbc.co.uk/news/technology-54423988

Thieme, M. (2022) Technology transformation at the Census Bureau: Building a modern, data-centric ecosystem. Retrieved from https://www.census.gov/newsroom/blogs/research-matters/2022/10/technology-transformation.html

Walsh, A. with AFP (2017) '198 million US voter records leaked'. Retrieved from https://www.dw.com/en/deep-root-analytics-behind-data-breach-on-198-million-us-voters-security-firm/a-39318788

Williams, J. D. (2011) The 2010 decennial census: Background and issues. Retrieved from https://www.census.gov/history/pdf/2010-background-crs.pdf

5

BIG DATA ANALYTICS AND CLOUD COMPUTING

CHAPTER CONTENTS

CHAPTER OBJECTIVES

In this chapter:

- You will learn the origin of cloud computing, its defining characteristics, and their implications for organizations.
- You will explore the trade-offs that come with outsourcing computing resources to the cloud.
- You will understand the interaction between cloud computing and big data analytics.
- You will reflect on the ethical considerations associated with cloud computing.

5.1 FOUNDATIONS

Cloud computing is a broad term for the delivery of hosted services over the internet. It is a key to the division of resources and hence to specialization and efficient operation. With cloud computing, organizations consume a range of computing resources, such as a virtual machine, storage, databases, analytics, and software as a utility — just like electricity — rather than having to build and maintain computing infrastructures in-house.

There are five essential characteristics of cloud computing:

1   *Business model: from a commodity to a service.* Users can provision computing resources, such as server time and network storage, automatically, without requiring human interaction with the cloud provider.
2   *Broad network access.* Cloud services are available over the network and can be accessed by diverse client platforms (e.g., thin clients, thick clients, mobile devices, and servers).
3   *Resource pooling.* The provider's computing resources are pooled to serve multiple consumers using a multi-tenant model, with different physical and virtual resources dynamically assigned and reassigned according to demand.
4   *Rapid elasticity.* This is one of the key characteristics of cloud computing, as defined by the National Institute of Standards and Technology (NIST). It refers to the ability of a cloud service to quickly and automatically scale up or down the amount of resources provided based on the demand. This allows users to easily allocate and de-allocate resources as needed, without having to go through a lengthy procurement process or make long-term commitments. In practical terms, this means that cloud users can dynamically adjust their computing resources, such as processing power, storage, and network bandwidth, to match their changing requirements. For example, if a company experiences a sudden spike in website traffic, they can quickly scale up their cloud resources to handle the increased load. Conversely, during periods of lower demand, they can scale down to reduce costs. Capabilities can be elastically provisioned and released, in near real time, to scale

rapidly up or down according to demand. To the consumer, the capabilities available for provisioning often appear to be unlimited and can be purchased in any quantity at any time.

5 *Measured service.* Cloud systems automatically monitor resource usage and bill accordingly, providing a predictable and consistent cost model in which users only pay for the resources they consume.

These characteristics enable cloud computing to offer several benefits over traditional IT solutions, including:

- *Greater efficiency and cost savings.* Cloud computing can help businesses save money on IT costs by eliminating the need to purchase and maintain hardware and software. It can therefore be more cost-effective than traditional on-premises big data analytics solutions.
- *Specialization and efficient use of resources.* By effectively outsourcing some of the big data analytics workload, cloud computing can make it easier to set up and manage big data analytics solutions.
- *Agility.* Cloud computing can help businesses be more agile by providing them with the ability to quickly scale up or down their IT resources as needed.
- *Scalability.* Cloud computing can help businesses scale up or down, to meet the precise needs of big data analytics workloads.
- *Reliability.* Cloud computing can help businesses improve the reliability of their IT systems by providing them with access to a robust and redundant infrastructure. The term 'redundant infrastructure' means that cloud service providers have implemented backup systems, resources, and processes to ensure high availability and reliability of their services, a redundancy designed to minimize downtime and ensure that applications and data remain accessible even in the event of hardware failures, network outages, or other unforeseen issues. Redundant infrastructure can be broken down into hardware redundancy, data redundancy, geographic redundancy, load balancing and redundant network connectivity.
- *Security.* Cloud computing can help businesses improve security for big data analytics by providing organizations with access to a variety of security features and controls.

As a result of these benefits, cloud computing is becoming increasingly popular with businesses of all sizes. In fact, a recent study by Gartner forecast that worldwide end-user spending on cloud computing would reach nearly $600 billion in 2023. This represents annual growth of almost 22%, up from $491 billion in 2022 (Gartner, 2023). Cloud computing is the driver of digital transformation through disruptive technologies such as generative artificial intelligence, Web3, and the metaverse.

The history of cloud computing is remarkable not only because of the ground-breaking technology it has ushered but also because it transformed the way the IT industry runs as a commercial enterprise. However, this development is not unprecedented. It fits into a pattern where technological and socio-economic change reinforce one another. To appreciate this process, consider the story of Chester Carlson (1906–68), an American inventor raised in an impoverished part of Seattle. The inventor of the first modern photocopying machine, Carlson's technological innovation would usher in new business practices on a global scale. Prior to Carlson, copying documents was an unpleasant and time-consuming affair, risking damage to original documents, and smearing users with unsavoury, foul-smelling chemicals. Despite the huge potential of his work, it took decades for Carlson and his partners to convince potential customers of the merit of this ground-breaking technology (Owen, 2004).

One of the decisive factors contributing to Carlson's commercial breakthrough in September 1959 was his partnership with a company that was soon to become the Xerox Corporation. Instead of selling the photocopying machine itself as a technological commodity, the idea was to sell the right to use the machine, practically leasing it to customers. Customers did not own the photocopier, but were allowed to use it for $25 per month, plus $0.04 per copy.

This novel arrangement made all the difference to customers. Xerox could now sell photocopying as a service, retaining both ownership rights and the responsibility to maintain the machines, assuming the risk that the machine would not be used as much as it could be (i.e., Xerox took on itself the machine's opportunity costs). Customers became users, paying in proportion to their use. They could also increase or decrease their use of the machine. By experimenting, many discovered that they could innovate their business processes, cutting costs or taking advantage of new opportunities by increasing the number of photocopies they made. Slowly but surely, Carlson's photocopier became an indispensable part of every workplace worldwide and a significant source of Xerox's revenues (Brooks, 1969).

5.1.1 Technology as a service

Just like the business innovation that turned Carlson's photocopier into a success, cloud computing, at its bare minimum, is about transforming the tech industry from one that sells commodities to one that sells services. This complicates the contractual arrangements considerably, but it also enables stakeholders to carve out the costs and responsibilities between them according to their needs and constraints. To appreciate the transformation ushered in by cloud services, consider what was at stake for an entrepreneur wanting to launch an online shop in the early 2000s (Lisdorf, 2021). First, they needed a website as an interface between themselves and their customers. Depending on their ambitions, they would acquire a couple of personal computers, or they might choose to assume more risk and order a computer rack and several computers from a wholesale provider. They would then need to find a space large enough to host their infrastructure, either a space they owned or one they rented. As their business grew, they would need to keep buying additional machines, licenses for software packages, memory, and physical space. They would need a system for backing up their file system, a cooling system, and insurance to protect against damage from flood, theft, and fire.

With the increase in one-off costs (so-called capital expenditures), regular costs would also increase. Rent for office space would be paid regularly, and specialists might need to be hired to configure, maintain, and upgrade the software in addition to employees for supporting functions such as accounting, finance, and marketing. Capital expenditures often go hand in hand with increasing operational expenses.

In contrast, consider the options facing entrepreneurs launching an online shop today. First, they must decide how much of the computing infrastructure they would want to acquire, and how much of it they would want to outsource, as it were, to a third party. At one extreme, just like in the past, they are free to purchase the infrastructure and the software and deploy the entire system in-house. The benefit of this route would be greater control over their system, allowing them to optimize it to their specific needs and constraints. They could also decide to procure remote servers on the cloud and install the software themselves. This would free them from having to purchase the property to house their servers. At the other extreme, entrepreneurs would need to subscribe to an existing e-commerce service provider such as Shopify or WIX, two companies that provide the entire technology stack needed for an online shop. End-users do not need to develop software or to purchase physical infrastructure. They just need to decide what kind of subscription they need, and configure such subscriptions to implement payment processes, reporting systems, customer relationship management systems, etc. Other services could be purchased to support the payment of wages, a call centre, and so on. Many of these services can be purchased at a regular fixed fee, whereas other services can be paid for on a pay-as-you-go basis. In other words, there is a whole range of routes that are open today, and the barriers to entry for any given industry are in this sense lower than they were in the past.

5.1.2 Origins and some defining properties

Cloud computing can be traced back at least to the emergence of the dot-com era in the late 1990s. Touted at the time under the name 'application service provider', it was considered more as an outsourcing business model than a technology. The idea was for software vendors to run their applications on their own servers locally, but to provide customers with access to those applications through communication protocols and application programming interfaces. These interfaces acted as gateways, exposing the services to users, while hiding the complexity of implementation on the servers. Gateways were also the place vendors could implement common business rules such as access control (who has access to the servers?), usage monitoring (how are the services being used and how often?), and service charging (how should customers be charged?). Consider a weather forecasting service provider, for example. The service publishes the API, with all the information necessary to make use of the interface and to invoke it. The customer then connects to the API remotely using the communication protocol. Using the interface, the customer can then invoke the service. The service then runs remotely and delivers the result back to the client: the weather forecast over the next couple of days, for example.

This rather basic business model has since then developed and in its new form is now known as cloud computing. From an economic perspective, it allows companies to out-source certain parts of the value chain: be it data, computing power, memory, or any other resources that run on external machines, also known as server nodes. A form of distributed computing, cloud computing divides computation labour between stakeholders, a system that can increase efficiency through specialization and economies of scale. This introduces a trade-off: outsourcing part of the value chain can incur transaction costs, and organiza-tions need to decide between keeping all of it in-house and outsourcing part of it, and if the latter, how much of it they wish to outsource. Cloud computing makes services avail-able to end-users, personal users, and businesses on demand. Examples include Gmail, iCloud, and Salesforce. It is basically an out-sourcing strategy whose purpose is to cut costs on hardware and IT support.

In its ideal form, the cloud is envisioned to turn computing into a public utility, an infra-structure not dissimilar to those providing electricity, water, and public transportation ser-vices. This idea suggests that all the complexity and effort of setting up the computing power, configuring and maintaining it, can be hidden from customers way up in the cloud. But like many cases in the economy, in which labour and resources are divided, this has both advantages and disadvantages. By concentrating computing resources in the hands of a rel-atively small number of providers, economies of scale and specialization lead to more effi-cient use of resources. Customers need only pay for the computing that they need, the problem of load balancing becomes easier to handle, and maintenance, update, configura-tion, and administrative costs can be outsourced to some extent.

On the other hand, the risk of a breakdown or security threat can have grave conse-quences for large parts of the service economy. The complexity of the system brings about the challenge of coordinating and managing a large number of distributed resources and components, numerous interconnected parts, each contributing to the system's overall func-tionality. Coordinating these elements efficiently and ensuring they work together seam-lessly can be a significant logistical challenge, also known as 'the problem of many hands'.

Cloud computing has three main deployment models: public, private, and hybrid. We also discuss the community cloud here.

- *Public* cloud computing is the most common type of cloud computing deployment model. In a public cloud, the cloud infrastructure is owned and operated by a third-party cloud service provider, and made publicly available. Public clouds are typically the most cost-effective option, as the cloud service provider can reap economies of scale and thus offer more value for money. This comes at a cost: public cloud providers are often limited with regard to their ability to cater to specific needs or atypical requirements. In addition, security issues can theoretically become more important for very large providers of a public good. Well known examples of private clouds are Amazon Web Services (AWS), Microsoft Azure, and Google Cloud Platform (GCP).
- *Private* cloud computing is when the end-user's organization owns and operates the cloud infrastructure. Private clouds are typically used by organizations that

require more control over their data and security than is possible with a public cloud. Private clouds can be more expensive than public clouds, but they offer robust security because the private cloud can be completely isolated, enhanced performance because there is no competition for resource-intensive workloads on a shared server, and complete control over resources. Examples include the HPE private cloud (Hewlett Packard), VMware vCloud Air, IBM Cloud Private, Oracle Cloud Infrastructure, and Dell EMC cloud products.

- *Community* cloud computing is a deployment model in which the cloud infrastructure is owned and operated by a group of organizations that share a common goal or interest. Community clouds are typically used by organizations that need to share data and resources, but do not want to make their data and resources publicly available. Community clouds can be more expensive than public clouds, but they offer increased security and compliance. Examples of community clouds include Nutanix Calm, Fujitsu InterConnect, and Cisco Intercloud.
- *Hybrid* cloud computing is a deployment model that combines two or more of the above deployment models. Hybrid clouds are typically used by organizations that need the flexibility of a public cloud, but also need the control and security of a private cloud. Hybrid clouds can be more complex to manage than other deployment models, but they offer several advantages, such as increased flexibility and scalability. Examples of hybrid clouds include VMware Cross-Cloud Architecture, IBM Cloud Pak for Multicloud, and Microsoft Azure Stack.

Each cloud computing deployment model has its own advantages and disadvantages. The best deployment model for an organization will depend on its specific needs. When deciding on the most suitable kind of deployment, organizations must weigh up the following factors:

- *Cost*. Public clouds are typically the most cost-effective option, while private clouds can be more expensive.
- *Security*. Private clouds offer more security than public clouds, but they can be more difficult to manage.
- *Compliance*. Public clouds may not be able to meet the compliance requirements of some organizations.
- *Flexibility*. Hybrid clouds offer the most flexibility, but they can be more complex to manage.

By considering these factors, organizations can choose the cloud computing deployment model that best meets their needs.

5.1.3 Drivers and barriers

Whereas much of the literature on cloud computing focuses on the advantages of cloud computing, this is a complex multi-dimensional problem of finding a balance between the competing needs and requirements of the organization, and thus there is no one-size-fits-all solution to the question of whether and how much of the technology to he outsource to the cloud. That said, there are typical patterns in which cases tend to fall, determining typical answers for each pattern.

However, the problem goes beyond the financial pros and cons of outsourcing or running servers in-house. An MIT survey in 2017 found that only 34% of the respondents cited cost savings as the primary driver of increased cloud usage, whereas 45% of the respondents cited the prime driver to be 'increased need for agility and speed' (Sadowski, 2017).

But there are additional factors influencing this decision. One such factor concerns the privacy and security of this move, issues about the regulation of data usage, the worry of being locked into a specific cloud provider, among others. Another important issue is that organizations are in a state of flux, and cloud computing could be catalyst for change. Recall the case of Carlson's photocopier (Section 5.1). Its availability had a direct influence on organizations' business processes, simply because generating an additional photocopy became much cheaper than before, and organizations could suddenly tweak their processes to rely on that new availability. A similar dynamic was identified a decade ago (McAfee, 2011), when most companies owned their software and hardware, housing them on the premises in data centres and other specialized facilities. Having deep expertise with on-premises computing, many IT professionals were reluctant to use cloud technology. But making the move allowed them to simplify processes. Take, for example, Balfour Beatty, a British multinational infrastructure group, which in the early 2000s replaced its on-premises FTP server with box.com, a cloud provider of access to file sharing services. Not only did users find it much easier to access information via web browsers and mobile devices, but the process of sharing files and collaborating with external users in an ad-hoc fashion became much more straightforward. The previous arrangement required the IT department to sign up each new user and manage their access rights on the FTP server. After moving to the cloud, users could take charge of this process, thereby obviating the need for the IT department to get involved. Thus, the cloud increased productivity and simplified processes in a way that was not necessarily anticipated at the outset.

Another factor is the impact on data analytics. One of the side effects of using cloud services is the granularity of data usage supplied by cloud providers. This data is used to enhance the understanding and prediction of customer behaviour, both online and offline. By keeping track of very large amounts of low-level transaction data, companies can now identify, monitor, and control suspicious patterns, take advantage of opportunities, and mitigate risks of which they were unaware. Numerous such side effects have now been documented, some of them beneficial and some not, but they are often hard to anticipate and therefore difficult to consider when balancing the costs and benefits of cloud computing.

Cloud computing is not an all-or-nothing affair, but a choice along a continuum: which parts of the computing stack will stay in-house, and which will be outsourced, available remotely over the network. The combination of software and hardware components that work together to support the operations of an information technology (IT) system or application in an organization is sometimes referred to as: IT infrastructure.

The central decision that organizations need to make is how much of the system to manage in-house, and how much to outsource.[1] This is a strategic decision for an organization, involving not only financial considerations, but also considerations around privacy, security, regulations, and ethics.

It is common to consider four different service models, lying on a continuum of possibilities. At one extreme, the leftmost column in Figure 5.1 shows the entire technology stack owned and managed in-house. This was the only model available to entrepreneurs before the advent of cloud computing, in the early 2000s, as described earlier. It is the model that provides the greatest control to users, but it also involves the greatest capital expenditure.

Moving from left to right, Figure 5.1 shows alternative service models, where customers relegate additional layers of the technology stack to the cloud vendor, while the vendor accepts increasing responsibility for the operation of the customer. At the extreme end of the spectrum in the rightmost column, the vendor provides the software-as-a-service (SaaS) service model, allowing users to launch their online business without purchasing or installing even one physical server.

Between the two extremes we find the platform-as-a-service (PaaS) and infrastructure-as-a-service (IaaS) models, each allowing the end-user different ways to strike a balance between capital expenditure and operational expenditure. For example, developers often need an operating system so they can develop applications and test them. In this case, they could use an IaaS, the most basic service model, providing computing resources and allowing users to install and manage the software they need. The system comes pre-installed with an operating system, much like a bare-bones computer. They can install software and develop it, but they are also responsible for maintaining the software they develop or deploy. An example is a Windows virtual machine.

In contrast, a data scientist might want to access a large database, pre-installed and pre-configured. She may not want direct access to the underlying operating system, or want to maintain and upgrade the database she is using. In this case, a PaaS might be the ideal service model, offering her access to the database. In this case, the vendor manages everything related to running and maintaining the database server, and the user is responsible only for the use and configuration of the server.

Each type of service model allocates the rights and responsibilities to the various computing resources between the parties.

There is an array of additional acronyms pertaining to cloud services, including but not limited to specialist cloud services such as the following:

- Machine learning as a service (MLaaS) and blockchain as a service (BaaS) provide users with machine learning and blockchain functionality (Singh, 2017).
- Robotics as a service (RaaS) denotes the contractual arrangement by which vendors lease robotic systems providing technical support, monitoring, maintenance, and other services.
- Function as a service (FaaS), also known as serverless computing, is the capability of writing a code that is triggered by a call from a client application, like a call to a web service API.

Technology Stack	In-house	Infrastructure as a Service	Platform as a Service	Software as a Service
	SELF MANAGED	SELF MANAGED	SELF MANAGED	
	SELF MANAGED	SELF MANAGED	SELF MANAGED	
	SELF MANAGED	SELF MANAGED		
	SELF MANAGED	SELF MANAGED		
	SELF MANAGED			
	SELF MANAGED			
	SELF MANAGED			
	SELF MANAGED			
	SELF MANAGED			
	SELF MANAGED			

Figure 5.1 Service models describe what proportion of the technology stack is being outsourced

The column on the left of Figure 5.1 enumerates the different parts of the 'technology stack', a system encompassing the entire set of technologies, tools, and frameworks that are used to build, operate, and maintain a specific software solution. A technology stack typically includes several layers, each responsible for specific functions. Some layers are physical (such as storage and networks), while others are conceptual abstractions (such as middleware and virtualization, see below). The stack is arranged along a value chain leading from the physical property housing the servers all the way to the interface interacting with the end-user. Figure 5.1 below enumerates different parts of the technology stack, as explained below:

Runtime: A runtime environment is a program that runs the code of an application, and it is responsible for executing the instructions of the program, line by line, the allocation and management of the memory associated with the application, the interface between the running code and the operating system, etc.

Middleware: Middleware is software that links applications to one another. It often encapsulates and simplifies complex underlying services or sequences of actions that must be run multiple times. Sometimes it codifies business rules or business processes that may change from time to time, such as certain requirements that need to be validated against the data, or a series of operations and tasks that need to be signed off in a particular order. These complex repetitive series of operations are encapsulated in the middleware, allowing each component to focus on its unique task, independently of the other components. One example of middleware is an ETL processing system, used to extract, transfer, and load data in preparation for analysis or processing. Other examples include message queue management systems for managing messages exchanged between applications, and integration and workflow software.

Operating system: Each computer has a set of resources and services used by its applications. Examples include the use of memory and computer processors interacting with the screen, keyboard, and other devices. The program that makes all these resources and services available to software application is called the operating system. It is a piece of software that provides a set of common functions that all applications can use.

Virtualization: Operating systems typically run on physical computers that need to be set up, plugged in, connected to the network, configured, and maintained. But it is also possible to create a piece of software that imitates a self-sufficient machine, a virtual computer running on a host computer. It is thus possible to set up multiple virtual computers with which users could interact remotely, with the state of each virtual computer saved in a single file. Allowing multiple virtual machines to be hosted on one physical machine is a game changer for cloud computing. Multiple users can work concurrently on a single physical machine, sharing its resources and services over the Internet in a matter of minutes, without having to buy and install multiple machines. This reduces space requirements, enabling a more efficient sharing of resources over time. The virtual and physical machines are all connected to one another over the same network infrastructure, allowing for greater flexibility and more efficient use of resources.

Networking: The network is a part of the infrastructure, responsible for the interconnectedness between various IT resources and responsible for the transmission of data from one point to another. Each resource is assigned an IP address, and the network determines how the endpoints contact one another. The network is organized in a hierarchic manner. The lowest level is sometimes called an entity, which can be a device or a computer, either a physical or a virtual machine

Storage: Data can be stored in different ways for different purposes, but all storage types share basic functions of storing and recovering and manipulating data, each type of storage using its own interfaces and protocols. Examples include file storage, which is structured hierarchically using files and folders, block storage, and object storage.

5.2 BIG DATA ANALYTICS AND CLOUD COMPUTING

An important contributing factor driving the integration of cloud computing and big data analytics has been the rise of the Internet of Things (IoT), a technology that equips a whole range of physical objects with miniature sensors, all connected to one another and exchanging data with other devices and systems over the networks. Collecting sensory information from their environment, over time these devices generate large quantities of data. Devices that are too small to process and store the data locally rely on remote servers with nearly unlimited computing and memory resources.

But the IoT is not the only technology combining cloud computing with big data analytics. Processing data at scale is a complex undertaking, requiring users to manage large clusters of servers, install software, manage failure recovery processes and replication tasks, and much more. The cloud insulates the users from this complexity.

5.2.1 Cloud computing and big-data-related roles and responsibilities

One of the consequences of cloud computing for big data analytics lies in the way it restructured roles and responsibilities associated with big data. By taking care of some of the tasks previously carried out by data engineers and data scientists, the cloud effectively reconfigures tasks associated with traditional organizational roles, as shown in. For example, data ingestion and preparation are now much more straightforward, allowing data scientists to write and submit data science jobs and have them executed remotely on the cloud. In this sense, data scientists become less dependent on data engineers and database administrators.

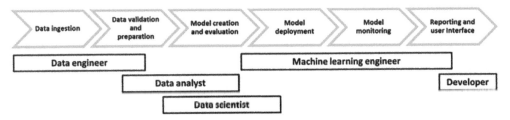

Figure 5.2 The traditional association between roles and the tasks they perform is being upended by cloud computing

In the same vein, data engineers can use pre-configured data modelling packages with frequently used models. These models generally deliver decent results without even the need for fine-tuning. This relieves engineers, at least to some extent, from their dependence on experts who understand the mathematical details of machine learning algorithms. Thus, the cloud facilitates a decoupling between the tasks of data engineers and those of data scientists, enabling smaller teams, requiring less specialization and facilitating the rise of what has recently been called the 'full stack' data scientist, an expert who can handle a data science project 'end-to-end': from data collection and ingestion, via feature engineering, model building and optimization, all the way to the actual deployment stage.

The transition from on-premises computing to cloud-driven systems led to sweeping structural changes in organizational roles and responsibilities. Database administrators have seen their work change substantially. Whereas the traditional database administrator would administer relational databases, the advent of the cloud saw a range of new types of databases becoming available. The database specialist must now understand a range of methods to store and organize data, how each method caters to specific tasks, and how to optimize the tools and methods for the task at hand.

Traditionally, data analysts would manually analyse data to make a single decision in a one-off or ad-hoc manner. They could, for instance, set up a model and fine-tune it, evaluate the results, interpret them, or use them to make predictions. In contrast, data scientists develop more generic processes or algorithms so that similar types of decisions can be made in a systematic way, continuously, over time. Whereas the data analyst's goal was to answer a specific question, the data scientist automates and optimizes the decision-making process so that the question can be addressed repeatedly. But the cloud is changing the way these roles are defined, with some roles disappearing completely, others appearing, and yet others converging or transforming.

These days, data scientists often act as a bridge between the business and the IT professionals, having to acquire a deep understanding of business processes and the skills of software developers and often those of statisticians. Data scientists typically work with production data, translating business requirements into code, building models, and communicating results to decision-makers. In short, the data scientist provides decision support services to the organization. This is different from simply constructing a model on a subset of the data. It includes building tools to evaluate the quality of the decision itself, the sources of potential errors and their magnitude, as well as possible constraints or limitations.

5.2.2 Processing big data on the cloud

There is a whole range of strategies to process very large quantities of data, sometimes known as autoscaling. The service provider must resize the cluster dynamically, fragment jobs down into tasks, and move tasks and data between nodes to process the data. Autoscaling can be carried out in various ways. First, it is possible to either scale up or scale out, and when scaling out, it is possible to scale out either with sharding or with data in situ. Which option is most appropriate depends on the problem, the context, and the resources at hand.

- *Scaling up.* The first option is to use more powerful processors, a greater number of processors, larger volumes of memory, faster networks, and wider bandwidths. Scaling up on-premises can be costly when the infrastructure is not used close to its full capacity. In this case, scaling up would involve renting appropriate resources from a cloud service provider. Scaling up is appropriate when the data is read multiple times. This happens often when machine learning algorithms need to be trained, which is why scaling up is common in machine learning. This approach is costly in terms of storage and computing power. It takes place on a single machine and so performance is bounded by the performance of the fastest machine available.
- *Scaling out with sharded data.* Fragmenting a job into smaller tasks that can be carried out independently of one another on multiple machines is called 'scaling out'. One way to do this is by partitioning a large table into smaller, more easily managed partitions or shards. Sharding is often contrasted with table normalization. Whereas normalization is a grouping of columns into separate tables, sharding is the process of grouping rows into horizontal partitions (also known as shards), where each shard is processed on a separate node. After the data is processed (in parallel), the results are combined, yielding a final outcome. This two-stage process of first partitioning and then combining the results is known as MapReduce, a process that the Hadoop Distributed File System (HDFS) can execute automatically. This method is costly in terms of storage but less costly than scaling up in terms of the computing power required. The bottleneck for scaling out is resource allocation when sharding the data. This can lead to inefficient use of resources and sub-optimal performance.

- *Scaling out without sharding.* When the data exists in its entirety in the cloud, network speed is high and the number of servers available on the cloud is in the hundreds of thousands. In such a case, it may be possible to optimize and automate resource allocation without sharding the data, maintaining a strict separation between the storage and the computing process. This setup is less costly than the previous ones in terms of storage and computing power, but it requires very fast networking capacity, and reading the data must keep up with the computation. There is no going back or rereading parts of the data.

5.3 INDUSTRY INSIGHTS

Businesses and organizations that are considering the adoption of cloud computing need to keep in mind a few things:

- The first choice that an organization needs to make is the type of cloud computing services it wishes to implement. Roughly stated, the choice is between public, private, and hybrid cloud services.
- The security and privacy requirements are central to the decision to adopt cloud computing. Cloud computing providers offer a variety of security features and controls, but it is important to choose a provider that can meet an organization's specific needs.
- The third strategic decision is to find the right balance between data accessibility and security. Cloud computing providers offer a variety of data replication and disaster recovery options, but it is important to choose a provider that can meet your specific needs.

Two popular cloud computing platforms are Amazon Web Services (AWS) and Microsoft Azure. Both platforms offer a wide range of services, including big data analytics.

AWS is one of the oldest and most mature cloud computing platforms. Its origins go back to the early 2000s in Amazon's SaaS offering, and it now offers a wide range of big data analytics services, including:

- Amazon Elastic MapReduce: a service that makes it easy to process large datasets using Hadoop and Spark.
- Amazon Redshift: a fully managed, petabyte-scale data warehouse service.
- Amazon Kinesis Data Analytics: a service that makes it easy to process streaming data.
- Amazon QuickSight: a business intelligence service that makes it easy to visualize and analyse data.

Microsoft Azure is a newer cloud computing platform than AWS, but it is growing rapidly. Azure offers a wide range of big data analytics services, including:

- Azure Databricks: a fully managed Spark service.
- Azure HDInsight: a fully managed Hadoop and Spark service.
- Azure Data Lake Analytics: a service that makes it easy to process large datasets using Apache Spark.
- Azure Machine Learning: a service that makes it easy to build and deploy machine learning models.

AWS and Azure offer a similar range of big data analytics services. However, there are some key differences between the two platforms. Although AWS tends to be more expensive than Azure, it also offers a wider range of features and perhaps more tailored support than Azure. Both AWS and Azure are popular platforms for big data analytics.

Google's cloud computing platform, Google Cloud Platform (GCP), has also emerged as a popular solution for businesses seeking infrastructure and services. Like AWS and Azure, GCP allows businesses to scale their computing resources up or down based on demand, enabling them to handle fluctuating workloads and manage costs effectively. Google achieves this scalability through technologies like Google Kubernetes Engine for container orchestration and autoscaling for virtual machine instances.

GCP also provides businesses with a wide range of services and tools to support their operations. From virtual machines and storage options to databases, machine learning tools, and data analytics services, GCP offers a comprehensive set of services to meet various business requirements. These services are designed to integrate seamlessly with each other and provide a unified environment for application development, deployment, and management. GCP also implements robust security measures to protect data and infrastructure, including data encryption, access controls, and compliance certifications. Other tools and services include Identity and Access Management and Cloud Security Command Centre to help businesses monitor and manage their security posture effectively.

GCP leverages Google's vast infrastructure and global network to deliver high-performance and low-latency services. GCP data centres are strategically located worldwide, allowing businesses to deploy applications closer to their users for improved performance and reduced latency. The global network backbone ensures reliable and fast connectivity between different regions.

GCP offers extensive support for open-source technologies, enabling businesses to leverage popular frameworks and tools. GCP supports a wide range of programming languages, containers, and development frameworks, allowing businesses to build and deploy applications using their preferred technologies. Google also actively contributes to open-source projects and offers managed services for popular frameworks like TensorFlow and Apache Spark.

When used together, cloud computing and big data analytics can be a powerful driver of innovation. For example, cloud computing can be used to store and process the massive amounts of data generated by organizations, data which can then be analysed using big data analytics to identify trends and patterns that can be used to improve marketing campaigns, product development, and customer service. More specifically, we can see how cloud computing and big data analytics can complement one another in the healthcare industry. Cloud computing can be used to store and process the vast amounts of medical data generated by electronic health records, which can then be analysed using big data analytics to identify patterns and trends that can improve patient diagnostic and health outcomes.

Cloud computing and big data analytics are still relatively new technologies, but they have the potential to revolutionize the way businesses operate. By working together, these two technologies can help businesses to make better decisions, improve efficiency, and gain a competitive edge. In 2015, Netflix used big data analytics to predict which movies and TV shows its users were most likely to watch. Both the storage and real-time processing of the data and the deployment of the predictive models were carried out in the cloud. The two technologies were used together to create personalized recommendations for each user. As a result of this initiative, Netflix saw a significant increase in user engagement and retention.

These are just examples of how cloud computing and big data analytics can create synergies, and when combined correctly, are able to improve business performance. As these technologies continue to evolve, we can expect to see even more innovative applications emerge.

5.4 ETHICS BY DESIGN

This chapter argues that cloud computing is a common way for organizations to store and process data. Together with cost savings, scalability, and flexibility, it is associated with some serious security, privacy, and ethical concerns. Taking the TAFARP data ethics by design framework, the three main areas of concern with respect to cloud computing are data security, data privacy, and responsibility, autonomy, and sustainable green cloud-computing.

5.4.1 Data security

When storing data in the cloud, an organization is entrusting it to a third-party provider. This makes trust an important part of the game, and organizations must be confident that the provider has taken appropriate security measures to protect the data. But there are several steps to assess the security of a cloud computing provider. First, providers can be certified by a reputable security organization, such as the Cloud Security Alliance, an organization dedicated to defining and raising awareness of best practices to help ensure a secure cloud computing environment. A trustworthy provider will also have security policies and procedures in place that should be consulted to make sure they are aligned with specific needs.

In addition to the provider's security measures, organizations must revisit their own data protection policies and be very clear what data they store in the cloud. Sensitive data can always be encrypted before being uploaded, as an additional security measure.

5.4.2 Privacy

Another concern with cloud computing is privacy. Storing data in the cloud amounts to sharing it with the provider and any other users with appropriate access rights. Uploading private details about so-called data subjects is a step that must be carefully weighed against the risks. To mitigate privacy concerns in cloud computing, one should first choose a provider that has a strong privacy policy. The contract, policy, and other paperwork that is exchanged should outline clearly how the provider collects, uses, and shares the data. You should also be careful about what data you share. If you are sharing sensitive data, you may want to consider using a pseudonym or a fake email address.

5.4.3 Responsibility and autonomy

Beyond data security and the privacy of data subjects, there are other concerns that are associated with cloud computing. One obvious concern is the implications for jobs. As more and more businesses move their IT operations to the cloud, there is less need for in-house IT staff, leading to job losses. Another concern is that cloud computing can influence environmental issues. The energy required to power server farms is significant, but it is very possible that centralizing computing power will in fact lead to more efficient solutions and an effective decrease in total greenhouse gas emissions.

Cloud computing is closely related to getting the balance right in terms of the division of rights and responsibilities of stakeholders with respect to limited (computing) resources. This is the question that faces both users and providers of cloud services, a question that is primarily an economic one, but it also has a normative, and thus ethical, dimension. In addition, by virtue of outsourcing different parts of the technical system to different stakeholders, the potential for a responsibility gap (Fosch-Villaronga and Millard, 2018) increases. With unanticipated consequences of cloud computing constantly emerging and the multiple stakeholder structure of the industry, regulation often lags behind the rapid pace of innovation in the cloud computing industry.

5.4.4 Sustainable green cloud computing

Green computing is the practice of using computing resources in an efficient and environmentally responsible manner. This can be done by using energy-efficient hardware and software, by reducing the amount of energy used by computers, and by recycling and disposing of computer equipment in an environmentally friendly way. Due to their high level of energy consumption, green computing is an especially urgent problem when it comes to cloud computing. On the other hand, cloud computing can be a more environmentally friendly way to use computing resources than traditional on-premises computing. This is because cloud computing providers can use economies of scale to purchase and operate more efficient computation power. Additionally, providers can build data centres near areas where renewable and recyclable energy is most readily available.

Organizations can choose a cloud computing provider that has a strong commitment to sustainability, even if there is scarce supply of renewable energy in their own vicinity. For example, some cloud computing providers offer virtual machines that are powered by renewable energy.

Some important considerations for ensuring security, privacy, and ethics when using cloud computing are the following:

- Organizations may want to choose a reputable cloud computing provider. For this, they would carry out careful research and choose a provider that has a good reputation for security and privacy.
- It is recommended to study the provider's terms of service very carefully, paying close attention to the provider's policies on data security and privacy.
- It is useful to think about what data one stores in the cloud. Only data that one is comfortable sharing with the provider and with other users should be uploaded.
- Not only sensitive but any type of data being uploaded should be encrypted prior to uploading.

SUMMARY

From a financial point of view, cloud computing is simply a problem of outsourcing computing services to a third party. It is therefore a technology that shares many features with the canonical make-or-buy dilemma, a dilemma that is central to corporate governance, one which has been discussed at length since Ronald Coase's landmark article *The Nature of the Firm*, published in 1937 (Coase, 1937). Though useful as a starting point, the chapter demonstrates that this is just part of the story. Rather than a binary decision to make or to buy, organizations must make strategic decisions that lie on a continuum along dimensions. This claim is supported by the results of the survey mentioned above, in which only a minority of respondents claimed that the decisive reason for their companies to move to the cloud stems from the desire to reduce costs. From an organizational perspective, adopting cloud computing is a strategic decision with potential ramifications for the very identity and culture of an organization.

Cloud computing offers enormous advantages, but also some costs in terms of security, privacy, and ethical concerns, issues that are specific to cloud computing. By carefully considering these concerns, organizations can make sure that cloud computing is a safe and ethical way to store and process data.

TEST YOUR KNOWLEDGE

1   Explain the concepts of operating expenditure and capital expenditure, and describe how they relate to cloud computing
2   Search the literature for two case studies of companies that migrated parts of their technology stack to the cloud, with different results and experiences. Then answer the following questions:

a What decisions did these organizations have to make when they first had to implement cloud computing? What choices did they have, what were the decisive criteria and what was the cost of making the transition to the cloud?

b How do the two organizations compare? In your answer, use the concepts and principles introduced in this chapter.

FURTHER READING (OPTIONAL)

Coase, Ronald H. 1937. The Nature of the Firm. Economica 4 (16): 386–405

de Bruin, B. and Floridi, L. (2017) The ethics of cloud computing. *Science and Engineering Ethics*, 23(1), 21–39.

Lakshmanan, V. (2018) *Data Science on the Google Cloud Platform: Implementing End-to-End Real-Time Data Pipelines: From Ingest to Machine Learning*. O'Reilly Media.

Murphy, B. and Rocchi, M. (2021) Ethics and cloud computing. In T. Lynn, J. G. Mooney, L. van der Werff and G. Fox (eds), *Data Privacy and Trust in Cloud Computing* (pp. 105–28). Cham: Springer.

NOTE

1 This decision depends on a range of constraints and affordances. Organizations need to identify the type of cloud-based services (and complementary technologies) that best address their business needs. They also need to identify appropriate practices that leverage these technologies.

REFERENCES

Brooks, J. (1969) *Business Adventures*. New York: Weybright & Talley.

Fosch-Villaronga, E. & Millard, C. (2018) Loud and cloud: Human responsibility for cloud robotics ecosystems. In J. L. Pons (ed.), *Inclusive Robotics for a Better Society: Selected Papers from INBOTS Conference* (pp. 109–12). Cham: Springer.

Gartner (2023) Gartner forecasts worldwide public cloud end-user spending to reach nearly $600 billion in 2023. Press release, 19 April. Retrieved from https://www.gartner.com/en/newsroom/press-releases/2023-04-19-gartner-forecasts-worldwide-public-cloud-end-user-spending-to-reach-nearly-600-billion-in-2023

Lisdorf, A. (2021) *Cloud Computing Basics*. Apress.

McAfee, A. (2011) What every CEO needs to know about the cloud. *Harvard Business Review*, 89(11), 124–32.

Owen, D. (2004) *Copies in Seconds: Chester Carlson and the Birth of the Xerox Machine*. New York: Simon & Schuster.

Sadowski, R. (2017) *Turns out, security drives cloud adoption.* Retrieved from https://cloud.google.com/blog/products/gcp/turns-out-security-drives-cloud-adoption-not-the-other-way-around

Singh, M. and Michels, J. D. (2017). Blockchain as a service: Providers and trust. Queen Mary School of Law Legal Studies Research Paper No. 269/2017. https://ssrn.com/abstract=3091223

6

BIG DATA ANALYTICS AND ACTIONABLE INSIGHTS

CHAPTER CONTENTS

CHAPTER OBJECTIVES

In this chapter:

- You will learn how big data analytics is used to draw insights using exploratory, descriptive, diagnostics, predictive, and prescriptive analytics.
- You will be introduced to practical methods of data preparation and pre-processing using Apache Spark.
- Finally, you will explore more ways of incorporating ethics by design and also touch on some industry insights.

6.1 THE PROMISE OF BIG DATA ANALYTICS

In earlier chapters, we explored the process of collecting, storing, and analysing large amounts of data The objective was to extract 'meaningful insights'. But what makes insights meaningful to organizations? This is the question we try to answer in this section.

For organizations, insights are meaningful to the extent that they can influence strategic decisions, decisions that are based on an understanding of their customers, operations, and markets. If the process of big data analytics can be used to meet their strategic goals, improve efficiency, and provide routes to a sustained competitive advantage, we would say that the insights are meaningful. Some of the strategic goals that can be met with big data analytics are the following:

1   *Improved understanding of customers and other stakeholders*. Organizations collect data from a variety of resources: from purchase history and customer surveys to public data on social media, and other resources. This data can provide a better understanding of customers' needs, choices, and preferences, allowing organizations to predict future behaviour and cater to customers' appetites in a variety of ways: organizations can improve marketing campaigns, segment their market, and cater their communication to each segment accordingly. These insights can also shape product development and customer service.

2   *Increased operational efficiency*. By analysing data from sensors and other devices, organizations can identify areas where they can improve their operations. This could include reducing costs, improving quality, or increasing productivity. Increased monitoring of operations, employees, and customers is, however, a mixed blessing, as operational efficiency can come at the cost of privacy, raising ethical concerns.

3   *Innovating products, services, and business models*. Analysing company data can inform market research and pave the way to new ways of generating revenue. These insights could drive innovation of products and services, adapting them to new needs and trends. It could also help companies enter new markets. By analysing their data, organizations can identify new channels for opportunities for innovation.

4   *Gaining a competitive advantage.* Big data analytics can yield insights that help organizations improve operations, make better decisions, and identify new opportunities. All of these can allow organizations to gain a competitive advantage over their rivals.

5   *Risk mitigation and control.* If data is the heartbeat of an organization, it is also a way to diagnose any worrying signs in advance. For example, through the operation of 'anomaly detection', organizations can identify potential risks and take steps to mitigate them.

Big data analytics is a powerful tool that can be used to achieve a wide range of strategic goals. Organizations can gain a competitive advantage and improve their bottom line by understanding the potential benefits of big data analytics and developing a clear strategy for its use. One example of a company that uses big data analytics is Uber Technologies Inc. (which we discuss further in Section 6.5), which started out primarily in the transportation industry, but with the pioneering ways it has used big data analytics it has now expanded into other revenue streams like Uber Eats (food deliveries), UberFresh (grocery deliveries), UberRush (courier service) and Uber Copter (helicopter services). Companies like Google, Amazon, X, formerly known as Twitter, Netflix, and Walmart owe their competitive advantage, at least in part, to data-driven insights. The promise of big data analytics and what it offers is not just for the commercial sector but applies to any sector that is able to tap into it; we see examples of this in the health sector, where data analytics has ushered in a transformation in diagnostics and disease prevention.

6.2 DATA WRANGLING EXERCISE

As discussed earlier in Chapter 2, data wrangling (or data munging) covers the procedures that are used to pre-process and transform data into a structured format, preparing it for processing and analysis from which actionable insights can be drawn. Data wrangling, cleaning, and general pre-processing constitute a large part of what data professionals do to get data ready to be processed and analysed and as such this is an important subject area. In this section we will use some data wrangling techniques. For these practical exercises we will use two main tools: OpenRefine and Apache Spark (which was introduced in Chapter 3).

OpenRefine is a free open-source powerful tool that is particularly useful for data cleaning and wrangling. It can also be used for deduplication (the elimination of duplicate data). Apache Spark can particularly handle large datasets as it distributes the data across multiple nodes, which in turn makes the processing of big data more efficient. In the following subsections there are hands-on exercises using both OpenRefine and Apache Spark (Karau et al., 2015).

6.2.1 Installing OpenRefine and downloading files for data wrangling

In this section we will demonstrate how to use OpenRefine to explore your data. To install OpenRefine, download the OpenRefine executable file from https://openrefine.org/ then

file. Unzip the archive, and double-click on openrefine.exe or refine.bat if the former does not work.

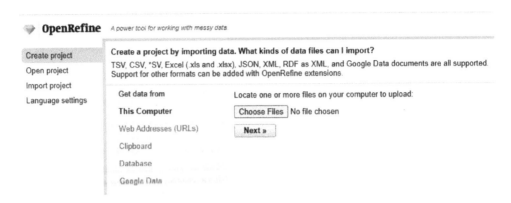

Figure 6.1   Screenshot of OpenRefine

To upload data for pre-processing into OpenRefine, you need to select the location of the data. OpenRefine gives five options for this:

- *This Computer.* This refers to the local machine that you are working on. If this option is selected, it allows you to manually choose the file from its location on your local machine.
- *Web Addresses (URLs).* With this option you can enter one or more web addresses and point to the data to be uploaded into OpenRefine.
- *Clipboard.* This provides an interface where you can paste data from the clipboard. This would usually be for small datasets as with the clipboard one is limited by the machine's available memory and address space.
- *Database.* OpenRefine provides connectors to four different database types: MySQL, PostgreSQL, MariaDB, and SQLite (see Figure 6.2).

Figure 6.2   OpenRefine database sources

- *Google Data.* This provides an interface to import a public Google spreadsheet by its URL.

OpenRefine takes in a wide range of file formats:

- Comma-separated values (CSV) or text-separated values (TSV)
- Text files
- Fixed-width columns
- JSON
- XML
- OpenDocument spreadsheet (ODS)
- Excel spreadsheet (XLS or XLSX)
- PC-Axis (PX)
- MARC
- RDF data (JSON-LD, N3, N-Triples, Turtle, RDF/XML)
- Wikitext.

Let us import a file into OpenRefine for data wrangling and pre-processing. Again, you can download a file from any open data portal, use an existing file you have access to, or download a file from one of the links provided on this book's online resources website.

For text files the default setting for OpenRefine is that columns are separated by commas (CSV); if that is not the case for your file you need to change this setting and others to the correct values. In Figure 6.3 we have uploaded a file that is separated by tabs and so the initial preview of the data does not correctly show the various fields. Once this is corrected from CSV to TSVC, the data preview shows all the various fields in the file (see Figure 6.4).

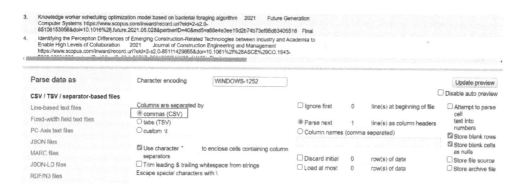

Figure 6.3   Data preview with incorrect settings

In subsequent sections, we use PySpark and OpenRefine to carry out some hands-on data wrangling and pre-processing.

6.2.2 Data exploration

One of the very first steps when it comes to wrangling and cleaning data is to explore the data. When it comes to big data, we need to appreciate that because of the large volumes of data involved the way we go about exploring the data might have to be different than when we are dealing with small datasets. With a small dataset, the file can be opened in Notepad,

| 2. | Identification of topic development process of knowledge and information science field based on the topic modeling (LDA) | 2021 | Iranian Journal of Information Processing and Management | https://www.scopus.com/inward/record.uri?eid=2-s2.0-85107476727&partnerID=40&md5=a1ae51f743590d0868f9c3cbd9344e5b | | Final |
| 3. | Knowledge worker scheduling optimization model based on heuristic | 2021 | Future Generation Computer Systems | https://www.scopus.com/inward/record.uri?eid=2-s2.0-85106153956&doi=10.1016%2f].future.2021.05.028&partnerID=40&md5=a38e4e3ee15:2b74b73ef95df3405516 | | Final |

Parse data as		Character encoding	WINDOWS-1252			Update preview

Disable auto preview

CSV / TSV / separator-based files

Line-based text files

Columns are separated by
○ commas (CSV)
◉ tabs (TSV)
○ custom \t

□ Ignore first   0   line(s) at beginning of file
◉ Parse next   1   line(s) as column headers
○ Column names (comma separated)

□ Attempt to parse cell text into numbers
☑ Store blank rows
☑ Store blank cells as nulls
□ Store file source
□ Store archive file

Fixed-width field text files
PC-Axis text files
JSON files
MARC files
JSON-LD files
RDF/N3 files

☑ Use character " to enclose cells containing column separators
□ Trim leading & trailing whitespace from strings
Escape special characters with \

□ Discard initial   0   row(s) of data
□ Load at most   0   row(s) of data

Figure 6.4 Data preview with correct settings

Notepad++, Textpad, Excel, or a similar application and visually explored. However, with large datasets these applications might not be able to handle the volume of the datasets involved. For instance, the maximum size of an Excel worksheet is a total of 1,048,576 rows by 16,384 columns. In Chapter 2, we gave an example about how during the Covid-19 pandemic there was an incident with Public Health England where Covid-19 test results across the country where being stored in the old format of Excel (which can only handle about 65,000 rows of data) and as a result of this the Covid-19 test results that were being collected were grossly underreported until the issue was spotted. So we see that the choice of application to use really does matter. How then do we explore the data when it comes to big data volumes? One way of doing this is to explore the data via programming code, so after you have uploaded the file into a development environment or computing platform like Jupyter, which we introduced in Chapter 2, you can write code to carry out your data exploration. You can also use existing tools which can handle large volumes of data such as OpenRefine and a host of others which cover a wide range and fall under both open source and commercial. Let us get started with our hands-on exploration.

First of all, we need a dataset to work with.

One of the initial files was originally downloaded from NHS Digital portal (NHS Digital, 2023) and is data about patients registered at GP practices; it has been made freely available so users can carry out their own analyses. The URL for the dataset can be found on this book's website. This dataset has already been pre-processed by NHS Digital and is reasonably clean. The second file we will use contains tweets on Covid-19 that were harvested online and has had no pre-processing or cleansing done to it.

For several of the Apache Spark hands-on exercises we also use the accidents dataset from the UK police open data portal that was first introduced in Chapter 3. Recall that it contains the columns depicted in Figure 6.5.

So, as described in Chapter 2, open a Jupyter Notebook, run the required configuration scripts, and import the necessary modules as depicted in Figure 6.6.

Once the environment is up and running, then again as demonstrated in Chapters 2 and 4, we need to upload our data (as seen in the previous chapters, there are a variety of ways of doing this, depending on the source of the data and so on). In Figure 6.7, the file which

```
root
 |-- Accident_Index: string (nullable = true)
 |-- Location_Easting_OSGR: integer (nullable = true)
 |-- Location_Northing_OSGR: integer (nullable = true)
 |-- Longitude: double (nullable = true)
 |-- Latitude: double (nullable = true)
 |-- Police_Force: integer (nullable = true)
 |-- Accident_Severity: integer (nullable = true)
 |-- Number_of_Vehicles: integer (nullable = true)
 |-- Number_of_Casualties: integer (nullable = true)
 |-- Date: string (nullable = true)
 |-- Day_of_Week: integer (nullable = true)
 |-- Time: string (nullable = true)
 |-- Local_Authority_(District): integer (nullable = true)
 |-- Local_Authority_(Highway): string (nullable = true)
 |-- 1st_Road_Class: integer (nullable = true)
 |-- 1st_Road_Number: integer (nullable = true)
 |-- Road_Type: integer (nullable = true)
 |-- Speed_limit: integer (nullable = true)
 |-- Junction_Detail: integer (nullable = true)
 |-- Junction_Control: integer (nullable = true)
 |-- 2nd_Road_Class: integer (nullable = true)
 |-- 2nd_Road_Number: integer (nullable = true)
 |-- Pedestrian_Crossing-Human_Control: integer (nullable = true)
 |-- Pedestrian_Crossing-Physical_Facilities: integer (nullable = true)
 |-- Light_Conditions: integer (nullable = true)
 |-- Weather_Conditions: integer (nullable = true)
 |-- Road_Surface_Conditions: integer (nullable = true)
 |-- Special_Conditions_at_Site: integer (nullable = true)
 |-- Carriageway_Hazards: integer (nullable = true)
 |-- Urban_or_Rural_Area: integer (nullable = true)
 |-- Did_Police_Officer_Attend_Scene_of_Accident: integer (nullable = true)
 |-- LSOA_of_Accident_Location: string (nullable = true)
```

Figure 6.5 Schema of the accident dataset

holds the data we want to explore is uploaded to HDFS and then uploaded into an RDD in the Jupyter Notebook.

Now we are ready to explore the data. Let us start by checking how many items are in each dataset (see Figure 6.8).

```
# Import necessary modules
from pyspark import SparkContext, Sparkconf
Conf = SparkConf().setAppName("appName")
sc = SparkContext(conf=conf)


# Define SQLContext
from pyspark.sql import SQLContext
sqlContext = SQLContext(sc)
```

Figure 6.6 Jupyter Notebook with required configurations for Apache Spark (PySpark)

```
hadoop fs -put corona_tweets_extended_16032020_1_final.csv

# load the data/ create RDD
# remember to change the location to yours for your file

gpPracPatients = sc.textFile("hdfs:///data/gp-reg-pat-prac-all.csv")

covidTweets = sc.textFile(("hdfs:///data/corona_tweets.csv")
```

Figure 6.7 Uploading the data into RDDs

```
gpPracPatients.count()

Output: 7464

covidTweets.count()

Output: 665953
```

Figure 6.8 Count of items in each dataset

Next, let us have a look at what it is contained in the datasets; we will output the first five items in each of the datasets (see Figure 6.9).

From Figure 6.9 we can see that each of the datasets has a header row and each column is separated by a comma. With this in mind we could choose to load the data into a

```
# return the first five items in the RDD
gpPracPatients.take(5)
```

```
Output:
['PUBLICATION,EXTRACT_DATE,TYPE,CCG_CODE,ONS_CCG_CODE,CODE,POSTCODE,SEX,
AGE,Number of patients',
 'GP_PRAC_PAT_LIST,01-May-17,GP,00C,E38000042,A83005,DL1 3RT,ALL,ALL,11673',
 'GP_PRAC_PAT_LIST,01-May-17,GP,00C,E38000042,A83006,DL3 6HZ,ALL,ALL,7954',
 'GP_PRAC_PAT_LIST,01-May-17,GP,00C,E38000042,A83010,DL3 9JP,ALL,ALL,14283',
 'GP_PRAC_PAT_LIST,01-May-17,GP,00C,E38000042,A83013,DL1 4YL,ALL,ALL,11192']
```

Figure 6.9   First five items in each of the datasets

DataFrame rather than a RDD like we have currently done. Recall that we discussed RDDs and DataFrames and the differences between them in Chapter 3. In Figure 6.10 we load the data directly into DataFrames.

```
gpPracPatientsDF=spark.read.option("header","true").option("delimiter",",").
option("inferSchema","true").csv("hdfs:///data/gp-reg-pat-prac-all.csv")

covidTweetsDF=spark.read.option("header","true").option("delimiter",",").
option("inferSchema","true").csv("hdfs:/// data/corona_tweets.csv")
```

Figure 6.10   Uploading the data directly into DataFrames

Again, as with the RDDs, we can explore the data in the DataFrames. In Figure 6.11 we return the count of items in one of the DataFrames and its schema.

For data pre-processing the schema can be extremely important, as we need each field type to have the correct data type. It can hinder analysis and processing if any of these are incorrect. For instance, if you have a field that holds data such as date of birth, if instead of having a date format in the schema it is a string, then that would limit what you can do with that field when it comes to processing and drawing out insights from it. Simple queries such as returning all the data within a certain date range would not return the correct data because the field is not seen as a date but a string. So, early on issues such as this need to be corrected. Another example would be a field that holds decimals but does not have a format that supports this. To illustrate one way to correct this using PySpark, we will correctly cast a *created* field from a string format to a date format as it represents the date the tweet was created. Figure 6.12 shows code to change the data type from string to date; the change can be seen in the schema that is also displayed in the figure.

```
covidTweetsDF.count()
```

Output: 665953

```
covidTweetsDF.printSchema
```

Output:
```
root
 |-- id: string (nullable = true)
 |-- user_description: string (nullable = true)
 |-- user_location: string (nullable = true)
 |-- coordinates: string (nullable = true)
 |-- text: string (nullable = true)
 |-- geo: string (nullable = true)
 |-- user_name: string (nullable = true)
 |-- user_created: string (nullable = true)
 |-- user_followers: string (nullable = true)
 |-- id_str: string (nullable = true)
 |-- created: string (nullable = true)
 |-- retweet_count: string (nullable = true)
 |-- user_bg_color: string (nullable = true)
 |-- polarity: string (nullable = true)
 |-- subjectivity: string (nullable = true)
```

Figure 6.11 Count of items in the DataFrame and its schema

To change the datatypes to other formats, all that needs to be done is to replace DateType in the code in Figure 6.12 with the relevant data type (e.g., IntegerType, BooleanType or StringType). We are able to use these because as part of the step where we set the configurations, we imported into the Jupyter Notebook the relevant library using

```
from pyspark.sql.types Import IntegerType, BooleanType, DateType
```

If you try to cast from one data type to another one that is inappropriate, you'll get an error message which can easily be resolved by changing the value to an appropriate data type.

6.2.3 Missing values

Ensuring that data is pre-processed well is extremely important because when it comes to big data analytics, as mentioned earlier, if the data being used is garbage then the phrase 'garbage in, garbage out' applies. Any insights drawn from analytics on that data will be wrong.

```
covidTweetsDF=covidTweetsDF.withColumn("created",covidTweetsDF.created.
cast(DateType()))


covidTweetsDF.printSchema()


Output:
root
 |-- id: string (nullable = true)
 |-- user_description: string (nullable = true)
 |-- user_location: string (nullable = true)
 |-- coordinates: string (nullable = true)
 |-- text: string (nullable = true)
 |-- geo: string (nullable = true)
 |-- user_name: string (nullable = true)
 |-- user_created: string (nullable = true)
 |-- user_followers: string (nullable = true)
 |-- id_str: string (nullable = true)
 |-- created: string (nullable = true)
 |-- retweet_count: string (nullable = true)
 |-- user_bg_color: string (nullable = true)
 |-- polarity: string (nullable = true)
 |-- subjectivity: string (nullable = true)
```

Figure 6.12   Casting datatypes

There are several ways to handle missing values in a dataset and the type of analytics to be used on the dataset will also contribute to what technique is chosen to handle the missing data. These are covered further in Chapters 7–10, which go into more detail on various analytic techniques. Some of the approaches for handling missing values are as follows:

- Deleting the missing values.
- Deleting the entire row with the missing values.
- Deleting the entire feature (as discussed above).
- Replacement of the missing values with a constant) e.g., the median, mean, or mode value).
- Replacement of the missing values with 0.
- Imputing the missing value (e.g., with the most frequent value or nearest neighbour imputations).

Figure 6.13 shows code to return the count of all null values in every field of the dataset. This code loops through every field in the DataFrame and sums up the number of null values present in each field and returns this value. The `show()` method at the end of the line of code is a useful one; it is an action (remember we discussed Apache Spark actions and transformations in Chapter 3). It allows you to see the output from your query without needing to create a new DataFrame. It can be particularly useful when troubleshooting and/or pre-processing, particularly if you want to see the data your change would affect prior to actually applying the change.

```
from pyspark.sql.functions import isnan, when, count, col

covidTweetsDF.select([count(when(col(c).isnull(),c)).alias(c) for c in
covidTweetsDF.columns]).show
```

Output:

```
+----+-----------------+-------------+-----------+       +----+---------+------------+---------------+------+-------+------------
-+-----------------+------------+-----------+
| id|user_description|user_location|coordinates|     text|       geo|user_name|user_created|user_followers|id_str|created|retweet_coun
t|user_bg_color|polarity|subjectivity|
+----+-----------------+-------------+-----------+       +----+---------+------------+---------------+------+-------+------------
-+-----------------+------------+-----------+
| 18|          222625|       279879|     437542|162054|442894|    212377|      210687|        209974|209715| 209618|       28018
9|      290365|  292141|      316971|
+----+-----------------+-------------+-----------+       +----+---------+------------+---------------+------+-------+------------
-+-----------------+------------+-----------+
```

Figure 6.13 Count of null values in every field in the DataFrame

Figure 6.14 shows the count of null values in a specific field; in this example we have specified the `geo` field.

```
from pyspark.sql.functions import isnan, when, count, col

covidTweetsDF.select([count(when(col('geo').isNull(),True))]).show()
```

Output:

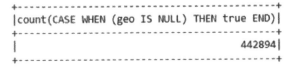

Figure 6.14 Count of null values in a specific field (`geo`) in the DataFrame

We can also use the PySpark `fillna()` and `fill()` functions to replace null or none values in integer columns. Both of these functions do exactly the same thing:

```
fillna(value, subset = None)

fill(value, subset = None)
```

In the syntax above `value` is the value you want to replace the null or none values in the dataset with, while `subset`, which is non-mandatory, allows you to specify which fields to apply this replacement to – if not specified it would be applied to all the fields in the dataset.

The following code snippet would replace all null or none values in integer fields with zero (add a `show()` to the end of the code if you just want to see what instances it would affect):

```
covidTweetsDF.na.fill(value=0)
```

To replace all null or none values but just for the specified field (in this case `retweet_count`) you would instead write:

```
covidTweetsDF.na.fill(value=0,subset=["retweet_count"])
```

We can also replace all the null or none values in a specific column with a value such as 'unknown':

```
covidTweetsDF.na.fill("unknown",["user_name"])
```

Figure 6.15 is an additional code sample that demonstrates data wrangling of a dataset using the `fillna` and `dropna` methods. As mentioned above the `fillna` method replaces null values with a specified value while the `dropna` method removes the rows with null values. Within the code there are checks for missing values, filling of missing values in some specific columns, dropping of rows with missing values, filtering of rows based on a condition and aggregation.

6.2.4 Deduplication

Deduplication is the process of removing duplicate instances of values from a dataset. When it comes to data wrangling in big data analytics, deduplication can be quite important for two main reasons. First, it can significantly reduce storage requirements. Second, failing to remove the duplicate data when analytics are carried out on a dataset it can skew results and result in incorrect insights and conclusions being drawn. A simple example of deduplication is shown in Figure 6.16 where the duplicate row with ID equal to 1 is removed.

```
# Import necessary modules
from pyspark.sql import SparkSession
from pyspark.sql.functions import *

# Create a Spark session
spark = SparkSession.builder.appName("HandsOnExercise").getOrCreate()

# Load the dataset into a Spark DataFrame (replace the path with yours)
accidents_2019DF=spark.read.option("header","true").option("delimiter",",").
option("inferSchema","true").csv("hdfs:///user/Accidents2019.csv")

# Check for missing values in the DataFrame
missing_values=accidents_2019DF.select([count(when(isnan(c) | col(c).isNull(),
c)).alias(c) for c in accidents_2019DF.columns])
missing_values.show()

# Fill missing values in specific columns;
# replace missing values in Location_Easting_OSGR with '0'
# replace missing values in Did_Police_Officer_Attend_Scene_of_Accident with
#"unknown"
accidents_2019DF=accidents_2019DF.fillna({"Location_Easting_OSGR":0,
"Did_Police_Officer_Attend_Scene_of_Accident": "unknown"})

# Check how many rows are in the dataset before doing any drops (deletes)
accidents_2019DF.count()

# Drop rows with missing values
accidents_2019DF = accidents_2019DF.dropna()

# Now re-check how many rows are left after the drop command
accidents_2019DF.count()

# Filter rows based on a condition
accidents_2019DF = accidents_2019DF.filter(col("column1") > 0)

# Group by a column and perform aggregation
grouped_accidents_df=accidents_2019DF.groupBy("Number_of_Casualties").
agg(avg("Day_of_Week"))

# View the new grouped DataFrame
grouped_accidents.show()
```

Figure 6.15 Data wrangling using Apache Spark fillna **and** dropna **methods**

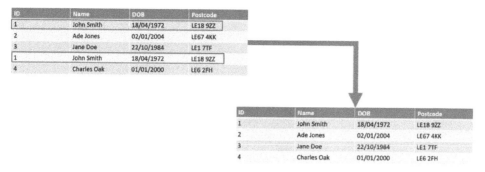

Figure 6.16   Deduplication

To use PySpark code for deduplication, we can check how many items are originally in our dataset, how many of them are distinct and then we can drop all the duplicates from the DataFrame. These steps are all depicted in the code snippets in Figure 6.17 where with the final line of code we check the count of items in the DataFrame after deduplication. In this example we see that the original number of items in the DataFrame was 555,709; after deduplication this drops to 503,842 items, with 51,867 duplicate items having been dropped.

```
covidTweetsDF.count()
```

```
Output: 555709
```

```
covidTweetsDF.distinct().count()
```

```
Output: 503842
```

```
covidTweetsDF_dedup = covidTweetsDF.drop_duplicates()
```

```
covidTweetsDF_dedup.count()
```

```
Output: 503842
```

Figure 6.17   Deduplication using PySpark

6.2.5 Grouping

Grouping and aggregating data can be informative and are useful processes during data wrangling and pre-processing. Let us demonstrate how to do this easily using OpenRefine. After uploading your data and creating a project from it, select the field you are interested in and right-click on the field name; this opens a drop-down list of functions that you can run (see Figure 6.18).

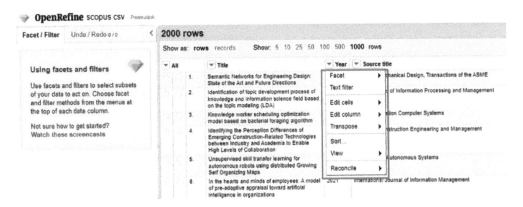

Figure 6.18 OpenRefine methods

The first of these methods is facet; this is said to be one of OpenRefine's strongest features. It provides functions to help find trends and patterns in the dataset. It also provides facilities for you to write your own custom facet. Figure 6.19 shows the various facets that are available in OpenRefine.

Figure 6.19 OpenRefine facets

A quick selection of `Text facet` within the `Year` field immediately returns the year field grouped together. Figure 6.20 shows that there are 12 options and the number of instances that fall under each of the options.

Figure 6.21 is an example of deduplication using Apache Spark using the `dropDuplicates` method. The `dropDuplicates()` command removes duplicate rows from a dataset, so that the newly created DataFrame does not include duplicate rows.

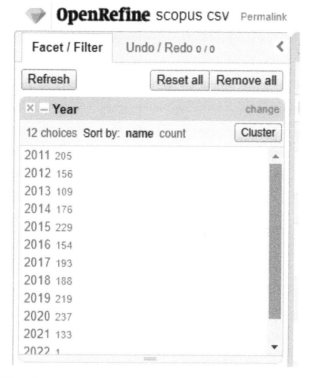

Figure 6.20   Text facet

6.2.6 Other data wrangling techniques (with Apache Spark hands-on exercises)

The data wrangling techniques covered so far are by no means exhaustive and you will find that the more you work with data, the more proficient you will become at data pre-processing, wrangling, and cleaning. Other useful techniques (some of which we will revisit in Chapters 7–10) that can be employed using PySpark code, OpenRefine, or a variety of other available tools, including the following:

- Concatenating data
- Merging data
- Grouping data
- Reshaping data
- Filtering data
- Extracting information from data (from text, dates, etc.)
- Standardizing textual data
- Normalization

```
from pyspark.sql import SparkSession
from pyspark.sql.functions import *


# Create a Spark session
spark = SparkSession.builder.appName("HandsOnExercise").getOrCreate()


# Load the dataset into a Spark DataFrame (replace the path with yours)
accidents_2019DF=spark.read.option("header","true").option("delimiter",",").
option("inferSchema","true").csv("hdfs:///user/Accidents2019.csv")


# Check how many rows are in the dataset before dropping exact duplicates
accidents_2019DF.count()


# Drop exact duplicate rows
accidents_2019DF = accidents_2019DF.dropDuplicates()


# Now re-check how many rows are left after the dropduplicates command
accidents_2019DF.count()


# Drop rows with duplicate values in specific columns Number_of_Casualties #
and Day_of_Week
accidents_2019DF=accidents_2019DF.dropDuplicates(subset=["Number_of_
Casualties", "Day_of_Week"])
```

Figure 6.21   Code using Apache Spark for data wrangling (deduplication)

Examples of Apache Spark code for some of these can be seen in Figures 6.22–6.25.

In the concatenation example in Figure 6.22, the methods `concat` and `split` are used. The `concat` command concatenates two or more columns into a new column while `split`, as its name suggests, splits the contents of a column on a specified delimiter.

In the hands-on exercise in Figure 6.23 the accident dataset is grouped based on two of the columns in the dataset (`Day_of_Week` and `Speed_limit`) using the `groupBy` function. This is then followed by aggregations that include counting the number of rows using `count("*").alias("count")`, taking the sum, average, maximum. and minimum of the values in the `Number_of_Casualties`. Figure 6.24 shows a screenshot of a subset of the values in the final aggregated DataFrame.

In the code in Figure 6.25 the `filter` function is used to filter the data based on a specific condition. In this example a simple condition where the day of the week is equal to 2 has been used. If required, the condition could be more complex; multiple conditions can also be combined.

```
from pyspark.sql import SparkSession
from pyspark.sql.functions import *


# Create a Spark session
spark = SparkSession.builder.appName("HandsOnExercise").getOrCreate()


# Load the dataset into a Spark DataFrame (replace the path with yours)
accidents_2019DF=spark.read.option("header","true").option("delimiter",",").
option("inferSchema","true").csv("hdfs:///user/Accidents2019.csv")


# Concatenate two columns into a new column
# concatenated_column_casultiesByWeek

accidents_2019DF=accidents_2019DF.withColumn("concatenated_column_
casultiesByWeek", concat(col("Number_of_Casualties"), lit(" "), col("Day_of_
Week")))


# Check that the new column "concatenated_column_casultiesByWeek" has been #
created and added to the DataFrame's schema
accidents_2019DF.printSchema()


# Split a column Local_Authority_(Highway)into multiple columns
accidents_2019DF=accidents_2019DF.withColumn("split_column_local_highway",
split(col("Local_Authority_(Highway)"), " "))
```

Figure 6.22   Code using Apache Spark for data wrangling (concatenation)

Now that we have gone through data wrangling and our data has been pre-processed, the next step is to process and apply various analytical techniques to draw out actionable insights from the data. Recall that in Chapter 1, we saw how one of the five Vs of big data analytics is value – which speaks to the end goal, the main aim of big data analytics, of drawing out insights from the data that help us to get value from the data.

6.3 FORMS OF BIG DATA ANALYTICS: EXPLORATORY, DESCRIPTIVE, DIAGNOSTIC, PREDICTIVE, PRESCRIPTIVE

In this section we will revisit the various big data analytics methods and processes first introduced in Chapter 2. We carry out some hands-on exercises to see how we can draw out insights from them. In Chapters 7–10 as we go into more detail on these, we carry out more in-depth exercises.

Exploratory analytics is all about carrying out initial investigations on data to discover trends and patterns which could help to highlight any anomalies. It also includes the use of

```
from pyspark.sql import SparkSession
from pyspark.sql.functions import *

# Create a Spark session
spark = SparkSession.builder.appName("HandsOnExercise").getOrCreate()

# Load the dataset into a Spark DataFrame (replace the path with yours)
accidents_2019DF=spark.read.option("header","true").option("delimiter",",").
option("inferSchema","true").csv("hdfs:///user/Accidents2019.csv")

# Display the schema and first five items in the dataset
print("Dataset Schema:")
accidents_2019DF.printSchema()
print("First five Items in the Dataset:")
accidents_2019DF.show(5)

# Group data based on two columns (Day_of_Week and Speed_limit) and perform #
aggregations
grouped_accident_DF=accidents_2019DF.groupBy("Day_of_Week", "Speed_limit")
aggregated_accident_data = grouped_accident_DF.agg(
    count("*").alias("count"),
    sum("Number_of_Casualties").alias("sum"),
    avg("Number_of_Casualties").alias("average"),
    max("Number_of_Casualties").alias("maximum"),
    min("Number_of_Casualties").alias("minimum")
)

# Display the aggregated accident data
print("Aggregated Accident Data:")
aggregated_accident_data.show()
```

Figure 6.23   Code using Apache Spark for data wrangling (grouping)

statistical functions such as count, maximum, minimum, average, standard deviation, and quantiles to check assumptions about the data. As mentioned previously in Chapter 2, descriptive analytics helps us to understand what happened in the past and can be used to monitor important metrics going forward.

Finally, exploratory and descriptive analytics usually also involve the use of visualizations and graphical representations to explore the data. In this section we will carry out some hands-on exploratory and descriptive analytics. The techniques that are typically used include the following:

```
# Display the aggregated accident data
print("Aggregated Accident Data:")
aggregated_accident_data.show()
```

Output:

```
Aggregated Accident Data:
+-----------+-----------+-----+-----+------------------+-------+-------+
|Day_of_Week|Speed_limit|count|  sum|           average|maximum|minimum|
+-----------+-----------+-----+-----+------------------+-------+-------+
|          3|         30|10479|12592|1.2016413779940833|     16|      1|
|          5|         40| 1497| 2073|1.3847695390781563|     19|      1|
|          6|         20| 1994| 2297|1.1519558676028083|      6|      1|
|          2|         40| 1419| 1962|1.3826638477801267|      8|      1|
|          7|         -1|   12|   13|1.0833333333333333|      2|      1|
|          1|         20| 1183| 1426|1.2054099746407438|      7|      1|
|          2|         60| 2093| 3163|1.5112279025322504|     12|      1|
|          7|         20| 1553| 1844|1.1873792659368962|      6|      1|
|          5|         30|10767|13050|1.2120367790470883|     13|      1|
|          7|         50|  663| 1077|1.6244343891402715|      7|      1|
|          4|         50|  678| 1032|1.5221238938053097|      9|      1|
|          7|         70|  949| 1595|1.6807165437302423|     11|      1|
|          4|         -1|   15|   16|1.0666666666666667|      2|      1|
|          6|         70| 1202| 1891|1.5732113144758735|     13|      1|
|          3|         20| 1704| 1981|1.1625586854460095|      7|      1|
|          7|         60| 1987| 3133|1.5767488676396577|     52|      1|
|          4|         30|10638|12794| 1.202669674750893|     10|      1|
|          4|         60| 1958| 2882|1.4719101123595506|      9|      1|
|          1|         50|  572|  894| 1.562937062937063|      9|      1|
|          6|         60| 2302| 3527|1.5321459600347525|     10|      1|
+-----------+-----------+-----+-----+------------------+-------+-------+
only showing top 20 rows
```

Figure 6.24   Subset of the values in the final aggregated aggregated_accident_
data **DataFrame from Figure 6.23**

- Missing values (see Section 6.2.3)
- Statistical measures
- Binning and distribution
- Visualizations
- Correlation
- Frequency tables

Diagnostic analytics helps us to understand why something happened in the past – it uses trends, patterns, and visualizations to answer the 'why' question. Some of the techniques used here include the use of statistical functions like count, maximum, minimum, average, top-*n*,

```
from pyspark.sql import SparkSession
from pyspark.sql.functions import *


# Create a Spark session
spark = SparkSession.builder.appName("HandsOnExercise").getOrCreate()


# Load the dataset into a Spark DataFrame (replace the path with yours)
accidents_2019DF=spark.read.option("header","true").option("delimiter",",").
option("inferSchema","true").csv("hdfs:///user/Accidents2019.csv")


# Display the DataFrame schema and the first five items in the data of the
#dataset
print("The dataset schema:")
accidents_2019DF.printSchema()
print("First five items in the dataset:")
accidents_2019DF.show(5)


# Check how many rows are in the dataset before filtering
accidents_2019DF.count()


# Filter data based on a condition - where day of the week is equal to 2
filtered_accident_data=accidents_2019DF.filter(accidents_2019DF["Day_of_Week"]
== "2")


# Now re-check how many rows have been picked up by filtering
filtered_accident_data.count()


# Display the filtered data
print("Filtered accident data:")
filtered_accident_data.show()
```

Figure 6.25 Code using Apache Spark for data wrangling (filtering)

and correlations. Linear algebraic computations are also used for diagnostic analytics; these include algorithms such as linear algebra, linear regression, and principal component analysis.

Predictive analytics, which we will go into in a lot of depth in Chapter 8, is used to predict what is likely to happen in the future. Techniques that are commonly used here include classification, clustering, and forecast models. These cover algorithms such as naïve Bayes, deep learning, random forest, and K-means.

Finally, we have prescriptive analytics, which is also predominantly implemented using machine learning algorithms (Burkov, 2019).

6.3.1 Hands-on general example

The first example that we will look at is based on data from the UK police open data portal. We will use the open data portal's API to pull data to analyse from the portal. Each step is clearly outlined and as such we encourage you to go through the steps too. We also encourage you to download a version of the dataset with parameters of interest to you from the open data portal at https://data.police.uk/.

We will be carrying out the analysis using a Jupyter Notebook as before, but the first step is to acquire the data that you want to analyse and draw insights from. So, we go to the relevant open data portal at https://data.police.uk/ and navigate to the API tab there, which contains guidance on how to use the API to pull data from the portal. Note that APIs can be updated and the commands to retrieve and process data from them can change; if this happens it should not be a problem, as what you need to do (and should always do) is go through the documentation, which will have been updated to reflect the current correct commands. To pull data (make requests for data) by using the API we need to first import the requests library into our Jupyter Notebook (see Figure 6.26).

```
import requests
```

Figure 6.26   Importing the required library

We are now ready to request the data that we need from the open data portal. So, based on the guidance on the API, we request stop and search data for January 2020 and January 2021 in the Leicestershire area (see Figure 6.27).

```
LeicesterStopSearch2020=requests.get("https://data.police.uk/api/
stops-force?force=leicestershire&date=2020-01")

LeicesterStopSearch2021=requests.get("https://data.police.uk/api/
stops-force?force=leicestershire&date=2021-01")

display(LeicesterStopSearch2020.json())
```

category	location_type	location	context	outcome_status	persistent_id	id	loc
anti-social-behaviour	Force	{'latitude': '52.640298', 'street': {'id': 883237, 'name': 'On or near Lethbridge Close'}, 'longitude': '-1.125483'}		None		80451527	
criminal-damage-arson	Force	{'latitude': '52.636256', 'street': {'id': 883316, 'name': 'On or near		{'category': 'Investigation complete; no suspect	63a969cb0278523b8aa5541d8f0c3a13228551fc752856c259d8e23c8596addf	80449754	

Figure 6.27   Requesting stop and search data

To create visualizations to explore the datasets and pull out insights, we can either write our own code (as in the examples in Chapter 3 and in Chapter 11, where we revisit visualizations) or use codeless visualization libraries like PixieDust (IBM, 2016) to generate quick visualizations from our data. PixieDust is an open-source Python helper library that works as an add-on to Jupyter Notebooks to improve the user experience of working with data. To install PixieDust from PyPI, the command to run in your Jupiter notebook is simply

```
pip install pixiedust
```

Once it is installed in your environment, whenever you want to use it you simply import it as you would do any other library (Figure 6.28).

```
import pixiedust
```

Once you have imported it, you use the `display` command to access it (see Figure 6.29).

```
import pixiedust
```
Pixiedust database opened successfully

Pixiedust version 1.1.15

Warning: You are not running the latest version of PixieDust. Current is 1.1.15, Latest is 1.1.19

Please copy and run the following command in a new cell to upgrade: `!pip install --user --upgrade pixiedust`

Please restart kernel after upgrading.

Figure 6.28   Importing PixieDust library

We can then start to explore and draw out insights from the data. Figure 6.29 shows the distribution of stop and searches across Leicestershire in January 2021 split by gender.

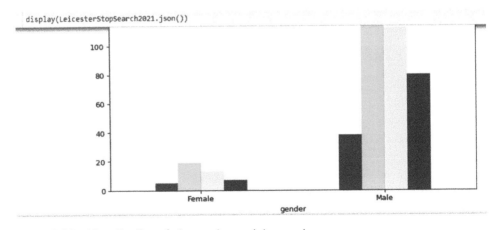

Figure 6.29   Visualization of stop and search by gender

Similarly, to explore crime rates in a particular location, we can request data for all crimes in January 2020 (pre-Covid) and January 2021 (during Covid) and then analyse the data to see if Covid appears to have had any impact. As a hands-on exercise write the code to pull the data for each of the periods for a location of your choice from the police open data portal (hint: read the API documentation on the open data portal website). Once you pull this data you can combine the results and create a new variable that holds the data from both periods, and then use PixieDust to plot this visualization as shown in Figure 6.30:

```
combined_results = crimes2020.json() + crimes2021.json()
display(combined_results)
```

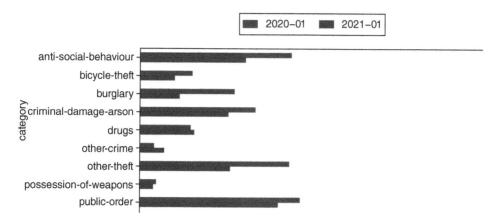

Figure 6.30   Visualization of crime categories, January 2020 and January 2021

We see from this that there was a decrease in the crime rates during the period with Covid. Further investigation could be carried out to explore whether there was a lockdown in place at the time and whether this could have contributed to the decrease. We can also use different types of visualizations; this is covered in more depth in Chapter 11. Figure 6.31 depicts the same crime categories with a different type of visualization.

From this we see that violent crime is by far the largest category of crime in this area, followed by public order, while possession of weapons is the least common. Pulling out insights like this can help the police and authorities in their planning. If the focus had been on seasonal trends in crime, this could also help with putting in place relevant deterrents in particular areas at during certain seasons.

In the next two subsections hands-on exercises for the various types of analysis will be carried out, we encourage you to do the exercises with datasets of your choice – datasets can also be downloaded from the links provided on this book's online resources website.

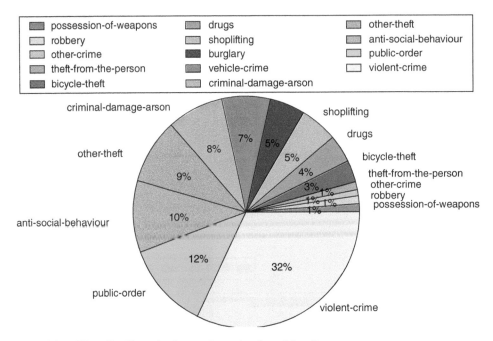

Figure 6.31   Visualization of crime categories (combined)

6.3.2 Hands-on general example (exploratory)

In this hands-on exercise some exploratory analysis is carried out (see Figure 6.32). This example on exploratory uses the accident dataset which has been used earlier (the details of how to access it can be found on this book's website). This dataset is from the UK Department of Transport open data portal. The initial exploration that is done after loading the data into a DataFrame (accidents_2019DF) includes displaying the schema of the DataFrame, displaying the first 5 rows of the DataFrame. Displaying summary statistics from the data, this includes returning for each numerical column; the count, mean, standard deviation, minimum and maximum values. In the code in Figure 6.32 we also as part of the exploratory analysis count the number of rows and columns in the DataFrame and check for missing values. The average number of casualties in the DataFrame were also computed, let's break down how this was done.

```
average_casualties=accidents_2019DF.select("Number_of_Casualties").
agg({"Number_of_Casualties": "avg"}).collect()[0][0]
```

From the DataFrame (accidents_2019DF) the column we are interested in is selected, i.e. ("Number_of_Casualties"). The aggregation method agg is then used to compute the average of all the values in the "Number_of_Casualties" column. We then use the collect() method to retrieve the average value that has been computed for the entire column across the whole dataset. collect()[0][0] is used to retrieve this average value from the first location (which is where it resides as it is a single value). Finally the "Police_Force" column is grouped using the groupBy operation.

In Figure 6.33 we see the output from grouping the police force.

```
from pyspark.sql import SparkSession
from pyspark.sql.functions import col

# Create a Spark session
spark = SparkSession.builder.appName("ExploratoryAnalysis").getOrCreate()

# Load the dataset into a Spark DataFrame (replace the path with yours)
accidents_2019DF=spark.read.option("header","true").option("delimiter",",").
option("inferSchema","true").csv("hdfs:///user/Accidents2019.csv")

# Display the schema of the DataFrame
accidents_2019DF.printSchema()

# Display the first five rows of the DataFrame
accidents_2019DF.show(5)

# Summary statistics
accidents_2019DF.describe().show()

# Count the number of rows in the DataFrame
accident_rows = accidents_2019DF.count()
print(accident_rows)

# Count the number of columns in the DataFrame
accident_columns = len(accidents_2019DF.columns)
print(accident_columns)

# Check for missing values
missing_accident_values=accidents_2019DF.select([col(c).isNull().cast("int").
alias(c) for c in accidents_2019DF.columns])
missing__accident_counts=missing_accident_values.agg(*[sum(col(c)).alias(c)
for c in missing_accident_values.columns])
missing__accident_counts.show()

# Computing the average number of casualties
average_casualties=accidents_2019DF.select("Number_of_Casualties").
agg({"Number_of_Casualties": "avg"}).collect()[0][0]
print("Average number of casualties:", average_casualties)

# Group the column "Police_Force" using the groupBy operation
police_force_counts = accidents_2019DF.groupBy("Police_Force").count()
police_force_counts.show()
```

Figure 6.32 Apache Spark code for exploratory analysis

```
police_force_counts = accidents_2019DF.groupBy("Police_Force").count()
police_force_counts.show()
```

Output:

```
+------------+-----+
|Police_Force|count|
+------------+-----+
|          31| 2354|
|          53|  845|
|          34| 1113|
|          44| 3657|
|          12| 1376|
|          91|  405|
|          22| 1879|
|          93|  344|
|          47| 3991|
|           1|25055|
|          52| 2935|
|          13| 3620|
|           6| 3622|
|          16| 2311|
|           3| 1025|
|          20| 5416|
|          40| 1390|
|          94|  304|
|          54| 1333|
|          96|  284|
+------------+-----+
only showing top 20 rows
```

Figure 6.33 Subset of the values in output from grouping the police force in Figure 6.32

6.3.3 Hands-on general example (descriptive)

Next, we go through a hands-on for descriptive analysis exercise (see Figure 6.34). The various tasks that fall under descriptive analysis include computing summary statistics such as count, mean, standard deviation, minimum, maximum, calculating correlation, skewness, and kurtosis (Lane et al., 2017). For these example we also use some methods from Pandas which is an open-source data manipulation and analysis library, so for instance when we use `describe()` to retrieve the statistical measures of the DataFrame we then convert the DataFrame to a Pandas one by calling the operation `toPandas()`, the output from a Pandas DataFrame tends to be formatted in a more visually appealing way than from a Apache Spark one.

```
from pyspark.sql import SparkSession
from pyspark.sql.functions import *

# import the pandas library
import pandas as pd

# Create a SparkSession
spark = SparkSession.builder.appName("DescriptiveAnalysis").getOrCreate()

# Load the dataset into a Spark DataFrame (replace the path with yours)
accidents_2019DF=spark.read.option("header","true").option("delimiter",",").
option("inferSchema","true").csv("hdfs:///user/Accidents2019.csv")

# Display the schema of the dataset
accidents_2019DF.printSchema()
```

Output:
```
root
 |-- accident_index: string (nullable = true)
 |-- accident_year: integer (nullable = true)
 |-- accident_reference: string (nullable = true)
 |-- location_easting_osgr: string (nullable = true)
 |-- location_northing_osgr: string (nullable = true)
 |-- longitude: string (nullable = true)
 |-- latitude: string (nullable = true)
 |-- police_force: integer (nullable = true)
 |-- accident_severity: integer (nullable = true)
```

```
# Show the first five rows of the dataset
accidents_2019DF.show(5)

# Compute summary statistics
# The function 'describe' returns the count, mean, stdev, min and max
summary_accident_statistics = accidents_2019DF.describe().toPandas()
print(summary_accident_statistics)
```

Output:

(Continued)

Figure 6.34   (Continued)

```
  summary accident_index            accident_year accident_reference  \
0   count           117536                  117536             117536
1    mean         Infinity                  2019.0           Infinity
2  stddev              NaN  1.6507734986587103E-13                NaN
3     min        2.01901E+12                   2019           06A152268
4     max   201998QC01004                     2019           98QC01004
```

```
  location_easting_osgr location_northing_osgr        longitude  \
0                117536                 117536           117536
1    452403.22471661505     278685.7364264561  -1.2494388302498534
2    95033.02483109804      150935.57622679     1.392355674940207
3                115167                 100007            -0.00014
4                  NULL                   NULL              NULL
```

```
            latitude       police_force    accident_severity  ...  \
0             117536             117536               117536   ...
1  52.395426913146245  28.228159882929486   2.776272801524639  ...
2  1.3595219725328034  24.62251884745595   0.4493191399549517  ...
3           49.91776                  1                    1   ...
4               NULL                 98                    3   ...
```

```
  pedestrian_crossing_physical_facilities   light_conditions  \
0                                  117536             117536
1                      1.1255785461475634  2.0468877620473727
2                       2.359613362714065  1.7311310115080945
3                                      -1                 -1
4                                       9                  7
```

```
  weather_conditions road_surface_conditions special_conditions_at_site  \
0             117536                  117536                     117536
1  1.653102028314729      1.3812789273073782        0.20928056084944188
2  1.8092019319529222     0.9133346423408452         1.215007042411138
3                  1                      -1                         -1
4                  9                       9                          9
```

```python
# Return the number of records in the accident DataFrame
accident_record_count = accidents_2019DF.count()
print("Record Count: ", accident_record_count)
```

Output:
Record Count: 117536

```python
# Calculate the mean of the Number_of_Casualties column
casualties_mean_value=accidents_2019DF.select(mean("Number_of_Casualties")).
collect()[0][0]
print(casualties_mean_value)
Output: 1.3030731010073509
```

```
# Calculate the standard deviation of the Number_of_Casualties column
casualties_stddev_value=accidents_2019DF.select(stddev("Number_of_
Casualties")).collect()[0][0]
print(casualties_stddev_value)
```

Output: 0.7543689060867705

```
# Calculate the minimum value of the Number_of_Casualties column
casualties_min_value=accidents_2019DF.select(min("Number_of_Casualties")).
collect()[0][0]
print(casualties_min_value)
```

Output: 1

```
# Calculate the maximum value of the Number_of_Casualties column
casualties_max_value=accidents_2019DF.select(max("Number_of_Casualties")).
collect()[0][0]
print(casualties_max_value)
```

Output: 52

```
# Calculate the skewness of the Number_of_Casualties column
casualties_skewness_value=accidents_2019DF.select(skewness("Number_of_
Casualties")).collect()[0][0]
print(casualties_skewness_value)
```
Output: 6.60403209122729

```
# Calculate the kurtosis of the Number_of_Casualties column
casualties_kurtosis_value=accidents_2019DF.select(kurtosis("Number_of_
Casualties")).collect()[0][0]
print(casualties_kurtosis_value)
```

Output: 210.12000558769066

```
# Perform a cross-tabulation of two columns Number_of_Casualties and
# Day_of_Week
casualties_days_cross_tab=accidents_2019DF.stat.crosstab("Number_of_
Casualties", "Day_of_Week")
casualties_days_cross_tab.show()
```
Output:

(Continued)

Figure 6.34   (Continued)

```
+----------------------------------+-----+-----+-----+-----+-----+-----+-----+
|Number_of_Casualties_Day_of_Week|    1|    2|    3|    4|    5|    6|    7|
+----------------------------------+-----+-----+-----+-----+-----+-----+-----+
|                                 5|   93|   74|   69|   70|   65|   92|  129|
|                                10|    0|    0|    0|    1|    0|    6|    2|
|                                25|    0|    0|    0|    0|    1|    0|    0|
|                                52|    0|    0|    0|    0|    0|    0|    1|
|                                20|    0|    0|    0|    0|    1|    0|    0|
|                                 1| 9837|13393|14278|14410|14562|15245|11866|
|                                 6|   41|   35|   26|   14|   19|   32|   46|
|                                 9|    1|    1|    2|    3|    2|    3|    5|
|                                13|    1|    0|    0|    0|    1|    2|    1|
|                                 2| 2009| 2277| 2400| 2407| 2474| 2648| 2479|
|                                12|    1|    1|    0|    1|    0|    1|    1|
|                                 7|   17|    5|    7|   10|    9|   14|   13|
|                                 3|  644|  626|  600|  626|  635|  763|  710|
|                                16|    0|    0|    1|    0|    0|    0|    0|
|                                11|    0|    0|    2|    0|    1|    2|    2|
|                                 8|    5|    5|    6|    3|    7|    3|    5|
|                                19|    1|    0|    0|    0|    1|    0|    0|
|                                 4|  285|  226|  207|  230|  195|  245|  296|
+----------------------------------+-----+-----+-----+-----+-----+-----+-----+
```

Figure 6.34   Apache Spark code for descriptive analysis with snippets of the outputs

6.3.4 Hands-on general example (diagnostic)

For the hands-on exercise on diagnostic analysis there are some functions that are applicable which we have used previously such as summary statistics. However, we do not repeat them here but focus on new functions which have not yet been used. These include identifying columns with high cardinality (columns that are very uncommon) and columns with low variance (Figure 6.35).

Hands-on exercises on predictive analysis are covered in Chapter 8, which delves deeper into machine learning. In Chapter 7, which focuses on graph analytics, Chapter 8 on machine learning, Chapter 9 on natural language processing, Chapter 10 on real-time data analytics, and finally Chapter 11 on big data visualizations, we will see many more examples of big data analytics and how actionable insights are drawn from them.

6.4 ETHICS BY DESIGN

Incorrect insights are costly for organizations because they lead to incorrect decisions and actions. For instance, major problems may result if a model is implemented based on biased data that disadvantages a section of the community when this is in areas that can potentially have a high impact on people's lives and well-being such as health, education, finances and/or the justice system. So how can ethics by design help in these types of situations? Again,

```
from pyspark.sql import SparkSession
from pyspark.sql.functions import *


# Create a SparkSession
spark = SparkSession.builder.appName("DiagnosticAnalysis").getOrCreate()


# Load the dataset into a Spark DataFrame (replace the path with yours)
accidents_2019DF=spark.read.option("header","true").option("delimiter",",").
option("inferSchema","true").csv("hdfs:///user/Accidents2019.csv")


# Identify columns with high cardinality
accidents_high_cardinality_columns = [col for col in accidents_2019DF.columns
if accidents_2019DF.select(col).distinct().count() > 100]

print(accidents_high_cardinality_columns)


Output:

['accident_index', 'accident_reference', 'location_easting_osgr', 'location_
northing_osgr', 'longitude', 'latitude', 'date', 'time', 'local_authority_
district', 'local_authority_ons_district', 'local_authority_highway', 'first_
road_number', 'second_road_number', 'lsoa_of_accident_location']



# Identify columns with low variance
accidents_low_variance_columns = [col for col in accidents_2019DF.columns if
accidents_2019DF.select(col).distinct().count() <= 1]

print(accidents_low_variance_columns)


Output:

['accident_year']
```

Figure 6.35 Apache Spark code for diagnostic analysis with snippets of the outputs

we will use the TAFARP Data Ethics by design framework which was first introduced in Chapter 2 (see Figure 2.14, p.44). The idea is that as each step of the pre-processing, processing, and analytics is being carried out the various areas in the TAFARP data ethics by design framework are explored in the context of the particular project that is being done.

So, for instance in the GCSE results example that was used, under fairness how representative was the data that was collected and used for the analytics? Was it a subset of the data that was collected that was used for the analytics? If so, what was done to ensure that it was fully representative of every part of society (e.g., in terms of gender, demographics, type of school, deprived/non-deprived area, and ethnicity)? If these questions and other related ones are not asked and dealt with, we could end up with data that is not truly representative of the whole society and insights that are incorrect, and this could end up disadvantaging a section of society. Imagine if these incorrect insights are then used to set policies and regulations that would have an impact on the education of young people – you might end up inadvertently disadvantaging a whole section of the community.

Under accountability, we need to ensure that there are effective processes in place to ensure that the project we are embarking on has good oversight and governance. If the data originates from public bodies (e.g., the original providers of the GCSE results data) the data governance team should usually include representation from the public who would also have oversight over what is being done and how it is being done. The processes for effective governance and oversight should be part and parcel of the project from start to finish.

Transparency is another key area when it comes to analytics and actionable insights. Transparency would help support the identification of and minimization of accidental bias and prejudices. Again, as mentioned earlier, there are many examples of this across various sections. Transparency can also help improve trust in the big data analytics and the insights generated from it. People can be understandably uncomfortable when there is a lack of transparency in how insights have been obtained from data, where the data was sourced from, and how it was sourced. This has particularly been the case when it comes to big data analytics and machine learning, where some describe machine learning models that are complex and too complicated to be easily understood by humans as black boxes. To solve this transparency problem, the field of explainable AI has become more and more popular in recent times.

The process of generating actionable insights from big data analytics raises several ethical issues that organizations must consider. Here are some of the main ethical concerns associated with this process:

- *Privacy and data protection.* Big data analytics often involves the collection and analysis of large volumes of personal data. Organizations need to ensure they have obtained proper consent for data collection and are handling the data in a secure and responsible manner. An ethical concern arises when the data is used without the knowledge or consent of individuals, or when data is re-identified or combined in ways that violate privacy expectations.

- *Fairness and data bias.* Bias in data analytics can lead to unfair or discriminatory outcomes. Biased data inputs or algorithms can perpetuate existing biases or create new ones. It is crucial to ensure that the data used for analysis is representative and unbiased, and that algorithms are designed and tested to minimize discriminatory impact.

- *Transparency and informed consent.* Organizations must be transparent about the data they collect, how it is used, and the potential consequences of analysis. Individuals should be fully informed and can provide informed consent for their data to be used in analytics. Transparency about the purposes, methods, and potential impact of data analysis is essential for maintaining trust and ethical practices.

- *Data ownership and intellectual property.* The ownership and intellectual property rights of the data used in big data analytics can be complex. Organizations need to ensure they have the proper rights and permissions to use the data and respect the ownership rights of individuals or entities. Unauthorized data appropriation or improper use of intellectual property can lead to ethical and legal concerns.

- *Data security and protection.* Big data analytics involve handling and processing large amounts of sensitive information. Organizations have a responsibility to protect the data from unauthorized access, breaches, or misuse. Implementing robust security measures and following best practices in data protection are essential to safeguard the privacy and confidentiality of individuals' data.

- *Social and economic implications.* Big data analytics can have wide-ranging social and economic implications. Ethical considerations arise when the insights derived from analytics are used to manipulate consumer behaviour, exploit vulnerable populations, or create unfair advantages in the market. Organizations should be mindful of the potential impact of their actions and strive to use analytics for the betterment of society while avoiding harm.

Addressing these ethical issues requires a proactive and responsible approach to big data analytics. Organizations should develop and adhere to clear ethical guidelines and standards, ensure transparency and accountability in data practices, and regularly assess the social, legal, and ethical implications of their analytics initiatives. Additionally, involving diverse perspectives and engaging in ongoing dialogue with stakeholders can help organizations navigate the complex ethical landscape of generating actionable insights from big data.

6.5 INDUSTRY INSIGHTS

When it comes to the use of big data analytics and the use of the insights drawn from it, it is phenomenal how these cut across different sectors and disciplines. There is almost no industry that is unaffected by it. For our industry insight in this chapter, we will focus on the transportation industry and the company Uber Technologies Inc. in particular. Uber is currently primarily known as a 'mobility as a service' provider, which you can use to book rides in a similar manner to a taxi but with additional functionality. The company has recently started to expand into other areas such as through Uber Eats (food deliveries), UberFresh (grocery deliveries), and UberRush (courier service). However, our focus in this chapter is on the transportation side of things. Uber's blog[1] on its big data platform describes how it pre-processes and stores over 100 petabytes of data, which it performs analytics on to draw out insights from. It started off in 2004 with data that could fit into traditional databases and used MySQL and PostgreSQL, but as it grew in leap and bounds these storage facilities became unsustainable and it passed through several generations of big data platforms using Hadoop for storage, Apache Spark for processing, Apache Kafka[2] for event messaging and some other big data technologies. The company is totally data-driven – everything about its operations and the remarkable success it has achieved has been driven by data. Its use of algorithms to draw out information from data include the following:

- Algorithms to match taxi drivers to passengers, based on models that predict timings and which driver is best suited for which job, based on both locations, traffic, time of day, and so on.
- Algorithms to calculate fares based on distance, traffic, GPS data, current demand, and so on.
- Real-time algorithms to increase and maintain positive user experiences.

Part of the secret of Uber's success is that as it has progressed, it has not rested on its laurels but continues to be extremely innovative in its use of big data technologies and analytics and the actionable insights it can draw from them.

Other examples of how organizations use big data analytics to achieve their strategic goals include:

- *Netflix*. Netflix uses big data analytics to recommend movies and TV shows to its users. By analysing data on what users have watched in the past, Netflix can predict what they are likely to enjoy in the future. This helps Netflix to keep its users engaged and subscribed.
- *Amazon*. Amazon uses big data analytics to personalize its shopping experience for its customers. By analysing data on what customers have purchased in the past, Amazon can recommend products that they are likely to be interested in. This helps Amazon to increase sales and customer satisfaction.
- *Walmart*. Walmart uses big data analytics to optimize its supply chain. By analysing data on sales, inventory, and weather, Walmart can ensure that it has the right products in the right stores at the right time. This helps Walmart to reduce costs and improve customer service.

These are just a few examples of how organizations are using big data analytics to achieve their strategic goals. As big data continues to grow in importance, we can expect to see even more innovative ways that organizations are using it to improve their businesses.

SUMMARY

In this chapter you were introduced to practical ways to prepare data using Apache Spark and OpenRefine. Using hands-on exercises, we explored how big data analytics is used to draw out insights. We explored a real-world example of how actionable insights can be used for competitive advantage by an organization. We also covered more ways of incorporating ethics by design. Subsequent chapters such as Chapter 8 will go into further details on these, but this chapter provides a good foundation for subsequent chapters to build on. This chapter also covered fundamental areas for data analytics such as data pre-processing and wrangling.

TEST YOUR KNOWLEDGE

1   What are the three strategic goals organizations wish to achieve from big data analytics?

2   List some techniques that can be used for data wrangling.

3   What are the forms of analytics?

4   Download a dataset of your choice from an open data portal, upload the data into a Jupyter Notebook and write code to do the following:

- Load the dataset into a DataFrame.
- Cast the data type of one of the fields into a new one.
- Count the number of instances that exist in the dataset.
- Drop all duplicate items.
- Replace all null or none values in integer fields with zero.

5   Download four datasets of your choice which have not been cleaned and use both OpenRefine and Apache Spark to identify data quality issues with the datasets.

FURTHER READING (OPTIONAL)

An insightful and interesting read that concisely covers how 45 companies have used big data analytics to draw out insights that have led to very successful outcomes for them:

Marr, B. (2016) *Big Data in Practice: How 45 Successful Companies Used Big Data Analytics to Deliver Extraordinary Results*. Chichester: John Wiley & Sons.

An interesting article on an explainable AI competition and black box models:

Rudin, C. and Radin, J. (2019) Why are we using black box models in AI when we don't need to? A lesson from an explainable AI competition. https://hdsr.mitpress.mit.edu/pub/f9kuryi8/release/8

Fantastic blog by Uber on how their big data platform has evolved over the years. A highly recommended read!

https://www.uber.com/en-GB/blog/uber-big-data-platform/

Interesting blog on Uber's use of data science to reinvent transportation:

ProjectPro (2023) How Uber uses data science to reinvent transportation? https://www.projectpro.io/article/how-uber-uses-data-science-to-reinvent-transportation/290

Interesting TED talk that demonstrates the use of big data to draw out actionable insights from public open data:

Wallington, B. (2014) How we found the worst place to park in New York City – using big data. https://www.ted.com/talks/ben_wellington_how_we_found_the_worst_place_to_park_in_new_york_city_using_big_data?language=en

NOTES

1   https://www.uber.com/en-GB/blog/uber-big-data-platform/

2   https://kafka.apache.org/

REFERENCES

Burkov, A. (2019) *The Hundred-Page Machine Learning Book*. Quebec City: Author.

IBM (2016) PixieDust documentation. Retrieved from https://pixiedust.github.io/pixiedust/

Karau, H., Konwinski, A., Wendell, P. and Zaharia, M. (2015) *Learning Spark: Lightning-Fast Data Analytics*. Sebastopol, CA: O'Reilly Media.

Lane, D., Scott, D., Hebl, M., Guerra, R., Osherson, D. and Zimmer, H. (2017) *Introduction to Statistics*. Retrieved from https://onlinestatbook.com/Online_Statistics_Education.pdf

NHS Digital (2023) *Patients registered at a GP practice metadata*. Retrieved from https://digital.nhs.uk/data-and-information/publications/statistical/patients-registered-at-a-gp-practice/metadata

7

GRAPH ANALYTICS

CHAPTER CONTENTS

CHAPTER OBJECTIVES

In this chapter:

- You will learn about graph analytics, associated technologies, and use cases.
- You will explore using Apache Spark GraphFrames on data that can be represented in graphical form.
- You will learn how to query and draw out insights using graph analytics.
- You will discover the potential advantages that graph analytics has in the area of ethics by design.

7.1 INTRODUCTION

Graph analytics plays a crucial role in the field of big data analytics and data science, paving the way for the exploration, understanding, and extraction of insights from complex relationships and interactions between entities within datasets. Graph analysis focuses on studying the structure and behaviour of interconnected entities, represented as nodes (vertices) and their connections (edges) and the computational techniques used to analyse and derive meaningful information from these networks.

The background to network analysis and graph analytics can be traced back to various disciplines, including social network analysis, graph theory, and computational biology. In recent years, with the explosion of data and the rise of big data technologies, graph analytics has gained significant attention due to its applicability in diverse domains such as social media analysis, fraud detection, recommendation systems, and supply chain optimization.

One of the key benefits of graph analytics is its ability to uncover hidden patterns, relationships, and insights that may not be apparent in traditional tabular data analysis. By representing data as networks, graph analytics allows for the identification of influential nodes, community detection, centrality analysis, and prediction of node behaviour. It provides a holistic view of the structure and dynamics of the data, enabling a deeper understanding of complex systems.

However, carrying out graph analytics also presents some challenges. One major challenge is the scalability of graph algorithms, especially when dealing with large-scale datasets. Analysing massive networks requires distributed computing frameworks and optimized algorithms to process and traverse the graphs efficiently. Another challenge is data quality and integrity, as network data often comes with noise, missing values, or inaccuracies. Data pre-processing and cleaning techniques specific to network data are required to ensure accurate analysis and reliable results.

In the field of graph analytics, several technologies and tools have emerged to facilitate the analysis and manipulation of large-scale networks. Among the commonly used technologies are the following:

- *Graph databases*. Graph databases, such as Neo4j, provide a scalable and efficient storage and querying solution for graph data. They offer specialized graph algorithms and query languages to perform complex graph analytics operations.
- *Graph processing frameworks*. Frameworks like Apache Spark GraphX and Apache Giraph enable distributed graph processing by leveraging parallel computing capabilities. They provide a scalable infrastructure for executing graph algorithms on large-scale datasets.
- *Network analysis libraries*. Network analysis libraries, such as NetworkX (Python) and igraph (R), offer a rich set of functions and algorithms for network analysis tasks. These libraries provide data structures and methods to compute centrality measures, perform community detection, and visualize networks.
- *Graph visualization tools*. Graph visualization tools like Gephi and Cytoscape allow researchers and analysts to visually explore and interact with networks. They offer a range of visualization techniques and layout algorithms to effectively present network structures and patterns.

Graph analytics is particularly good for understanding relationships and structures between entities. Examples of graph data structures include social networks such as Facebook and LinkedIn, where people are connected via relationships. A graph is made up of a set of vertices (nodes) and a set of edges that connect the vertices in various ways. Graph analytics uses various algorithms to explore the relationships that exist between these entities (edges). Graph analytics will be explored using libraries such as the Apache Spark GraphFrames. This chapter addresses ways to run analytics on datasets that are in graphical form, such as social networks. It covers how to analyse existing graphs and how to draw out useful information to inform decision-making and extract actionable insights. Common use cases include the following:

- *Network infrastructure analysis*. Graph analytics is utilized in analysing network infrastructure, such as telecommunications networks, internet routers, and power grids. It assists in optimizing network performance, identifying network bottlenecks, detecting anomalies or attacks, and planning network expansions.
- *Social media*. Graph analytics is extensively used to analyse social media to map out and analyse relationships between individuals, communities, and organizations. It helps identify influential users, detect communities or groups, analyse information flow, and predict user behaviour on social media platforms.
- *Fraud detection*. Graph analytics is valuable in detecting and preventing fraud by analysing patterns of fraudulent activities. By modelling relationships between entities such as customers, accounts, transactions, and IP addresses, graph analytics can identify suspicious connections and uncover complex fraud networks.

- *Recommendation systems*. Graph analytics is employed in recommendation systems to provide personalized and relevant recommendations to users. By analysing the connections between users, items, and their interactions, graph algorithms can generate accurate recommendations based on the behaviour and preferences of similar users.
- *Supply chain optimization*. Graph analytics helps optimize supply chain networks by analysing the relationships between suppliers, manufacturers, distributors, and customers. It enables efficient route planning, demand forecasting, inventory management, and identifying bottlenecks or vulnerabilities in the supply chain.
- *IoT analytics*. With the proliferation of Internet of Things devices, graph analytics is used to analyse the relationships between devices, sensors, and users. It enables real-time monitoring, anomaly detection, predictive maintenance, and optimization of IoT networks and systems.
- *Knowledge graphs*. Graph analytics is used to build and query knowledge graphs, which represent interconnected concepts and relationships. Knowledge graphs enhance search engines, chatbots, and question-answering systems by providing structured information and context-aware answers.
- *Bioinformatics*. Graph analytics is applied to analyse biological networks, such as protein–protein interactions, gene regulatory networks, and metabolic pathways. It helps uncover relationships between genes, identify biomarkers, understand disease mechanisms, and support drug discovery and development.

These are just a few examples of the diverse applications of graph analytics. The ability to model and analyse complex relationships and interconnected data makes graph analytics a powerful tool for gaining insights, making informed decisions, and solving complex problems in various domains. These examples illustrate the powerful role of graph analytics, a framework designed to extract valuable insights from complex interconnected data. While offering benefits like pattern discovery and understanding complex relationships, graph analytics also presents challenges in terms of scalability and data quality. With the advancements in technology and the availability of specialized tools and frameworks, graph analytics has become an essential approach for analysing and leveraging the inherent structure in network data.

Foundational to graph analytics is the concept of graphs and so we will touch briefly on this. As mentioned earlier, a graph is a set of vertices connected to each other via edges. The idea behind graph analytics is to first identify graph structures in the data. There are different types of graphs, including the following:

- *Directed graphs*. Here the edges are all directed from one vertex to another (see Figure 7.1). In a directed graph each edge has a direction, that is, there is a clear source vertex and a clear destination vertex for every edge. For instance,

in the simple example in Figure 7.1, for the edge d1, the source vertex is n1
and the destination vertex is n3.

- *Undirected graphs*. Here the edges have no defined direction so are deemed to be
  bidirectional. So in the example in Figure 7.2, the edges e1 and e2 have no
  defined source or destination vertices – there is a two-way connection between
  each set of vertices.

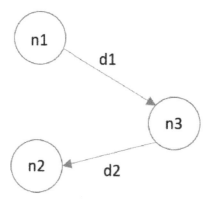

Figure 7.1   Simple directed graph

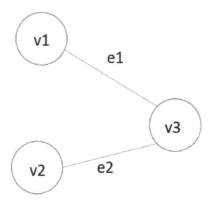

Figure 7.2   Simple undirected graph

- *Cyclic graphs*. These contain at least one graph cycle. For instance, in Figure 7.3,
  there is a graph cycle formed by the directed edges between vertices v4, n1, n3,
  n2, v3, and then back to v4.

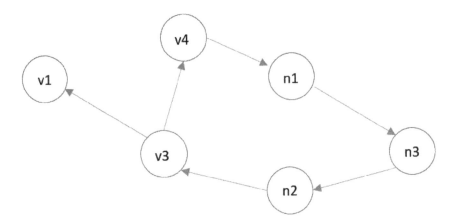

Figure 7.3 Simple cyclic graph

- *Acyclic/tree graphs*. These contain no graph cycle (Figure 7.4). Unlike in cyclic graphs, there is no way to transverse from any vertex back to itself. Acyclic graphs are commonly used in a number of algorithms and data structures to solve problems efficiently, in terms of computational power and reducing unnecessary complexity.

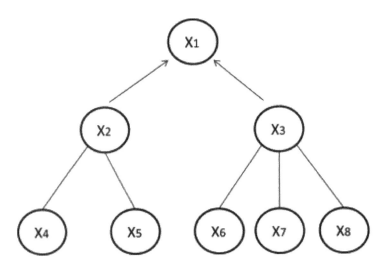

Figure 7.4 Simple acyclic graph

- *Weighted graphs*. These have weights assigned to edges or vertices (Figure 7.5). The weights represent some attribute. For instance, in a transportation network the weights might represent distance from one location to another. There are specific algorithms used to process and analyse weighted graphs which take these weights into account.

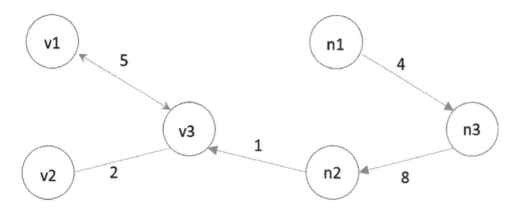

Figure 7.5 Simple weighted graph

- *Unweighted graphs*. In these graphs, all edges/vertices have no weights.

It is important to be able to distinguish between the different types of graphs when it comes to graph analytics for big data because it enables better problem-specific analysis, performance optimization, efficient processing, and extraction of insights.

Some common graph analytics analysis procedures are as follows:

- *Graph search*. This algorithm searches through the vertices of the graph and is also known as graph traversal.
- *Shortest paths*. This algorithm finds the path between two vertices with the least edges.
- *PageRank*. Originally used by Google to rank the importance of web pages based on counting the quality and links to a page, this procedure can be applied to any graphical structure.
- *Triangle count*. This algorithm counts the number of triangles for each node in the graph.
- *Connected components*. This algorithm works out the set of connected subgraphs in the graph, that is, vertices with a path (edge) between them.
- *Label propagation algorithm*. This algorithm is used to find communities in a graph.
- *Strongly connected components*. This differs from the connected components algorithm in that here there is a path between all pairs of vertices.

As part of the hands-on exercises in this chapter we will go through how to use some of these graph analytics algorithms on graph data structures.

7.2 GRAPH PROCESSING FRAMEWORKS

There are various graph processing frameworks which help to facilitate graph analytics for big data. In this chapter we will use Apache Spark's GraphFrames (Guller, 2015) for our hands-on exercises. However, we briefly mention a few other frameworks first.

7.2.1 GraphX

GraphX is Apache Spark's API for graphs and graph-parallel computation. It extends Spark RDD (which we discussed in Chapter 3) to produce a new abstraction, the resilient distributed graph (RDG). It is based on a property graph model $G = (V, E)$, where each vertex V is represented as an (id, attribute/data) pair and each edge E as an (src, dst, attribute/data) tuple. When using GraphX, it is important to remember that you need to name the id column for your vertices id. This id must uniquely represent a vertex. Similarly, for the edges the column name for the source vertices must be src and the destination dst.

GraphX has a list of built-in algorithms, including the following:

- PageRank
- Connected components
- Label propagation algorithm
- SVD++
- Strongly connected components
- Triangle count

7.2.2 GraphFrames

GraphFrames is a package for Apache Spark which provides DataFrame-based graphs. GraphFrames represent graphs: vertices (e.g., users) and edges (e.g., relationships between users) and are based on DataFrames, while GraphX is based on RDDS. It provides APIs for graph processing in Scala, Python, and Java. GraphFrames is a graph processing package developed by Databricks, an American enterprise software company founded by the creators of Apache Spark. Using the package involves installation followed by import. The code to install GraphFrames via your Jupyter Notebook is

```
pip install graphframes
```

GraphFrames comes with a number of standard graph algorithms built in, including:

- Breadth-first search
- Connected components
- Strongly connected components
- Label propagation algorithm
- PageRank

- Shortest paths
- Triangle count

As mentioned for Apache Spark GraphX, when using GraphFrames, you must name the id column for your vertices `id`. This id must uniquely represent a vertex. Similarly, for the edges the column name for the source vertices must be `src` and the destination `dst`.

7.2.3 Other frameworks

In terms of being able to handle the computation power and performance requirements for graph analytics for big data, with Apache Spark the GraphFrame is created from two DataFrames, namely, the edge and vertex DataFrames. Recall from Chapter 3 that DataFrames like RDDs have partitions and are distributed by design. Hence, they are able to compute extremely fast and efficiently. However, in addition to using Apache Spark libraries for your graph analytics as we do in the hands-on exercises, there are other tools and technologies available for this. One of the most popular is Neo4j. Neo4j is a graph database management system that provides graph algorithms that enable fast queries to be run on complex graph datasets. If you are interested in learning more about it, there are tutorials, white papers, and a lot of other useful resources for this online. Other graph processing frameworks include Apache Flink Gelly (Apache Software Foundation, n.d.) and Apache Giraph (Apache Software Foundation, 2020).

7.3 GRAPH ANALYTICS HANDS-ON EXERCISES

In this section, we start to carry out some hands-on exercises using Apache Spark GraphFrames. There is no substitute for working through and practising yourself, so do follow along in your environment. Also, try to do additional ones using datasets of your choice. The more you practise, the more comfortable and better you will become at it.

7.3.1 Exploratory and descriptive graph analytics

As mentioned in Chapters 2 and 6, exploratory and descriptive graph analytics for big data is about analysing, exploring, and carrying out initial investigations on a graph or network to discover insights, trends, and patterns. The main objective of exploratory and descriptive graph analytics is to understand the data (i.e., the graph or network). The discoveries made at this stage will then help inform further processes and analyses that are carried out. We will now go through some hands-on exercises to carry out exploratory and descriptive graph analytics.

Let us start by opening up a Jupyter Notebook (this was introduced in Chapter 3; see Figure 7.6). Once the Jupyter Notebook is opened, the first step is to run the necessary configurations (see Chapter 3) and then import the relevant library:

```
from graphframes import *
```

Figure 7.6   Opening up a new Jupyter Notebook

To create the graph we start by defining the vertices and edges (see Figure 7.7). We create the vertices from a DataFrame made up of a collection of id, name, and age. Next, we create the edge DataFrame (Figure 7.8).

```
# Create a Vertex DataFrame with unique ID column "id"
v = spark.createDataFrame([
  ("a", "Alice", 34),
  ("b", "Bob", 36),
  ("c", "Charlie", 30),
], ["id", "name", "age"])


v.show()

Output:
```

```
+---+-------+---+
| id|   name|age|
+---+-------+---+
|  a|  Alice| 34|
|  b|    Bob| 36|
|  c|Charlie| 30|
+---+-------+---+
```

Figure 7.7   Creating the vertex DataFrame

Now that we have the vertex and edge DataFrames we can use the GraphFrames library to create the GraphFrame that represents the graph (Figure 7.9).

```
# Create an Edge DataFrame
e = spark.createDataFrame([
  ("a", "b", "friend"),
  ("b", "c", "follow"),
  ("c", "b", "follow"),
], ["src", "dst", "relationship"])
```

```
e.show()
```

Output:

```
+---+---+------------+
|src|dst|relationship|
+---+---+------------+
|  a|  b|      friend|
|  b|  c|      follow|
|  c|  b|      follow|
+---+---+------------+
```

Figure 7.8 Creating the edge DataFrame

```
# Create GraphFrame from the Vertex and Edge DataFrames
g = GraphFrame(v, e)
```

```
g
```

Output:

```
GraphFrame(v:[id: string, name: string ... 1 more field], e:[src: string, dst:
string ... 1 more field])
```

Figure 7.9 Creating the graph DataFrame from the vertex and edge DataFrames

The degree of a vertex is the number of edges that are attached to it. The indegree of a vertex is the number of edges coming into the vertex, while the outdegree is the number of edges coming out of the vertex. Let us now apply this to the hands-on exercise. Figure 7.10 shows the indegrees and outdegrees of the vertices, while Figure 7.11 shows the degrees.

```
# Query: Get indegree of each vertex.
g.inDegrees.show()
```

```
+---+--------+
| id|inDegree|
+---+--------+
|  c|       1|
|  b|       2|
+---+--------+
```

```
# Query: Get outdegree of each vertex.
g.outDegrees.show()
```

```
+---+---------+
| id|outDegree|
+---+---------+
|  c|        1|
|  b|        1|
|  a|        1|
+---+---------+
```

Figure 7.10   The indegrees and outdegrees of the GraphFrame

```
# Query: Get degree of each vertex.
g.degrees.show()
```

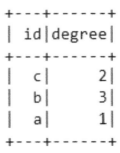

```
+---+------+
| id|degree|
+---+------+
|  c|     2|
|  b|     3|
|  a|     1|
+---+------+
```

Figure 7.11   The degrees of the GraphFrame

Let us go through some other queries using the current GraphFrame that we have defined. To count the number of 'follow' relationships in the graph, we can use the `filter` method and the `count()` action as shown in Figure 7.12.

```
# Query: Count the number of "follow" connections in the graph.
g.edges.filter("relationship = 'follow'").count()


Output: 2
```

Figure 7.12 Counting the number of 'follow' relationships in the GraphFrame g

```
# Find the youngest user's age in the graph.
# This queries the vertex DataFrame.

g.vertices.groupBy().min("age").show()
```
```
                    +---------+
                    |min(age)|
                    +---------+
                    |      30|
                    +---------+
```

Figure 7.13 Finding the youngest user's age in the GraphFrame g

We can also run other queries like the one in Figure 7.13 where we find the minimum age present in the graph.

Let us now look at another related example. Within the GraphFrames library there is a pre-defined friend GraphFrame which we will load and use next (Figure 7.14). Having loaded it, we will run a series of queries on it. In Figure 7.15 we display all the vertices in the graph, in Figure 7.16 we display all the edges, and in Figure 7.17 we display the subgraph of users older than 30, and edges of type 'friend'.

```
# import pre-defined friend example
from graphframes.examples import Graphs

g = Graphs(sqlContext).friends()   # Get example graph

display(g)

GraphFrame(v:[id: string, name: string ... 1 more field], e:[src: string, dst:
string ... 1 more field])
```

Figure 7.14 Importing pre-defined friend GraphFrame

```
g.vertices.show()
```

```
+---+-------+---+
| id|   name|age|
+---+-------+---+
|  a|  Alice| 34|
|  b|    Bob| 36|
|  c|Charlie| 30|
|  d|  David| 29|
|  e| Esther| 32|
|  f|  Fanny| 36|
+---+-------+---+
```

Figure 7.15   Displaying the vertices of GraphFrame g

```
g.edges.show()
```

```
+---+---+------------+
|src|dst|relationship|
+---+---+------------+
|  a|  b|      friend|
|  b|  c|      follow|
|  c|  b|      follow|
|  f|  c|      follow|
|  e|  f|      follow|
|  e|  d|      friend|
|  d|  a|      friend|
+---+---+------------+
```

Figure 7.16   Displaying the vertices of GraphFrame g

Next let us visualize the GraphFrames. For this we will use the PixieDust library (IBM, 2016) which was first introduced in Chapter 3. To use PixieDust, we import the library (see Figure 7.18)

Then we plot our visualization by calling the display method and passing in as input parameter the variable we want to visualize. Then we choose the type of visualization we want, in this case a graph (Figure 7.19).

```
v2 = g.vertices.filter("age > 30")
e2 = g.edges.filter("relationship = 'friend'")
g2 = GraphFrame(v2, e2)

v2.show()
```

```
+---+------+---+
| id|  name|age|
+---+------+---+
|  a| Alice| 34|
|  b|   Bob| 36|
|  e|Esther| 32|
|  f| Fanny| 36|
+---+------+---+
```

```
e2.show()
```

```
+---+---+------------+
|src|dst|relationship|
+---+---+------------+
|  a|  b|      friend|
|  e|  d|      friend|
|  d|  a|      friend|
+---+---+------------+
```

Figure 7.17   Selecting a subgraph of users older than 30 and with relationship equal to 'friend', then display the vertices and edges of the subgraph

```
import pixiedust
```

Pixiedust database opened successfully

Pixiedust version 1.1.15

Figure 7.18   Importing PixieDust

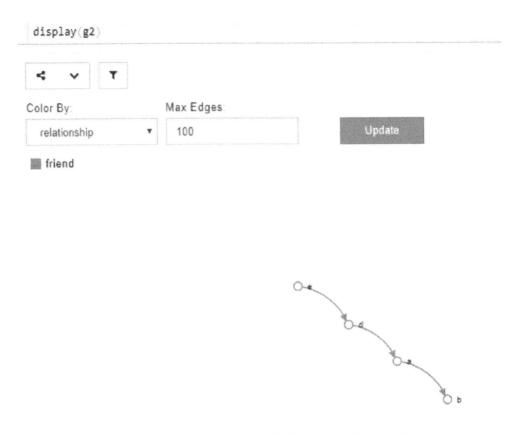

Figure 7.19 Displaying the GraphFrame g2, with its four vertices and three edges

We can also use motifs (GraphFrames, n.d.) to find patterns in GraphFrames. In the example in Figure 7.20 we use motifs to select a subgraph based on edges e of type 'follow' pointing from a younger user a to an older user b.

In Figure 7.21 we then create a new GraphFrame g2, using the paths DataFrame to create the edges DataFrame and the vertices from GraphFrames g Finally, we visualize GraphFrames g (Figure 7.22) and g2 (Figure 7.23).

In a subsequent hands-on section, we carry out more exploratory graph analytics on a larger dataset; the initial datasets that we are using here are to illustrate concepts which we will bring together in a later exercise. To conclude this section let us carry out some final exploratory graph analytics (see Figure 7.24).

7.3.2 Predictive graph analytics

Predictive graph analytics, as mentioned in Chapter 6 and covered again in Chapter 8, is used to predict what is likely to happen in the future. In certain situations, being able to predict likely outcomes from graphs and networks is extremely powerful. For example, predictive graph analytics can be used to forecast user preferences in social networks, as in the LinkedIn connections recommendation system.

```
# Select subgraph based on edges "e" of type "follow"
# pointing from a younger user "a" to an older user "b".

paths = g.find("(a)-[e]->(b)")\
   .filter("e.relationship = 'follow'")\
   .filter("a.age < b.age")

paths
```

```
Output:
DataFrame[a: struct<id:string,name:string,age:bigint>,
e: struct<src:string,dst:string,relationship:string>, b: struct<id:string,nam
e:string,age:bigint>]
```

```
paths.show()
```

```
+-----------------+---------------+--------------+
|                a|              e|             b|
+-----------------+---------------+--------------+
| [e, Esther, 32]|[e, f, follow]|[f, Fanny, 36]|
|[c, Charlie, 30]|[c, b, follow]|  [b, Bob, 36]|
+-----------------+---------------+--------------+
```

Figure 7.20 Using motifs to find patterns

As with the preceding subsection, we will start off with a simple hands-on exercise to illustrate this and step through it. In this example we will use the pre-defined friend example which we used earlier. We will add a new label to it which will take the value 1 if a person's age is greater than 30 and 0 otherwise. We will then split the dataset into test and training data, use the training data to define a logistic model which we will then use to predict the label of the test data. In Chapter 8 we will cover this in a lot more detail.

Step 1. Import the required libraries.

```
from pyspark.ml.feature import VectorAssembler, StringIndexer,
Imputer

from pyspark.ml.classification import LogisticRegression

from pyspark.sql.functions import col
```

Step 2. Import the pre-defined friend example into a GraphFrame and display the edges and vertices of g.

```
# "paths" contains vertex info. Extract the edges.
e2 = paths.select("e.src", "e.dst", "e.relationship")

# Construct the subgraph
g2 = GraphFrame(g.vertices, e2)

e2.show()
```

```
+---+---+------------+
|src|dst|relationship|
+---+---+------------+
|  e|  f|      follow|
|  c|  b|      follow|
+---+---+------------+
```

```
g.vertices.show()
```

```
+---+-------+---+
| id|   name|age|
+---+-------+---+
|  a|  Alice| 34|
|  b|    Bob| 36|
|  c|Charlie| 30|
|  d|  David| 29|
|  e| Esther| 32|
|  f|  Fanny| 36|
+---+-------+---+
```

Figure 7.21 Creating a new GraphFrame g2

```
from graphframes.examples import Graphs

g = Graphs(sqlContext).friends()  # Get example graph

print('vertices:')

g.vertices.show()

print('edges:')

g.edges.show()
```

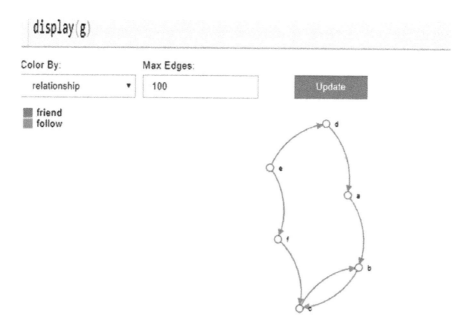

Figure 7.22 Visualizing GraphFrame g

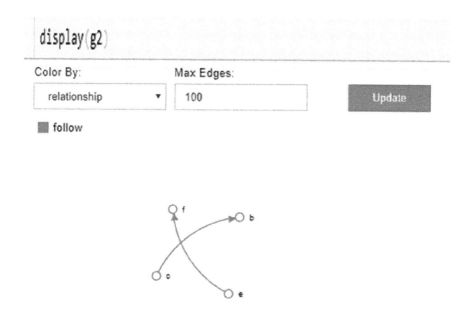

Figure 7.23 Visualizing GraphFrame g2

```
# Display the number of vertices and edges in the graph
num_vertices = g.vertices.count()
num_edges = g.edges.count()
print("Number of vertices:", num_vertices)
print("Number of edges:", num_edges)

# Compute and display the degree distribution of the vertices
degree_distribution = g.degrees.groupBy("degree").count().orderBy("degree")
degree_distribution.show()

# Find the top-k vertices with the highest degree
top_k_vertices = g.degrees.orderBy("degree", ascending=False).limit(10)
top_k_vertices.show()
```

```
Number of vertices: 6
Number of edges: 7
+------+-----+
|degree|count|
+------+-----+
|     2|    4|
|     3|    2|
+------+-----+

+---+------+
| id|degree|
+---+------+
|  c|     3|
|  b|     3|
|  f|     2|
|  e|     2|
|  d|     2|
|  a|     2|
+---+------+
```

Figure 7.24 Number of vertices, edges, degree distribution and top-k vertices with highest degrees

```
vertices:
+---+-------+---+
| id|   name|age|
+---+-------+---+
|  a|  Alice| 34|
|  b|    Bob| 36|
|  c|Charlie| 30|
|  d|  David| 29|
|  e| Esther| 32|
|  f|  Fanny| 36|
+---+-------+---+
```

```
edges:
+---+---+------------+
|src|dst|relationship|
+---+---+------------+
|  a|  b|      friend|
|  b|  c|      follow|
|  c|  b|      follow|
|  f|  c|      follow|
|  e|  f|      follow|
|  e|  d|      friend|
|  d|  a|      friend|
+---+---+------------+
```

Step 3. Add a feature to the vertices representing a binary label (if age is greater 30 it will take value 1, otherwise 0), then display the new vertices with the added label.

```
labeled_vertices=g.vertices.withColumn("label",(g.vertices.age>30).
cast("int"))

print('labeled_vertices:')

labeled_vertices.show()
```

```
labeled_vertices:
+---+-------+---+-----+
| id|   name|age|label|
+---+-------+---+-----+
|  a|  Alice| 34|    1|
|  b|    Bob| 36|    1|
|  c|Charlie| 30|    0|
|  d|  David| 29|    0|
|  e| Esther| 32|    1|
|  f|  Fanny| 36|    1|
+---+-------+---+-----+
```

Step 4. Prepare the feature vectors for predictive analysis.

```
assembler = VectorAssembler(inputCols=["age"],
outputCol="features")

features_df = assembler.transform(labeled_vertices)
```

Step 5. Split the data into training and test sets (defined ratio means 70% of the data will randomly be allocated to the train_data variable and 30% to the test_data variable) then display the training and test data.

```
train_data, test_data = features_df.randomSplit([0.7, 0.3],
seed=42)

print('train data:')

train_data.show()

print('test data:')

test_data.show()
```

```
train data:
+---+-------+---+-----+--------+
| id|   name|age|label|features|
+---+-------+---+-----+--------+
|  a|  Alice| 34|    1|  [34.0]|
|  b|    Bob| 36|    1|  [36.0]|
|  c|Charlie| 30|    0|  [30.0]|
|  d|  David| 29|    0|  [29.0]|
|  f|  Fanny| 36|    1|  [36.0]|
+---+-------+---+-----+--------+

test data:
+---+------+---+-----+--------+
| id|  name|age|label|features|
+---+------+---+-----+--------+
|  e|Esther| 32|    1|  [32.0]|
+---+------+---+-----+--------+
```

Step 6. Define and train a logistic regression model.

```
lr = LogisticRegression(featuresCol="features", labelCol="label")

model = lr.fit(train_data)
```

Step 7. Make predictions on the test data.

```
predictions = model.transform(test_data)
```

Step 8. Display the predicted labels.

```
predictions.select("name", "age", "prediction").show()
```

```
+------+---+----------+
|  name|age|prediction|
+------+---+----------+
|Esther| 32|       1.0|
+------+---+----------+
```

In this example our model correctly predicted Esther's label as 1, which is correct as her age is greater than 30.

7.4 GRAPH ANALYTICS ALGORITHMS

There are several graph algorithms that are used for analysing graphs and networks. In this section we explore a few of the popular ones with hands-on exercises. Figure 7.25 shows the example graph in tabular and graphical form that we will be using for this purpose.

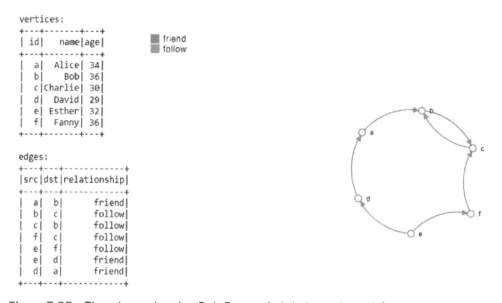

Figure 7.25   The edge and vertex DataFrames in tabular and graph form

7.4.1 PageRank

The PageRank algorithm was developed by Larry Page and Sergey Brin, the founders of Google, to measure the importance of web pages on the World Wide Web, and it has had a tremendous impact on web searching. Still using the pre-defined friend example as the source of our graph, we run the PageRank algorithm on the GraphFrame (Figure 7.26). From the PageRank results, we can see that vertex b has the highest ranking, closely followed by c. In PageRank, a higher score typically indicates that a vertex is more important or central in the network, so in this example b is more significant in the network than c.

```
pr_results = g.pageRank(resetProbability=0.01, maxIter=20)
pr_results.vertices.select("id","pagerank").show()
```

```
+---+--------------------+
| id|            pagerank|
+---+--------------------+
|  b|   2.9701000000000004|
|  e|0.010000000000000021|
|  a|  0.02480050000000005|
|  f|0.014950000000000031|
|  d|0.014950000000000031|
|  c|   2.9651995000000007|
+---+--------------------+
```

Figure 7.26   PageRank applied to the simple relationship GraphFrame

7.4.2 Breadth-first search

The breadth-first search (BFS)_ algorithm traverses a graph in breadth-first manner, exploring all the neighbours of a node before moving to the next level.

In Figure 7.27, a BFS traversal is done on the graph, starting from the vertices that satisfy the given vertex condition and exploring the graph based on the specified edge condition. In this exercise, the starting condition is specified as name=Alice, which means that the traversal will begin from the vertex where the name property is equal to Alice. The edge condition is specified as age < 32, which means that during the traversal, only edges with a property age less than 32 will be considered. This condition filters out edges based on the age property of the edges. The result of the BFS traversal is stored in the paths variable, which represents a DataFrame containing the paths explored during the BFS traversal. Finally, the show method is called on the paths DataFrame to display the result. What this result depicts is a subgraph of the friend graph that includes all the people who are friends of Alice and are younger than 32, this can be used for further analysis or visualization. BFS is a useful and effective algorithm for exploring a graph and pulling out data which meet certain conditions.

```
paths = g.bfs("name='Alice'", "age < 32")
paths.show()
```

```
+-------------+-------------+-----------+--------------+---------------+
|         from|           e0|         v1|            e1|             to|
+-------------+-------------+-----------+--------------+---------------+
|[a, Alice, 34]|[a, b, friend]|[b, Bob, 36]|[b, c, follow]|[c, Charlie, 30]|
+-------------+-------------+-----------+--------------+---------------+
```

Figure 7.27 Breadth-first search applied to the simple relationship GraphFrame

7.4.3 Strongly connected components

This algorithm aims to identify strongly connected components in a graph. Strongly con-nected components are subsets of vertices in a directed graph where every vertex in the subset is reachable from every other vertex.

In Figure 7.28 the strongly connected components algorithm is applied to the graph and returns a DataFrame with a new `component` column. Each row in the resultant table represents a vertex in the graph and the component it belongs to. From the table we can see that vertices c and b belong to the same strongly connected component. This means that there is a strong connection between c and b, b can be reached from c and vice versa using the directed edges in the graph. It should be noted that the values of the components are just labels and identifiers used to identify the different strongly connected components in the graph.

```
result = g.stronglyConnectedComponents(maxIter=10)
result.select("id", "component").orderBy("component").show()
```

```
+---+--------------+
| id|     component|
+---+--------------+
|  f|    412316860416|
|  e|    670014898176|
|  d|    807453851648|
|  c|  1047972020224|
|  b|  1047972020224|
|  a|  1460288880640|
+---+--------------+
```

Figure 7.28 Strongly connected components applied to the simple relationship GraphFrame

7.4.4 Label propagation algorithm

The label propagation algorithm is a graph clustering algorithm which is used to assign labels to vertices in such a way as to maximize label agreement for neighbouring vertices. The labels of vertices are labelled based on that of their neighbours. A simple way to think about this is by imagining a group of people in a social network (e.g., Facebook) with interests (labels) which can be shared with others. To start off with, each person (node) will have their own label, and as interactions happen labels might be updated based on influences from others. Overtime we will then be left with a spread of labels this will include some groups where people with similar labels are grouped together in communities within the network. The label propagation algorithm help find these groupings in a network. In Figure 7.29 the label propagation for detecting communities in networks is executed and it returns the vertex ids with the new label column. This result shows us that the algorithm has grouped nodes f and d into the same community because they have characteristics that are similar to each other. This is also the case with nodes a and c.

```
result = g.labelPropagation(maxIter=5)
result.select("id","label").show()

+---+-------------+
| id|        label|
+---+-------------+
|  b|1047972020224|
|  e| 412316860416|
|  a|1382979469312|
|  f| 670014898176|
|  d| 670014898176|
|  c|1382979469312|
+---+-------------+
```

Figure 7.29 Label propagation applied to the simple relationship GraphFrame

7.4.5 Shortest paths

The shortest paths algorithm computes the shortest paths between vertices. In Figure 7.30 the code computes the shortest paths between the vertices.

7.4.6 Triangle count

A triangle in a graph is a set of three vertices connected by edges forming a closed loop. The triangle count algorithm determines the number of triangles each vertex is part of in a triangle.

```
results = g.shortestPaths(landmarks=["a", "d"])
results.select("id","distances").show()
+---+----------------+
| id|       distances|
+---+----------------+
|  b|              []|
|  e|[d -> 1, a -> 2]|
|  a|        [a -> 0]|
|  f|              []|
|  d|[d -> 0, a -> 1]|
|  c|              []|
+---+----------------+
```

Figure 7.30 Shortest paths algorithm applied to the simple relationship GraphFrame

In Figure 7.31 the algorithm counts the number of triangles in the graph that each vertex belongs to; in this case there are no triangles in the graph hence the result is zero for each vertex.

```
results=g.triangleCount()
results.select("id","count").show()

+---+-----+
| id|count|
+---+-----+
|  f|    0|
|  e|    0|
|  d|    0|
|  c|    0|
|  b|    0|
|  a|    0|
+---+-----+
```

Figure 7.31 Triangle count algorithm applied to the simple relationship GraphFrame

7.5 MORE GRAPH ANALYTICS HANDS-ON EXERCISES

So far, the hands-on exercises we have done have been on small and simple datasets. However, graph analytics is also used on big data, for instance on social media network datasets like the large Facebook page to page network. In the next hands-on exercise, we will use some aeroplane and flight datasets. The datasets can be downloaded from the links provided on this book's online resources website.

The datasets are from open data portals and consist of two main files. The first file is a global list of airports with their unique IATA code (e.g. London Heathrow is LHR, Murtala Muhammed International Airport in Lagos is LOS, and O'Hare International Airport in Chicago is ORD). As it is unique, the IATA code makes an excellent vertex id.

• The Airport Dataset (Source: https://openflights.org/data).

The second file contains origin airport IDs (i.e., the source airport code), the destination airport code, the departure delay, and a few other fields such as the destination city name (https://www.transtats.bts.gov/ot_delay/ot_delaycause1.asp). This file has been pre-processed and the src and dst identified and labelled. Remember that the edges DataFrame must have these fields.

The steps to be taken to create the GraphFrame from this data are as follows:

• Download the relevant datasets.
• Prepare and load the datasets.
• Create the vertices DataFrame from the airports data (remember to rename columns to src and dst).
• Create the edges DataFrame from the flights data (remember to rename the appropriate column to id).
• Create the GraphFrames from the vertices and edges DataFrames.
• Run queries.

We now go through the Apache Spark code needed for the various steps.

Step 1. Upload the airport data into a DataFrame and display the first five items in it. Remember to replace 'path' with the actual path and location of the file in your environment (Figure 7.32).

Step 2. Create the trip vertex from the uploaded airport data. Recall that the vertex must have an id column, so we rename the IATA column to id. Also display the first five items in the vertex (Figure 7.33).

Step 3. We can upload the data for the edges DataFrame in a similar manner to that of the vertices DataFrame. However, in Figure 7.34 we use a different command to demonstrate another way of uploading the data. Again, remember to replace the path and filename with the ones in your environment. We also display the first five items in the edge DataFrame.

Step 4. Then we create the GraphFrame (tripGraph) from the vertex and edge DataFrames (Figure 7.35).

Step 5. Next, we use PixieDust to visualize the GraphFrame (Figure 7.36).

```
airports=spark.read.option("header","true").csv("hdfs:///path/airports2.csv")

airports.take(5)
```

Output:

```
[Row(AirportID='1', Name='Goroka Airport', City='Goroka', Country='Papua
New Guinea', IATA='GKA', ICAO='AYGA', Latitude='-6.081689835',
Longitude='145.3919983', Altitude='5282', Timezone='10', DST='U',
TzDatabaseTimeZone='Pacific/Port_Moresby', Type='airport',
Source='OurAirports'),

Row(AirportID='2', Name='Madang Airport', City='Madang', Country='Papua
New Guinea', IATA='MAG', ICAO='AYMD', Latitude='-5.207079887',
Longitude='145.7890015', Altitude='20', Timezone='10', DST='U',
TzDatabaseTimeZone='Pacific/Port_Moresby', Type='airport',
Source='OurAirports'),

 Row(AirportID='3', Name='Mount Hagen Kagamuga Airport', City='Mount Hagen',
Country='Papua New Guinea', IATA='HGU', ICAO='AYMH', Latitude='-5.826789856',
Longitude='144.2960052', Altitude='5388', Timezone='10', DST='U',
TzDatabaseTimeZone='Pacific/Port_Moresby', Type='airport',
Source='OurAirports'),

Row(AirportID='4', Name='Nadzab Airport', City='Nadzab', Country='Papua
New Guinea', IATA='LAE', ICAO='AYNZ', Latitude='-6.569803',
Longitude='146.725977', Altitude='239', Timezone='10', DST='U',
TzDatabaseTimeZone='Pacific/Port_Moresby', Type='airport',
Source='OurAirports'),

Row(AirportID='5', Name='Port Moresby Jacksons International Airport',
City='Port Moresby', Country='Papua New Guinea', IATA='POM', ICAO='AYPY',
Latitude='-9.443380356', Longitude='147.2200012', Altitude='146',
Timezone='10', DST='U', TzDatabaseTimeZone='Pacific/Port_Moresby',
Type='airport', Source='OurAirports')]
```

Figure 7.32 Upload the airports data

Step 6. To demonstrate how graph analytics can be used to draw out insights from data, we next run a series of queries on the GraphFrames (see Figure 7.37).

Let us now run some more specific queries on the graph, focusing on Detroit (Figure 7.38). We can see that a number of flights from Detroit appear to generally have delays. This insight can help the airport management in trying to address what the issues and bottlenecks causing this might be. It can also help customers plan their trip: for example, does additional time need to be factored in, and which flights should perhaps be avoided from Detroit? (See Figure 7.39.)

```
tripVertices = airports.withColumnRenamed("IATA", "id").distinct()
```

```
tripVertices.take(5)
```

Output:

```
[Row(AirportID='28', Name='CFB Bagotville', City='Bagotville',
Country='Canada', id='YBG', ICAO='CYBG', Latitude='48.33060074',
Longitude='-70.99639893', Altitude='522', Timezone='-5', DST='A',
TzDatabaseTimeZone='America/Toronto', Type='airport', Source='OurAirports'),

Row(AirportID='91', Name='Moosonee Airport', City='Moosonee',
Country='Canada', id='YMO', ICAO='CYMO', Latitude='51.29109955',
Longitude='-80.60700334', Altitude='30', Timezone='-5', DST='A',
TzDatabaseTimeZone='America/Toronto', Type='airport', Source='OurAirports'),

Row(AirportID='156', Name='Vancouver International Airport', City='Vancouver',
Country='Canada', id='YVR', ICAO='CYVR', Latitude='49.19390106',
Longitude='-123.1839981', Altitude='14', Timezone='-8', DST='A',
TzDatabaseTimeZone='America/Vancouver', Type='airport', Source='OurAirports'),

Row(AirportID='221', Name='Mohamed Boudiaf International Airport',
City='Constantine', Country='Algeria', id='CZL', ICAO='DABC',
Latitude='36.27600098', Longitude='6.620389938', Altitude='2265',
Timezone='1', DST='N', TzDatabaseTimeZone='Africa/Algiers', Type='airport',
Source='OurAirports'),

Row(AirportID='290', Name='Gafsa Ksar International Airport', City='Gafsa',
Country='Tunisia', id='GAF', ICAO='DTTF', Latitude='34.42200089',
Longitude='8.822500229', Altitude='1060', Timezone='1', DST='E',
TzDatabaseTimeZone='Africa/Tunis', Type='airport', Source='OurAirports')]
```

Figure 7.33 **Create the vertices DataFrame,** tripVertices, **from the loaded data and rename the IATA column to** id

```
tripVertices = airports.withColumnRenamed("IATA", "id").distinct()
```

```
tripVertices.take(5)
```

Output:

```
[Row(ORIGIN_AIRPORT_ID='ABE', src='ABE', dst='DTW', DEST_CITY_NAME='Detroit
, MI', DEST_STATE_ABR='MI', DEP_DELAY=21),

Row(ORIGIN_AIRPORT_ID='ABE', src='ABE', dst='DTW', DEST_CITY_NAME='Detroit
, MI', DEST_STATE_ABR='MI', DEP_DELAY=561),

Row(ORIGIN_AIRPORT_ID='ABE', src='ABE', dst='DTW', DEST_CITY_NAME='Detroit
, MI', DEST_STATE_ABR='MI', DEP_DELAY=-4),
```

```
Row(ORIGIN_AIRPORT_ID='ABE', src='ABE', dst='DTW', DEST_CITY_NAME='Detroit
, MI', DEST_STATE_ABR='MI', DEP_DELAY=-2),
```

```
Row(ORIGIN_AIRPORT_ID='ABE', src='ABE', dst='DTW', DEST_CITY_NAME='Detroit
, MI', DEST_STATE_ABR='MI', DEP_DELAY=236)]
```

Figure 7.34 **Create the edges DataFrame** tripEdges **from the loaded data**

```
tripGraph = GraphFrame(tripVertices, tripEdges)
```

Figure 7.35 **Create the** tripGraph **GraphFrame from the vertex and edge DataFrames**

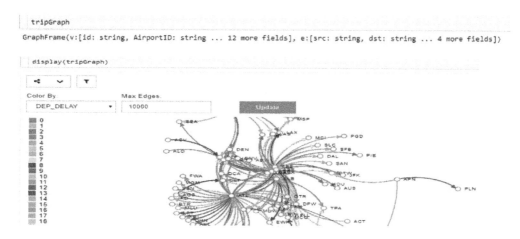

Figure 7.36 **Visualizing the tripGraph GraphFrames**

```
# how many airports and trips are in the dataset?
```

```
print("Airports: %d" % tripGraph.vertices.count())
print("Trips: %d" % tripGraph.edges.count())
```

```
Output:
  Airports: 7184
  Trips: 570131
```

```
# what is the longest delay?
```

```
longestDelay = tripGraph.edges.groupBy().max("DEP_DELAY").first()
longestDelay
```

(Continued)

Figure 7.37 (Continued)

Output:
```
    Row(max(DEP_DELAY)=2007)
```

```
# what is the shortest delay?
```

```
shortestDelay = tripGraph.edges.groupBy().min("DEP_DELAY").first()
shortestDelay
```

Output:
```
 Row(min(DEP_DELAY)=50)
```

```
# how many flights were on time or early
print("On-time / Early Flights: %d" % tripGraph.edges.filter("DEP_DELAY <=
0").count())
```

```
# how many flights were delayed?
```

```
print("Delayed Flights: %d" % tripGraph.edges.filter("DEP_DELAY > 0").count())
```

Output:
```
  On-time / Early Flights: 369073
  Delayed Flights: 183732
```

Figure 7.37 Number of airports and trips in the GraphFrame, longest and shortest delays and on-time/early flights versus delayed flights

```
# What flights departing Detroit (DTW) are most likely to have significant
delays
# Delay can be <= 0 meaning the flight left on time or early, then display 10
of them
```

```
tripGraph.edges.filter("src='DTW' and DEP_DELAY>0").groupBy("src", "dst").
avg("DEP_DELAY").take(10)
```

Output:
```
[Row(src='DTW', dst='MKE', avg(DEP_DELAY)=54.828125),
 Row(src='DTW', dst='PHL', avg(DEP_DELAY)=54.45161290322581),
 Row(src='DTW', dst='GRR', avg(DEP_DELAY)=65.15151515151516),
 Row(src='DTW', dst='ATW', avg(DEP_DELAY)=78.09677419354838),
 Row(src='DTW', dst='BGM', avg(DEP_DELAY)=40.958333333333336),
```

```
Row(src='DTW', dst='CIU', avg(DEP_DELAY)=71.76470588235294),

Row(src='DTW', dst='GRB', avg(DEP_DELAY)=49.5),

Row(src='DTW', dst='SBN', avg(DEP_DELAY)=61.68888888888889),

Row(src='DTW', dst='ALB', avg(DEP_DELAY)=46.48275862068966),

Row(src='DTW', dst='AUS', avg(DEP_DELAY)=40.54545454545455)]
```

```
# which destinations have delays? Display 5 of them
```

```
tripDelays = tripGraph.edges.filter("DEP_DELAY > 0").take(5)
tripDelays
```

```
Output:
```

```
[Row(ORIGIN_AIRPORT_ID='ABE', src='ABE', dst='DTW', DEST_CITY_NAME='Detroit,
MI', DEST_STATE_ABR='MI', DEP_DELAY=21),

Row(ORIGIN_AIRPORT_ID='ABE', src='ABE', dst='DTW', DEST_CITY_NAME='Detroit,
MI', DEST_STATE_ABR='MI', DEP_DELAY=561),

Row(ORIGIN_AIRPORT_ID='ABE', src='ABE', dst='DTW', DEST_CITY_NAME='Detroit,
MI', DEST_STATE_ABR='MI', DEP_DELAY=236),

Row(ORIGIN_AIRPORT_ID='ABE', src='ABE', dst='DTW', DEST_CITY_NAME='Detroit,
MI', DEST_STATE_ABR='MI', DEP_DELAY=32),

Row(ORIGIN_AIRPORT_ID='ABE', src='ABE', dst='DTW', DEST_CITY_NAME='Detroit,
MI', DEST_STATE_ABR='MI', DEP_DELAY=12)]
```

Figure 7.38 Using `filter` to return data where the source is Detroit 'DTW' and there is a flight delay

```
# What destinations tend to have significant delays going from Detroit? Display
5 of them.
```

```
tripGraph.edges.filter("src = 'DTW' and DEP_DELAY > 100").take(5)
```

```
Output:
```

```
[Row(ORIGIN_AIRPORT_ID='DTW', src='DTW', dst='DFW', DEST_CITY_NAME='Dallas/
Fort Worth, TX', DEST_STATE_ABR='TX', DEP_DELAY=124),

Row(ORIGIN_AIRPORT_ID='DTW', src='DTW', dst='MIA', DEST_CITY_NAME='Miami, FL',
DEST_STATE_ABR='FL', DEP_DELAY=149),

Row(ORIGIN_AIRPORT_ID='DTW', src='DTW', dst='MIA', DEST_CITY_NAME='Miami, FL',
DEST_STATE_ABR='FL', DEP_DELAY=122),

Row(ORIGIN_AIRPORT_ID='DTW', src='DTW', dst='MIA', DEST_CITY_NAME='Miami, FL',
DEST_STATE_ABR='FL', DEP_DELAY=273),

Row(ORIGIN_AIRPORT_ID='DTW', src='DTW', dst='MIA', DEST_CITY_NAME='Miami, FL',
DEST_STATE_ABR='FL', DEP_DELAY=112)]
```

(Continued)

Figure 7.39 (Continued)

```
#inDegrees: Incoming connections to the airport
#outDegrees: Outgoing connections from the airport
#degrees: Total connections to and from the airport


tripGraph.degrees.sort(("degree")).limit(4).take(4)


Output:
[Row(id='YNG', degree=4),
 Row(id='BFF', degree=7),
 Row(id='HGR', degree=18),
 Row(id='ADK', degree=18)]


tripGraph.inDegrees.sort(("InDegree")).limit(4).take(4)


Output:
[Row(id='YNG', inDegree=2),
 Row(id='BFF', inDegree=4),
 Row(id='HGR', inDegree=9),
 Row(id='ADK', inDegree=9)]


tripGraph.outDegrees.sort(("OutDegree")).limit(4).take(4)


Output:
[Row(id='YNG', outDegree=2),
 Row(id='BFF', outDegree=3),
 Row(id='HGR', outDegree=9),
 Row(id='ADK', outDegree=9)]
```

Figure 7.39 Using `filter` to return data where the source is Detroit (DTW) and there is significant flight delay (any departure delay greater than 100 is taken to be significant)

In Figure 7.39 we also use the degrees to work out the total number of connections to and from an airport. Degrees give the total number of connections (regardless of direction of travel). Indegrees give the number of incoming connections, and outdegrees the number of outgoing connections.

We then run the PageRank algorithm to determine the airport with the most important ranking in the dataset. Figure 7.40 shows the top five results in descending order. The most significant airport (edge) in the dataset is Hartsfield Jackson Atlanta International with a page rank value of 83.32. It is closely followed by Chicago O'Hare International with a page rank value of 73.08. The third airport in terms of importance is Dallas Fort Worth International with a page rank value of 69.57. One thing all these airports have in common is that they are busy international airports with lots of connecting flights both into and out of them. So, the page ranking algorithm has factored all of this in and ranked them.

```
# Which is most important ranking - using PageRank algorithm


ranks = tripGraph.pageRank(resetProbability=0.15, maxIter=5)
ranks.vertices.orderBy(ranks.vertices.pagerank.desc()).limit(5).take(5)
```

Output:

```
[Row(AirportID='3682', Name='Hartsfield Jackson Atlanta International
Airport', City='Atlanta', Country='United States', id='ATL', ICAO='KATL',
Latitude='33.63669968', Longitude='-84.42810059', Altitude='1026',
Timezone='-5', DST='A', TzDatabaseTimeZone='America/New_York', Type='airport',
Source='OurAirports', pagerank=83.3167772224317),

Row(AirportID='3830', Name="Chicago O'Hare International Airport",
City='Chicago', Country='United States', id='ORD', ICAO='KORD',
Latitude='41.97859955', Longitude='-87.90480042', Altitude='672',
Timezone='-6', DST='A', TzDatabaseTimeZone='America/Chicago', Type='airport',
Source='OurAirports', pagerank=73.08026635608465),

Row(AirportID='3670', Name='Dallas Fort Worth International Airport',
City='Dallas-Fort Worth', Country='United States', id='DFW', ICAO='KDFW',
Latitude='32.89680099', Longitude='-97.03800201', Altitude='607',
Timezone='-6', DST='A', TzDatabaseTimeZone='America/Chicago', Type='airport',
Source='OurAirports', pagerank=69.57309240166732),

Row(AirportID='3751', Name='Denver International Airport', City='Denver',
Country='United States', id='DEN', ICAO='KDEN', Latitude='39.86169815',
Longitude='-104.6729965', Altitude='5431', Timezone='-7', DST='A',
TzDatabaseTimeZone='America/Denver', Type='airport', Source='OurAirports',
pagerank=50.34723954232367),

Row(AirportID='3876', Name='Charlotte Douglas International Airport',
City='Charlotte', Country='United States', id='CLT', ICAO='KCLT',
Latitude='35.2140007', Longitude='-80.94309998', Altitude='748',
Timezone='-5', DST='A', TzDatabaseTimeZone='America/New_York', Type='airport',
Source='OurAirports', pagerank=48.667931262612505)]
```

Figure 7.40 PageRank algorithm on the `tripGraph` **GraphFrame**

The PageRank algorithm outputs a probability distribution used to represent the likelihood that a person randomly selecting a flight will arrive at any airport. The PageRank computations require several passes, called 'iterations', and as such for large datasets can be quite computationally intensive.

Some additional queries can be seen in Figure 7.41. These return the ten most popular flights both into and out of the airports.

As mentioned earlier with big data analytics, visualizations can be extremely useful and so we have an entire chapter (Chapter 11) on visualizations for big data analytics. So far in this chapter we have, however, used PixieDust which is a Python library to plot some visualizations. Figure 7.42 depicts a visualization of the GraphFrame. We have chosen to represent delays in different colours, so if for instance the edge between two airports is red in colour, then we can tell from the legend that the delay is 23.

```
# Show the top 10 most popular flights (single city hops)

topTrips.orderBy(topTrips.trips.desc()).limit(10).take(10)

Output:
[Row(src='SFO', dst='LAX', trips=1235),
 Row(src='LAX', dst='SFO', trips=1233),
 Row(src='ORD', dst='LGA', trips=1200),
 Row(src='LGA', dst='ORD', trips=1194),
 Row(src='LAX', dst='JFK', trips=1037),
 Row(src='JFK', dst='LAX', trips=1037),
 Row(src='LAS', dst='LAX', trips=1019),
 Row(src='LAX', dst='LAS', trips=1017),
 Row(src='HNL', dst='OGG', trips=810),
 Row(src='OGG', dst='HNL', trips=810)]


# inDeg (flights into the airport) and outDeg (flights leaving the airport)

inDeg = tripGraph.inDegrees
outDeg = tripGraph.outDegrees
inDeg.take(5)

Output:
[Row(id='BGM', inDegree=58),
 Row(id='PSE', inDegree=69),
 Row(id='INL', inDegree=53),
 Row(id='MSY', inDegree=4654),
 Row(id='PPG', inDegree=10)]


outDeg.take(5)

Output:
[Row(id='BGM', outDegree=58),
 Row(id='INL', outDegree=53),
 Row(id='PSE', outDegree=70),
 Row(id='MSY', outDegree=4650),
 Row(id='PPG', outDegree=10)]
```

Figure 7.41 The ten most popular flights into and out of airports (inDegrees) and out of airports (outDegrees)

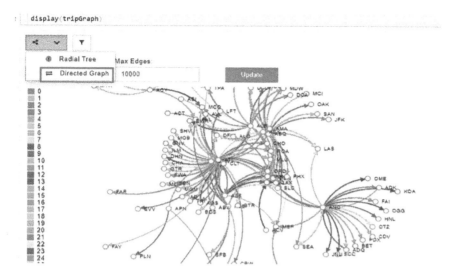

```
: | display(tripGraph)
```

Figure 7.42   Visualization of the GraphFrame (directed graph)

In Figures 7.43–7.46 we use PixieDust to plot some maps. The figures show how to choose the parameters, and there are various types of maps that can be plotted. For instance, you could choose clusters which would show you how many airports are in that region, or you could choose density maps as in Figure 7.46. The trick is to make choices that can be used for actionable insights and good decision-making.

7.6 ETHICS BY DESIGN

Ethics by design needs to be at the forefront of graph analytics. As in other chapters, the elements highlighted by the TAFARP data ethics by design framework are also very important here: transparency, accountability, fairness, autonomy, responsibility, and privacy (see Figure 2.14, p. 44). Graph analytics, however, has an additional dimension to ethics by design that we have not come across in any other chapter. Graph data structures, by their very nature, contain context about the data within them. If you think about a graph data structure, it is made up of edges and vertices. It is not only about the data but also about the context in which the data exists. For instance, what are the edges (relationships) between the vertices (nodes)? This brings an additional layer of understanding and transparency to the context of the data. This is increasingly being seen as an aspect of graphs that could potentially help to provide trustworthy ethical AI (O'Shee, 2022). Work is also now being carried out on how graph algorithms can be used in conjunction with other more traditional machine learning algorithms to provide more context, and to enrich the understanding of the data and its

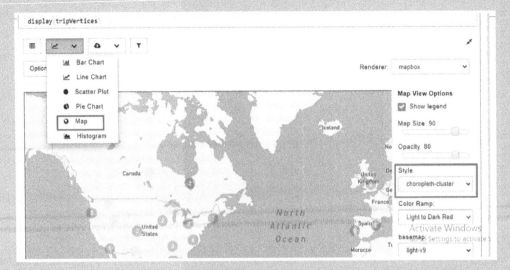

Figure 7.43 **Visualization of the GraphFrame (map) – clustered on light background**

Figure 7.44 **Visualization of the GraphFrame (map) – choosing parameters to plot**

domain to help improve outcomes (Needham and Hodler, n.d.). This emerging area is helping showcase the importance and relevance of graph analytics across different areas. Graph analytics raises specific ethical considerations due to the relational nature of the data involved and the potential impact on individuals and communities. In contrast to other datasets that provide data about isolated entities (individuals, organizations, etc.), graph analysis requires information about the relationships between those entities, such as information about friendships and interactions. This kind of data can be especially sensitive. Here are some key ethical considerations specific to these fields:

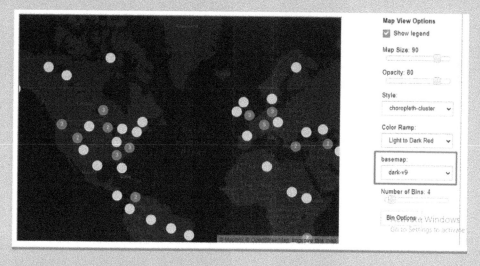

Figure 7.45 Visualization of the GraphFrame (map) – clustered on dark background

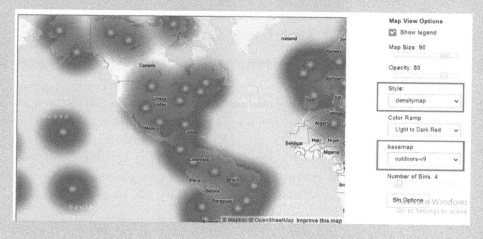

Figure 7.46 Visualization of the GraphFrame (map) – density map

- *Privacy and informed consent.* Social network analysis often relies on collecting and analysing personal data, such as social media posts, connections, and interactions. Respecting individuals' privacy rights and obtaining informed consent are essential. It is crucial to inform individuals about the purpose and scope of data collection, the types of analysis performed, and any potential implications of the analysis.
- *Network bias and discrimination.* Graph analytics can uncover patterns of relationships and interactions, but there is a risk of perpetuating biases or discrimination. Care should be taken to ensure that the analysis and algorithms used are fair and unbiased. Bias detection and mitigation techniques should be employed to prevent the amplification of existing inequalities or unfair treatment.

- *Data ownership and intellectual property*. The ownership and intellectual property rights of network data can be complex, especially in social network analysis where the data may involve multiple individuals or entities. It is essential to respect the rights and permissions associated with the data and to adhere to legal and ethical standards regarding data ownership and intellectual property.
- *Data accuracy and integrity*. Graph analytics heavily relies on the quality and accuracy of the data. Ensuring data accuracy and integrity is crucial to avoid drawing incorrect or misleading conclusions. It is necessary to implement data validation and verification processes, address data biases or errors, and transparently document data sources and pre-processing steps.
- *Data security and confidentiality*. Networks and social connections can contain sensitive information, and protecting the security and confidentiality of the data is paramount. Appropriate security measures should be in place to prevent unauthorized access, data breaches, or misuse of personal information. Data anonymization and aggregation techniques can be employed to protect individuals' identities.
- *Impact on individuals and communities*. Social network analysis can have significant implications for individuals and communities. Analysing and visualizing network structures may reveal personal or sensitive information that individuals may not have intended to share. Ethical considerations involve minimizing harm, ensuring responsible use of the insights derived, and considering the potential impact on individuals' reputation, relationships, and well-being.
- *Transparency and accountability*. Openness, transparency, and accountability are crucial in graph analytics and social network analysis. It is important to provide clear explanations of the analysis methodology, algorithms used, and any assumptions made. Documentation of data sources, pre-processing steps, and analysis procedures helps ensure reproducibility and allows for independent scrutiny.

7.7 INDUSTRY INSIGHTS

The graph analytics market is a rapidly emerging area of data analytics. It is currently expected to reach $2.03 billion by 2028 (Graph Analytics Market Research, 2023). This means that more companies are beginning to focus on this area. For our industry insights, there were a number of companies we could have chosen – Neo4j Inc., TigerGraph Inc., Oracle Corporation, and IBM Corporation to name but a few. We focus on Perspectives from the Tom Sawyer Software Corporation. Tom Sawyer is a leading provider of software that enables the development of flexible graph and data analysis and visualization applications. Perspectives is a low-code graph visualization and analysis development platform that allows developers to develop custom applications for solving big data problems in short time frames (see the further reading section at the end of this chapter). Perspectives contains about 27 different features, among them data extraction, predictive analytics, and workflow management, that make it possible for users to draw insights from their data that could lead to actionable insights, better decision-making, and, in some cases, competitive advantage. Perspectives has been future-proofed by virtue of having been made low-code – the direction of travel in many areas, as previously hinted, is low-code and even no-code. Again, this is an interesting observation in the technology world (another example of a product that does this well is PixieDust, which we used extensively earlier on in this chapter). In the further reading section, we have added links to some interesting articles exploring this.

SUMMARY

In this chapter we discussed graph analytics for big data, different types of graphs, and why being able to distinguish between them is important for graph analytics. We also touched on exploratory, descriptive, and predictive graph analytics, along with various graph analytics algorithms such as PageRank, breadth-first search, and shortest paths. We carried out hands-on exercises with visualizations to enhance the insights derived from the analytics. Finally, we discussed ethics by design and industry insights in this area.

TEST YOUR KNOWLEDGE

1   What are some of the advantages of graph analytics?
2   Upload a graph dataset of your choice and do the following:
  •   Work out how many edges are going into each vertex.
  •   Work out how many edges are going out each vertex.
  •   Work out which edge is the most important.
3   Plot a visualization of the graph from the previous task.
4   What advantage do graph data structures have when it comes to ethics by design?
5   Describe three ways in which you can use graph analytics.
6   Upload a graph data structure, create a GraphFrame, and then apply the following graph analytics algorithms to the GraphFrame:
  •   Graph search
  •   Shortest paths
  •   PageRank
  •   Triangle count
  •   Connected components
  •   Label propagation algorithm
  •   Strongly connected components

FURTHER READING (OPTIONAL)

An interesting read on the role of graph databases in big data analytics:

Gaur, C. (2022) Role of graph databases in big data analytics. Retrieved from https://www. xenonstack.com/insights/graph-databases-big-data

An example of a system designed for big data analytics using AWS:

Sood, L. (2022) Designing an educational big data analysis architecture with AWS. Retrieved from https://aws.amazon.com/blogs/publicsector/designing-educational-big-data-analysis-architecture-aws/

Interesting article on why graph analytics for big data is on the rise:

Morgan, L. (2021) Why using graph analytics for big data is on the rise. Retrieved from https://www.techtarget.com/searchbusinessanalytics/feature/Why-using-graph-analytics-for-big-data-is-on-the-rise

Brief write-up on when, why, and how to use graph analytics for big data:

Shetty, S. (2017) When, why and how to use graph analytics for your big data. Retrieved from https://hub.packtpub.com/when-why-and-how-to-use-graph-analytics-for-your-big-data/

Very brief video with overview of Perspectives from the Tom Sawyer Corporation:

https://youtu.be/0CfLE0f5AvA

Articles that explore whether no code is the future of software:

Kostereva, K. (2022) No-code is the future of software: Here are five critical things to drive success in 2022 and beyond. Retrieved from https://www.forbes.com/sites/forbestechcouncil/2022/03/18/no-code-is-the-future-of-software-here-are-five-critical-things-to-drive-success-in-2022-and-beyond/

Goel, P. (2022) Are low-code and no-code platforms the next big thing in the IT sector? Retrieved from https://www.entrepreneur.com/en-in/news-and-trends/are-low-code-and-no-code-platforms-the-next-big-thing-in/436896

Pajorska, Z. (2022) Is low-code/no-code the future? 5 most important trends. Retrieved from https://stratoflow.com/is-low-code-no-code-the-future/

REFERENCES

Apache Software Foundation (2020) Welcome to Apache Giraph! Retrieved from https://bit.ly/3PT0qYb

Apache Software Foundation (n.d.) Gelly: Flink Graph API. Retrieved from https://nightlies.apache.org/flink/flink-docs-master/docs/libs/gelly/overview/

Graph Analytics Market Research (2023) *Global Graph Analytics Market: Analysis By Component, By Deployment, By Enterprise Size, By Application, By Industry Vertical, By Region, Size and Trends with Impact of COVID-19 and Forecast up to 2028.* Research and Markets. Retrieved from https://www.researchandmarkets.com/reports/4850847/graph-analytics-market-by-component-deployment

GraphFrames (n.d.) GraphFrames User Guide: Motif finding. Retrieved from https://graphframes.github.io/graphframes/docs/_site/user-guide.html#motif-finding

Guller, M. (2015) *Big Data Analytics with Spark. A Practitioner's Guide to Using Spark for Large Scale Data Analysis.* Apress.

IBM (2016) PixieDust documentation. Retrieved from https://pixiedust.github.io/pixiedust/

Needham, M. and Hodler, A. (n.d.) *How Graph Algorithms Improve Machine Learning.* O'Reilly.

O'Shee, K. D. (2022) Are graphs the missing key to trustworthy, ethical AI? *The AI Journal.* https://aijourn.com/are-graphs-the-missing-key-to-trustworthy-ethical-ai/

8

MACHINE LEARNING

CHAPTER CONTENTS

CHAPTER OBJECTIVES

In this chapter:

- You will explore the history and emergence of machine learning, its advantages, and use cases.
- You will learn about various machine learning algorithms and go through various practical implementations of a few of them.
- Finally, you will examine some ethical issues and industry insights in the context of machine learning.

8.1 INTRODUCTION

In this chapter we build on the foundations laid in earlier chapters, in particular Chapter 3 where we introduced Apache Spark and its libraries (including the MLlib machine learning library) and Chapter 6 in which as part of the discussion on big data analytics and actionable insights some data pre-processing techniques were explored.

Machine learning, a subfield of artificial intelligence (AI), has revolutionized the way we approach complex problems and make data-driven decisions. With its ability to automatically learn patterns and make predictions from data, machine learning has become a cornerstone technology across various industries. The roots of machine learning can be traced back to the early days of computing. In the 1950s and 1960s, researchers began exploring the concept of creating intelligent machines that could learn and adapt (Russell and Norvig, 2003). The term AI was promoted by John McCarthy, widely recognized as one of the founding fathers of AI, in 1956 at a conference on the campus of Dartmouth College.

One of the earliest theoretical milestones of machine learning (Marr, 2016; Turing, 1950) is Alan Turing's famous (and today controversial) 'Turing test' from 1950. In his seminal paper (Turing, 1950), Turing reflects on the possibility of distinguishing between a human and an intelligent machine. The Turing test involves three participants: a human interrogator and two interviewees, one human and the other an intelligent machine. The interrogator can interview the two interviewees via text messaging, without knowing which is human and which is the machine. If the interrogator cannot tell them apart, the machine is said to pass the Turing test for intelligent machines.

This milestone paper was closely followed by computer scientist Arthur Lee Samuel's learning program, a project that is said to have popularized the term 'machine learning' in the late 1950s. Samuel's machine was programmed to play the game of checkers, making it the first known computer learning program. The field gained momentum with the development of algorithms like the perceptron by Frank Rosenblatt, which laid the foundation for neural networks. Over the years, advancements in computational power, data availability, and algorithmic innovations propelled machine learning to new heights. The chess-playing expert Deep Blue, a machine developed at IBM, became the first to win a chess game against a reigning world champion under regular time controls. The late 2000s witnessed an explosion of deep learning and reinforcement learning algorithms that may transform society in ways that are still hard to predict. Today, machine learning has become a powerful tool for solving complex problems:

- *Pattern recognition and prediction.* Machine learning algorithms excel at identifying patterns and trends in large datasets. They can automatically learn from historical data and make accurate predictions or classifications, enabling businesses to gain valuable insights and make informed decisions.
- *Scalability and efficiency.* Machine learning algorithms can process and analyse vast amounts of data in a relatively short period. By automating tasks that would be time-consuming or infeasible for humans, machine learning allows for scalable and efficient data analysis.
- *Adaptability and learning.* Machine learning models can learn and adapt as new data becomes available. They can continuously update their knowledge and improve their performance, making them suitable for dynamic and evolving environments.
- *Handling complex and nonlinear relationships.* Machine learning techniques can effectively model complex and nonlinear relationships between variables. They can capture intricate patterns that may not be apparent through traditional analytical approaches.

Machine learning finds applications in diverse domains, empowering organizations to solve complex problems and make data-driven decisions. Here are some notable use cases:

- *Healthcare.* Machine learning is used in medical diagnosis, predicting disease outcomes, drug discovery, and personalized medicine. It enables early detection of diseases, improves patient monitoring, and assists in identifying optimal treatment plans.
- *Finance.* Machine learning algorithms are employed in fraud detection, credit scoring, algorithmic trading, and risk assessment. They help detect fraudulent transactions, analyse market trends, and optimize investment strategies.
- *Marketing and sales.* Machine learning enables personalized marketing campaigns, customer segmentation, churn prediction, and recommendation systems. It helps businesses target the right audience, improve customer satisfaction, and optimize marketing strategies.
- *Autonomous vehicles.* Machine learning plays a vital role in the development of self-driving cars. It enables object detection, scene understanding, and decision-making capabilities necessary for safe and efficient autonomous navigation.
- *Natural language processing.* Machine learning techniques are used in speech recognition, language translation, sentiment analysis, and chatbots. They enhance human–computer interaction and enable the understanding and processing of human language.

Machine learning is crucial for solving of many big data analytics problems. This chapter will cover the more common machine learning algorithms used for big data analytics, including supervised and unsupervised learning algorithms. It will also cover the use of popular machine learning libraries in Apache Spark and Python for big data analytics

8.1.1 Challenges of machine learning for big data

Machine learning enables users to make sense of big data, transforming data into predictions and insights that inform their decisions. In this chapter we explore various machine learning algorithms and techniques and will see that it is important to have large enough datasets when training models using these algorithms, otherwise results could become either biased, unreliable, or invalid. Some of the sources of inaccuracy can include:

- *Incorrect results*. When a machine learning algorithm is trained with a dataset that is too small, one that does not represent the population or is biased, its predictions are unreliable or invalid, leading to false conclusions.
- *Overfitting*. Overfitting occurs when a machine learning model learns too much from the training data to the extent that it starts to capture irrelevant patterns. In other words, the model becomes overly complex and starts fitting the training data too closely, losing its ability to generalize well to new, unseen data. This leads to poor performance when the model is applied to the test or validation data.
- *Underfitting*. Underfitting occurs when a machine learning model is too simple or lacks the capacity to capture the underlying patterns in the data. It fails to capture the complexity of the problem, resulting in poor performance on both the training and test data.
- *Bias*. Bias can occur when the dataset is not representative of the entire population that is being model. So, for instance, a facial recognition model that has been trained based on data that is not fully representative of the entire population can end up being inaccurate for certain groups in the community (Coe & Atay, 2021).
- *Handling rare occurrences*. Small datasets may fail to capture rare but important events, leading to problems with anomaly detection, for example, where the model fails to predict or address rare occurrences.

Another class of challenges stem from the machine learning workflow itself: the process of collecting data, analysing it and identifying patterns in vast volumes of data, and then making sense of those patterns. These challenges include:

- *Interpretability*. Models that are trained on big data can be complex, and this can lead to 'black box' models which work and seem to make correct predictions but are hard to understand. The decision-making processes are not clear. It is increasingly important that models are interpretable and transparent; some of the issues that this raises are treated in the ethics by design sections in various chapters of this book. Explainable AI is a whole subset of AI that focuses on this and continues to gain traction. For more on this see Molnar (2023).

- *Privacy and security.* When dealing with big data, it must be recognized that the data can contain sensitive and confidential information that needs to be handled appropriately and with care. For instance, vast amounts of data were used to train ChatGPT, which is a chatbot powered by AI that is adept at answering questions, generating responses, and interacting in a conversational way. In instances where some of this data has been sourced by harvesting data, it can become a challenge to ensure that sensitive or confidential data is not released in error.
- *Scalability.* In Chapter 1, we touched on scalability when considering the enablers of big data. As data volumes continue to increase exponentially, it can become more difficult to process and draw out insights from the data in reasonable amounts of time. Machine learning algorithms need to be able to handle these vast amounts of data.
- *Data quality.* Big data can have data quality issues, including missing values, noise, and outliers, and all of these must be handled in pre-processing steps appropriately. In Chapter 6 we looked at some techniques to tackle some of these, and we consider more data pre-processing techniques in this chapter and in Chapter 9.
- *Feature selection.* As the amount of data increases there tends to be an increase in the number of available features, and this in turn can make it more difficult to select the features that are most relevant to train the model. Discarding the wrong features can result in the loss of important information, so getting this right is key. Removing unnecessary features also helps to reduce the computational cost of the algorithms. In this chapter we will consider some feature selection techniques.
- *Algorithm selection.* Machine learning algorithms all have their pros and cons, and as data increases selecting the correct algorithm for a particular problem and dataset can be challenging. Additionally, not all machine learning algorithms are suitable for large-scale data because of computational constraints.

8.2 CATEGORIES OF MACHINE LEARNING

Machine learning can be categorized into different types, primarily supervised learning, unsupervised learning, semi-supervised learning, and reinforcement learning (see Figure 8.1). In this section we will examine these categories and work through some hands-on implementations for them.

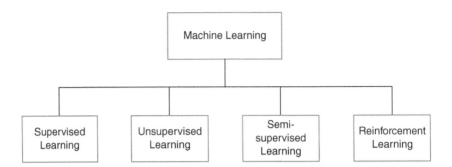

Figure 8.1 Categories of machine learning

Machine learning is an interdisciplinary field, and it overlaps with some aspects of mathematics, computer science, and statistics. In this book, in keeping with the hands-on approach, the focus is on equipping you to carry out hands-on analytics with existing libraries to implement models and use them. There are several libraries for machine learning and below we list some of the more popular ones:

- General machine learning frameworks
  - Numpy
  - Scikit-learn
  - NLTK

- Data analysis and visualization tools
  - Jupyter Notebook
  - Matplotlib
  - Pandas

Some of the above general machine learning frameworks and data analysis and visualizations tools are used in the hands-on exercises in this chapter and some subsequent ones.

Additional ones like Weka, Tableau, and KNIME are not used but are applications that you might want to explore. Weka provides a collection of machine learning algorithms for data mining, Tableau is a popular visual analytics platform, as are Power BI and Grafana. KNIME is a GUI-based data analytics platform.

8.2.1 Supervised learning

Supervised learning is a type of machine learning where the dataset to be used to train the model includes the target (this could, for instance, be what the model is predicting). This type of dataset is known as labelled data. In supervised machine learning what we are trying to do is estimate from the available data a function f that would best give the value of the output Y given input X:

$$Y=f(X).$$

As the function f is just an estimate, it will not be perfect and there will also be errors introduced that are independent of the input, but Y the point is that from using that function we will be able to predict the value of the output given a new set of inputs X.

The different machine learning algorithms approach how to work out the function f in different ways but the overarching goal is the same.

So, for supervised learning, for the data that we have (which we are going to use to estimate the function f), we know what the output Y for every input X is. This is why it is called 'supervised' learning: because as the algorithm estimates the function, that is, training is taking place and the algorithm iteratively learns as it makes predictions that are checked against what the actual value should be, and this continues until a model whose performance is acceptable is obtained from the process. Supervised learning generally falls into two categories: classification, where the output Y is a category such as yes/no; and regression, where the output Y is a real value such as height or salary (see Figure 8.2). Examples of classification include identify fraud detection and spam filters, while examples of regression include market forecasting and predicting house prices.

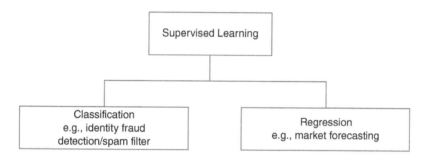

Figure 8.2   Types of supervised learning

Examples of supervised machine learning algorithms include:

- Linear regression
- Logistic regression
- Decision trees
- Random forests
- Naïve Bayes
- Support vector machines

8.2.2 Unsupervised learning

Unlike in supervised learning, where you have both input X and output Y and you are trying to estimate a function f, in unsupervised learning you only have the input X you do not know what the output Y is. What this means is that with unsupervised learning, the algorithm tries to find patterns and/or groupings without any output labels being available. Unsupervised learning can generally be categorized into clustering or association (see Figure 8.3). In clustering the algorithm looks to group the data into clusters based on some inherent characteristics – for instance, in customer segmentation where customers are placed in groups based on some similar traits. With association the algorithm is identifying rules that apply to most of the data. For example, in the identification of rules that can be used for product placement, if it is identified that customers who buy cereal are likely to buy sugar then that insight can factor into where and how both products are placed in a store.

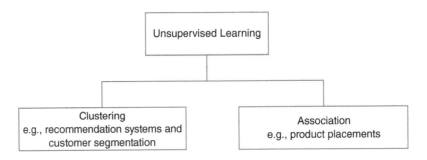

Figure 8.3 **Types of unsupervised learning**

Examples of unsupervised learning algorithms include

- *K*-means
- Hierarchical clustering
- Gaussian mixture models
- Apriori algorithm

8.2.3 Semi-supervised learning

Semi-supervised learning sits in between supervised learning and unsupervised learning. This is because with semi-supervised learning you have the input X and a small amount of Y; in real-life applications you sometimes have situations where most of the data is not labelled (i.e., it does not have outputs corresponding to the inputs) because labelling can be time-consuming and expensive and require specialists (domain experts) to provide the information. In instances like this, what you might end up with is a small amount of the output Y being present and labelled. In this situation the approach to take which would give the best results would be a hybrid one where you use both supervised and unsupervised learning algorithms. This will give you the benefits of both supervised and unsupervised learning.

8.2.4 Reinforcement learning

In reinforcement learning, an intelligent agent (the program) interacts with its environment and learns the best ways to engage in the environment through a reward system. Whenever the correct decisions are made, a reward is given for the success, and this reinforces the correct choices, and the intelligent agent learns from that. An example of the use of reinforcement learning is in financial trading where the reward function is calculated based on how profitable or not the transaction was.

8.3 DATA PRE-PROCESSING FOR MACHINE LEARNING

In Chapter 6 we covered data pre-processing and cleaning; this is important when it comes to machine learning, so do revisit Section 6.2 if you need to. In that section we went through various pre-processing techniques, including data exploration, handling missing data, and deduplication. Getting this right can make all the difference between being able to train a model with good performance and not. There are additional aspects of pre-processing that are specifically relevant to machine learning, we discuss these in this section and in Chapter 9.

8.3.1 Feature selection

Feature selection is all about selecting the best features from the available set of features in a dataset for use in machine learning algorithms. As mentioned earlier in the chapter, it is very important to get this right. If irrelevant features are left in the dataset, it can unnecessarily increase the complexity of the model, and yet if important features are removed, this can have a detrimental impact on the trained model as important information will have been lost. When feature selection is done correctly it results in improved performance of the model. The following processes can be used for feature selection:

- *Removal of features.* The decision to remove features can be made for various reasons, including when two features are highly correlated (see Section 8.4.2), making one of them redundant. A feature might also be removed when it has a lot of missing values or when it is not relevant (e.g., identifiers that do not have any contextual meaning in the dataset).
- *Recoding of features.* This involves mapping features to a set of required values; for instance, an additional feature can be created from age that classes a person as an adult or child.
- *Combining of features.* This tends to be done when a composite value that can be derived from two or more existing features is needed.

8.3.2 Feature engineering

Feature engineering is about transformation of raw data into relevant features for machine learning algorithms. The main aim is to get the data into suitable formats for the use by the machine learning algorithms. Some of the processes used for this are as follows:

● *Feature scaling.* In machine learning feature scaling is the process of making feature values fall into a specific range or scale. Sometimes in datasets features have very different scales or ranges and if not adjusted this could cause one set of features to dominate the analysis just because it is within a larger scale or range. Hence, feature scaling ensures no feature has a disproportionate impact on the outputs and for comparison purposes like is being compared with like. Two of the techniques for feature scaling in machine learning are normalization and standardization. With normalization the data is scaled to lie between 0 and 1. With standardization the data is scaled to have a mean of 0 and a standard deviation of 1.

● *Encoding categorical variables.* When input features are categorical, it is usual to need to encode them into numerical representations as most machine learning algorithms need the inputs in that form. There are several techniques for doing this encoding, including one-hot encoding and feature hashing.

● *Feature extraction.* This is the process used to extract useful features from the input data in natural language processing; these features are subsequently used to train machine learning models (Sarkar, 2019). For more detail see Chapter 9.

● *Feature selection.* As already mentioned, selecting the right features is part of the machine learning workflow. When done correctly, it helps to reduce computational complexity and improve the model performance.

8.3.3 Data quality issues

Identifying and resolving data quality issues is very important when it comes to the data that is used to fit machine learning models. If the data quality is substandard the model generated from this data will be too (Chapter 6 discusses quality issues and potential resolutions in data wrangling).

8.3.4 Exploratory data analysis

Exploratory data analysis is all about carrying out initial investigations on data to discover trends and patterns which could help to highlight any anomalies. Exploratory data analysis leads to better understanding of the data. It was covered in detail in Chapter 6 and is included here for completeness. See Section 6.3 for detailed information, including hands-on exercises.

In terms of pre-processing, an additional process is dimension reduction, which is used to reduce the number of features in a dataset while keeping relevant features (Uberoi, 2023).

8.4 MODEL TRAINING AND EVALUATION

In the various hands-on exercises in this chapter (and in Chapter 9) we will practise training various models. As well as following the exercises, it is important that you read the documentation for the various techniques and algorithms. For this chapter, you should familiarize yourself with the Apache Spark MLlib web page and refer to it often (https://spark. apache.org/mllib/). Before we start on the hands-on exercises, we will explore correlation and model evaluation metrics.

8.4.1 Prediction errors, overfitting, and underfitting

There are mainly three types of errors in supervised learning: irreducible error, bias error, and variance error. Irreducible error, as the name implies, is a product of the process out of our control. Bias error refers to the difference between the average prediction from the model and the actual value. When bias error is high the model is not well fitted to the training data (this is related to underfitting, described below). Variance error, on the other hand, is when the model is too well fitted to the training data but cannot generalize to unseen data (this is related to overfitting, described below). There is a trade-off between bias error and variance error inasmuch as reducing one increases the other.

Underfitting refers to the case where the algorithm is unable to produce a good estimate of the relationship between the input and the output, which means that even against the training data the model will not be suitable. Underfitting is very easy to spot, and the fix will usually be to try a different algorithm.

Overfitting, on the other hand, refers to a model that cannot generalize and is too well fitted to the training data (the training data is the portion of the input which has been put aside to train the model). Being too well fitted to the training data means that the model is fitted even to the noise in the training data and so has high accuracy, but it cannot generalize when applied to new input data that it has not previously seen and so its accuracy will be poor. Overfitting can be hard to spot and deal with. One way of trying to avoid overfitting is to split the input data not just into a training set and a test set, but also to include a validation set which serves as data that the model will not have previously seen. Another approach to combat overfitting is also to use a resampling technique like *k*-fold cross validation,[1] which is used to test how the model will perform on unseen data.

8.4.2 Correlation

Correlation coefficients are used to measure the strength of the relationship between two numeric variables. Correlation can be used as an aid in feature selection; for instance, when trying to predict a target variable, you might want to choose the features that are most highly correlated to that target. The type of feature selection method used is determined to a large extent by the type of input and output variables (i.e., numerical or categorical).

Correlation is a measure of the *linear* relationship between two variables (e.g. children's age and height). It takes values strictly between –1 and +1. A value of –1 (+1) denotes a perfect negative (positive) correlation, so that as one value increases the other decreases (increases). A value between ±0.5 and ±1 denotes strong correlation, between ±0.3 and ±0.5 moderate correlation, and below ±0.3 low correlation, while a value of 0 denotes no linear correlation.

In addition to producing individual correlation coefficients that display the correlation between two features, it is possible and useful in machine learning to generate a correlation matrix which is a square matrix which depicts the pairwise correlations between all the features in a dataset. In the example in Figure 8.4, from the correlation matrix we see the following:

- Features 1 and 2 have a strong positive correlation of 0.6, so as feature 1 increases, so does feature 2.
- Features 1 and 3 have a strong negative correlation of –0.7, so as feature 1 decreases, so does feature 3.
- Features 2 and 3 have a low correlation of 0.1.

	Feature 1	Feature 2	Feature 3
Feature 1	1	0.6	-0.7
Feature 2	0.6	1	0.1
Feature 3	-0.7	0.1	1

Figure 8.4   Example of a correlation matrix

In the hands-on exercises in subsequent sections of the chapter some practical coding for correlations will be done.

8.4.3 Model evaluation metrics

An evaluation metric quantifies the performance of a predictive model. This usually involves the following steps:

- Train the model on a dataset (training dataset).
- Use the model to make predictions using a test dataset not used during training.
- Compare the predictions to the expected values in the test dataset.

Some evaluation metrics can be seen in Figure 8.5.

The choice of which evaluation metrics to use for a machine learning model is an important one and in this subsection we discuss how to make this choice and consider some common evaluation metrics. The choice of which metric to use will depend on the type of problem you are trying to solve. Figure 8.5 depicts some of the evaluation metrics for classification, regression, and clustering. We discuss a few of these below and in the hands-on exercises. For further information on evaluation metrics see Burkov (2019).

- *Classification accuracy.* This is the percentage of correct predictions for the test data. It can be calculated easily by dividing the number of correct predictions by the number of total predictions:

Classification	Regression	Clustering
Accuracy	Mean Squared Error (MSE)	Silhouette Coefficient
Precision	Mean Absolute Error (MAE)	Adjusted Rand Index
Recall	R-squared (R²)	Dunn Index
F1-score	Root Mean Squared Error (RMSE)	
ROC-AUC		

Figure 8.5   Evaluation or performance metrics

$$\text{Accuracy} = \frac{\text{Number of correct predictions}}{\text{Total number of predictions}}$$

Mean absolute error (MAE). The MAE is the average absolute difference between the original values O_i and the predicted values P_i:

$$\text{MAE} = \frac{1}{N} \sum |P_i - O_i|$$

It thus gives a measure how far the predictions are from the actual values. However, it does not give any indication whether the model is underpredicting or overpredicting. It is often used for regression models.

- Root mean square error (RMSE). The RMSE takes the difference for each observed and predicted value and divides the sum of the differences by the number of observations:

$$\text{RM}\sqrt{\frac{\sum (P_i - O_i)^2}{n}}$$

The main difference between the MAE and RMSE is the contribution of individual error values to the final error value. For the MAE the contribution follows a linear pattern (e.g., an error of 40 contributes twice as much as an error of 20). This is not the case for the RMSE, where the squaring effect means that large errors are magnified, and small errors ignored. The MAE should be used for models where the error follows a linear pattern, while the RMSE should be used for models where large errors must be penalized but small errors can be tolerated.

8.5 MACHINE LEARNING TECHNIQUES FOR BIG DATA WITH HANDS-ON EXERCISES

In this section we will carry out some hands-on exercises. The hands-on exercises cover both supervised and unsupervised learning, two fundamental approaches to machine learning. For the exercises based on supervised learning, Figure 8.6 depicts a summary of the general steps that are taken.

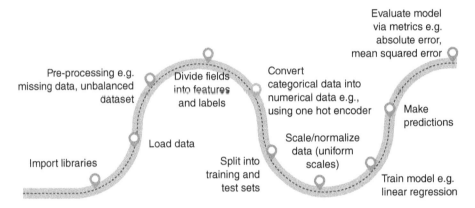

Figure 8.6   Supervised learning

For each of the hands-on exercise we will need a Jupyter Notebook to do our coding in, so let us start by opening a Jupyter Notebook (this was introduced in Chapter 3), this is depicted in Figure 8.7.

Figure 8.7   Opening up a new Jupyter Notebook

8.5.1 Supervised learning algorithms

Supervised learning is a type of machine learning where the model learns from labelled training data. In this approach, the training data consists of input features and corresponding target labels or outputs. The goal is to build a model that can accurately predict the correct output for new, unseen inputs. The model learns the relationship between the input features and the target labels by minimizing the error between its predictions and the actual labels in the training data. Supervised learning is commonly used for tasks such as classification, regression, and sequence prediction, where the model learns to make predictions based on known examples.

Linear regression

Linear regression is a machine learning algorithm that models a linear relationship between the inputs and output variable. For the hands-on exercise we will use the Apache Spark MLlib linear regression algorithm to predict loan amounts. Once a Jupyter Notebook is opened, the relevant libraries are imported and the dataset loaded into a DataFrame (Figure 8.8).

```
from pyspark.mllib.regression import LabeledPoint
from pyspark.ml.regression import LinearRegression
```

Figure 8.8   Import the relevant libraries

The next step is to choose the features to be included. The original dataset has lots of columns, many of which are not needed. As described below, correlation can be used to help select the features that are important, that is, have a large impact on the label that we are trying to predict. To illustrate this, in Figure 8.9 we check the strength of the relationship between individual features and the label (loan amount). The chosen features all have a positive correlation with the loan amount (with varying strengths). Instead of checking individual features we could also write code to return a correlation matrix to show the correlations between all the fields in the dataset.

The dataset is for a lending club and, based on relevant features in the dataset, we want to predict loan amounts that members will be given. Using the `printSchema()` command, we can see the full schema of the dataset. To simplify our example, we choose a few features to train our model; the target variable (label) is `loan_amnt` (the loan amount). Figure 8.10 shows the choice of features to be included.

Define `feature_columns` by removing the last column, which is the label, that is, the output to be predicted (see Figure 8.11).

We now need to transform the input into the format required by the machine learning algorithm. To help with this we import `VectorAssembler`,[2] which is a feature transformer that merges multiple columns into a vector column (see Figure 8.12).

Next, the `VectorAssembler` function is used to create the `features` vector column by merging the input feature columns (see Figure 8.13).

The `randomSplit` command is then used to split into the training and test datasets (Figure 8.14).

```
root
 |-- id: string (nullable = true)
 |-- member_id: string (nullable = true)
 |-- loan_amnt: integer (nullable = true)
 |-- funded_amnt: integer (nullable = true)
 |-- funded_amnt_inv: integer (nullable = true)
 |-- term: string (nullable = true)
 |-- int_rate: string (nullable = true)
 |-- installment: double (nullable = true)
 |-- grade: string (nullable = true)
 |-- sub_grade: string (nullable = true)
 |-- emp_title: string (nullable = true)
 |-- emp_length: string (nullable = true)
 |-- home_ownership: string (nullable = true)
 |-- annual_inc: double (nullable = true)
 |-- verification_status: string (nullable = true)
 |-- issue_d: string (nullable = true)
 |-- loan_status: string (nullable = true)
 |-- pymnt_plan: string (nullable = true)
 |-- url: string (nullable = true)
 |-- desc: string (nullable = true)
 |-- purpose: string (nullable = true)
 |-- title: string (nullable = true)
 |-- zip_code: string (nullable = true)
 |-- addr_state: string (nullable = true)
 |-- dti: double (nullable = true)
 |-- delinq_2yrs: integer (nullable = true)
 |-- earliest_cr_line: string (nullable = true)
 |-- inq_last_6mths: integer (nullable = true)
 |-- mths_since_last_delinq: integer (nullable = true)
 |-- mths_since_last_record: integer (nullable = true)
 |-- open_acc: integer (nullable = true)
 |-- pub_rec: integer (nullable = true)
 |-- revol_bal: integer (nullable = true)
 |-- revol_util: string (nullable = true)
 |-- total_acc: integer (nullable = true)
 |-- initial_list_status: string (nullable = true)
 |-- out_prncp: double (nullable = true)
 |-- out_prncp_inv: double (nullable = true)
 |-- total_pymnt: double (nullable = true)
 |-- total_pymnt_inv: double (nullable = true)
 |-- total_rec_prncp: double (nullable = true)
 |-- total_rec_int: double (nullable = true)
```

```
|-- total_rec_late_fee: double (nullable = true)
|-- recoveries: double (nullable = true)
|-- collection_recovery_fee: double (nullable = true)
|-- last_pymnt_d: string (nullable = true)
|-- last_pymnt_amnt: double (nullable = true)
|-- next_pymnt_d: string (nullable = true)
|-- last_credit_pull_d: string (nullable = true)
|-- collections_12_mths_ex_med: integer (nullable = true)
|-- mths_since_last_major_derog: integer (nullable = true)
|-- policy_code: integer (nullable = true)
|-- application_type: string (nullable = true)
|-- annual_inc_joint: string (nullable = true)
|-- dti_joint: string (nullable = true)
|-- verification_status_joint: string (nullable = true)
|-- acc_now_delinq: integer (nullable = true)
|-- tot_coll_amt: integer (nullable = true)
|-- tot_cur_bal: integer (nullable = true)
|-- open_acc_6m: string (nullable = true)
|-- open_act_il: string (nullable = true)
|-- open_il_12m: string (nullable = true)
|-- open_il_24m: string (nullable = true)
|-- mths_since_rcnt_il: string (nullable = true)
|-- total_bal_il: string (nullable = true)
|-- il_util: string (nullable = true)
|-- open_rv_12m: string (nullable = true)
|-- open_rv_24m: string (nullable = true)
|-- max_bal_bc: string (nullable = true)
|-- all_util: string (nullable = true)
|-- total_rev_hi_lim: integer (nullable = true)
|-- inq_fi: string (nullable = true)
|-- total_cu_tl: string (nullable = true)
|-- inq_last_12m: string (nullable = true)
|-- acc_open_past_24mths: integer (nullable = true)
|-- avg_cur_bal: integer (nullable = true)
|-- bc_open_to_buy: integer (nullable = true)
|-- bc_util: double (nullable = true)
|-- chargeoff_within_12_mths: integer (nullable = true)
|-- delinq_amnt: integer (nullable = true)
|-- mo_sin_old_il_acct: integer (nullable = true)
|-- mo_sin_old_rev_tl_op: integer (nullable = true)
|-- mo_sin_rcnt_rev_tl_op: integer (nullable = true)
|-- mo_sin_rcnt_tl: integer (nullable = true)
```

(Continued)

Figure 8.9 (Continued)

```
|-- mort_acc: integer (nullable = true)
|-- mths_since_recent_bc: integer (nullable = true)
|-- mths_since_recent_bc_dlq: integer (nullable = true)
|-- mths_since_recent_inq: integer (nullable = true)
|-- mths_since_recent_revol_delinq: integer (nullable = true)
|-- num_accts_ever_120_pd: integer (nullable = true)
|-- num_actv_bc_tl: integer (nullable = true)
|-- num_actv_rev_tl: integer (nullable = true)
|-- num_bc_sats: integer (nullable = true)
|-- num_bc_tl: integer (nullable = true)
|-- num_il_tl: integer (nullable = true)
|-- num_op_rev_tl: integer (nullable = true)
|-- num_rev_accts: integer (nullable = true)
|-- num_rev_tl_bal_gt_0: integer (nullable = true)
|-- num_sats: integer (nullable = true)
|-- num_tl_120dpd_2m: integer (nullable = true)
|-- num_tl_30dpd: integer (nullable = true)
|-- num_tl_90g_dpd_24m: integer (nullable = true)
|-- num_tl_op_past_12m: integer (nullable = true)
|-- pct_tl_nvr_dlq: double (nullable = true)
|-- percent_bc_gt_75: double (nullable = true)
|-- pub_rec_bankruptcies: integer (nullable = true)
|-- tax_liens: integer (nullable = true)
|-- tot_hi_cred_lim: integer (nullable = true)
|-- total_bal_ex_mort: integer (nullable = true)
|-- total_bc_limit: integer (nullable = true)
|-- total_il_high_credit_limit: integer (nullable = true)
|-- revol_bal_joint: string (nullable = true)
|-- sec_app_earliest_cr_line: string (nullable = true)
|-- sec_app_inq_last_6mths: string (nullable = true)
|-- sec_app_mort_acc: string (nullable = true)
|-- sec_app_open_acc: string (nullable = true)
|-- sec_app_revol_util: string (nullable = true)
|-- sec_app_open_act_il: string (nullable = true)
|-- sec_app_num_rev_accts: string (nullable = true)
|-- sec_app_chargeoff_within_12_mths: string (nullable = true)
|-- sec_app_collections_12_mths_ex_med: string (nullable = true)
|-- sec_app_mths_since_last_major_derog: string (nullable = true)
|-- hardship_flag: string (nullable = true)
|-- hardship_type: string (nullable = true)
|-- hardship_reason: string (nullable = true)
```

```
|-- hardship_status: string (nullable = true)
|-- deferral_term: integer (nullable = true)
|-- hardship_amount: double (nullable = true)
|-- hardship_start_date: string (nullable = true)
|-- hardship_end_date: string (nullable = true)
|-- payment_plan_start_date: string (nullable = true)
|-- hardship_length: integer (nullable = true)
|-- hardship_dpd: integer (nullable = true)
|-- hardship_loan_status: string (nullable = true)
|-- orig_projected_additional_accrued_interest: double (nullable = true)
|-- hardship_payoff_balance_amount: double (nullable = true)
|-- hardship_last_payment_amount: double (nullable = true)
|-- debt_settlement_flag: string (nullable = true)
|-- debt_settlement_flag_date: string (nullable = true)
|-- settlement_status: string (nullable = true)
|-- settlement_date: string (nullable = true)
|-- settlement_amount: double (nullable = true)
|-- settlement_percentage: double (nullable = true)
|-- settlement_term: integer (nullable = true)


from pyspark.ml.stat import Correlation


data_ml.stat.corr("annual_inc","loan_amnt")


Output:
0.3919615305715742


data_ml.stat.corr("last_pymnt_amnt","loan_amnt")


Output:
0.4243182145422379


data_ml.stat.corr("installment","loan_amnt")


Output:
0.9478973044210571


data.stat.corr("total_pymnt","loan_amnt")


Output:
0.8930317733309153
```

Figure 8.9 **Full schema and correlations between individual features and the label**
(`loan_amnt`)

```
data_ml=data.selectExpr("installment","annual_inc","total_rec_late_fee","last_
pymnt_amnt","delinq_amnt","loan_amnt")
```

```
data_ml
```

```
Output:
DataFrame[installment: double, annual_inc: double, total_rec_late_fee: double,
last_pymnt_amnt: double, delinq_amnt: int, loan_amnt: int]
```

```
data_ml.printSchema()
```

```
Output:
root
 |-- installment: double (nullable = true)
 |-- annual_inc: double (nullable = true)
 |-- total_rec_late_fee: double (nullable = true)
 |-- last_pymnt_amnt: double (nullable = true)
 |-- delinq_amnt: integer (nullable = true)
 |-- loan_amnt: integer (nullable = true)
```

```
data_ml.show()
Output:
```

```
+-----------+----------+------------------+---------------+-----------+---------+
|installment|annual_inc|total_rec_late_fee|last_pymnt_amnt|delinq_amnt|loan_amnt|
+-----------+----------+------------------+---------------+-----------+---------+
|     321.08|   58000.0|               0.0|         321.08|          0|    10400|
|     336.64|   78000.0|               0.0|       12017.81|          0|    15000|
|     326.53|   69000.0|               0.0|        9338.58|          0|     9600|
|      260.2|   50000.0|               0.0|           17.7|          0|     7650|
|     319.08|  125000.0|               0.0|         319.08|          0|    12800|
|     516.36|   63800.0|               0.0|       17813.19|          0|    21425|
|     578.22|   75000.0|               0.0|       10888.01|          0|    17000|
|     800.71|   72000.0|               0.0|         800.71|          0|    23325|
|      83.03|   89000.0|               0.0|        2294.26|          0|     2500|
|     468.17|   60000.0|               0.0|           50.0|          0|    12975|
|     172.98|   26000.0|               0.0|           43.4|          0|     5250|
|      351.4|  109777.0|               0.0|        4935.54|          0|    16000|
|      332.1|   90000.0|               0.0|          332.1|          0|    10000|
|     581.95|   55000.0|               0.0|         581.95|          0|    21075|
|      70.31|   37000.0|               0.0|        1255.43|          0|     2000|
|     194.99|  120000.0|               0.0|          578.3|          0|     6000|
|       97.5|   60000.0|               0.0|        1117.63|          0|     3000|
|      69.33|   32200.0|               0.0|        1897.69|          0|     2000|
|     140.61|   50000.0|              15.0|         1606.9|          0|     4000|
|      601.7|   67000.0|               0.0|       24652.44|          0|    28000|
+-----------+----------+------------------+---------------+-----------+---------+
only showing top 20 rows
```

Figure 8.10 Features selected

```
# create features array (all fields except last field)

feature_columns = data_ml.columns[:-1]

feature_columns
```

Output:
```
['installment',
 'annual_inc',
 'total_rec_late_fee',
 'last_pymnt_amnt',
 'delinq_amnt']
```

Figure 8.11   Removing label

```
from pyspark.ml.feature import VectorAssembler

# creating a features array by passing a list of features to the
VectorAssembler class
#outputCol="festures" -> name of output vector that combines all the values

assembler=VectorAssembler(inputCols=feature_columns,outputCol="features")
```

Figure 8.12   Applying VectorAssembler to the input columns

```
data2 = assembler.transform(data_ml)

data2.show()
```

Output:

installment	annual_inc	total_rec_late_fee	last_pymnt_amnt	delinq_amnt	loan_amnt	features
321.08	58000.0	0.0	321.08	0	10400	[321.08,58000.0,0...|
336.64	78000.0	0.0	12017.81	0	15000	[336.64,78000.0,0...|
326.53	69000.0	0.0	9338.58	0	9600	[326.53,69000.0,0...|
260.2	50000.0	0.0	17.7	0	7650	[260.2,50000.0,0,...|
319.08	125000.0	0.0	319.08	0	12800	[319.08,125000.0,0...|
516.36	63800.0	0.0	17813.19	0	21425	[516.36,63800.0,0...|
578.22	75000.0	0.0	10888.01	0	17000	[578.22,75000.0,0...|
800.71	72000.0	0.0	800.71	0	23325	[800.71,72000.0,0...|
83.03	89000.0	0.0	2294.26	0	2500	[83.03,89000.0,0....|
468.17	60000.0	0.0	50.0	0	12975	[468.17,60000.0,0...|
172.98	26000.0	0.0	43.4	0	5250	[172.98,26000.0,0...|
351.4	109777.0	0.0	4935.54	0	16000	[351.4,109777.0,0...|
332.1	90000.0	0.0	332.1	0	10000	[332.1,90000.0,0,...|
581.95	55000.0	0.0	581.95	0	21075	[581.95,55000.0,0...|
70.31	37000.0	0.0	1255.43	0	2000	[70.31,37000.0,0....|
194.99	120000.0	0.0	578.3	0	6000	[194.99,120000.0,...|
97.5	60000.0	0.0	1117.63	0	3000	[97.5,60000.0,0.0...|
69.33	32200.0	0.0	1897.69	0	2000	[69.33,32200.0,0,...|
140.61	50000.0	15.0	1606.9	0	4000	[140.61,50000.0,1...|
601.7	67000.0	0.0	24652.44	0	28000	[601.7,67000.0,0....|

only showing top 20 rows

Figure 8.13   Creating the vector column using VectorAssembler

```
train, test = data2.randomSplit([0.7,0.3])
```

Figure 8.14   Creating training and test datasets

Now the linear regression algorithm can be applied to fit the model and the model then used to make predictions (see Figure 8.15).

Figure 8.16 shows the loan amount and the predicted values. Figure 8.17 shows some evaluation metrics.

Logistic regression

Logistic regression is used to analyse the relationship between a dependent variable and one or more independent variables. The main objective of logistic regression is to fit the model that best predicts the probability of the dependent variable being a particular value, given the values of the independent variables.

For our logistic regression example, we will use the popular Titanic dataset. The Titanic Disaster Dataset is an iconic dataset in the field of data science and machine learning. It comprises information about the passengers on board the RMS Titanic, which tragically sank on its maiden voyage in April 1912 after colliding with an iceberg. This dataset serves as a historical record and has been widely used for educational and analytical purposes. The dataset provides details on various attributes of the passengers, including their age, gender, class of ticket, number of siblings or spouses aboard, number of parents or children aboard,

```
# using the linear regression algorithm, specify feature columns name and the
label name
algorithm = LinearRegression(featuresCol="features", labelCol="loan_amnt")


# train the model using the fit method on the train dataset
LRModel = algorithm.fit(train)


# make predictions using the model on the test dataset
predictions = LRModel.transform(test)
```

Figure 8.15 Fitting the model and using it to make predictions

```
predictions.show()
+-----------+---------+------------------+---------------+----------+---------+--------------------+------------------+
|installment|annual_inc|total_rec_late_fee|last_pymnt_amnt|deling_amnt|loan_amnt|            features|        prediction|
+-----------+---------+------------------+---------------+----------+---------+--------------------+------------------+
|      30.88|  33000.0|               0.0|         122.25|         0|     1000|[30.88,33000.0,0....| 1369.1942103805433|
|      31.11|  60000.0|               0.0|         391.12|         0|     1000|[31.11,60000.0,0....| 1504.5841199343683|
|      31.43|  85000.0|               0.0|        1008.38|         0|     1000|[31.43,85000.0,0....| 1671.6369177281686|
|      31.88|  45000.0|               0.0|          31.84|         0|     1000|[31.88,45000.0,0....| 1435.5951400607914|
|      32.95|  30000.0|               0.0|         630.27|         0|     1000|[32.95,30000.0,0....| 1475.6054462925814|
|      33.45|  61000.0|               0.0|         227.32|         0|     1000|[33.45,61000.0,0....| 1564.4333012678028|
|      33.69|  11000.0|               0.0|          12.99|         0|     1000|[33.69,11000.0,15...| 1562.4453443095235|
|      33.69|  16000.0|               0.0|          33.65|         0|     1000|[33.69,16000.0,0....| 1384.7702575861315|
|      33.69|  29750.0|               0.0|         562.71|         0|     1000|[33.69,29750.0,0....| 1490.8798928433628|
|      33.69|  40000.0|               0.0|         200.75|         0|     1000|[33.69,40000.0,0....| 1491.2372520175854|
|      33.87|  75000.0|               0.0|         133.14|         0|     1000|[33.87,75000.0,0....| 1619.7229443971669|
|      34.33|  30000.0|               0.0|         617.85|         0|     1000|[34.33,30000.0,0....| 1517.5662814820685|
|      34.33|  54000.0|               0.0|         352.83|         0|     1000|[34.33,54000.0,0....| 1579.0458721354294|
|      34.33|  60000.0|               0.0|          34.26|         0|     1000|[34.33,60000.0,0....| 1568.1476109895732|
|      34.33|  60000.0|               0.0|         090.02|         0|     1000|[34.33,60000.0,0....| 1667.6504366766644|
|      34.33|  75500.0|               0.0|          34.26|         0|     1000|[34.33,75500.0,0....| 1625.6722760290506|
|      34.33|  95000.0|               0.0|         326.4|          0|     1000|[34.33,95000.0,0....| 1728.4562993109835|
|      34.33| 110000.0|               0.0|          34.26|         0|     1000|[34.33,110000.0,0....|  1753.711846600791|
|      34.67|  23000.0|               0.0|         620.58|         0|     1000|[34.67,23000.0,0....| 1502.5061921048518|
|      34.67|  36340.0|               0.0|          34.67|         0|     1000|[34.67,36340.0,0....| 1491.016252937606|
+-----------+---------+------------------+---------------+----------+---------+--------------------+------------------+
only showing top 20 rows
```

Figure 8.16 The actual loan amount and the predicted loan amount

```
from pyspark.ml.evaluation import RegressionEvaluator


# Mean Absolute Error (R2)
evaluator=RegressionEvaluator(labelCol="loan_amnt",predictionCol=
"prediction", metricName="r2")
r2 = evaluator.evaluate(predictions)
print(" Mean Absolute Error (R2) on test data = %g" % r2)


Output:
Mean Absolute Error (R2) on test data = 0.903805


# Mean Squared Error (MSE)

evaluator=RegressionEvaluator(labelCol="loan_amnt",predictionCol=
"prediction",metricName="mse")
mse = evaluator.evaluate(predictions)
print(" Mean Squared Error (MSE) on test data = %g" % mse)


Output:
Mean Squared Error (MSE) on test data = 6.86036e+06


#Root Mean Squared Error (RMSE)

evaluator=RegressionEvaluator(labelCol="loan_amnt",predictionCol="prediction",
metricName="rmse")
rmse = evaluator.evaluate(predictions)
print("Root Mean Squared Error (RMSE) on test data = %g" % rmse)


Output:
Root Mean Squared Error (RMSE) on test data = 2619.23
```

Figure 8.17 Evaluation metrics

ticket fare, cabin number, and whether they survived or not. Let us start with considering the schema of the dataset, as it is presented in Figure 8.18. This shows all the features in the dataset and their datatypes; for instance, Age can be seen to be of data type double, while Sex is of type string. This schema also shows that all the features have nullable = true, which means they can have null values. This dataset can be downloaded using the link provided on this book's online resources website.

In what follows, we demonstrate the process of developing the algorithm, a process that involves troubleshooting and a range of procedures to resolve issues such as missing data, incorrect data types and the need to encode categorical data types prior to passing them into the machine learning algorithm. Troubleshooting is an invaluable skillset for a developer or analyst to have.

Our first task is to develop a model to 'predict' whether a passenger survives the disaster of the Titanic, given the passenger's features (age, sex etc). Our first code implements a simple binary classification model (to predict either 'survived' or 'did not survive'), the name of the model is a logistic regression model (see Figure 8.19).

```
root
 |-- PassengerId: integer (nullable = true)
 |-- Survived: integer (nullable = true)
 |-- Pclass: double (nullable = true)
 |-- Name: string (nullable = true)
 |-- Sex: string (nullable = true)
 |-- Age: double (nullable = true)
 |-- SibSp: double (nullable = true)
 |-- Parch: double (nullable = true)
 |-- Ticket: string (nullable = true)
 |-- Fare: double (nullable = true)
 |-- Cabin: string (nullable = true)
 |-- Embarked: string (nullable = true)
 |-- SexIndex: double (nullable = false)
 |-- Parch_imputed: double (nullable = true)
 |-- Fare_imputed: double (nullable = true)
 |-- SibSp_imputed: double (nullable = true)
 |-- Age_imputed: double (nullable = true)
 |-- Pclass_imputed: double (nullable = true)
```

Figure 8.18   Schema of the Titanic dataset

```
from pyspark.sql import SparkSession
from pyspark.ml.feature import VectorAssembler
from pyspark.ml.classification import LogisticRegression

# Create a SparkSession
spark = SparkSession.builder.appName("LogisticRegressionHandsOn").getOrCreate()

# Load the Titanic dataset from CSV
titanic_data = spark.read.csv("titanic.csv", header=True, inferSchema=True)

# Select relevant features and target variable
selected_features = ["Age", "Fare", "Pclass", "Sex", "SibSp", "Parch"]
target_variable = "Survived"

# Create a vector assembler to combine features into a feature vector
assembler=VectorAssembler(inputCols=selected_features, outputCol="features")
feature_vector=assembler.transform(titanic_data).select("features", target_
variable)
```

```
# Split the data into training and testing sets
(training_data, testing_data) = feature_vector.randomSplit([0.8, 0.2], seed=42)

# Create a Logistic Regression model
lr = LogisticRegression(labelCol=target_variable, featuresCol="features")

# Fit the model to the training data
lr_model = lr.fit(training_data)

# Make predictions on the testing data
predictions = lr_model.transform(testing_data)

# Evaluate the model's performance
accuracy = predictions.filter(predictions[target_variable] ==
predictions["prediction"]).count() / float(predictions.count())
print("Accuracy: {:.2%}".format(accuracy))
```

```
Error Message:
Py4JJavaError: An error occurred while calling o1675.transform.
: java.lang.IllegalArgumentException: Data type string of column Sex is not
supported.
```

Figure 8.19 Logistic regression code for Titanic data with error message

When we run the code in Figure 8.19, we get an error message which indicates that we need to encode the Sex feature which currently holds string values, that is, it is a categorical variable, while the algorithm needs numeric values. To fix this we use the StringIndexer transformer to encode the categorical Sex variable in Figure 8.20 (see highlighted text).

With the amended code, the initial error message is gone. However, we now have a new error message (see Figure 8.20). This error message indicates that VectorAssembler is having problems with the null values. As seen in the section on pre-processing (Section 8.3), this can be handled in different ways. In this hands-on exercise two techniques are used. First we drop rows with null values and then we also add an Imputer transformer to handle missing values by replacing null values with the mean value of the feature (see highlighted rows in Figure 8.21).

The error message in Figure 8.21 alerts us that the previous error has now been resolved but we still have another error. This time around we have a few features that are of the wrong data types (e.g., PClass should be a double or float but is of type int). To resolve this, we cast the affected columns as shown in the highlighted text in Figure 8.22.

Learning to troubleshoot is an important skill, and the more you do hands-on exercises and actively troubleshoot the more confident and better you will become at it.

```
from pyspark.sql import SparkSession
from pyspark.ml.feature import VectorAssembler, StringIndexer
from pyspark.ml.classification import LogisticRegression

# Create a SparkSession
spark = SparkSession.builder.appName("LogisticRegressionHandsOn").getOrCreate()

# Load the Titanic dataset from CSV
titanic_data = spark.read.csv("titanic.csv", header=True, inferSchema=True)

# Select relevant features and target variable
selected_features = ["Age", "Fare", "Pclass", "SibSp", "Parch"]
target_variable = "Survived"

# Convert categorical variable 'Sex' to numerical values
indexer = StringIndexer(inputCol="Sex", outputCol="SexIndex")
titanic_data = indexer.fit(titanic_data).transform(titanic_data)

# Create a vector assembler to combine features into a feature vector
assembler = VectorAssembler(inputCols=selected_features + ["SexIndex"],
outputCol="features")
feature_vector = assembler.transform(titanic_data).select("features", target_variable)

# Split the data into training and testing sets
(training_data, testing_data) = feature_vector.randomSplit([0.8, 0.2], seed=42)

# Create a Logistic Regression model
lr = LogisticRegression(labelCol=target_variable, featuresCol="features")

# Fit the model to the training data
lr_model = lr.fit(training_data)

# Make predictions on the testing data
predictions = lr_model.transform(testing_data)

# Evaluate the model's performance
accuracy = predictions.filter(predictions[target_variable] == predictions["prediction"]).
count() / float(predictions.count())
print("Accuracy: {:.2%}".format(accuracy))

Error Message:
Caused by: org.apache.spark.SparkException: Encountered null while assembling a row with
handleInvalid = "keep". Consider removing nulls from dataset or using handleInvalid =
"keep" or "skip".
```

Figure 8.20 Logistic regression code for Titanic data with another error message

```python
from pyspark.sql import SparkSession
from pyspark.ml.feature import VectorAssembler, StringIndexer, Imputer
from pyspark.ml.classification import LogisticRegression

# Create a SparkSession
spark = SparkSession.builder.appName("LogisticRegressionHandsOn").getOrCreate()

# Load the Titanic dataset from CSV
titanic_data = spark.read.csv("titanic.csv", header=True, inferSchema=True)

# Select relevant features and target variable
selected_features = ["Age", "Fare", "Pclass", "SibSp", "Parch"]
target_variable = "Survived"

# Drop rows with null values
titanic_data=titanic_data.dropna(subset=selected_features + [target_variable])

# Convert categorical variable 'Sex' to numerical values
indexer = StringIndexer(inputCol="Sex", outputCol="SexIndex")
titanic_data = indexer.fit(titanic_data).transform(titanic_data)

# Handle missing values in selected features
imputer = Imputer(inputCols=selected_features, outputCols=[f"{col}_imputed" for col in
selected_features])
titanic_data=imputer.setStrategy("mean").fit(titanic_data).transform(titanic_data)

# Create a vector assembler to combine features into a feature vector
assembler = VectorAssembler(inputCols=[f"{col}_imputed" for col in selected_
features] + ["SexIndex"],
                            outputCol="features")
feature_vector = assembler.transform(titanic_data).select("features", target_
variable)

# Split the data into training and testing sets
(training_data, testing_data) = feature_vector.randomSplit([0.8, 0.2], seed=42)

# Create a Logistic Regression model
lr = LogisticRegression(labelCol=target_variable, featuresCol="features")

# Fit the model to the training data
lr_model = lr.fit(training_data)

# Make predictions on the testing data
predictions = lr_model.transform(testing_data)
```

(Continued)

Figure 8.21 (Continued)

```
# Evaluate the model's performance
accuracy = predictions.filter(predictions[target_variable] ==
predictions["prediction"]).count() / float(predictions.count())
print("Accuracy: {:.2%}".format(accuracy))


Error Message:
Py4JJavaError: An error occurred while calling o1917.fit.
: java.lang.IllegalArgumentException: requirement failed: Column Pclass must
be of type equal to one of the following types: [double, float] but was
actually of type int.
```

Figure 8.21 Logistic regression code for Titanic data with a third error message

```
from pyspark.sql import SparkSession
from pyspark.ml.feature import VectorAssembler, StringIndexer, Imputer
from pyspark.ml.classification import LogisticRegression
from pyspark.sql.functions import col


# Create a spark session
spark=SparkSession.builder.appName("LogisticRegressionHandsOn").getOrCreate()


# Load the Titanic dataset from CSV
titanic_data = spark.read.csv("titanic.csv", header=True, inferSchema=True)


# Select relevant features and target variable
selected_features = ["Age", "Fare", "Pclass", "SibSp", "Parch"]
target_variable = "Survived"


# Drop rows with null values
titanic_data=titanic_data.dropna(subset=selected_features + [target_variable])


# Convert categorical variable 'Sex' to numerical values
indexer = StringIndexer(inputCol="Sex", outputCol="SexIndex")
titanic_data = indexer.fit(titanic_data).transform(titanic_data)


# Cast the "Pclass" column to double type
titanic_data=titanic_data.withColumn("Pclass", col("Pclass").cast("double"))


# Cast the "SibSp" column to double type
titanic_data= titanic_data.withColumn("SibSp", col("SibSp").cast("double"))
```

```
# Cast the "Parch" column to double type
titanic_data= titanic_data.withColumn("Parch", col("Parch").cast("double"))
```

```
# Handle missing values in selected features
imputer = Imputer(inputCols=selected_features, outputCols=[f"{col}_imputed"
for col in selected_features])
titanic_data = imputer.setStrategy("mean").fit(titanic_data).transform(titanic_
data)
```

```
# Create a vector assembler to combine features into a feature vector
assembler = VectorAssembler(inputCols=[f"{col}_imputed" for col in selected_
features] + ["SexIndex"],
                            outputCol="features")
feature_vector=assembler.transform(titanic_data).select("features", target_
variable)
```

```
# Split the data into training and testing sets
(training_data, testing_data) = feature_vector.randomSplit([0.8, 0.2],
seed=42)
```

```
# Create a Logistic Regression model
lr = LogisticRegression(labelCol=target_variable, featuresCol="features")
```

```
# Fit the model to the training data
lr_model = lr.fit(training_data)
```

```
# Make predictions on the testing data
predictions = lr_model.transform(testing_data)
```

```
# Evaluate the model's performance
accuracy = predictions.filter(predictions[target_variable] ==
predictions["prediction"]).count() / float(predictions.count())
print("Accuracy: {:.2%}".format(accuracy))
```

```
Output:
Accuracy: 80.60%
```

Figure 8.22 **Final working logistic regression code for Titanic data (with output)**

An alternative to the logistic regression model is the naïve Bayes model. Similar to the logistic model, this approach is designed to develop a model that can predict outcomes in a dataset. In the following hands-on exercise we will use naïve Bayes to implement a spam filter, to distinguish between spam text messages and good ones (Figure 8.23). The dataset used for this example is the SMS Spam Collection (Almeida and Hidalgo, 2012), which is a public set of SMS labelled messages for mobile phone spam research.

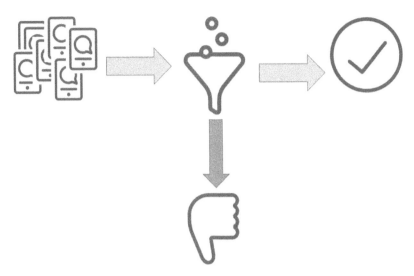

Figure 8.23   Spam filter

As usual we import the relevant libraries into the Jupyter Notebook (see Figure 8.24). Then we load the data into an RDD (Figure 8.25). Remember to change this path to the path where your file is.

The data currently holds both spam text messages and ham (good) text messages. To eventually be able to train the model we need to split these up. So, in Figure 8.27 we create an RDD with just spam using the `filter` transformation. To understand the code, you need to understand the raw data that has been uploaded into the RDD.

Figure 8.26 shows a snippet of the data in the file. What you have are two columns separated by a tab: the first column holds a label which is either `ham` (for good messages) or `spam` (for junk messages) and the second column holds the actual text message. With this in mind we can now examine the code in Figure 8.26.

Now we split the data in the original RDD using tab as the delimiter and then only return data where the first column holds the value `spam`. Where this criterion is met, the relevant row is copied into the new RDD `spamRDD1` (see Figure 8.27). The new RDD has every row with first column equal to `spam` (see Figure 8.28).

Next, we create a new RDD `spam` which contains the contents of the second column in `spamRDD1`, that is, just the actual SMS text without the label `spam` from the first column (Figure 8.29). We then do the same for the ham messages (Figure 8.30).

```
from pyspark.mllib.regression import LabeledPoint
from pyspark.mllib.classification import NaiveBayes
from pyspark.mllib.feature import HashingTF
```

Figure 8.24   Importing relevant libraries

```
inputRdd = sc.textFile("hdfs:///data/SMSSpamCollection.txt")
```

```
inputRdd.first()
```

Output:

'ham\tGo until jurong point, crazy.. Available only in bugis n great world la
e buffet... Cine there got amore wat...'

Figure 8.25 Uploading data and viewing the first line of the contents of the RDD

ham	Wait that's still not all that clear, were you not sure about me being..
ham	Yeah he got in at 2 and was v apologetic...
spam	Free entry in 2 a wkly comp to win FA Cup final tkts 21st May 2005.
ham	I see the letter B on my car …
ham	Nah I don't think he goes to usf, he lives around here though
spam	FreeMsg Hey there darling it's been 3 week's now and no word back! I'd
ham	Even my brother is not like to speak with me. They treat me like aids
ham	As per your request 'Melle Melle (Oru Minnaminunginte Nurungu Vettam)'
spam	WINNER!! As a valued network customer you have been selected to

Figure 8.26 Snippet of raw data in the file

```
# create a new RDD spamRDD1
spamRDD1 = inputRdd.filter(lambda x: x.split("\t")[0] == 'spam')
```

Figure 8.27 Creating an RDD with just spam labels and messages using filter

"spam\tFree entry in 2 a wkly comp to win FA Cup final tkts 21st May 2005.
Text FA to 87121 to receive entry question(std txt rate)T&C's apply
08452810075over18's",

 "spam\tFreeMsg Hey there darling it's been 3 week's now and no word back!
I'd like some fun you up for it still? Tb ok! XxX std chgs to send, £1.50 to
rcv",

 'spam\tWINNER!! As a valued network customer you have been selected to
receivea £900 prize reward! To claim call 09061701461. Claim code KL341.
Valid 12 hours only.',

 'spam\tHad your mobile 11 months or more? U R entitled to Update to the
latest colour mobiles with camera for Free! Call The Mobile Update Co FREE on
08002986030',

 'spam\tSIX chances to win CASH! From 100 to 20,000 pounds txt> CSH11 and
send to 87575. Cost 150p/day, 6days, 16+ TsandCs apply Reply HL 4 info',

 'spam\tURGENT! You have won a 1 week FREE membership in our £100,000 Prize
Jackpot! Txt the word: CLAIM to No: 81010 T&C www.dbuk.net LCCLTD POBOX
4403LDNW1A7RW18',

 'spam\tXXXMobileMovieClub: To use your credit, click the WAP link in
the next txt message or click here>> http://wap. xxxmobilemovieclub.
com?n=QJKGIGHJJGCBL',

Figure 8.28 Snippet showing contents of spamRDD1

```
spam = spamRDD1.map(lambda x : x.split("\t")[1])
```

Figure 8.29 Creating an RDD with just spam messages (labels have been dropped)

```
hamRDD1 = inputRdd.filter(lambda x: x.split("\t")[0] == 'ham')
ham = hamRDD1.map(lambda x : x.split("\t")[1])
```

Figure 8.30 Creating an RDD with ham messages

We now have RDDs that hold the spam and ham messages. However, we still have the challenge that these text messages are in English. For the machine learning algorithm to be able to use them to train a model we need to convert these to numeric data. There are different algorithms for doing this, and in this exercise we will use the HashingTF[3] function. This function maps words into vectors of features.

First, we define the HashingTF instance which we will use (Figure 8.31). Next, each text message is split into words, and each word is then mapped to one feature. The HashingTF instance tf is applied to the contents of the spam and ham RDDs which are split into words by using space (i.e. " ") as a delimiter (see Figure 8.32). If we look at the contents of the newly created RDDs we will see that the words from the messages have been mapped to vector of features (see Figure 8.33).

```
tf = HashingTF(numFeatures = 100)
```

Figure 8.31 Creating a HashingTF instance to map SMS text to vectors of 100 features

```
spamFeatures = spam.map(lambda sms: tf.transform(sms.split(" ")))

hamFeatures = ham.map(lambda sms: tf.transform(sms.split(" ")))
```

Figure 8.32 Splitting the messages into words and mapping them to features using the HashingTF instance

```
spamFeatures.take(5)
```

```
Output:
[SparseVector(100, {4: 1.0, 5: 1.0, 8: 1.0, 9: 2.0, 24: 2.0, 27: 1.0, 33:
1.0, 42: 1.0, 47: 1.0, 48: 1.0, 52: 1.0, 55: 1.0, 59: 1.0, 61: 1.0, 62: 1.0,
65: 4.0, 68: 1.0, 69: 1.0, 71: 1.0, 83: 1.0, 88: 1.0, 89: 2.0}),
```

```
SparseVector(100, {1: 1.0, 3: 1.0, 9: 1.0, 15: 1.0, 21: 1.0, 23: 1.0, 24:
1.0, 27: 2.0, 35: 1.0, 36: 1.0, 37: 1.0, 39: 1.0, 40: 1.0, 45: 1.0, 49: 1.0,
55: 1.0, 65: 3.0, 66: 1.0, 67: 2.0, 72: 1.0, 76: 1.0, 79: 1.0, 82: 1.0, 84:
1.0, 87: 1.0, 89: 1.0, 94: 1.0, 96: 1.0}),
SparseVector(100, {0: 1.0, 4: 2.0, 8: 1.0, 20: 1.0, 21: 1.0, 22: 2.0, 24:
1.0, 27: 1.0, 37: 1.0, 40: 1.0, 43: 2.0, 51: 1.0, 56: 1.0, 62: 1.0, 65: 2.0,
70: 1.0, 72: 1.0, 82: 1.0, 84: 2.0, 88: 1.0, 89: 1.0}),
SparseVector(100, {2: 1.0, 3: 1.0, 8: 2.0, 10: 1.0, 11: 1.0, 14: 1.0, 17:
1.0, 18: 1.0, 19: 1.0, 27: 1.0, 28: 1.0, 40: 1.0, 42: 1.0, 44: 1.0, 47: 1.0,
59: 1.0, 62: 1.0, 65: 2.0, 67: 1.0, 69: 2.0, 81: 1.0, 84: 2.0, 95: 2.0,
98: 1.0}),
SparseVector(100, {1: 2.0, 4: 1.0, 10: 1.0, 11: 1.0, 16: 1.0, 20: 1.0, 21:
1.0, 30: 1.0, 33: 2.0, 34: 1.0, 37: 1.0, 48: 1.0, 52: 1.0, 55: 1.0, 62: 1.0,
63: 1.0, 65: 3.0, 66: 1.0, 84: 1.0, 86: 1.0, 93: 1.0, 97: 1.0})]
```

Figure 8.33 Snippets of contents of `spamFeatures`

We now need to start to think about how we would use the data to train the naïve Bayes model. We currently have two different datasets, one with ham and one with spam. To come up with a good model we will need to train it using a mixture of both ham and spam data. However, to evaluate the accuracy and performance of our model we would need to be able to differentiate between which vector features were originally spam and which ham. If we were to combine the data now (i.e., `spamFeatures` and `hamFeatures`) we would not be able to tell what the original labels were, so to help us with this, we will use `LabeledPoint`[4] to add labels to the data prior to combining them (Figure 8.34). If we look at the contents of `positiveExamples` we can see the `LabeledPoint` that has been added (Figure 8.35).

```
# use LabeledPoint to add the label 1 to all the ham features
positiveExamples=spamFeatures.map(lambda features: LabeledPoint(1, features))

# use LabeledPoint to add the label 0 to all the ham features
negativeExamples=hamFeatures.map(lambda features: LabeledPoint(0, features))
```

Figure 8.34 Using `LabeledPoint` to add labels

```
positiveExamples.take(5)
```

Output:
```
[LabeledPoint(1.0, (100,[4,5,8,9,24,27,33,42,47,48,52,55,59,61,62,65,68,69,71
,83,88,89],[1.0,1.0,1.0,2.0,2.0,1.0,1.0,1.0,1.0,1.0,1.0,1.0,1.0,1.0,1.0,4.0,1
.0,1.0,1.0,1.0,1.0,2.0])),
 LabeledPoint(1.0, (100,[1,3,9,15,21,23,24,27,35,36,37,39,40,45,49,55,65,66,6
7,72,76,79,82,84,87,89,94,96],[1.0,1.0,1.0,1.0,1.0,1.0,1.0,2.0,1.0,1.0,1.0,1.
0,1.0,1.0,1.0,3.0,1.0,2.0,1.0,1.0,1.0,1.0,1.0,1.0,1.0,1.0])),
```

(Continued)

Figure 8.35 (Continued)

```
 LabeledPoint(1.0, (100,[0,4,8,20,21,22,24,27,37,40,43,51,56,62,65,70,72,82,8
4,88,89],[1.0,2.0,1.0,1.0,1.0,2.0,1.0,1.0,1.0,1.0,2.0,1.0,1.0,1.0,2.0,1.0,1.0
,1.0,2.0,1.0,1.0])),
 LabeledPoint(1.0, (100,[2,3,8,10,11,14,17,18,19,27,28,40,42,44,47,59,62,65,6
7,69,81,84,95,98],[1.0,1.0,2.0,1.0,1.0,1.0,1.0,1.0,1.0,1.0,1.0,1.0,1.0,1.0,1.
0,1.0,1.0,2.0,1.0,2.0,1.0,2.0,2.0,1.0])),
 LabeledPoint(1.0, (100,[1,4,10,11,16,20,21,30,33,34,37,48,52,55,62,63,65,66,
84,86,93,97],[2.0,1.0,1.0,1.0,1.0,1.0,1.0,1.0,2.0,1.0,1.0,1.0,1.0,1.0,1.0,1.0
,3.0,1.0,1.0,1.0,1.0,1.0]))]
```

Figure 8.35 Spam features with `LabeledPoint`

We are now ready to combine the spam and ham data (Figure 8.36). Having done so, we split the data into training data (to fit the model) and test data (Figure 8.37). We then train the model by applying the Apache Spark `NaiveBayes` algorithm to the training data (Figure 8.38).

```
training_data = positiveExamples.union(negativeExamples)
```

Figure 8.36 Combining the spam and ham labelled data

```
trainset, testset = training_data.randomSplit([0.6, 0.4])
```

Figure 8.37 Using `randomSplit` to split into training and test datasets

```
model = NaiveBayes.train(trainset,1.0)
```

Figure 8.38 Training the model

Next, we use model for prediction using the test data; the original label (`x.label` in Figure 8.39) is also returned so that it can be compared to the predicted labels. The returned values in Figure 8.40 show the predicted label followed by the original label.

```
predictionLabel = testset.map(lambda x: (model.predict(x.features), x.label))
```

Figure 8.39 Predicting using the model on the test data

```
predictionLabel.take(20)

[(1.0, 1.0),
 (0.0, 1.0),
 (1.0, 1.0),
```

```
(0.0, 1.0),
(0.0, 1.0),
(1.0, 1.0),
(1.0, 1.0),
(1.0, 1.0),
(1.0, 1.0),
(0.0, 1.0),
(1.0, 1.0),
(0.0, 1.0),
(0.0, 1.0),
(1.0, 1.0),
(0.0, 1.0),
(0.0, 1.0),
(0.0, 1.0),
(0.0, 1.0),
(0.0, 1.0),
(0.0, 1.0)]
```

Figure 8.40 The values of the predicted labels and the original labels

Finally, let us calculate the accuracy of the model by dividing the total count where the predicted label is equal to the actual label by the total number of instances in the entire test dataset. Figure 8.41 shows that the model has an accuracy of 90.2%, which means that 90.2% of the time the model made the correct prediction.

```
accuracy = 1.0 * predictionLabel.filter(lambda x: (x[0]==x[1])).count()/
testset.count()

print(accuracy)

Output:
0.901646639964397
```

Figure 8.41 Calculating the accuracy of the model

8.5.2 Unsupervised learning algorithms

Unsupervised learning is a type of machine learning where the model learns patterns and structures in the data without any explicit target labels or outputs. In this approach, the model explores the data and identifies inherent patterns, clusters, or relationships among the data points. Unsupervised learning algorithms aim to discover hidden structures or insights in the data that may not be apparent to humans. It can be used for tasks such as clustering, anomaly detection, dimensionality reduction, and recommendation systems. Unsupervised learning is particularly useful when the data is unlabelled or when the objective is to gain a deeper understanding of the data without specific prediction goals.

Recommendation engine

Collaborative filtering[5] is commonly used for recommender systems. These techniques aim to fill in the missing entries of a user–item association matrix. The Apache Spark MLlib library supports model-based collaborative filtering, in which users and products are described by a small set of latent factors that can be used to predict missing entries. The library uses the alternating least squares (ALS) algorithm to learn these latent factors. The implementation in MLlib has the following parameters:

- `numBlocks` is the number of blocks used to parallelize computation (set to −1 to autoconfigure).
- `rank` is the number of features to use (also referred to as the number of latent factors).
- `iterations` is the number of iterations of ALS to run. ALS typically converges to a reasonable solution in 20 iterations or fewer.
- `lambda` specifies the regularization parameter in ALS.
- `implicitPrefs` specifies whether to use the explicit feedback ALS variant or one adapted for implicit feedback data.
- `alpha` is a parameter applicable to the implicit feedback variant of ALS that governs the baseline confidence in preference observations.

Apache Spark uses the ALS technique for collaborative filtering and its recommendation module. So, in this hands-on exercise we will use the ALS technique from the Apache Spark MLlib library (see Figure 8.42). See Koren et al. (2009) for an interesting discussion on recommendation systems.

Collaborative Filtering (Recommendation)

Widely used application of machine learning used in various domains.

Spark uses the ALS (Alternating Least Squares) technique for collaborative filtering / its recommendation module.

ALS is an algorithm that performs matrix factorisation.

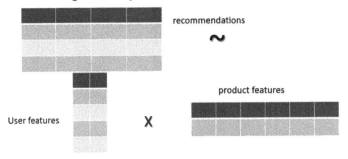

Figure 8.42   Collaborative filtering

The dataset we will be using is the MovieLens dataset,[6] which is a collection of millions of movie ratings collected from various users.

Once the Jupyter Notebook is opened, the first step is to run the necessary configurations (see Chapter 3) and then import the relevant libraries (see Figure 8.43).

```
from pyspark.mllib.recommendation import ALS, MatrixFactorizationModel, Rating
```

Figure 8.43 Importing the relevant libraries

Next, we load the data (Figure 8.44), in this case into an RDD which we have called `data` (recall that we first came across RDDs in Chapter 3) using the `textFile` method of the SparkContext `sc` (which was set in the configuration). When we view this data (remember to change the path to where the data is located in your environment), we see that we have a user id for the person who gave the rating, a movie id for the movie the rated, the rating that they gave the movie, and a timestamp.

```
data = sc.textFile("hdfs:///data/ml-1m/ratings.dat")
```

Figure 8.44 Loading the data into an RDD

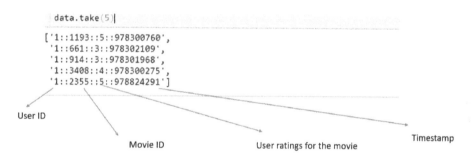

Figure 8.45 Viewing the contents of the RDD

We then parse the data into user id, movie id, user ratings, and timestamp columns using the `Rating`[7] function imported from the MLlib recommendation library. The `Rating` class represents a tuple with `user`, `product`, and `rating` fields (see Figure 8.46). So in Figure 8.46, we split the contents of the RDD based on the `::` and delimiter then pass the values in the first location into the `Rating` tuple's `user` field, the second into its `product` field, and the third into the `rating` field.

```
ratings = data.map(lambda l: l.split('::')).map(lambda l: Rating(int(l[0]),
int(l[1]), float(l[2])))
```

```
ratings.take(5)
```

(Continued)

Figure 8.46 (Continued)

```
Output:
[Rating(user=1, product=1193, rating=5.0),
 Rating(user=1, product=661, rating=3.0),
 Rating(user=1, product=914, rating=3.0),
 Rating(user=1, product=3408, rating=4.0),
 Rating(user=1, product=2355, rating=5.0)]
```

Figure 8.46 Parsing the data

Next, we split the data into training and testing datasets. To do so, we use the `ratings.randomSplit` function which would randomly split the data based on whatever proportion we specify. In Figure 8.47 we have specified a ratio of 70% for the training dataset and 30% for the test dataset. Now we are ready to train the model using the ALS algorithm from the MLlib library (see Figure 8.48).

```
train, test = ratings.randomSplit([0.7,0.3])


train.take(3)


Output:
[Rating(user=1, product=1193, rating=5.0),
 Rating(user=1, product=661, rating=3.0),
 Rating(user=1, product=3408, rating=4.0)]


test.take(3)


Output:
[Rating(user=1, product=914, rating=3.0),
 Rating(user=1, product=1287, rating=5.0),
 Rating(user=1, product=919, rating=4.0)]
```

Figure 8.47 Splitting the data into training and test datasets

```
rank = 10
numIterations = 10
model = ALS.train(ratings, rank, numIterations)
```

Figure 8.48 Training the model using ALS

We now prepare the test data which we will be using. To do this we create a new RDD `testdata` from the test RDD which will contain the user id and the product (i.e., the movie id; see Figure 8.49). Note that we have dropped the rating, as we want the trained model to predict the ratings of the test data so we can compare the predicted values to the actual values.

```
testdata = test.map(lambda p: (p[0], p[1]))

testdata.take(3)
```

Output:

```
[(1, 914), (1, 1287), (1, 919)]
```

Figure 8.49 Preparing the test data

We are now ready to use the trained model to predict the ratings for the test data. In Figure 8.50 we use the `predictAll` function of the module and pass in the testdata, and then use the `map` transformation to return the user id, movie id, and the newly predicted rating.

```
predictions = model.predictAll(testdata).map(lambda r: ((r[0], r[1], r[2])))

predictions.take(5)
```

Output:

```
[((3456, 480), 5.1995111194353649),
 ((3456, 32), 3.747468143908443),
 ((3456, 1396), 4.34045137419666895),
 ((3456, 1909), 4.186176644697877),
 ((3456, 1591), 3.6128257906491443)]
```

Figure 8.50 Testing the model

Having obtained predicted ratings, we compare the original ratings from the test dataset with the predicted ratings (Figure 8.51). We use the `map` transformation to return the user id, movie id, and the original rating from the test RDD, and then join that to the predictions on the user id and movie id. We can now compare the original ratings with the predicted ones. Figure 8.51 uses the `take()` function to return only five of the rows in the dataset. To determine how good our model is we can check its accuracy of the model, using all the predicted ratings and the actual ratings to determine mean squared error (Figure 8.52). In Section 8.4.3 we discussed some metrics, including this one, for evaluating models.

```
ratesAndPreds = ratings.map(lambda r: ((r[0],r[1],r[2]))).join(predictions)

ratesAndPreds.take(5)
```

Output:

```
[((2, 2355), (5.0, 3.872994306831986)),
```

(Continued)

Figure 8.51 (Continued)

```
((2, 2268), (5.0, 4.313960065784085)),
((2, 368), (4.0, 3.4616764210431823)),
((2, 1968), (2.0, 4.589717788448755)),
((4, 1615), (5.0, 2.74238729682978))]
```

Figure 8.51 Comparing the predicted ratings with the original ratings

```
MSE = ratesAndPreds.map(lambda r: (r[1][0] - r[1][1])**2).mean()
print("Mean Squared Error = " + str(MSE))
```

```
Output:
Mean Squared Error = 0.8192093577752585
```

Figure 8.52 Evaluating the accuracy of the model using the MSE

K-means clustering

K-means clustering is a widely used clustering technique which determines *K* clusters based on Euclidean distances. Figure 8.53 shows the steps involved. At the end of the process each point is assigned to the cluster of its nearest centroid. For our hands-on exercise we will use a well-known example based on the iris dataset (Fisher, 1988) which is a dataset that contains three classes, where each class refers to a type of iris plant. We use two methods, first we use scikit-learn,[8] which is a free software machine learning library for Python, and then we use Apache Spark.

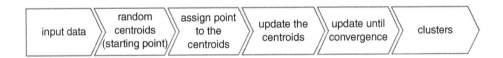

Figure 8.53 Steps for *K*-means clustering

As usual, we import the relevant libraries (Figure 8.54). Next, we import the iris dataset. Figure 8.55 depicts this and also shows some of the contents of the dataset. The iris dataset consists of four features (length and width of sepals and petals) and a label which defines the flowers species (*Iris setosa, Iris virginica,* and *Iris versicolor*). We then split the data into features (input) and labels (output). Next, we train the KMeans model (Figure 8.57). Figure 8.58 shows the predicted label values. Finally, we can plot the data points and see the three clusters and their centroids (Figure 8.59).

```
import numpy as np
import pandas as pd
from sklearn.datasets import make_blobs
from sklearn.cluster import KMeans
from matplotlib import pyplot as plt
%matplotlib inline
```

Figure 8.54 Importing relevant libraries

```
# load the iris dataset
import seaborn as sns

iris_df = sns.load_dataset("iris")
iris_df
```

Output:

	sepal_length	sepal_width	petal_length	petal_width	species
0	5.1	3.5	1.4	0.2	setosa
1	4.9	3.0	1.4	0.2	setosa
2	4.7	3.2	1.3	0.2	setosa
3	4.6	3.1	1.5	0.2	setosa
4	5.0	3.6	1.4	0.2	setosa
...	...	...	...	...	...
145	6.7	3.0	5.2	2.3	virginica
146	6.3	2.5	5.0	1.9	virginica
147	6.5	3.0	5.2	2.0	virginica
148	6.2	3.4	5.4	2.3	virginica
149	5.9	3.0	5.1	1.8	virginica

Figure 8.55 Uploading the iris dataset

```
features = iris_df.drop(["species"], axis=1)
labels = iris_df.filter(["species"], axis=1)

features
```

(Continued)

Figure 8.56 (Continued)

Output:

	sepal_length	sepal_width	petal_length	petal_width
0	5.1	3.5	1.4	0.2
1	4.9	3.0	1.4	0.2
2	4.7	3.2	1.3	0.2
3	4.6	3.1	1.5	0.2
4	5.0	3.6	1.4	0.2
...	...	...	...	...
145	6.7	3.0	5.2	2.3
146	6.3	2.5	5.0	1.9
147	6.5	3.0	5.2	2.0
148	6.2	3.4	5.4	2.3
149	5.9	3.0	5.1	1.8

labels

Output:

	species
0	setosa
1	setosa
2	setosa
3	setosa
4	setosa
...	...
145	virginica
146	virginica
147	virginica
148	virginica
149	virginica

Figure 8.56 Splitting into features and labels

```
features1 = features.values
km_model = KMeans(n_clusters=4)
km_model.fit(features1)
```

Output:
```
KMeans(algorithm='auto', copy_x=True, init='k-means++', max_iter=300,
        n_clusters=4, n_init=10, n_jobs=None, precompute_distances='auto',
        random_state=None, tol=0.0001, verbose=0)
```

Figure 8.57 Training the KMeans model

```
print(km_model.labels_)
```

Output:

```
[0 0 0 0 0 0 0 0 0 0 0 0 0 0 0 0 0 0 0 0 0 0 0 0 0 0 0 0 0 0 0 0 0 0 0 0
 0 0 0 0 0 0 0 0 0 0 0 0 0 1 1 1 3 1 3 1 3 1 3 1 3 3 3 3 1 3 1 3 3 1 3 1 3 1 1
 1 1 1 1 3 3 3 3 1 3 1 1 1 3 3 3 1 3 3 3 3 3 1 3 3 2 1 2 2 2 2 3 2 2 2 1
 1 2 1 1 2 2 2 2 1 2 1 2 1 2 2 1 1 2 2 2 2 2 1 1 2 2 2 1 2 2 2 1 2 2 2 1 1
 2 1]
```

Figure 8.58   The predicted label values

```
plt.scatter(features1[:,0], features1[:,1], c=km_model.labels_,
cmap='rainbow')
```

```
# plot the centroids
plt.scatter(km_model.cluster_centers_[:,0], km_model.cluster_centers_[:,1],
s=100, c='black')
```

Output:

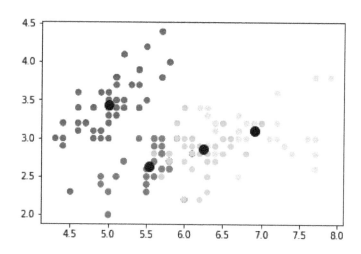

Figure 8.59   Clusters and their centroids

In Figure 8.60 we carry out the same *K*-means clustering exercise using the Apache Spark MLlib KMeans library.

```
from pyspark.sql import SparkSession
from pyspark.ml.feature import VectorAssembler
from pyspark.ml.clustering import KMeans
import matplotlib.pyplot as plt
import numpy as np
```

(Continued)

Figure 8.60 **(Continued)**

```python
# Create a Spark session
spark=SparkSession.builder.appName("KMeansClusteringHandsOn").getOrCreate()

# Load the Iris dataset
iris_df = spark.read.csv("iris.csv", header=True, inferSchema=True)

# Prepare the feature vector
assembler=VectorAssembler(inputCols=iris_df.columns[:-1],
outputCol="features")
feature_vector = assembler.transform(iris_df)

# Train the K-means model
kmeans = KMeans(k=3, seed=123)
model = kmeans.fit(feature_vector)

# Get the cluster centers
centers = np.array(model.clusterCenters())

# Assign clusters to the data points
predictions = model.transform(feature_vector)

# Extract predicted labels and convert them to a Pandas DataFrame
labels = predictions.select("prediction").toPandas()

# Extract feature vectors and convert them to a Pandas DataFrame
features = predictions.select("features").toPandas()

# Plotting the clusters
plt.figure(figsize=(10, 6))

# Plot the data points
plt.scatter(features["features"].apply(lambda x: x[0]), features["features"].
apply(lambda x: x[1]), c=labels["prediction"])

# Plot the cluster centers
plt.scatter(centers[:, 0], centers[:, 1], c='red', marker='x', s=200,
label='Cluster Centers')

plt.xlabel("Feature 1")
plt.ylabel("Feature 2")
plt.title("K-means Clustering on Iris Dataset")
plt.legend()
plt.show()
```

Output:

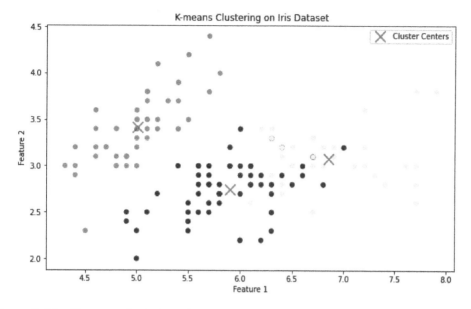

Figure 8.60 *K*-means clustering with the iris dataset using Apache Spark MLlib

8.6 ETHICS BY DESIGN

When it comes to machine learning (and AI in general), giving serious consideration to ethical issues cannot be overemphasized. Fortunately, because of the increasing prominence and use of machine learning algorithms in everyday life, this is being given more focus than ever before. Again, as our main reference framework we will use the TAFARP data ethics by design framework (see Figure 2.14, p. 44).

The United Nations Educational, Scientific and Cultural Organization (UNESCO) has a list of artificial intelligence ethical dilemmas.[9] In this chapter we focus on these dilemmas using the TAFARP data ethics by design framework.

- *Biased AI*. This is a very important issue and relates to elements in the TAFARP framework, the most obvious one being fairness. Where there is bias, maintaining fairness becomes an issue. UNESCO provides an example of biased AI, claiming that if you type 'greatest leaders of all time' into a search engine, you will probably get a list dominated by names of prominent men.
- In 2018 Amazon had to scrap a secret AI recruiting tool that was biased against women. In this case this happened because the data that had itself been used to train the model was biased towards and dominated by men. There have also been cases raised of racial bias in AI and machine learning. Some of the areas raised here are quite disturbing; for example, self-driving cars recognize white pedestrians better than black ones and a criminal risk assessment technology was giving blacks harsher sentences.[10] How do we combat these and other related issues? Ethics by design would go a long way to help. Right from the design stage it raises questions such as: What are the potential biases here? Is

the system fair? Is there transparency? If these and related questions are asked after the systems have already been implemented, it is already too late.

- *Autonomous cars* (i.e., self-driving cars). The concern here is what happens when moral decisions need to be made. If a driver decides to swerve into a pole instead of hitting a child on the road, the driver has taken a moral decision to shift the risk from the child on the road to themselves and everyone in the car with them. How would this be handled when it is not a human making the decision but an algorithm? In terms of the TAFARP data ethics by design framework, this speaks to responsibility and accountability.
- *AI in the court of law*. Again although advantages can be pointed out there are many concerns that this raises: issues around fairness, privacy, transparency, and responsibility. Some have also raised issues around human rights in this space. A famous example is the controversy around COMPAS (Correctional Offender Management Profiling for Alternative Sanctions) AI, a software used in the criminal justice system, particularly in the context of bail and sentencing decisions. COMPAS is a proprietary algorithm developed by a private company called Northpointe (now known as Equivant) that aims to predict the likelihood of a defendant reoffending if released before trial or sentencing. The case raised serious fairness concerns, namely the potential for bias in its predictions. Critics argued that the algorithm may exhibit racial or socioeconomic bias, leading to unequal treatment of defendants. Some studies have suggested that COMPAS may be more likely to falsely label Black defendants as high risk and White defendants as low risk. Another issue was that of lack of transparency: the inner workings of the COMPAS algorithm are proprietary and not disclosed to the public. This lack of transparency raises concerns about accountability and the potential for hidden biases or flaws within the model that can be identified only by examining the source code itself.

Ethics by design is and remains a very important area that needs to be prioritized in the design of every system and every project that has to do with machine learning.

8.7 INDUSTRY INSIGHTS

PayPal has access to data on more than 350 million consumers and merchants in over 200 markets, and it uses the vast amount of data at its disposal together with machine learning to help detect and prevent fraud, as well as to promote good practice, innovation, and competitive advantage.[11] Using machine learning algorithms, PayPal can assess in real time whether a customer is legitimate or not. Companies that fail to use machine learning in this way run the risk of being left behind and possibly going out of business (see Golsefid, n.d.).

Recommendation systems are another area in which companies are using machine learning for competitive advantage. Examples of companies doing innovative and interesting things in this space are Amazon, Netflix, Spotify, YouTube, and Google. Amazon's recommendation engines have been so successful that it was estimated in 2021 that 35% of all sales were generated by recommendation engines (Arora, 2021). Every one of these companies continues to benefit as a result of their embracing machine learning and being pace-setters for others.

SUMMARY

In this chapter we have discussed the various types of machine learning, their roles and the challenges facing the big data analyst. We reviewed pre-processing then explored correlations and model evaluation metrics, followed by a series of hands-on exercises. We also considered prediction errors, overfitting, and underfitting. Finally, we considered some important ethics by design issues and industry insights.

TEST YOUR KNOWLEDGE

1 What are the main differences between supervised and unsupervised learning?

2 Upload a dataset of your choice and do the following:

- Choose an appropriate machine learning algorithm for it, and explain the choice you made.
- If the algorithm you choose is supervised, use a function to choose your features.

3 Why was machine learning introduced?

4 List five use cases for machine learning.

5 List two potential ethical challenges for the use of machine learning.

6 Read the Apache Spark MLlib documentation[12] on decision trees, random forest, and support vector machines and, using a similar approach to the hands-on exercises in this chapter, train models using these techniques.

FURTHER READING (OPTIONAL)

Interesting TED talk on how to keep human bias out of AI:

Sharma, K. (2018) How to keep human bias out of AI. https://www.ted.com/talks/kriti_sharma_how_to_keep_human_bias_out_of_ai?language=en

An article on AI and the law:

Toews, R. (2019) AI will transform the field of law. *Forbes*, 19 December. https://www.forbes.com/sites/robtoews/2019/12/19/ai-will-transform-the-field-of-law/

NOTES

1 https://scikit-learn.org/stable/modules/cross_validation.html

2 https://spark.apache.org/docs/3.1.3/api/python/reference/api/pyspark.ml.feature.VectorAssembler.html

3 https://spark.apache.org/docs/latest/api/python/reference/api/pyspark.ml.feature.HashingTF.html

4 https://spark.apache.org/docs/latest/api/python/reference/api/pyspark.mllib.regression.LabeledPoint.html

5 https://spark.apache.org/docs/latest/mllib-collaborative-filtering.html

6 https://grouplens.org/datasets/movielens/

7 https://spark.apache.org/docs/latest/api/python/reference/api/pyspark.mllib.recommendation.Rating.html

8 https://scikit-learn.org/stable/

9 https://en.unesco.org/artificial-intelligence/ethics/cases

10 https://www.credera.com/insights/racial-bias-in-machine-learning-and-artificial-intelligence

11 https://www.paypal.com/us/brc/article/paypal-machine-learning-stop-fraud

12 https://spark.apache.org/mllib/

REFERENCES

Almeida, T. and Hidalgo, J. (2012) SMS Spam Collection. UCI Machine Learning Repository. https://doi.org/10.24432/C5CC84.

Alpaydin, E. (2016) *Machine Learning*. Cambridge, MA: MIT Press.

Arora, S. (2021) Recommendation engines: How Amazon and Netflix are winning the personalization battle. Retrieved from https://www.spiceworks.com/marketing/customer-experience/articles/recommendation-engines-how-amazon-and-netflix-are-winning-the-personalization-battle/

Burkov, A. (2019) *The Hundred-Page Machine Learning Book*. Quebec City: Author.

Coe, J. and Atay, M. (2021) Evaluating impact of race in facial recognition across machine learning and deep learning algorithms. *Computers,* 10(9), 113.

Fisher, R. A. (1988) Iris. UCI Machine Learning Repository. https://doi.org/10.24432/C56C76

Golsefid, S. (n.d.) More data, more insight: What does more data mean for boosting your fraud prevention? Retrieved from https://www.paypalobjects.com/ecm_assets/More%20Data%20More%20Insight%20White%20Paper-v2.pdf

Koren, Y., Bell, R. and Volinsky, C. (2009) Matrix factorization techniques for recommender systems. *Computer,* 42(8), 30–37. https://doi.org/10.1109/MC.2009.26

Marr, B. (2016) A short history of machine learning – every manager should read. Retrieved from https://www.forbes.com/sites/bernardmarr/2016/02/19/a-short-history-of-machine-learning-every-manager-should-read/

Molnar, C. (2023) *Interpretable Machine Learning: A Guide for Making Black Box Models Explainable (2nd edn)*. christophm.github.io/interpretable-ml-book/

Russell, S. and Norvig, P. (2003) *Artificial Intelligence: A Modern Approach*. Harlow: Pearson Education.

Sarkar, D. (2019) *Text Analytics with Python: A Practical Real-World Approach to Gaining Actionable Insights from your Data*. Apress.

Turing, A. M. (1950) Computing machinery and intelligence. *Mind,* 59(236), 433–60. http://www.jstor.org/stable/2251299

Uberoi, A. (2023) Introduction to dimension reduction. GeeksforGeeks. https://www.geeksforgeeks.org/dimensionality-reduction/

9

NATURAL LANGUAGE PROCESSING

CHAPTER CONTENTS

CHAPTER OBJECTIVES

In this chapter:

- You will learn about natural language processing (NLP) and how it is used for big data analytics.
- You will be introduced to NLP and its importance for big data.
- You will also be introduced to a few pre-processing algorithms for NLP such as tokenization and lemmatization.
- You will explore some NLP feature extraction techniques.
- You will learn about some techniques that fall under NLP such as sentiment analysis and topic modelling and use them in hands-on exercises.
- You will also consider some of the ethical issues that can arise from the use of NLP.

9.1 INTRODUCTION TO NLP FOR BIG DATA

Natural language processing (NLP) falls under machine learning (see Chapter 8) and provides methods to help analyse the contents of natural textual data and large amounts of unstructured data. NLP is used in text mining, topic modelling, text summarization, opinion mining, and many other techniques. It is increasingly becoming more important when it comes to big data analytics. This chapter introduces this important aspect of big data analytics and covers aspects of NLP such as sentiment analysis and tokenization using NLP libraries. NLP is a branch of AI that focuses predominantly on how to process and analyse large amounts of natural language. It can be used to automatically find relevant information in large amounts of text, it can also be used to identify trends in various areas early on, areas such as customers sentiments about a company's products and services, key influencers for specific topics in social media, virtual assistants, and NLP chatbots.

9.2 PRE-PROCESSING ALGORITHMS FOR NLP

We first touched on the importance of pre-processing in big data analytics in Chapter 2 where we discussed data wrangling (munging) and general cleaning and pre-processing. This is one step that is crucial when it comes to NLP as it deals with text and language. If you think about written text, it can be full of punctuation, misspelt words, and the like. Before feeding this data into a machine learning algorithm or analysing this data, it needs to be cleansed. In this section we focus on this crucial step and highlight some of the common algorithms that fall under it.

9.2.1 Tokenization

In NLP, tokenization has to do with splitting text up into the smallest units in it called tokens. There could be various reasons to want to do this, for example as part of the process of pre-processing or cleaning up the input text, or to pave the way to counting the number of occurrences of tokens or perhaps even to make it possible to categorize tokens. How do we carry it out in practice? We will use two different libraries to demonstrate how it can be done. The first one is TextBlob,[1] which is a Python library which provides an API for many NLP tasks, and which we will also use later in this chapter for sentiment analysis. The second library that we consider is the NLTK (Natural Language Toolkit) library which, as its name suggests, is a Python natural language library.

We start, as usual, by opening up a Jupyter Notebook (this was introduced in Chapter 3), as depicted in Figure 9.1, and importing the relevant libraries (Figure 9.2). We then import the text. This could be manually inputted text as shown in Figure 9.3 or it could be a much larger dataset from a file, a database, and so on. Once this is done, we then simply call the words method from the TextBlob object (Figure 9.4).

Figure 9.1   Opening a new Jupyter Notebook

```
import textblob
from textblob import TextBlob
```

Figure 9.2   Importing the relevant libraries (TextBlob)

```
input_text = "This is text to demonstrate tokenisation!!!! Big data analytics
is so, much fun....."
```

Figure 9.3   Importing the input text

```
TextBlob(input_text).words

Output:
WordList(['This', 'is', 'text', 'to', 'demonstrate', 'tokenisation', 'Big',
'data', 'analytics', 'is', 'so', 'much', 'fun'])
```

Figure 9.4   Tokenization of the input text (TextBlob)

We can do the same thing with the NLTK library. As with TextBlob, we need to import the relevant libraries (Figure 9.5). The NLTK library gives us two objects: one that splits up into sentences and the other into words (see Figure 9.6).

```
import nltk
from nltk import sent_tokenize
from nltk import word_tokenize
```

Figure 9.5   Importing the relevant libraries (NLTK)

```
tokens_sent = nltk.sent_tokenize(input_text)
print(tokens sent)
```

```
Output:
['This is text to demonstrate tokenisation!!!!', 'Big data analytics is so,
much fun.....']
```

```
tokens_word = nltk.word_tokenize(input_text)
print(tokens_word)
```

```
Output:
['This', 'is', 'text', 'to', 'demonstrate', 'tokenisation', '!', '!', '!',
'!', 'Big', 'data', 'analytics', 'is', 'so', ',', 'much', 'fun', '...', '..']
```

Figure 9.6   Tokenization of the input text into sentences and words (NLTK)

However, simply using Python libraries would not handle big data as efficiently as Apache Spark would. This is because Apache Spark is distributed and hence able to process large amounts of data in parallel. Figure 9.7 shows PySpark code for tokenization using the `Tokenizer` class. The code in Figure 9.7 gives the output in Figure 9.8. The words have all been tokenized and the sentences broken down into individual tokens (words) using the `Tokenizer` class.

9.2.2 Stemming

One of the important tasks of Natural Language processing is to reduce words to their base or root form, often by removing affixes (such as prefixes and suffixes). The resulting form, known as the 'stem', may not always be a valid word, but it represents the core meaning of the word. For example, applying stemming to the words 'running', 'runner', and 'ran' would result in the common stem 'run'.

Stemming is used in NLP to normalize text data and reduce the dimensionality of the feature space. Converting different forms of a word into a common base form is an important step, one used in text analysis, information retrieval, and sentiment analysis, where recognizing the core meaning of words is more important than linguistic variations.

```
from pyspark.ml.feature import Tokenizer


# create a dataframe with an id and a text column
df = spark.createDataFrame([(0,"This is text to demonstrate tokenisation"),
(1, "Big data analytics is so much fun")], ["id", "text"])


# create a Tokenizer instance and transform the text column
# inputCol, the name of the input column in the DataFrame
# outputCol, the name of the output column where the tokenised words will be
stored
tokenizer = Tokenizer(inputCol="text", outputCol="words")
tokenized_df = tokenizer.transform(df)


# show the results
tokenized_df.show(truncate=False)
```

Figure 9.7 **PySpark code for tokenization**

```
+---+------------------------------------------+--------------------------------------------------+
|id |text                                      |words                                             |
+---+------------------------------------------+--------------------------------------------------+
|0  |This is text to demonstate tokenisation   |[this, is, text, to, demonstate, tokenisation]    |
|1  |Big data analytics is so much fun         |[big, data, analytics, is, so, much, fun]         |
+---+------------------------------------------+--------------------------------------------------+
```

Figure 9.8 **Output from PySpark code for tokenization (see Figure 9.7)**

Different algorithms can be used to carry out stemming; we will focus on two from the NLTK library, the PorterStemmer[2], and the SnowballStemmer[3] algorithms. We do not go into their technical details in this book; however, more information can be found on them using the provided links.

As usual, we import the relevant libraries and then run the code to process the stemming. In Figure 9.9 we use the PorterStemmer algorithm, and in Figure 9.10 the SnowballStemmer algorithm.

```
from nltk.stem import PorterStemmer


PorterStemmer = PorterStemmer()
word = ("environment")
PorterStemmer.stem(word)


Output:
'environ'
```

Figure 9.9 **Stemming (PorterStemmer)**

```
from nltk.stem.snowball import SnowballStemmer

SnowballStemmer = SnowballStemmer(language = "english")
word = "environment"
SnowballStemmer.stem(word)

Output:
'environ'
```

Figure 9.10   Stemming (SnowballStemmer)

It is interesting to note that stemming does not use lexical knowledge to work out the base word and, as such, when it removes the inflections of a word this can sometimes result in incorrect words (see Figure 9.11). Lemmatization, which we look at in the next subsection, resolves this issue.

```
from nltk.stem import PorterStemmer

PorterStemmer = PorterStemmer()
word = ("education")
PorterStemmer.stem(word)

Output:
'educ'

from nltk.stem.snowball import SnowballStemmer

SnowballStemmer = SnowballStemmer(language = "english")
word = "education"
SnowballStemmer.stem(word)

Output:
'educ'
```

Figure 9.11   Stemming can result in incorrect base words

9.2.3 Lemmatization

As mentioned earlier, lemmatization not only finds the related base word like stemming does, but also uses lexical knowledge bases to get the correct word. For our examples we will use functions from TextBlob and the NLTK library. The results from these in Figure 9.12 show that for the word 'Education', unlike with stemming, which returned root words of 'educ', lemmatization using both libraries correctly returns 'Education' as the base word.

```
import nltk
from nltk.stem import WordNetLemmatizer
lemmatizer = WordNetLemmatizer()


print(lemmatizer.lemmatize("education"))


Output:
education


from textblob import TextBlob, Word


word = 'education'
w = Word(word)
w.lemmatize()


Output:
Education
```

Figure 9.12 Lemmatization (NLTK and TextBlob)

9.2.4 Part-of-speech tagging

The final pre-processing algorithm that we look at is part-of-speech (POS) tagging. In POS tagging a piece of text is broken down into individual words and each of these words is then assigned a POS tag. These POS tags represent adjectives, nouns, verbs, pronouns, prepositions, conjunctions, and so on. Figure 9.13 shows code for POS tagging and the output from the code.

Here, the sentence 'Big data analytics is so much fun' is broken down into the following POS tags (the POS tags are underlined):

Big: NNP (proper noun, singular)

data: NNS (noun, plural)

analytics: NNS (noun, plural)

is: VBZ (verb, present tense, third person singular)

```
import nltk

# Input sentence
sentence = "Big data analytics is so much fun"

# Tokenize the sentence into words
tokens = nltk.word_tokenize(sentence)

# Perform POS tagging
pos_tags = nltk.pos_tag(tokens)

# Print the POS tags
for token, pos_tag in pos_tags:
    print(f"{token}: {pos_tag}")
```

Output:

```
Big: NNP
data: NNS
analytics: NNS
is: VBZ
so: RB
much: JJ
fun: NN
```

Figure 9.13   Part-of-speech tagging code and its output

so: RB (adverb)

much: JJ (adjective)

fun: NN (noun, singular)

The above results are interesting, for instance 'Big' is tagged as a noun. However, as 'Big' is an adjective the expectation is that it would be tagged as one. This illustrates that the specific POS tagging model and its training data can lead to different interpretation of words based on context. 'Big' could for instance be interpreted as a proper noun because it is common for it to be used as part of a proper noun like 'Big Data'.

Knowing the POS tags for words can be important in NLP algorithms in working out what surrounding words are, and sentence structures.

9.3 FEATURE EXTRACTION TECHNIQUES

We now turn to feature extraction – the process used to extract useful features from the input data in NLP, which are then subsequently used to train machine learning models (Sarkar, 2019). In this chapter, as the focus is on NLP, we limit the discussion on feature extraction techniques to text-based ones; three commonly used ones are the bag-of-words model, term frequency–inverse document frequency (TF-IDF), and word embeddings. Other feature extraction techniques include statistical features, deep-learning-based features, image-based features, transform-based features, and frequency-based features. Further sources of information on these other techniques can be found in Hardeniya (2015).

The bag-of-words is perhaps the simplest technique of all the various approaches. It is also commonly used. In using it, text is represented as a bag (collection) of individual words. This collection does not take into consideration context, grammar, or the order of words. As with most NLP techniques, the input text or corpus (this is a collection of text) is pre-processed to remove words that are not significant (stop words), punctuation, and carry out general cleaning of the input text. A simple example that illustrates bag-of-words is as follows:

1   *Input text.* 'Learning big data analytics is so so amazing! There's so much to explore, and the insights from it are fantastic, simply fantastic and amazing!!!'
2   *Pre-processing.* Convert the text to lower case, remove punctuation, and eliminate stop words. The output from this step is 'learning big data analytics amazing much explore insights fantastic simply fantastic amazing'.
3   *Vocabulary creation.* List all unique words from step 2. The output from this step is ['learning big data analytics amazing much explore insights fantastic simply fantastic amazing'].
    Feature extraction. Create a feature vector that represents the bag-of-words. Count the occurrence of each word in the document, then assign the count to the corresponding index in the feature vector. The output from step 4 is [1, 1, 1, 1, 2, 1, 1, 1, 2, 1]: 'learning' has one occurrence, 'big' has one occurrence, 'data' has one occurrence, 'analytics' has one occurrence, 'amazing' has two occurrences, 'much' has one occurrence, 'explore' has one occurrence, 'insights' has one occurrence, 'fantastic' has two occurrences, and 'simply' has one occurrence.

In Figure 9.14, we use sklearn,[4] which is a popular free Python machine learning library. It provides many supervised and unsupervised algorithms, including many for NLP.

9.4 SENTIMENT ANALYSIS

Having looked at some of the common algorithms for pre-processing the input text in NLP and feature extraction, we now move on to a popularly used NLP algorithm: sentiment analysis. Sentiment analysis makes it possible to analyse and mine opinions, sentiments, and even emotions from texts. The analysis usually results in determining the polarity of a piece

```
import numpy as np
from sklearn.feature_extraction.text import CountVectorizer


vectorizer = CountVectorizer()


# input text
text = np.array(['Learning big data analytics is so so amazing! There's so
much to explore, and the insights from it are fantastic, simply fantastic and
amazing!!!'])


# fit the bag of words model
bag = vectorizer.fit_transform(docs)


# display the feature names
print('feature names:')
print(vectorizer.get_feature_names())


# display the feature vector
print('bag of words feature vector:')
print(bag.toarray())
```

Output

```
feature names: ['amazing', 'analytics', 'and', 'are', 'big', 'data',
'explore', 'fantastic', 'from', 'insights', 'is', 'it', 'learning', 'much',
'simply', 'so', 'the', 'theres', 'to']
bag of words feature vector: [[2 1 2 1 1 1 1 2 1 1 1 1 1 1 1 3 1 1 1]]
```

Figure 9.14 Bag-of-words code with output

of text, that is, whether it is positive, neutral, or negative. A simple illustration of this can be seen in Figure 9.15.

Sentiment analysis, also known as opinion mining, is a powerful technique in natural language processing (NLP) that aims to understand and extract sentiments, emotions, and opinions expressed in textual data. It plays a crucial role in various industries, enabling businesses and researchers to gain valuable insights from the vast amounts of text data generated online. Sentiment analysis is implemented in the following contexts:

Social Media Monitoring: Businesses use sentiment analysis to track and analyse customer feedback, comments, and reviews on social media platforms. This allows them to understand public perception, identify trends, and respond to customer concerns in real time.

Customer Feedback Analysis: Companies utilize sentiment analysis to process customer surveys, reviews, and feedback forms. By categorizing sentiments as positive,

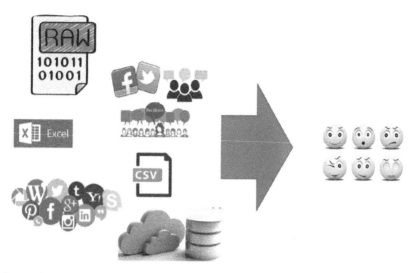

Figure 9.15 Simple pictorial depiction of sentiment analysis showing a few potential input data sources and output sentiments

negative, or neutral, organizations can gauge customer satisfaction, identify areas for improvement, and tailor their products or services accordingly.

Brand Reputation Management: Sentiment analysis helps businesses monitor and manage their brand reputation online. By analysing sentiment trends, companies can proactively address negative feedback, protect their brand image, and enhance customer loyalty.

Market Research and Product Development: Sentiment analysis is employed to gather insights into consumer preferences, opinions, and trends. This information aids in the development of new products or services that align with customer needs and desires.

Political Analysis and Public Opinion: Sentiment analysis is used in political campaigns to gauge public sentiment towards candidates, parties, and policies. It provides valuable insights for campaign strategy, messaging, and targeting.

Active and ongoing research in sentiment analysis includes the following:

Aspect-Based Sentiment Analysis: This field focuses on extracting sentiment at a more granular level, identifying sentiments related to specific aspects or features of a product or service. For instance, in a restaurant review, it might analyse sentiments about food quality, service, and ambience separately.

Emotion Detection: Some research in sentiment analysis goes beyond basic positive/ negative sentiment classification and aims to detect specific emotions like happiness, anger, sadness, etc., expressed in text.

Multimodal Sentiment Analysis: This area combines text with other forms of data (images, audio, video) to perform sentiment analysis. It's particularly relevant in analysing social media content where multiple types of media are often present.

As the examples above show, sentiment analysis has emerged as an important tool in extracting valuable insights from textual data, offering applications in marketing, customer service, market research, and more. Ongoing research in sentiment analysis continues to refine and expand its capabilities, paving the way for even more sophisticated and accurate sentiment analysis techniques in the future. As the volume of text data continues to grow, the importance of sentiment analysis in understanding public sentiment and making informed decisions will only continue to rise.

9.4.1 Machine-learning-based approach

There are several approaches to sentiment analysis. These can broadly be categorized into three main ones: the machine learning approach, the lexicon-based approach, and the hybrid approach. Each of these approaches then further splits into other techniques. Under the machine learning approach, there are both supervised learning and unsupervised learning techniques for sentiment analysis. The differences between supervised and unsupervised learning were covered in Chapter 8, where we also looked at some of the specific machine learning algorithms such as naïve Bayes. The machine learning approach involves the training of a model which can be used to classify the sentiments of texts. There are also hybrid approaches which combine elements of both the machine learning and the lexicon- or rule-based approach. Figure 9.16 brings together some of the elements such as pre-processing and tokenization that we have touched on earlier in this chapter and shows where they fit in the process of sentiment analysis using the machine learning approach.

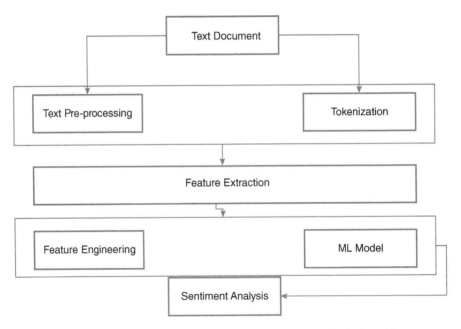

Figure 9.16 Diagram illustrating the process of sentiment analysis (machine-learning-based approach)

In Figure 9.16 the input text goes through some pre-processing which include tasks such as removing stop words and stemming. The pre-processed text is then split up into tokens (as seen in Section 9.2.1). The tokens are then used as features for the next step, the feature extraction step, which uses various techniques such as bag-of-words and TF-IDF. The relevant features are then transformed into the numerical features and the model trained.

9.4.2 The lexicon-based approach

Lexicon-based techniques use adjectives and adverbs to discover the semantic orientation of the text. For calculating any text orientation, adjective and adverb combinations are extracted with their sentiment orientation value. The lexicon-based approach can be further broken down into the dictionary-based approach and the corpus-based approach. In the dictionary-based approach, a dictionary is created by taking a few words initially. Then an online dictionary, thesaurus or WordNet can be used to expand that dictionary by incorporating synonyms and antonyms of those words. The dictionary is expanded until no new words can be added to it. On the other hand, in the corpus-based approach the sentiment orientation of context-specific words is found, and these can in turn be further split into the semantic and the statistical corpus-based approaches. As the names imply, statistical techniques are used in the statistical corpus-based approach, while in the semantic corpus-based approach sentiment values are assigned to words and the words which are semantically closer to such words – this can be done by finding synonyms and antonyms with respect to those words (Gupta and Agrwal, 2020). This is summarized in Figure 9.17.

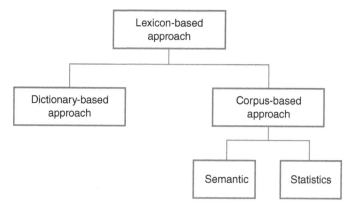

Figure 9.17 The lexicon-based approach

As in the machine-learning-based approach, the input text is initially pre-processed to clean it; this could involve the removal of stop words, punctuation, and so on. Scoring is then done on the aggregated words based on the lexicon, which is a collection of words and phrases with predefined sentiment scores. An overall polarity based on these scores is then given to the text and this could be positive, negative, or neutral.

In the hands-on exercises in this chapter, we focus mainly on the use of the lexicon-based approach.

9.4.3 Hands-on exercises on sentiment analysis

In the rest of this section, we cover two of the most popular Python libraries for sentiment analysis and use them to carry out some hands-on exercises:

- TextBlob is a Python library which provides an API for many natural language processing tasks, including sentiment analysis. It uses a lexicon-based approach to sentiment analysis and has two implementations: NaiveBayesAnalyzer, which is trained on a movie reviews corpus, and PatternAnalyzer, based on a pattern library.
- Valence Aware Dictionary and sEntiment Reasoner (Vader)[5] is a lexicon and rule-based sentiment analysis tool that is specifically attuned to sentiments expressed in social media.

To kick off the hands-on exercises we will start with a simple example where, using a news API, we fetch news articles and then use the TextBlob library to analyse the polarity of their content and headlines. Note that we can apply this to any piece of text.

```
https://newsapi.org
```

Figure 9.18   News API site

The News API site[6] (see Figure 9.18) provides access to vast amounts of worldwide news using a JSON API. Using a Jupyter Notebook (this was first introduced in Chapter 3), we will pull news data using a specific keyword and then use a sentiment analysis library to work out the polarity of the various articles. The main steps that we will be following in this hands-on exercise can be summarized as follows:

1   Pull data directly using an API (news API).
2   Use TextBlob for sentiment analysis.
3   Do some visualizations on the results.

So let us begin by opening up a new Jupyter Notebook to do our coding in (see Figure 9.1).

Once the Jupyter Notebook is created and opened, we execute the necessary configurations and import the relevant libraries. The first library to import is the News API library (see Figure 9.18), which allows us to connect and pull news articles from the News API site. In Figure 9.19 we have also imported the datetime[7] library (which provides modules for manipulating dates and times) and pandas[8] (which is a popular Python data analysis library).

```
from newsapi import NewsApiClient
import datetime as dt
import pandas as pd
```

Figure 9.19   Import the required libraries

Whenever you are connecting to any site or using any API, one of the first things to do is to go through the documentation. The documentation will tell you how to connect to the site and use the various facilities that are available. The documentation of the News API shows how to connect to it to retrieve articles; for our example what you need is to pass your unique `api_key` (which you receive when you register on the site) into the `NewsAPIClient` function as shown in Figure 9.20.

```
newsapi = NewsApiClient(api_key='xxxxxxxxxxxxxxxxxxxxxxx')
```

Figure 9.20   Connecting to the News API site

We are now ready to pull the required data from the News API site. From the documentation on the site, we are using the `get_everything` method to return the requested data. The method takes in some parameters such as the date range for the news articles we want to retrieve and the language the articles need to be in (see Figure 9.21). Figure 9.22 shows the data returned.

```
data = newsapi.get_everything(q='covid-19',
                             #sources='bbc-news,the-verge',
                             #domains='bbc.co.uk,www.saga.co.uk',
                             from_param='2023-02-20',
                             to='2023-03-12',
                             language='en',
                             sort_by='relevancy',
                             page=5)
```

Figure 9.21   Retrieving data (news articles)

Next, to simplify the sentiment analysis step, we will extract the news articles and store them in a DataFrame (remember we covered Apache Spark DataFrames in Chapter 3). In this case we could create an Apache Spark DataFrame, but let us use a different type of DataFrame – a pandas DataFrame (this is to illustrate that there are different ways of doing the same thing; see Figure 9.23). To create this, we call the relevant method from the pandas library which we imported in the first cell of our Jupyter Notebook (see Figure 9.19). The documentation for the pandas API can be found on the pandas website.[9]

```
data.keys()
```

```
Output:
dict_keys(['status', 'totalResults', 'articles'])
```

```
data['status']
```

```
Output:
'ok'
```

```
data['totalResults']
```

```
Output:
142466
```

```
data['articles']
```

```
Output:
[{'source': {'id': None, 'name': 'Gizmodo.com'},
  'author': 'Matt Novak',
  'title': 'Twitter Launches Five-Strike System to Ban Users Who Spread
Covid-19 Lies',
  'description': 'Twitter will ban users who spread misinformation about the
coronavirus pandemic and covid-19 vaccines under a new five-strike system,
according to a new blog post from the social media company. Twitter bans all
medical information that's "demonstrably false o…',
  'url': 'https://gizmodo.com/twitter-launches-five-strike-system-to-ban-
users-who-sp-1846386340',
  'urlToImage': 'https://i.kinja-img.com/gawker-media/image/upload/c_fill,f_
auto,fl_progressive,g_center,h_675,pg_1,q_80,w_1200/rk8mwlqkppdbr8yvfokk.jpg',
  'publishedAt': '2021-03-02T11:00:00Z',
  'content': 'Twitter will ban users who spread misinformation about the
coronavirus pandemic and covid-19 vaccines under a new five-strike system,
according to a new blog post from the social media company. Twitt… [+2847
chars]'}…
```

Figure 9.22 Inspecting the returned data

Now that we have the news data in the pandas DataFrame, we are now ready to perform sentiment analysis on it. The Python library that we will be using in this example is TextBlob, and again to know what methods it provides and how to use them you should look through the documentation for it.

In the example in Figure 9.24, we are applying the TextBlob sentiment method to the first news article's title and so the results that we get in terms of polarity and subjectivity are just for a single record (i.e., the first article). Polarity determines whether a text is positive, negative, or neutral, and for TextBlob it is a float which ranges from –1 (negative statement) to

```
#save copy of articles to new list
articles = data['articles']


#create a pandas dataframe df from the articles data returned from the newsAPI
df = pd.DataFrame(articles)


df
```

Output:

	source	author	title	description	url	urlT
0	{'id': 'cnn', 'name': 'CNN'}	By <a href="/profiles/melissa-mahtani" target=...	Here's where things stand	Senate Democrats are racing to pass their vers...	https://www.cnn.com/politics/live-news/stimulu...	https://cdn.cnn.com/cnnnext/dam/assets/21C
1	{'id': 'cnn', 'name': 'CNN'}	None	Doctor: Fighting insurance company on Covid ca...	Dr. Andrew Carroll describes to CNN's Brianna ...	https://www.cnn.com/videos/health/2021/03/04/c...	https://cdn.cnn.com/cnnnext/dam/assets/21C
2	{'id': 'cnn', 'name': 'CNN'}	None	Why this Republican is urging the GOP to suppo...	Jeff Williams, the mayor of Arlington, Texas, ...	https://www.cnn.com/videos/politics/2021/03/03...	https://cdn.cnn.com/cnnnext/dam/assets/21C
3	{'id': 'cnn', 'name': 'CNN'}	Christina Maxouris, CNN	US is at a tipping point of another Covid-19 s...	With each day and each vaccination, the US inc...	https://www.cnn.com/2021/03/07/health/us-coron...	https://cdn.cnn.com/cnnnext/dam/assets/21C
4	{'id': 'cnn', 'name': 'CNN'}	None	See what Bill Gates thinks of Biden's stimulus...	CNN's Fareed Zakaria asks Bill Gates whether h...	https://www.cnn.com/videos/economy/2021/03/01/...	https://cdn.cnn.com/cnnnext/dam/assets/21C
5	{'id': 'cnn', 'name': 'CNN'}	None	Bloopers, snafus and viral goofs: Inside pande...	CNN's Brian Stelter shows you how television p...	https://www.cnn.com/videos/media/2021/03/07/st...	https://cdn.cnn.com/cnnnext/dam/assets/21C

Figure 9.23 Creating a pandas DataFrame from the articles and viewing snippets from its contents

```
# Textblob for sentiment analysis
from textblob import TextBlob


blob = TextBlob(df.title[0])
sent = blob.sentiment


polarity=sent.polarity,
subjectivity=sent.subjectivity


# return the values returned by TextBlob for the polarity and subjectivity


polarity, subjectivity
```

Output:
```
((0.0,), (0.1,))
```

Figure 9.24 Sentiment analysis and the results for the title of the first article

+1 (positive statement). Subjectivity, on the other hand, refers to whether a text expresses personal opinion or factual information, and for Textblob it is a float which ranges from 0 (very objective) to 1 (very subjective).

In this case, though, we do not just want the polarity and subjectivity for one article, we want them for all the articles that were retrieved, that is, all the articles in the DataFrame. To achieve this, we can add additional columns to the DataFrame to hold the values of the respective polarity and subjectivity for all the articles' titles and descriptions.

Figure 9.25 shows how this is achieved. The first new column that is added to the DataFrame is called the `polarity_title`, and the values in it are obtained by applying the TextBlob method to all of the titles of the articles in the DataFrame. The next three columns, `subjectivity_title`, `polarity_description`, and `subjectivity_description`, are retrieved in a similar manner. For the final column, keyword, all its values are set to covid-19 as a reminder of the keyword that was used to retrieve the news articles in the first place.

```
# add sentiment analysis fields to the dataframe
df['polarity_title'] = df['title'].apply(lambda tweet: TextBlob(tweet).
sentiment.polarity)

df['subjectivity_title'] = df['title'].apply(lambda tweet: TextBlob(tweet).
sentiment.subjectivity)

df['polarity_description'] = df['description'].apply(lambda tweet:
TextBlob(tweet).sentiment.polarity)

df['subjectivity_description'] = df['description'].apply(lambda tweet:
TextBlob(tweet).sentiment.subjectivity)

df['keyword'] = 'covid-19'
```

Figure 9.25 Adding new columns to the DataFrame with the polarity and subjectivity values

If we now look at a snippet of the contents of the DataFrame, we can see that all the new columns have been added and populated with the respective values (Figure 9.26). As mentioned above and in the TextBlob documentation, the polarity and subjectivity values that have been returned are floats. What if we are interested in being able to see at a glance the description of the polarity (i.e., whether it is positive, negative or neutral) and not so much in the actual float value? To achieve this, we can once again add some additional columns to hold the information that we need (see Figure 9.27). Where the polarity value is less than zero we set the description in the new column to negative, where it is greater than zero to positive, and where it is zero to neutral.

We have returned the polarity and subjectivity for every news article title and description that we retrieved from the News API site, which was the objective that we set out to achieve. Let us now apply some simple visualizations to our results (the important topic of visualizations is treated in depth in Chapter 11). The two libraries that we will use for the visualizations here are ones we used in Chapters 3 and 6,

	urlToImage	publishedAt	content	polarity_title	subjectivity_title	polarity_description	subjectivity_description	keyword
	dn.cnn.com/cnnnext/dam/assets/2103051...	2021-03-06T13:39:58Z	The Senate is voting into Saturday morning on ...	0.000000	0.000000	0.500000	0.900000	covid-19
	dn.cnn.com/cnnnext/dam/assets/2103041...	2021-03-04T20:35:37Z	None	0.000000	0.000000	0.000000	0.000000	covid-19
	dn.cnn.com/cnnnext/dam/assets/2103031...	2021-03-03T19:59:36Z	None	0.000000	0.000000	0.000000	0.000000	covid-19
	dn.cnn.com/cnnnext/dam/assets/2103041...	2021-03-07T08:26:26Z	(CNN)With each day and each vaccination, the U...	0.000000	1.000000	-0.875000	1.000000	covid-19
	dn.cnn.com/cnnnext/dam/assets/2102280...	2021-03-01T20:21:13Z	None	0.000000	0.000000	-0.250000	1.000000	covid-19
	dn.cnn.com/cnnnext/dam/assets/2103071...	2021-03-07T18:44:48Z	None	0.000000	0.000000	0.000000	0.000000	covid-19

Figure 9.26   Updated contents of the DataFrame

```
# add new columns to data frame with polarity descriptions
df.loc[df.polarity_title < 0, 'polarity_title_desc' ] = 'negative'
df.loc[df.polarity_title == 0, 'polarity_title_desc' ] = 'neutral'
df.loc[df.polarity_title > 0, 'polarity_title_desc' ] = 'positive'

df.loc[df.polarity_description < 0, 'polarity_description_desc' ] = 'negative'
df.loc[df.polarity_description == 0, 'polarity_description_desc' ] = 'neutral'
df.loc[df.polarity_description > 0, 'polarity_description_desc' ] = 'positive'

df
```

Output:

lishedAt	content	polarity_title	subjectivity_title	polarity_description	subjectivity_description	keyword	polarity_title_desc	polarity_description_desc
2021-03-13:39:58Z	The Senate is voting into Saturday morning on ...	0.000000	0.000000	0.500000	0.900000	covid-19	neutral	positive
2021-03-20:35:37Z	None	0.000000	0.000000	0.000000	0.000000	covid-19	neutral	neutral
2021-03-19:59:36Z	None	0.000000	0.000000	0.000000	0.000000	covid-19	neutral	neutral
2021-03-08:26:26Z	(CNN)With each day and each vaccination, the U...	0.000000	1.000000	-0.875000	1.000000	covid-19	neutral	negative
2021-03-20:21:13Z	None	0.000000	0.000000	-0.250000	1.000000	covid-19	neutral	negative
2021-03-18:44:48Z	None	0.000000	0.000000	0.000000	0.000000	covid-19	neutral	neutral

Figure 9.27   Adding new columns with the polarity descriptions (positive, negative, or neutral)

```
# draw pie chart for polarity [-1, 1] -1 =>  negative, + 1 => positive, 0
=> neutral
  df.polarity_title_desc.value_counts().plot(kind='pie', autopct='%1.0f%%')
```

Output:

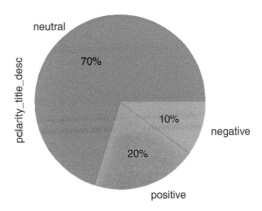

```
  df.polarity_description_desc.value_counts().plot(kind='pie',
autopct='%1.0f%%')
```

Output:

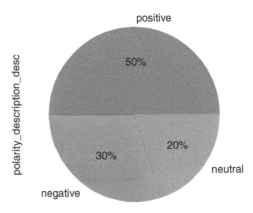

Figure 9.28 Visualization of the sentiment analysis results using PyPlot

PixieDust[10] and matplotlib.[11] After importing the matplotlib library the simple code depicted in Figure 9.28 can be used to plot pie charts that show the ratio of the various polarity descriptions for news titles and news descriptions. In this case it is interesting to see that a much higher percentage of the news titles (i.e., the headlines) were neutral in comparison to the actual news descriptions (i.e., the content of the articles).

Some research has been done into why sentiment analysis of news headlines and the actual contents of the news might have different sentiments. In one particularly interesting paper on sentiment analysis Reis et al. (2015) investigate possible strategies used by online news corporations in the design of their headlines to attract clicks and catch people's attention; some of these might explain the difference in the sentiments of new headlines and the actual content of the news.

The next set of visualizations were done using PixieDust, which provides facilities to produce various types of visualizations without writing a single line of code. All you have to do to use it is install the library (as described in Chapter 2) and then import it in the Jupyter Notebook before you use it (see Figures 9.29 and 9.30). To load it you then simply use the command `display` and pass in the variable holding the data you want to visualize. In this example we have used it to plot both pie charts and a clustered histogram which depicts the polarity of the news articles against that of the news headlines.

```
# import the pixiedust library
import pixiedust

display(df)

Output:
```

Figure 9.29 Visualization of the sentiment analysis results using PixieDust (pie chart)

For our next hands-on exercise, we will carry out sentiment analysis using TextBlob again, but this time on larger amounts of data in files. The steps involved are as follows:

1   Upload text files for analysis.
2   Use Textblob for sentiment analysis.
3   Visualization of the results as a word cloud.

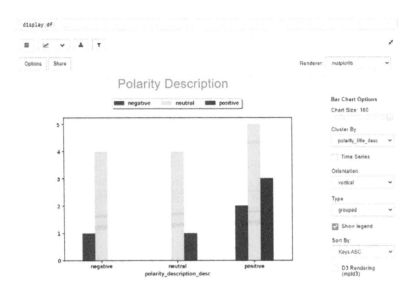

Figure 9.30 Visualization of the sentiment analysis results using PixieDust (histogram and clustering)

We start by carrying out sentiment analysis on manually inputted text, and then move on to much larger files.

```
# import the relevant libraries
import nltk
import matplotlib
import pandas



# perform sentiment analysis on text inputted by a user
from textblob import TextBlob

input_text = "big data analytics is fantastic!!!"

blob = TextBlob(input_text) #pass the input text to Textblob

polarity = (blob.sentiment.polarity) #get a polarity score

print(polarity)

Output:
0.390625
```

Figure 9.31 Sentiment analysis on manually inputted text (polarity)

For the text entered in Figure 9.31 we can see that the polarity is 0.39, which for TextBlob means that the text is positive, which is as expected for what is clearly a positive statement. Play around with various statements and see if the polarity you get is what you would expect based on whether the text you enter is positive, negative, or neutral.

Let us now turn the subjectivity of the same inputted text. Remember that subjectivity quantifies the amount of personal opinion and factual information in the text. The closer the subjectivity is to 1, the more personal the opinion is in the text, and the closer it is to 0, the more factual it is. From Figure 9.32 we see that the subjectivity is 0.5, half-way between 1 and 0.

```
from textblob import TextBlob

input_text = "big data analytics is fantastic!!!"

blob = TextBlob(input_text) #pass the input text to TextBlob

polarity = blob.sentiment.polarity #get a polarity score

subjectivity = blob.sentiment.subjectivity #get a subjectivity score

if polarity > 0:
  sentiment = "Positive"
elif polarity < 0:
    sentiment = "Negative"
else:
    sentiment = "Neutral"

print('Polarity: ' + str(polarity))

print('Subjectivity: ' + str(subjectivity))

print('sentiment: ' + str(sentiment))

Output:
Polarity: 0.390625
Subjectivity: 0.5
sentiment: Positive
```

Figure 9.32 Sentiment analysis on manually inputted text (polarity and subjectivity)

Let us now move on to carry out sentiment analysis on larger amounts of data. Let us start off by having a go with the Shakespeare sonnets dataset which we first came across in Chapter 3. First, let us upload the file to be analysed (see Figure 9.33). Then, using similar code to that used for the manually inputted text, let us apply sentiment analysis to the entire contents of the Shakespeare file. From Figure 9.34, we see that overall Shakespeare's sonnets have a positive polarity and hold more personal opinion than factual information.

```
# upload the text file to be analysed
with open(r'shakespeare.txt') as f:
    input_text = f.read()
    print(input_text)


Output:
1609


THE SONNETS


by William Shakespeare



                  1
    From fairest creatures we desire increase,
    That thereby beauty's rose might never die,
    But as the riper should by time decease,
    His tender heir might bear his memory:
    But thou contracted to thine own bright eyes,
    Feed'st thy light's flame with self-substantial fuel,
    Making a famine where abundance lies,
    Thy self thy foe, to thy sweet self too cruel:
    Thou that art now the world's fresh ornament,
    And only herald to the gaudy spring,
```

Figure 9.33 Uploading and viewing snippets of the contents of the Shakespeare file

As in our previous example, it can be useful to also apply some visualizations to our results, in this case a word cloud. So first we create a pandas DataFrame from our input text (Figure 9.35, in this case the contents of the Shakespeare file). Then we import the matplotlib library to plot the word cloud from the words in the input file. Again, remember that going through documentation is essential and this will enable you to see what types of visualizations are available and how to go about plotting them. The word cloud output is shown in Figure 9.36. The size of each word in the word cloud corresponds to the frequency (i.e. number of times the word occurs) of the specific word in the input text. So in the word cloud in Figure 9.36, we can see that some of the words that occur the most in Shakespeare's sonnets are 'thy', 'thou', 'the', 'made', 'sonnets', and 'pray'.

```
from textblob import TextBlob

with open(r'shakespeare.txt') as f:
    input_text = f.read()

blob = TextBlob(input_text) #pass the input text to TextBlob

polarity = blob.sentiment.polarity #get a polarity score

polarity = round(polarity, 2) # round to 2 decimal places

subjectivity = blob.sentiment.subjectivity #get a subjectivity score

subjectivity = round(subjectivity, 2) # round to 2 decimal places

if polarity > 0:
  sentiment = "Positive"
elif polarity < 0:
  sentiment = "Negative"
else:
    sentiment = "Neutral"

print('Polarity: ' + str(polarity))

print('Subjectivity: ' + str(subjectivity))

print('Sentiment: ' + sentiment)

Output:
Polarity: 0.16
Subjectivity: 0.53
Sentiment: Positive
```

Figure 9.34 Applying sentiment analysis to the contents of the Shakespeare file

```
  # create dataframe from input text to use for word cloud
import pandas as pd
df = pd.DataFrame(input_text)
```

Figure 9.35 Creating a pandas DataFrame from the contents of the input file

```
# Word cloud
# import the relevant libraries
from wordcloud import WordCloud
import matplotlib.pyplot as plt


# Create and generate a word cloud image:
wordcloud = WordCloud().generate(str(df))

# Display the generated image:
plt.imshow(wordcloud, interpolation='bilinear')
plt.axis("off")
plt.show()
```

Output:

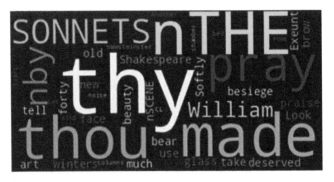

Figure 9.36   Plotting the word cloud

So far for all the sentiment analysis that we have carried out we have used the TextBlob library. In the next example we use Vader. As in the previous hands-on exercises, we start by importing the relevant libraries, including vaderSentiment which holds the modules that we need to carry out the sentiment analysis on the text using Vader (Figure 9.37). Then we apply sentiment analysis to the inputted text in a similar manner to previous examples (see Figure 9.38).

```
# import the relevant libraries
import nltk
import matplotlib
import pandas
import vaderSentiment
```

Figure 9.37   Importing the relevant libraries

```
from vaderSentiment.vaderSentiment import SentimentIntensityAnalyzer
analyzer = SentimentIntensityAnalyzer()


input_text = "big data analytics is fantastic!!!"


# function to calculate vader sentiment
def vadersentimentanalysis(review):
    vs = analyzer.polarity_scores(review)
    return vs['compound']


polarity = vadersentimentanalysis(input_text)


if polarity >= 0.05:
  sentiment = "Positive"
elif polarity <= -0.05:
    sentiment = "Negative"
else:
    sentiment = "Neutral"


print('Polarity: ' + str(polarity))


print('sentiment: ' + str(sentiment))


Output:
Polarity: 0.6679
sentiment: Positive
```

Figure 9.38 Sentiment analysis using Vader

Using Vader, we see that the polarity is again positive (Figure 9.38), which is consistent with the results that we got using TextBlob earlier. The results for Vader are interpreted in a different way from TextBlob: with Vader the polarity is said to be positive if the compound score is greater than or equal to 0.05, neutral if the compound score is less than 0.05 in absolute value, and negative if the compound score is less than or equal to –0.05.

Sentiment analysis is not limited to just manually inputted text or text files; it can be applied to any form of textual data. It can be applied to data in databases, data in the cloud, data submitted using forms, customer feedback, X (formerly known as Twitter) feeds, and so on. In the next hands-on exercise, we will consider sentiment analysis on some X (formerly known as Twitter) feeds. The steps that are followed can be summarized as follows:

1   Use X (formerly known as Twitter) developer account keys and the Tweepy Python library to harvest tweets for analysis.

2   Use Textblob for sentiment analysis.

To be able to directly harvest X (formerly known as Twitter) feeds you will need to register for an X (formerly known as Twitter) developer account.[12] Once your registration is successful, you will be sent a set of keys (consumer key, consumer secret, access key, and access secret) whose values are unique to your account. These keys are what you use to access the X (formerly known as Twitter) API and harvest tweets. In this hands-on exercise we also use Tweepy,[13] which is an easy-to-use Python library to access the X (formerly known as Twitter) API.

As always, we start by importing the relevant libraries (Figure 9.39). Next, we use the X (formerly known as Twitter) keys to extract tweets from the X (formerly known as Twitter) API (Figure 9.40). We then use TextBlob to analyse the harvested tweets and return their polarities and subjectivity (see Figure 9.41).

```
import dataset
from textblob import TextBlob
import pandas as pd
import tweepy
```

Figure 9.39 Importing the relevant libraries

```
# Replace the Xs with the credentials from X (formerly known as Twitter)
consumer_key = "XXXXXXXXXXXXXXXXXXXXXXXXXXXXXXXXXXXXXXXXX"
consumer_secret = " XXXXXXXXXXXXXXXXXXXXXXXXXXXXXXXXXXXXXXXXXXXXXX"
access_key="XXXXXXXXXXXXXXXXXXXXXXXXXXXXXXXXXXXXXXXXXXX"
access_secret = " XXXXXXXXXXXXXXXXXXXXXXXXXXXXXXXXXXXXXXXXXX "


# Function to extract tweets
def get_tweets(username):

# Authorization to consumer key and consumer secret
    auth = tweepy.OAuthHandler(consumer_key, consumer_secret)

# Access to user's access key and access secret
    auth.set_access_token(access_key, access_secret)

# Calling api
    api = tweepy.API(auth)

# 500 tweets to be extracted
    number_of_tweets=500
    tweets = api.user_timeline(screen_name=username)

# Empty Array
    tmp=[]
```

Figure 9.40 Using keys and Tweepy to harvest tweets from the X (formerly known as Twitter) API

```
# create array of tweet information: username,
# tweet id, date/time, text
    tweets_info = [tweet.created_at for tweet in tweets]
    tweets_for_csv = [tweet.text for tweet in tweets]
    for j in tweets_for_csv:
        # Textblob for sentiment analysis
        blob = TextBlob(j)
        sent = blob.sentiment

# Appending tweets to the empty array tmp
        tmp.append(j)
        tmp.append(sent.polarity)
        tmp.append(sent.subjectivity)
        df = pd.DataFrame(tmp)


# Printing the tweets
    print(tmp)

# Driver code
if __name__ == '__main__':

# Here goes the X (formerly known as Twitter) handle for the user
# whose tweets are to be extracted.
    get_tweets("@bigdata")
```

Output:

['🆕 post 🦷 Entity resolution (ER) combines big data, real-time
processing & AI to tackle complex problems. Learn how… https://t.
co/wyZZ6fjS9M', -0.15, 0.25, "🆕 Newsletter 📩🚀 Learn what Apple's job
postings & patent filings reveal about their AI ambitions. Plus learn
why mod… https://t.co/eu9MRhU3ZF", 0.0, 0.0, "#TheDataExchangePod: Dive
into the future of AI with #Mojo, a language combining #Python's usability
& C's speed.… https://t.co/DCyaRWRLm0", 0.0, 0.125, 'George Washington
Gale Ferris Jr. 🎡🎡 the man who reinvented the wheel \nhttps://t.co/
M4Sp09z81o via @CBSSunday', 0.0, 0.0, "#TheDataExchangePod: Dive into the
future of AI with #Mojo, a language combining #Python's usability &
C's speed.… https://t.co/BSapA7890t", 0.0, 0.125, '"To apply for a U.S.
green card, you have to fill out an I-485 form, which is 20 pages long — not
including the 44… https://t.co/LxCpH8gmcr', -0.125, 0.35, "🆕 Newsletter 📩
🚀 Learn what Apple's job postings & patent filings reveal about their
AI ambitions. Plus learn why mod… https://t.co/f3Mwt3zBrr", 0.0, 0.0,
"#TheDataExchangePod: Dive into the future of AI with #Mojo, a language
combining #Python's usability & C's speed.… https://t.co/qwqiY6Ejfq",
0.0, 0.125, 'Happy Friday and\xa0Slava Ukraini 🇺🇦 #Ukraine
#UkraineRussiaWar https://t.co/wjnoXf0GuB', 0.8, 1.0, '🔒 Join

(Continued)

Figure 9.41 (Continued)

our illustrious roster of speakers 🔥 today is the last day to submit a talk to the first @AIConference 📅 ⌛\n🌐 https://t.co/mILOw6Qj4S', 0.125, 0.19999999999999998, "🆕Newsletter 📬🔬 Learn what Apple's job postings & patent filings reveal about their AI ambitions. Plus learn why mod… https://t.co/ewjiC7VRgD", 0.0, 0.0, "#TheDataExchangePod: Dive into the future of AI with #Mojo, a language combining #Python's usability & C's speed.… https://t.co/nlfco2Ta3l", 0.0, 0.125, "RT @psb_dc: Decoding #Apple's #AI Ambitions \n\n#BigTech cc @data_nerd @HaroldSinnott @FGraillot @SpirosMargaris @AkwyZ @Xbond49 \n\nhttps://t.…", 0.0, 0.0, "🆕Newsletter 📬🔬 Learn what Apple's job postings & patent filings reveal about their AI ambitions. Plus learn why mod… https://t.co/M8rTKb6Hvs", 0.0, 0.0, "#TheDataExchangePod: Dive into the future of AI with #Mojo, a language combining #Python's usability & C's speed.… https://t.co/jwfDoYwKhU", 0.0, 0.125, 'Extinction Rebellion 🚒 #SanFrancisco version\nhttps://t.co/NWFTjS2vse', 0.0, 0.0, 'RT @dkaloniuk: So many experts in the Prigozhin-Putin conflict in the media now. So many opinions on what that means for Russia, Ukraine, a…', 0.5, 0.5, '#TheDataExchangePod 👨 Andrew Feldman @ CerebrasSystems dives into the future of #AI with custom #LLMs. We discuss Ce… https://t.co/HoubT5tqiM', 0.0, 0.125, '#TheDataExchangePod 👨 Andrew Feldman @CerebrasSystems dives into the future of #AI with custom #LLMs. We discuss Ce… https://t.co/JCNetMS97L', 0.0, 0.125, "The stock market is so lit right now that it's practically on fire. #Litquidity is at an all-time high\n\nThis is an… https://t.co/pvZiJ5plPI", 0.22285714285714286, 0.5378571428571428]

Figure 9.41 Sentiment analysis applied to tweets

At times when you try to import libraries you might find that you are unable to do so because the library has not been installed in your environment. When this is the case all you need to do is install the relevant library using the pip command. Below are the commands that you would need to run some of the libraries that we have used in the hands-on exercise in your environment prior to importing these libraries if they have not already been installed in your environment:

- !pip install textblob[14]
- !pip install nltk[15]
- !pip install matplotlib[16]
- !pip install pandas[17]
- !pip install vaderSentiment[18]

As sentiment analysis is one of the most commonly used NLP techniques, in addition to writing code and applying it to your datasets (which is how you would normally use it on large datasets) there are also various sites where you can run analysis on texts in an online environment. These include the following:

- https://monkeylearn.com/sentiment-analysis-online/
- https://awario.com/blog/sentiment-analysis-tools/
- https://www.danielsoper.com/sentimentanalysis/default.aspx

9.5 TOPIC MODELLING

Topic modelling is a technique in NLP used to discover topics and themes within a collection of texts. It helps to determine the main themes in collections. Topic modelling can be used for semantic searches and for the identification of hidden relationships. The most popular algorithm for topic modelling is latent Dirichlet allocation (LDA). As with other algorithms, we do not go into its technical details but demonstrate how to use it in a hands-on exercise. For further details, see the original LDA paper by Blei et al. (2003) and the Apache Spark API documentation.[19]

9.5.1 Latent Dirichlet allocation

Figure 9.42 depicts the steps in LDA. As with most algorithms in NLP, once the documents or texts to be processed are uploaded the next step is pre-processing, to clean and prepare the texts or documents to be used in the training of the LDA model. The model takes in input parameters such as the number of topics to discover and the number of iterations to run. Once the model is trained it can then be used to assign topics based on probabilities for each document.

Figure 9.42 Steps in topic modelling using the LDA algorithm

For our hands-on exercise on topic modelling, we use methods from the Apache Spark MLlib library including LDA; the full code can be seen in Figure 9.43. For the hands-on exercise the dataset that we are using is crime outcomes, Figure 9.44 shows a snippet of this dataset.

The code for topic modelling of the Crime Outcomes dataset using LDA can be seen in Figure 9.44.

Let us look at the code from Figure 9.43 in detail. After importing the relevant libraries and initializing the spark session, the next step is to create a DataFrame from the input file which is then tokenized. A snippet of the results after tokenization is shown in Figure 9.45. This is displayed by using the command

```
tokenizedData.show(truncate=False)
```

After the input has been split into tokens, further pre-processing is carried out through the removal of stop words. To see the output from this step run the command

```
filteredData.show(truncate=False)
```

The next step in the process is then to convert the words into a feature vector; this is important as the training algorithm cannot use words, so we use various methods to convert into a format (numeric data) that the algorithms can work with. In this case we used

```python
from pyspark.ml.feature import CountVectorizer, Tokenizer, StopWordsRemover
from pyspark.ml.clustering import LDA
from pyspark.sql import SparkSession

# Initialize SparkSession
spark = SparkSession.builder.appName("LDA-HandsOn").getOrCreate()

# Create a DataFrame from File with the Data
crimes_df = spark.read.text("LondonCrimeOutcomes.csv")

# Tokenize the text data
tokenizer = Tokenizer(inputCol="value", outputCol="tokens")
tokenized_df = tokenizer.transform(crimes_df)

# Remove stop words
stopWordsRemover=StopWordsRemover(inputCol="tokens",
outputCol="filteredTokens")
filtered_df = stopWordsRemover.transform(tokenized_df)

# CountVectorizer to convert words into a feature vector
cv = CountVectorizer(inputCol="filteredTokens", outputCol="features")
cvModel = cv.fit(filtered_df)
vectorizedData = cvModel.transform(filtered_df)

# Train LDA model
lda = LDA(k=3, maxIter=10)
ldaModel = lda.fit(vectorizedData)

# Display topics and their corresponding word probabilities
topics = ldaModel.describeTopics(5)
print("The topics described by their top-weighted terms:")
topics.show(truncate=False)

# Display assigned topics for each document
transformed = ldaModel.transform(vectorizedData)
print("Documents assigned to topics:")
transformed.select("value", "topicDistribution").show(truncate=False)
```

Figure 9.43 Topic modelling using LDA

```
Offender given a caution
Court result unavailable
Status update unavailable
Court result unavailable
Court result unavailable
Formal action is not in the public interest
Status update unavailable
Court result unavailable
Investigation complete; no suspect identified
Investigation complete; no suspect identified
Investigation complete; no suspect identified
Investigation complete; no suspect identified
Status update unavailable
Awaiting court outcome
Status update unavailable
Status update unavailable
Unable to prosecute suspect
Unable to prosecute suspect
```

Figure 9.44   Snippet of the crime outcomes dataset

```
+--------------------------------------------+----------------------------------------------------+
|value                                       |tokens                                              |
+--------------------------------------------+----------------------------------------------------+
|Last outcome category                       |[last, outcome, category]                           |
|Investigation complete; no suspect identified|[investigation, complete;, no, suspect, identified]|
|Investigation complete; no suspect identified|[investigation, complete;, no, suspect, identified]|
|Investigation complete; no suspect identified|[investigation, complete;, no, suspect, identified]|
|Investigation complete; no suspect identified|[investigation, complete;, no, suspect, identified]|
|Unable to prosecute suspect                 |[unable, to, prosecute, suspect]                    |
|Unable to prosecute suspect                 |[unable, to, prosecute, suspect]                    |
|Offender given penalty notice               |[offender, given, penalty, notice]                  |
|Status update unavailable                   |[status, update, unavailable]                       |
|Status update unavailable                   |[status, update, unavailable]                       |
|Status update unavailable                   |[status, update, unavailable]                       |
|Investigation complete; no suspect identified|[investigation, complete;, no, suspect, identified]|
|Investigation complete; no suspect identified|[investigation, complete;, no, suspect, identified]|
|Investigation complete; no suspect identified|[investigation, complete;, no, suspect, identified]|
|Investigation complete; no suspect identified|[investigation, complete;, no, suspect, identified]|
|Investigation complete; no suspect identified|[investigation, complete;, no, suspect, identified]|
|Investigation complete; no suspect identified|[investigation, complete;, no, suspect, identified]|
|Status update unavailable                   |[status, update, unavailable]                       |
|Status update unavailable                   |[status, update, unavailable]                       |
|Investigation complete; no suspect identified|[investigation, complete;, no, suspect, identified]|
+--------------------------------------------+----------------------------------------------------+
only showing top 20 rows
```

Figure 9.45   Output from tokenization

CountVectorizer,[20] which converts documents into a feature vector ready to be used to train the LDA model. In training the model in this hands-on exercise, two input parameters are passed in; the number of topics (3) and the number of iterations (10). The trained model is then used to extract the top words for each topic and we see the assigned topics for each entered document.

Finally, we visualize the output in Figure 9.46 using the matplotlib.pyplot[21] library:

```
import matplotlib.pyplot as plt


# Extract topic distribution values from DataFrame
topic_distributions = transformed.select("topicDistribution").collect()

# Create a list of topic probabilities for each document
document_probabilities = [row[0] for row in topic_distributions]

# Plot the topic distributions for each document
for i, probabilities in enumerate(document_probabilities):
    topics = range(len(probabilities))
    plt.bar(topics, probabilities)
    plt.xlabel("Topic")
    plt.ylabel("Probability")
    plt.title("Topic Distribution - Document {i+1}")
    plt.xticks(topics)
    plt.show()
```

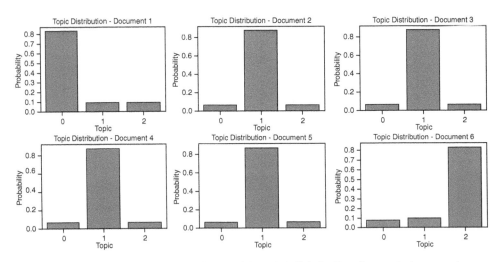

Figure 9.46   Code for and small snippet of the plot distribution for each document

Another technique for topic modelling is non-negative matrix factorization, discussed by Gillis (2021).

9.6 OTHER NLP ALGORITHMS AND TOOLS/FRAMEWORKS FOR NLP IN BIG DATA

There are a number of other NLP algorithms that are used for big data analytics, including the following:

- Keyword extraction algorithms[22] such as Rapid Automatic Keyword (RAKE), TextRank, Term Frequency
- Knowledge Graphs[23]
- Text Summarization[24]

Tools and frameworks for NLP in big data include the following:

- Natural Language Toolkit (NLTK) – this was used in some of the hands-on exercises in this chapter
- scikit-learn[25] – used and mentioned earlier, this is a popular free Python machine learning library providing many supervised and unsupervised algorithms, including many for NLP
- Stanford CoreNLP[26]
- Apache OpenNLP[27]
- spaCy[28]

9.7 ETHICS BY DESIGN

For this section on ethics by design we focus on ChatGPT.[29] This is a chatbot powered by AI that is very adept at answering questions, generating responses, and interacting in a conversational way. Within days of its release, it had taken the world by storm and become a viral sensation. It is expected to generate $1 billion in revenue by 2024 (Yao, 2022). ChatGPT is extremely impressive and can produce essays, respond conversationally, debug code, and do a host of other things. However, the ethical side of things also needs to be considered. Questions have been asked since its emergence over whether it would lead to AI-assisted plagiarism (Hern, 2022). It has certainly raised concerns across academia, and some tutors have already started to report catching students who have submitted essays/assignments that they got ChatGPT to produce. One such example covered by the *New York Post* (Mitchell, 2022) was reported for an assessment in which students were asked to write a 500-word essay on the eighteenth-century philosopher David Hume and the paradox of horror.

As a test of sorts, I asked chatGPT to write a 500-word essay on the eighteenth-century philosopher David Hume and the paradox of horror. The results can be seen in Figure 9.47.

David Hume was an 18th-century Scottish philosopher, historian, and economist, who is widely considered one of the most influential thinkers in the history of philosophy. One of the most interesting aspects of Hume's work is his exploration of human emotions, including the paradox of horror, which he described in his essay 'Of Tragedy'.

The paradox of horror is the idea that we can experience pleasure from things that would otherwise be considered horrific, such as tragedies, horror films, or other types of media that depict violence or suffering. Hume argues that this paradox arises from the fact that we are naturally drawn to novelty and variety, and that we enjoy the emotional stimulation that comes from experiencing something that is different from our everyday lives.

Hume notes that tragedies and other forms of horror can be enjoyable because they allow us to experience strong emotions in a controlled environment. We know that the events depicted in a tragedy are not real, and that we are not in danger ourselves, so we can experience the emotional intensity of the story without fear of harm. In this way, we can satisfy our natural desire for novelty and excitement without putting ourselves in danger.

However, Hume also notes that this enjoyment is not without limits. He argues that there is a point beyond which the horror becomes too intense, and the pleasure we derive from it is replaced by feelings of disgust and revulsion. This is why, he says, most tragedies and horror films are carefully crafted to balance the emotional intensity with moments of relief and resolution.

Hume's insights into the paradox of horror have been widely discussed and debated by philosophers and scholars over the centuries. Some have argued that his theory is incomplete or oversimplified, while others have found it to be a useful tool for understanding the complex relationship between emotion and media.

One of the most interesting aspects of Hume's theory is its relevance to contemporary debates about the effects of violent media on individuals and society. While some have argued that exposure to violent media can lead to desensitization and an increase in aggressive behavior, others have pointed out that people have been enjoying violent stories and entertainment for centuries without becoming violent themselves. Hume's theory of the paradox of horror suggests that this enjoyment may be a natural and healthy part of the human experience, as long as it is balanced with moments of relief and resolution.

In conclusion, David Hume's exploration of the paradox of horror offers a fascinating insight into the complex relationship between human emotions and the media we consume. His theory suggests that our natural desire for novelty and excitement can lead us to enjoy stories and entertainment that would otherwise be considered horrific, but that there is a limit beyond which this enjoyment becomes replaced by feelings of disgust and revulsion. This theory has been widely discussed and debated by scholars over the centuries and remains relevant to contemporary debates about the effects of violent media on individuals and society.

Figure 9.47 ChatGPT's response to 'write a 500-word essay on the 18th-century philosopher David Hume and the paradox of horror'

As this is not an area that I am an expert in I decided to ask ChatGPT to 'write a 500-word essay on the origins of machine learning', and what I found was each time I asked the question a well-written essay was delivered and each time the results were totally unique. This could potentially mean that someone who wants to cheat with this does not even have to fear that it can get picked up as plagiarism if ChatGPT gives a unique answer to the same question every time it is asked (see Figure 9.48 for one of the answers it generated). It is obvious why this is a concern and, referring to the TAFARP data ethics by design framework (Figure 2.14, p. 44), it raises issues around transparency, accountability, fairness, and responsibility.

Machine learning is a field of computer science that has gained popularity over the years due to its ability to allow computers to learn from data, without being explicitly programmed. Machine learning has become a critical part of modern technology, from image recognition and speech processing to natural language processing and autonomous vehicles.

The origins of machine learning can be traced back to the early days of artificial intelligence research, which dates back to the 1950s. At the time, researchers were interested in building machines that could mimic human intelligence. One of the earliest examples of machine learning was the perceptron, which was developed by Frank Rosenblatt in 1958. The perceptron was a simple neural network that was able to learn to classify images based on their features.

In the following decades, researchers continued to explore different types of machine learning algorithms. One of the most significant breakthroughs was the development of decision trees, which were introduced by Ross Quinlan in 1986. Decision trees are a type of supervised learning algorithm that can be used to classify data based on a set of rules.

Another key development in machine learning was the introduction of artificial neural networks in the 1980s. Neural networks are modeled after the structure of the human brain, and they consist of layers of interconnected nodes that can learn to recognize patterns in data. One of the most significant achievements in the field of neural networks was the development of the backpropagation algorithm, which allowed researchers to train networks with multiple layers.

The late 1990s and early 2000s saw the emergence of support vector machines, which are a type of supervised learning algorithm that can be used to classify data. Support vector machines are based on the idea of finding a hyperplane that separates data into different classes. This technique has proven to be effective in a wide range of applications, including image recognition and text classification.

In recent years, the development of deep learning has revolutionized the field of machine learning. Deep learning is a type of neural network that consists of many layers, allowing it to learn complex representations of data. Deep learning has been particularly successful in applications such as image and speech recognition, natural language processing, and autonomous vehicles.

Overall, the field of machine learning has undergone significant developments over the years, starting with the perceptron in the 1950s and continuing with neural networks, decision trees, support vector machines, and deep learning. As computers continue to become more powerful and the amount of data that is generated continues to increase, machine learning will undoubtedly continue to play a critical role in the development of new technologies.

Figure 9.48   ChatGPT's response to 'write a 500-word essay on the origins of machine learning'

The company that created the bot has said that it is working on a system to statistically watermark the outputs in a way that is not noticeable to readers but would be to those looking for signs of machine-generated text. While it is great that the company is now looking into this, an ethics by design approach would have been even better. With an ethics by design approach issues such as these would have been identified and combated during the design and implementation of the chatbot prior to its release. These are without a doubt very exciting times in the world of AI, machine learning, and specifically NLP, but to ensure that the systems that are built and released are assets to humanity and do not end up bringing harm, ethics by design must be at the forefront as these systems are envisioned, designed, and developed.

9.8 INDUSTRY INSIGHTS

The use of NLP for big data analytics is an emerging area, and for our industry insight we will focus on the company Alexandria Technology,[30] which is a pioneer in artificial intelligence NLP. Alexandria Technology uses NLP to analyse extremely large amounts of data (big data) to provide insights to help aid investment decisions in the financial sector. Its products include providing a single platform for its clients which classifies sentiments and themes for all document types including long-form reports, social media, and other similar sources. It protects positions by monitoring chatrooms and blogs so that organizations can be proactive and not just reactive. It provides real-time Environment, Social, and Governance (ESG) insights, deep thematic sentiments, and so on. This demonstrates what is needed in the big data era that we are in. Organizations that do not take advantage of the big data they can access to innovate and produce useful insights are unlikely to have a competitive advantage and might find that they struggle to survive.

SUMMARY

In this chapter we discussed NLP and went through common NLP algorithms used for pre-processing such as stemming and tokenization. We also covered sentiment analysis using different algorithms and carried out hands-on exercises to mine opinions from text and use visualizations to represent the mined sentiments. We also explored topic modelling. Finally, we considered related ethics by design issues and some industry insights in this space.

TEST YOUR KNOWLEDGE

1   Write down three ways in which you can use sentiment analysis.
2   Use the Tweepy API to harvest some tweets and then:
   •   Apply tokenization, stemming and lemmatization algorithms to the harvested tweets.
   •   Perform sentiment analysis on the cleaned input using TextBlob and Vader.
   •   Add additional columns with the polarity descriptions positive, negative, and neutral.
   •   Use visualizations to compare the results obtained using TextBlob and Vader.
3   Upload a large dataset of your choice and apply topic modelling to identify the top five themes in the text.

FURTHER READING (OPTIONAL)

Article on combining big data with NLP:

SafeNet Consulting (2018) The 3 hardest challenges of combining big data with natural language processing. Retrieved from https://safenetconsulting.com/challenges-natural-language-processing-evolving-world/

Interesting article on 2023 tech innovations, including chatGPT (our focus in the ethics by design section in this chapter):

Ovide, S. (2023) 2023 tech innovations probably won't change your life. *Washington Post*, 3 January. https://www.washingtonpost.com/technology/2023/01/03/2023-tech-predictions/

Article on the ChatGPT chatbot:

Shankland, S. (2023) Why we're obsessed with the mind-blowing ChatGPT AI chatbot. Retrieved from https://www.cnet.com/tech/computing/why-everyones-obsessed-with-chatgpt-a-mind-blowing-ai-chatbot/

NOTES

1   https://textblob.readthedocs.io/en/dev/quickstart.html
2   https://www.nltk.org/howto/stem.html
3   https://www.nltk.org/api/nltk.stem.snowball.html
4   https://scikit-learn.org/stable/
5   https://pypi.org/project/vaderSentiment/
6   https://newsapi.org
7   https://docs.python.org/3/library/datetime.html
8   https://pandas.pydata.org/
9   https://pandas.pydata.org/docs/reference/index.html
10 https://pixiedust.github.io/pixiedust/
11 https://matplotlib.org/stable/api/_as_gen/matplotlib.pyplot.plot.html
12 https://developer.twitter.com/en/docs/twitter-api/getting-started/getting-access-to-the-twitter-api
13 https://www.tweepy.org/
14 https://pypi.org/project/textblob/
15 https://pypi.org/project/nltk/
16 https://pypi.org/project/matplotlib/
17 https://pypi.org/project/pandas/
18 https://pypi.org/project/vaderSentiment/
19 https://spark.apache.org/docs/latest/api/python/reference/api/pyspark.ml.clustering.LDA.html
20 https://spark.apache.org/docs/latest/api/python/reference/api/pyspark.ml.feature.CountVectorizer.html
21 https://matplotlib.org/3.5.3/api/_as_gen/matplotlib.pyplot.html
22 https://medium.com/mlearning-ai/10-popular-keyword-extraction-algorithms-in-natural-language-processing-8975ada5750c
23 https://www.analyticsvidhya.com/blog/2019/10/how-to-build-knowledge-graph-text-using-spacy/
24 https://www.machinelearningplus.com/nlp/text-summarization-approaches-nlp-example/
25 https://scikit-learn.org/
26 https://nlp.stanford.edu/software/
27 https://opennlp.apache.org/

28 https://spacy.io/
29 https://openai.com/blog/chatgpt/
30 https://www.alexandriatechnology.com/

REFERENCES

Blei, D. M., Ng, A. Y. and Jordan, M. I. (2003) Latent Dirichlet allocation. *Journal of Machine Learning Research*, 3, 993–1022.

Gillis, N. (2021) *Nonnegative Matrix Factorization*. Philadelphia: Society for Industrial and Applied Mathematics.

Gupta, L., Gasparyan, A. Y., Misra, D. P., Agarwal, V., Zimba, O. and Yessirkepov, M. (2020) Information and misinformation on COVID-19: A cross-sectional survey study. *Journal of Korean Medical Science*, 35(27), e256. https://doi.org/10.3346/jkms.2020.35.e256

Hardeniya, N. (2015). NLTK Essentials: Build Cool NLP and Machine Learning Applications Using NLTK and Other Python Libraries. Packt Open Source. Birmingham: Packt Publ.

Hern, A. (2022) AI-assisted plagiarism? ChatGPT bot says it has an answer for that. *Guardian*, 31 December. https://www.theguardian.com/technology/2022/dec/31/ai-assisted-plagiarism-chatgpt-bot-says-it-has-an-answer-for-that

Mitchell, A. (2022) Professor catches student cheating with ChatGPT: 'I feel abject terror'. *New York Post*, 26 December. https://nypost.com/2022/12/26/students-using-chatgpt-to-cheat-professor-warns/

Reis, J., Benevenuto, F., Vaz de Melo, P., Prates, R., Kwak, H. and An, J. (2015) Breaking the News: First Impressions Matter on Online News. In *Proceedings of the Ninth International Conference on Web and Social Media* (pp. 357–66). Palo Alto, CA: AAAI Press. https://ink.library.smu.edu.sg/sis_research/5339

Sarkar, D. (2019) *Text Analytics with Python: A Practical Real-World Approach to Gaining Actionable Insights from your Data*. Apress.

Yao, D. (2022) OpenAI sees ChatGPT revenue of $1 billion in 2024. Retrieved from https://aibusiness.com/nlp/openai-sees-chatgpt-revenue-of-1-billion-in-2024

10

REAL-TIME DATA ANALYTICS

CHAPTER CONTENTS

CHAPTER OBJECTIVES

In this chapter:

- You will learn about real-time analytics in big data.
- You will learn about the advantages and disadvantages of real-time data analytics.
- You will explore various real-time analytics use cases.
- You will use Apache Spark Streaming to carry out some hands-on real-time analytics using the X, formerly known as Twitter API and from Google Trends.
- Finally, ethical challenges when it comes to real-time data analytics and industry insights will be highlighted.

10.1 WHAT IS REAL-TIME DATA ANALYTICS?

Real-time data analytics refers to the processing and drawing of insights from data as the data is received (streamed). So instead of performing analytics on static data or data at rest, the processing happens in real time. Data sources for this are varied. Examples include data feeds from social media, which are constantly updated, and data from the health and transportation sectors. Being able to process data as it is generated has many benefits, contributing to organizations' competitive advantage. However, there are also many challenges to overcome. Among these challenges are the handling of large amounts of streaming data at times from various sources and the need for scalability and resilience. This chapter teaches both the theoretical aspects of real-time big data analytics and covers how to go about it, using Apache Spark Streaming (first seen in Chapter 3) to illustrate it. Figure 10.1 depicts the typical stages of a big data real-time analytics cycle.

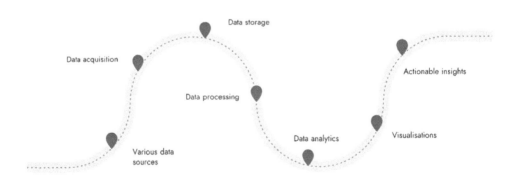

Figure 10.1 Big data real-time analytics

There are many advantages to real-time data analytics, perhaps the most obvious one being that you get insights in real time, which in turn means that timely intervention can be put in place where relevant.

An example of this can be seen in the Apple Watch fall detection functionality. As a smart device it uses real-time data for a range of purposes, one of which is detecting whether the owner has fallen and needs help. When it detects a hard fall, the Apple Watch taps the user on the wrist, sounds an alarm, and displays an alert. If the user does not respond and remains immobile, the Watch dials emergency services to get help and sends a message to all the user's emergency contacts along with the location to let them know the situation.

While the Apple Watch is an interesting example, it deals with relatively small amounts of data. An example of a use case for real-time big data analytics is in its use in real-time traffic information. Google Maps, which is a navigational application, relies heavily on real-time big data analytics; it is said to be used by more than a billion people across the globe every month and is used in over 220 countries and territories (Sohom Mukherjee, 2023).

The main disadvantage of real-time big data analytics is that because everything is in real time, if an error is not caught before the process kicks off, it is unlikely to be caught, or by the time it is, it is too late as the output is likely to have already been disseminated. This highlights the need for well-thought-out designs in terms of the actual implementation of the real-time data analytics architecture but also in terms of incorporating ethics by design, to avoid things going wrong further down the line.

There are specialist infrastructures for real-time big data analytics. Recall that in Chapter 4 big data storage was explored. For real-time big data analytics there are storage systems that have been designed specifically to handle real-time data, a common one being Apache Kafka, which we consider in more detail later in this chapter. Apache Kafka is primarily a distributed streaming platform but can also serve as a real-time big data storage system. We also encountered Apache HBase,[1] which is the open-source Hadoop database; it is distributed and scalable, which makes it ideal for use as a real-time big data store. Apache Cassandra[2] is an open-source NoSQL database which, because it is distributed with low latency, works well for real-time big data. Other storage systems include Apache Druid,[3] SingleStoreDB,[4] Google Cloud Bigtable,[5] and Apache Ignite.[6]

In addition to storage, there are specific data-processing frameworks for real-time big data analytics such as Apache Spark (which is used extensively in this book), Apache Flink,[7] Apache Storm,[8] Google Cloud Dataflow,[9] Apache Samza,[10] and Microsoft Azure Stream Analytics.[11] Finally, there are also real-time big data visualization tools such as Tableau,[12] Power BI,[13] and Grafana.[14]

The various additional real-time big data storage systems, data-processing frameworks, and big data visualization tools have been mentioned for completeness and links to their websites given so that these can be referenced for further information.

10.2 REAL-TIME ANALYTICS WITH APACHE SPARK

Apache Spark Streaming, first seen in Section 3.5, is used for processing real-time data from various sources and is a key extension to the Spark Core API. While extensions such as MLLIB and Apache SQL work typically work on static data, Spark Streaming enables real-time processing.

The design goals for Spark Streaming included the following:

- Low latency
- One-time-only event processing
- Scalability
- Integration with Spark Core API.

In the same way as SparkContext is the entry point for Spark Core and SQLContext is the entry point for Spark SQL, the entry point for Spark Streaming is StreamingContext. So, StreamingContext is like a control center for processing real time data. StreamingContext represents a connection to a Spark cluster using an existing SparkContext, specifying the time interval in seconds for the streaming of data into batches; this argument is called the batchDuration. As the data flows through the StreamingContext facilitates the collection of the data and breaks it down into smaller chunks (batches) and then processes each of these batches individually.

These batches are called discretized streams (DStreams). DStreams are basic abstractions in Spark Streaming; they are a continuous sequence of RDDs created from a continuous stream of data. Each RDD represents a time window. DStreams can be created either from streaming data sources (e.g., X, formerly known as Twitter) or from transformations on other DStreams. They support two operations: transformations (lazy evaluation applies) and output operations.

We will start with a simple hands-on example to illustrate this, using the command prompt and a Jupyter Notebook. Using the command prompt, open up a port and manually enter data into it (this to mimic real-time data; see Figure 10.2).

```
$ nc - lk 99992
one one
how
world
cat cat dog
testing testing testing
computing is fun!
one one one
```

Figure 10.2 Command prompt with port 9992 opened and used to stream words

10.2.1 Hands-on exercise 1

In the Jupyter Notebook the relevant configurations need to be set and the StreamingContext defined. Additional code is then written to watch the port that has been opened in the console and read the data streaming through it. A number of transformations are then used to count the occurrence of the words streaming through and DStreams used to output this values every 10 seconds (the batchDuration was set to 10 seconds when the Streaming Context was defined (see first line of code in Figure 10.3),

```
from pyspark.streaming import StreamingContext
ssc = StreamingContext(sc, 10)

lines = ssc.socketTextStream('localhost', 9992)

counts = lines.flatMap(lambda line: line.split(" ")).map(lambda x: (x,1)) \
.reduceByKey(lambda a,b: a+b)

counts

counts.pprint()

Output:
-----------------------------------------
Time: 2023-06-24 19:49:00
-----------------------------------------


-----------------------------------------
Time: 2023-06-24 19:49:10
-----------------------------------------
('cat', 2)
('one', 2)
('world', 1)
('how', 1)
('dog', 1)


-----------------------------------------
Time: 2023-06-24 19:49:20
-----------------------------------------
('testing', 3)


-----------------------------------------
Time: 2023-06-24 19:49:30
-----------------------------------------
('one', 3)
('computing', 1)
('fun!', 1)
('is', 1)


-----------------------------------------
Time: 2023-06-24 19:49:40
-----------------------------------------
```

Figure 10.3 Apache Spark Streaming: simple example

10.2.2 Hands-on exercise 2

In this exercise, we will harvest tweets from X (formerly known as Twitter) using the Python Tweepy library,[15] which is a library for accessing the X (formerly known as Twitter) API. Access to the API requires the user to register for an X (formerly known as Twitter) developer account.[16] (You may already have done so while working through Chapter 9.) The code in Figure 10.4 is then used to harvest tweets from the X (formerly known as Twitter) API using the Tweepy library (this needs to be installed in your environment). The search query is used to track and filter the tweets to be harvested. If, for instance, we were interested in tweets to do with the economy, we could assign search_query = 'economy'; in the examples in Figures 10.4 and 10.5 the search query that has been used is 'big data analytics'. You would also need to replace the placeholders 'your_consumer_key', 'your_consumer_secret', 'your_access_token', and 'your_access_token_secret' with the keys that you receive with your X (formerly known as Twitter) development registration.

```
from pyspark.sql import SparkSession
import tweepy

# X (formerly known as Twitter) API credentials
consumer_key = 'your_consumer_key'
consumer_secret = 'your_consumer_secret'
access_token = 'your_access_token'
access_token_secret = 'your_access_token_secret'

# Create a SparkSession
spark = SparkSession.builder \
    .appName("TwitterHarvester") \
    .getOrCreate()

# Set X (formerly known as Twitter) API credentials
auth = tweepy.OAuthHandler(consumer_key, consumer_secret)
auth.set_access_token(access_token, access_token_secret)

# Create the X (formerly known as Twitter) API object
api = tweepy.API(auth)

# Define the search query
search_query = 'big data analytics' #replace this with your search phrase

# Harvest tweets
tweets = api.search(q=search_query, count=100)
```

```
# Create an RDD from the tweets
tweets_rdd = spark.sparkContext.parallelize(tweets)


# Convert the RDD to a DataFrame
tweets_df = spark.createDataFrame(tweets_rdd)


# Display the entire DataFrame
tweets_df.show()
```

Output:

```
/usr/spark2.4.3/python/lib/pyspark.zip/pyspark/sql/session.py in
_interSchema(self, rdd, samplingRatio, names)
    375                    break
    376              else:
--> 377    raise ValueError("Some of types cannot be determined by the "
    378          "first 100 rows, please try again with sampling")
    379          else:


ValueError: Some of types cannot be determined by the first 100 rows,
please try again with sampling
```

Figure 10.4   Source code to retrieve tweets from X (formerly known as Twitter) and stream them using Apache Spark (error message)

In Figure 10.4, running the highlighted line of code `tweets_df= spark.createData-Frame(tweets_rdd)` which creates a DataFrame `tweets_df` from the harvested tweets results in an error, and this is a good example where some troubleshooting is required. The ability to troubleshoot is one that will serve you well in any form of programming, and the more you practise, the better you become. So, troubleshooting the error in Figure 10.4, the main error message states that `Some of types cannot be determined by the first 100 rows, please try again with sampling`. When you read that, what do you think it means? In creating the DataFrame we have not explicitly defined the schema (i.e., the data types of the various columns that would be created from the RDD containing the tweets); this has been done by using the `createDataFrame` method and only passing in the RDD as the input argument `spark.create-DataFrame(tweets_rdd)`. So, to implicitly determine the data types of the various columns, it uses by default the first 100 rows to try to work out what these should be; however, for these tweets the first 100 rows are not enough to determine these datatypes, hence the error message. This error can be resolved in various ways, two of which are as follows:

- We can explicitly define the schema and pass it in as an input argument when using the `createDataFrame` method, for example `spark.`

createDataFrame(tweets_rdd, mySchema), where mySchema is our predefined schema.

- We can use a different method to create the DataFrame which allows us to change the number of rows that are sampled to work out what the schema (data types) should be. This approach is followed in Figure 10.5 with tweets_df = tweets_rdd.toDF(sampleRatio=0.01); the ratio to use has now been set as we create the DataFrame and can be adjusted to an amount that is sufficient for sampling.

```python
from pyspark.sql import SparkSession
import tweepy

# X (formerly known as Twitter) API credentials
consumer_key = 'your_consumer_key'
consumer_secret = 'your_consumer_secret'
access_token = 'your_access_token'
access_token_secret = 'your_access_token_secret'

# Create a SparkSession
spark = SparkSession.builder \
    .appName("TwitterHarvester") \
    .getOrCreate()

# Set X (formerly known as Twitter) API credentials
auth = tweepy.OAuthHandler(consumer_key, consumer_secret)
auth.set_access_token(access_token, access_token_secret)

# Create the X (formerly known as Twitter) API object
api = tweepy.API(auth)

# Define the search query
search_query = 'big data analytics' #replace this with your search query

# Harvest tweets
tweets = api.search(q=search_query, count=100)

# Create an RDD from the tweets
tweets_rdd = spark.sparkContext.parallelize(tweets)

# Convert the RDD to a DataFrame
tweets_df = tweets_rdd.toDF(sampleRatio=0.01)
```

```
# Display the first 2 items in the DataFrame
tweets_df.take(2)
```

Output:

```
[Row(_json={'metadata': '{result_type=recent, iso_language_code=en}', 'in_
reply_to_status_id_str': None, 'in_reply_to_status_id': None, 'in_reply_to_
user_id_str': None, 'created_at': 'Sun Jun 25 22:43:17 +0000 2023', 'source':
'<a href="http://twitter.com/download/iphone" rel="nofollow">Twitter for
iPhone</a>', 'retweeted_status': '{metadata={result_type=recent, iso_language_
code=en}, in_reply_to_status_id_str=null, in_reply_to_status_id=null,
in_reply_to_user_id_str=null, created_at=Thu Jun 01 09:13:52 +0000 2023,
source=<a href="http://twitter.com/download/iphone" rel="nofollow">Twitter
for iPhone</a>, retweet_count=12087, retweeted=false, geo=null, is_quote_
status=false, in_reply_to_screen_name=null, id_str=1664198566926077953,
in_reply_to_user_id=null, favorite_count=21319, place=null, text=If you're
interested in LEARNING all of these for FREE:\n\nProduct management\
nProject management \nBusiness analytics… https://t.co/cOyIiapsxH,
id=1664198566926077953, lang=en, favorited=false, possibly_sensitive=false,
coordinates=null, truncated=true, entities={urls=[[expanded_url=https://
twitter.com/i/web/status/1664198566926077953, display_url=twitter.com/i/web/
status/1…, indices=[116, 139], url=https://t.co/cOyIiapsxH}], has . . .
```

Figure 10.5   Source code to retrieve tweets from Twitter and stream them using Apache Spark (with partial display of the first two items in the created DataFrame)

If you are unsure of the meaning of an error message, Stack Overflow[17] is an excellent resource for getting answers to technical questions. Stack Overflow has over 100 million visitors a month and since 2008 has provided help more than 45.1 billion times.

The stages that are followed in Figures 10.4 and 10.5 are also depicted in diagrammatic form in Figure 10.6.

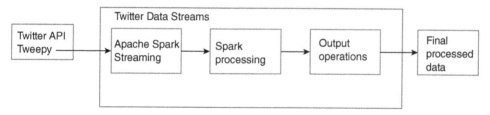

Figure 10.6   Diagram depicting steps in process to retrieve tweets from X (formerly known as Twitter) and stream them using Apache Spark

10.2.3 Hands-on exercise 3

We can also retrieve data from Google Trends[18] and stream it using Apache Spark Streaming. In this exercise, using a few lines of code, we demonstrate simple retrieval and visualization of data using Google Trends. Google Trends provides data and information on search trends over a period of time: it returns the frequency of a search time relative to the total search in that period. The pytrends[19] Python library can be used to retrieve data from Google Trends. The source code for this can be seen in Figure 10.7.

10.3 REAL-TIME ANALYTICS WITH APACHE KAFKA, X (FORMERLY KNOWN AS TWITTER) AND GOOGLE TRENDS

In this section we discuss the inclusion of an additional element to the hands-on exercises in Sections 10.2.2 and 10.2.3. Instead of pulling information directly from X (formerly known as Twitter) and converting the tweets into a DataFrame to be ingested by Apache Spark, we include Apache Kafka in our architecture

'Apache Kafka is an open-source distributed event streaming platform used by thousands of companies for high-performance data pipelines, streaming analytics, data integration, and mission-critical applications.'[20] The advantage of using it in combination with Apache Spark is that it temporarily stores the tweets that are being harvested, and it provides the system with fault tolerance; if one of the Apache Spark nodes should fail, for instance, the system

```
import pytrends
from pytrends.request import TrendReq
import matplotlib.pyplot as plt


# Set up pytrends
# TrendReq takes two parameters, language and time zone
pytrends = TrendReq(hl='en-Us', tz=360)


# The keyword to be analysed
main_keyword = 'big data analytics'


# The data for interest over time
pytrends.build_payload(kw_list=[main_keyword])
interest_over_time_df = pytrends.interest_over_time()


# Plot the data
plt.plot(interest_over_time_df.index, interest_over_time_df[main_keyword])
plt.xlabel('Time')
plt.ylabel('Interest')
plt.title('Interest over Time for "{}"'.format(main_keyword))
plt.show()
```

Output:

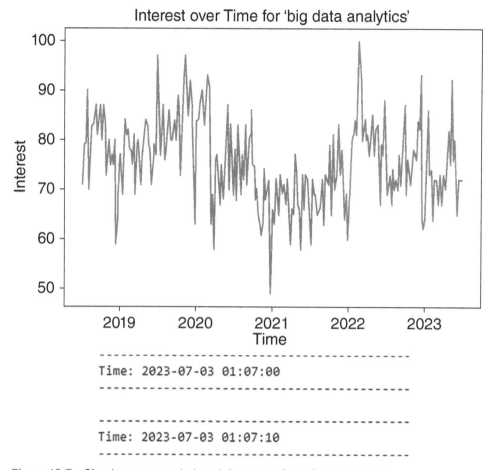

```
---------------------------------------
Time: 2023-07-03 01:07:00
---------------------------------------


---------------------------------------
Time: 2023-07-03 01:07:10
---------------------------------------
```

Figure 10.7 Simple source code to retrieve data from Google Trends

would be able to recover and carry on. It is also highly scalable. Adding Apache Kafka to the architecture for harvesting tweets, the architecture is now as depicted in Figure 10.8.

As in the previous exercise, Tweepy is used to harvest the tweets from the X (formerly known as Twitter) API. These tweets are then published to an Apache Kafka topic which performs the function of the message queue. Apache Spark then reads the messages from a Kafka consumer which is implemented in Apache Spark. The data is then processed in Spark and then output to a data pipeline – in this case the screen, but it could be a dashboard, database, application, etc. The Kafka home page is at https://kafka.apache.org/ and within that the documentation can be found at https://kafka.apache.org/documentation/. See these for further information on Kafka and for specific instructions on setting up the Kafka topic and producer in the environment you are working in. For this example, the environment provided by CloudxLab[21] has been used. CloudxLab is a cloud-based virtual lab for practising big data (Hadoop, Spark etc.),

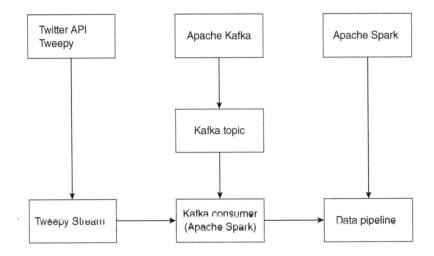

Figure 10.8 Diagram depicting the steps in the process of retrieving tweets from X (formerly known as Twitter) and streaming them using Apache Kafka and Apache Spark

machine learning, and deep learning) technologies. Below is an example of setting up Kafka using a web console.

Step 1. Include the Kafka binaries in the path, for this specific environment

```
export PATH=$PATH:/usr/hdp/current/kafka-broker/bin
```

Step 2: Create the topic (again for this specific environment). The topic has been named `bigdata_topic` for this example:

```
kafka-topics.sh --create --zookeeper localhost:2181

--replication-factor 1 --partitions 1 --topic bigdata_topic
```

Step 3: Check that your topic has been created, this lists all the topics on this localhost

```
kafka-topics.sh  --list --zookeeper localhost:2181
```

Figure 10.9 depicts the steps for the use of Apache Kafka as a distributed streaming platform in the example from hands-on exercise 2 where we harvested tweets using the Tweepy API and Apache Spark.

Similarly, Figure 10.10 depicts the steps to retrieve data from Google Trends and stream the retrieved data using Apache Kafka and Apache Spark Streaming.

As mentioned earlier, there are many other distributed streaming platforms. Some, such as Apache Pulsar, follow very similar steps to Apache Kafka.

10.5 COMMON REAL-TIME BIG DATA ANALYTICS USE CASES

In this section we explore some real-life use cases of big data real-time analytics from various sectors.

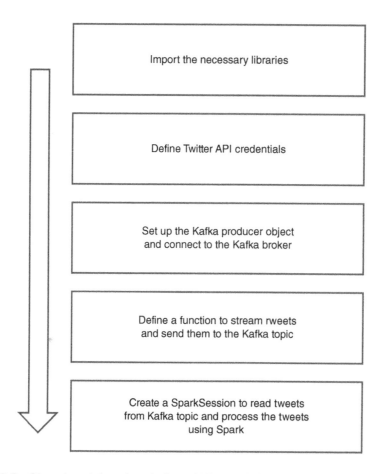

Figure 10.9   Steps to retrieve tweets from X (formerly known as Twitter) and stream them using Apache Kafka and Apache Spark

10.5.1 Financial analytics and fraud detection

When it comes to stock trading and the stock markets, as technology has advanced and data become more readily available in a timely fashion, so have the best ways to work in the sector. Access to real-time market data helps analysts and traders to respond appropriately and better. The United Fintech website[22] lists five benefits of using real-time market data as follows: speed and response time, workflow streamlining, data analysis, increased service quality, and cost reduction. Another common use case in the financial sector is fraud detection. Real-time data can be analysed in near real time to see if trends and patterns are normal or out of the ordinary, and this can be used to flag potential issues. An interesting Telus International article[23] on how AI is transforming fraud detection in banks highlights how some of this is done through analytics and models that centre on building purchase profiles, developing fraud scores, and fraud investigation, so that anything out of the ordinary gets picked up even in real time. In some situations, particularly when dealing with large amounts of money, if things are picked up after the fact it could be too late.

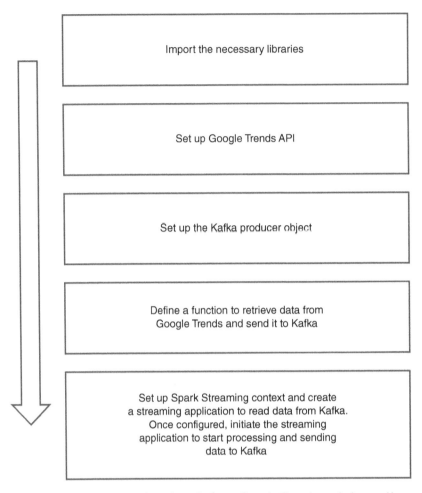

Figure 10.10   Steps to retrieve tweets from Google Trends and stream them using Apache Kafka and Apache Spark

10.5.2 Retail sector

An example of a company that has excelled at using real-time data analytics to drive efficiencies, effectiveness, customer satisfaction, and competitive advantage is Walmart. Bernard Marr, an author in the fields of business and technology, describes Walmart in his blog (Marr, 2021) as the world's largest retailer and goes into some detail on how it has harnessed data to its advantage. For example, the Data Café holds vast amounts of data from across Walmart stores, acquiring information from 200 sources, including economic, social media, and meteorological data. It also has algorithms that can in microseconds come up with insights and solutions. Other retailers such as Amazon and Netflix have also used and continue to use real-time data analytics to achieve outstanding results.

10.5.3 Social media data

Social media has revolutionized the way we access information in real time. The consumption of news and current affairs no longer requires us to wait for the mainstream broadcasters, with news often rapidly going viral through social media. Some other social media outlets like Facebook and Instagram have also changed how we relate to and connect with others and pass information around. This is potentially a double-edged sword, with many citing social media as a potential source of anxiety and mental health issues for some (Robinson and Smith, 2023). There have also been cases like the Facebook–Cambridge Analytica data scandal (Confessore, 2018) where the personal data of millions of Facebook users was collected and used without their consent in ways that raised serious ethical issues. There have also been several cases of the spread of misinformation using social media. However, when used in appropriate ways real-time big data analytics has had a tremendous impact.

10.5.4 Real-time dashboards and visualizations

As in many sectors, the health sector is one in which real-time dashboards and visualizations are used to facilitate efficient and optimized decision-making in real time. One example of this is the WaitLess app, which was developed to harness real-time information about accident and emergency and urgent treatment centres. This data is combined with traffic information and provides insights that help patients access the fastest place for minor emergencies from their location (Care Quality Commission, 2022).

Other use cases, some of which have been mentioned earlier in this chapter and in Chapter 1, include real-time recommendation engines, cybersecurity and threat detection, the Internet of Things, and location applications.

10.6 ETHICS BY DESIGN

Ethics by design is an important concept for real-time analytics, especially as the outputs from the processing are disseminated in real time (or near real time) without any opportunity to pause and make corrections. As in previous chapters, we use the TAFARP framework (Figure 2.14, p. 44) as the basis for exploring and putting in place the ethics by design elements right from the very start of any project:

- *Transparency and fairness.* When it comes to real-time analytics, as the insights from the data are disseminated in real time (or near real time), extra care needs to be taken with regard to the source of the data. With real-time analytics there is no time to observe the insights and correct any issues, because dissemination takes place in real time. So it is very important to ask questions such as: What is the data source? Is it bias-free? Is it fully representative? Is it transparent?

- *Accountability and responsibility.* Similarly, you cannot afford to leave accountability and responsibility as afterthoughts in the process because once it kicks off the end-user sees the results from the data processing in real time or near real time, and there is no pause button that gives you a chance to examine the results and fix any issues. This makes getting the data ethics checks here incredibly important.

- *Fairness and privacy.* Again, because the end results are disseminated almost immediately, getting issues such as fairness (e.g., no bias) and privacy correct right from the start of the process are important. If you notice that there is a problem after the information has already been disseminated and are at that point trying to correct the issue, it could turn out to be too late and be a costly mistake.

10.7 INDUSTRY INSIGHTS

For this chapter's industry insights, we consider how Walmart, currently the largest retailer in the world, harnesses the power of real-time big data analytics and uses it for competitive advantage and to stay at the top of the game in its areas of service provision.

An article online discusses how Walmart uses analytics to deliver extraordinary results[24] and highlights how vast amounts of data are collected about customers from various sources such as from point-of-sale systems, social media, loyalty cards, and customer feedback. All this data analytics, including real-time analytics, is used to draw out insights to drive optimal pricing of goods, market strategies, product placement, and so on. One of the other areas highlighted is Walmart's use of analytics for supply chain optimization; this includes real-time data on travel routes for delivery vans and real-time monitoring and management of inventory levels. Using real-time big data analytics allows the company to react to changes rapidly.

To illustrate how different elements are interlinked and especially how important ethical issues are, not just in designing systems but also how it continues to remain important even afterwards, consider the true story of a woman who sued Walmart over beauty product placement (Meza, 2018). She alleged that the retailer was promoting racial stereotypes as it had placed beauty products targeted towards African Americans behind a locked glass case (including a comb for 48 cents which she wanted to buy) while more expensive products (which were not targeted at African Americans) were placed on open shelving. From our perspective a learning point here is that ethical issues are extremely important and need to be well thought out.

SUMMARY

In this chapter we discussed real-time big data analytics, including its main advantages and disadvantages. We considered several use cases such as financial analytics, fraud detection, social media data, and the retail industry. Hands-on exercises using Apache Spark and Apache Kafka were also explored. The chapter concluded with a discussion on ethics by design and industry insights in this context.

TEST YOUR KNOWLEDGE

1 Using Apache Spark, set up a system to harvest tweets that contain the word 'strike' or 'strikes' and group them by the half hour.
2 Using Apache Spark, set up a system to collect data from Google Trends on a topic of your choice.
3 List three use cases of real-time big data analytics

FURTHER READING (OPTIONAL)

Interesting presentations on real-time fraud detection:

Lin, P., Tyagi, E. and Kattamuri, P. (n.d.) How to build a serverless real-time credit card fraud detection solution. *YouTube*. Retrieved from https://www.youtube.com/watch?v=qQnxq3COr9Q

Liu, B. (2019) Real time fraud detection at scale – integrating real time deep link graph analytics with Spark. *YouTube*. Retrieved from https://www.youtube.com/watch?v=yzKZWI9IwnA

Article on how Netflix built its real-time data infrastructure:

Anadiotis, G. (2022) How Netflix built its real-time data infrastructure. Retrieved from https://venturebeat.com/data-infrastructure/how-netflix-built-its-real-time-data-infrastructure/

Short article on how Walmart uses big data to help customers:

https://corporate.walmart.com/news/2017/08/07/5-ways-walmart-uses-big-data-to-help-customers

Interesting book with chapters on how 45 successful companies used big data analytics to deliver outstanding results:

Marr, B. (2016) *Big Data in Practice: How 45 Successful Companies Used Big Data Analytics to Deliver Extraordinary Results*. Chichester: John Wiley & Sons.

NOTES

1 https://hbase.apache.org/
2 https://cassandra.apache.org/_/index.html
3 https://druid.apache.org/

4   https://www.singlestore.com/
5   https://cloud.google.com/bigtable
6   https://ignite.apache.org/
7   https://flink.apache.org/
8   https://storm.apache.org/
9   https://cloud.google.com/dataflow
10 https://samza.apache.org/
11 https://azure.microsoft.com/en-gb/products/stream-analytics/
12 https://www.tableau.com/
13 https://powerbi.microsoft.com/en-gb/
14 https://grafana.com/
15 https://www.tweepy.org/
16 https://developer.twitter.com/en/docs/twitter-api/getting-started/getting-access-to-the-twitter-api
17 https://stackoverflow.com/
18 https://trends.google.com/home
19 https://pypi.org/project/pytrends/
20 https://kafka.apache.org/
21 https://cloudxlab.com/
22 https://unitedfintech.com/blog/5-benefits-of-real-time-market-data/
23 https://www.telusinternational.com/insights/trust-and-safety/article/ai-fraud-detection-in-banks
24 https://www.projectpro.io/article/how-big-data-analysis-helped-increase-walmarts-sales-turnover/109

REFERENCES

Care Quality Commission (2022) Real time urgent and emergency care waiting times. Retrieved from https://www.cqc.org.uk/publications/themes-care/real-time-urgent-emergency-care-waiting-times

Confessore, N. (2018) Cambridge Analytica scandal fallout. *New York Times*. Retrieved from https://www.nytimes.com/2018/04/04/us/politics/cambridge-analytica-scandal-fallout.html

Marr, B. (2021) Walmart: Big data analytics at the world's biggest retailer. Retrieved from https://bernardmarr.com/walmart-big-data-analytics-at-the-worlds-biggest-retailer/

Meza, S. (2018) Woman sues Walmart for 'segregated' beauty products, alleges racial discrimination. *Newsweek*, 27 January. Retrieved from https://www.newsweek.com/walmart-segregation-racial-discrimination-beauty-products-792931

Robinson, L. and Smith, M. (2023) Social media and mental health. Retrieved from https://www.helpguide.org/articles/mental-health/social-media-and-mental-health.htm

Sohom Mukherjee, C. Z. (2023) 29 Google Maps statistics. Retrieved from https://www.onthemap.com/blog/google-maps-statistics/

11

BIG DATA ANALYTICS AND VISUALIZATION

CHAPTER CONTENTS

CHAPTER OBJECTIVES

In this chapter:

- You will learn about the purpose of data visualization and what makes it effective.
- You will be introduced to its history, past and present, and some emerging data visualization trends.
- You will revisit some of the techniques used to visualize data.

11.1 INTRODUCTION

Data visualization aims to transform complex data into a visual format that conveys a clear and compelling story. Big data visualization uses imagery and graphics, communication strategies involving static and interactive prompts to represent relationships or patterns in the data, communicating and making it possible for an audience to identify patterns, trends, and relationships that may be difficult to see in raw data. Data visualization has three primary purposes.

The first is *communicating insights*. Ultimately, big data analytics depends on the ability to communicate, broadcasting information from an author to their audience as well as a multi-way exchange between peers. Effective communication of data-driven insights changes from one setting to another. Stakeholders may have different expectations and attitudes. Engineers may be more interested in the underlying methodology. Managers may want to understand the big picture or the bottom line. Policy-makers want to know how the insights might inform their decisions. A visual representation is effective to the extent that it helps viewers find whatever they are looking for, usually trying to understand how the data affects their choices, decisions, actions, and behaviour. To be effective, the data analyst must extract only what is necessary out of raw data, filtering out the meaningful gist from the noise while staying true to the data. This balancing act, between 'letting the data speak for itself' and extracting the needle from the haystack, is at the heart of data visualization. And the sweet spot depends greatly on your audience, their prior knowledge, expectations and values, and the way they will use the information you provide.

The second purpose is *exploring and analysing data more intuitively*. Visual representations can help viewers identify patterns, trends, outliers, or anomalies that are harder to spot in the raw data. Interactive visualizations invite users to manipulate and explore the data in real time, enabling them to gain deeper insights and identify hidden relationships.

One dramatic example of using visualization as a tool for exploration and creating new insights can be seen in John Snow's use of data visualization in the mid-nineteenth century. Snow is regarded as a founding father of contemporary epidemiology due to his meticulous data collection and acerbic visualization techniques. His visualization led him to identify the source of cholera outbreaks in Soho, London, in 1854, which turned out to be an innocent-looking water pump. Once its handle was removed, the pump could no longer be used, and the spread of the disease was successfully contained. To identify the offending pump, Snow collected data about the precise location where cholera incidents occurred.

Figure 11.1 Extract from the original map by John Snow showing the clusters of cholera cases (indicated by stacked rectangles) in the London epidemic. The offending pump is visible on the corner of Cambridge Street and Broad Street (Snow, 1854).

These incidents were not randomly scattered but were centralized around specific water pumps (see Figure 11.1). Snow devised a simple yet effective visualization technique whereby cholera incidences were illustrated on a map as stacked rectangles: the number of rectangles was equal to the number of incidences, and their location on the map denoted where the incidents occurred. The visualization made it clear that flats on the southern side of Broad Street had many more incidents than those on the northern side. Only by studying this visualization carefully did he reach this life-saving insight. In this sense, we say that visualizations do not function solely as a vehicle to carry and communicate information but much more as a tool to generate new types of knowledge, an understanding that comes into existence through the process of committing the data onto the paper, organizing it in a meaningful manner, and exploring it systematically.

A second example is much closer to our time, an insight described in the PhD thesis of one of the authors of this book (Engel, 2023). The visualizations in Figure 11.2 represent two different email communication networks. An email communication network consists of nodes and ties, the nodes representing individual email users, and the lines connecting two nodes representing an email exchanged between users. The two visualizations were constructed from two separate kinds of emails: one visualization was constructed from single-recipient emails only, while the other was constructed from multiple-recipient emails only.

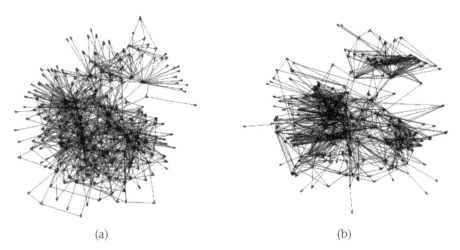

(a)   (b)

Figure 11.2   Two networks constructed from (a) single-recipient and (b) multiple-recipient emails. All emails sent and received between members of the same email users within the same period; each network is constructed from emails with a different range of number of recipients. Notice the open, fan-like structures in (a) and closed, triangle-like structures in (b).

Some important similarities and differences are revealed by studying both networks visually. Although the users in both networks are the same, the single-recipient email network exhibits open, fan-like structures, whereas the multiple-recipient email network exhibits closed, triangular structures. These different patterns raise many interesting theoretical questions about the mechanisms that underlie different network structures. But identifying these structures depends on the construction of the visualization. This example illustrates once again how visualizations are not just a way to communicate existing knowledge but also an engine generating new knowledge.

The third purpose of data visualization is *predicting, modelling, and forecasting*. By visualizing data trends and relationships, data scientists can build models and predict future outcomes. These models can be used to make strategic decisions and plans based on data-driven insights.

Overall, the purpose of data visualization is to make the insights buried deep in the data more accessible and understandable to a wider audience. But it also helps analysts reflect on, explore, and analyse complex data in an intuitive way, representing the data in a way that facilitates informed decisions and predictions. Of course, these goals are not exclusive to data visualization, but are the goals of big data analysis in general. Hence, visualization should not be treated as an afterthought, add-on, or merely the product of the analytic process. Instead, visualization is better thought of as an integral part of the analytic process itself, a framework designed to reflect, inform, and guide the analysis process. It allows the analyst make sense of their analysis, test a hypothesis, confirm suspicions, or lay doubts to rest. Creating a visual depiction of the data encourages visual exploration, thought experiments, and idea generation. It facilitates brainstorming and clarifies what is at stake.

Facts and figures are the vessel that carry your arguments to the hearts and minds of your audience. To do so, they must be convincing, appealing, memorable, and clear. The distinction between excellent and poorly designed visualizations can mean the difference between a very influential or obscure study, a grant or contract gained or lost, or a successful or unsuccessful job interview. Many tutorials concentrate on creating aesthetic effects, but reflecting on why some decisions are more effective than others. There is a real danger in using poorly designed visualizations, visualizations that may induce misunderstandings and confusion, and it is for this reason that data visualization comes with its own ethical dilemmas, which are discussed more below.

11.2 BIG DATA VISUALIZATION AS THE ART OF STORYTELLING

One of the common refrains about big data is that we ought to 'let the data speak for itself', without forcing on it our own expectations, interpretations, theories, and prejudices. But if we let the data speak for itself, your audience will not necessarily distinguish between information that is relevant and information that is not. Extracting meaningful insights from masses of data is often compared to the art of storytelling. Surprisingly, a range of concepts from data science have their origin in concepts that are frequently used in stories (Paulos, 2010). The notions of probability, repetition, prediction, trends, and recurrent patterns, found in a world that appears unruly and random, lie at the very heart of storytelling. Probability appears in the tension between the 'ordinary', 'commonplace', and 'just-so stories', on the one hand, and 'peculiar', 'strange', and 'deviant', on the other. The idea of probability also appears in storytelling under the guise of words such as 'chance', 'destiny', 'fate', 'odds', 'fortune', 'luck', and 'happenstance'.

The power and inevitability of plot twist require at least some kind of reasoning about probability. Even the notion of hypothesis testing has a natural incarnation in concepts that are fundamental to storytelling. In statistical terms, hypothesis testing is related to two types of errors. We make a Type I error when we believe the evidence for a relationship or event in the data and that relationship or event is not there. We make a Type II error when we fail to observe evidence for an event that is there. These two types of errors can be traced back to Aesop's Fables, a collection attributed to the ancient Greek storyteller Aesop (620–564 BCE). In one of the fables, 'The Boy Who Cried Wolf' (numbered 210 in the Perry Index), a shepherd alarms the local villagers repeatedly, falsely telling them that he saw a wolf, and the wolf is about to attack the villagers' flock. The villagers run to help the shepherd, only to discover that it was a case of false alarm. After several such false alarms, the villagers become desensitized to the boy's calls for help. Eventually, when the wolf appears and attacks the flock, the villagers ignore the shepherd's calls. From the point of view of statistical testing, the villagers make two different mistakes on two separate occasions. At first, they are subject to a false alarm, believing the shepherd's warnings when those warnings do not represent reality. The villagers have thereby committed a Type I error. Later, they ignore his cries for help when the wolf threatens their flock, thereby committing a Type II error.

These examples illustrate how statistical concepts are deeply embedded within the stories upon which generations have been educated, demonstrating the naturalness of notions found in quantitative analysis. The magic of data visualization is to reclaim this naturalness and make hidden structures and relationships evident and plain to see.

11.2.1 Visuals telling a story: sexual bias in admission to the University of California, Berkeley?

For a more contemporary example, consider a famous case of alleged sex discrimination in admission to graduate studies at the University of California, Berkeley, in the admissions cycle for the fall term of 1973 (Bickel, 1975). The Graduate Division of the University received 12,763 complete applications for entry, on which a decision had to be made whether to admit or deny admission. Ideally, we would like to assess whether the sex of the applicant influenced this decision. Based on these figures alone, it would not be possible to judge with any certainty which factors influenced the admission board. It would, perhaps, be possible to judge if there is a statistically relevant association between the sex of the applicant and the decision made. Identifying such an association would merit further investigation as to whether discrimination existed in selection. The most straightforward approach would be to aggregate all the data for all applications to the 101 graduate departments and interdepartmental majors. Table 11.1 is based on the aggregate data of a total of 4526 applicants (of them 1835 female and 2691 male) to graduate school at Berkeley for the six largest departments in the fall of 1973. It is clear that the admission rate among male candidates is higher than that of female candidates. To extract a meaningful conclusion from these numbers, one would have to assume that in any given discipline male and female applicants are on average alike in all relevant ways, for example in terms of their abilities, qualifications, and any other property deemed legitimately pertinent to the decision of whether to accept them or not. But there is another assumption: the sex ratios of applicants do not vary between the more selective and the less selective departments. Suppose one group consistently applies to more selective departments than another group. In that case, we should hardly be surprised that fewer members of that group were accepted to the department.

Table 11.1 Total admission rate for six largest departments in the graduate
school at Berkeley, 1973

Applicants to graduate school at Berkeley for the six largest departments in 1973 by admission and sex					
Male candidates			Female candidates		
Applicants	Admissions	Rate	Applicants	Admissions	Rate
2691	1198	44.52%	1835	557	30.35%

To judge the merit of the second assumption, Table 11.2 disaggregates the data, associating the rate of admissions with sex and with the department. We immediately see
that departments vary in their selectiveness. Whereas departments A and B admit over
60% of the applicants, the other departments admit as few as 7% of their applicants.
Further scrutiny shows that male applicants tend to apply to the less selective departments A and B, whereas female candidates tend to apply to the more selective departments. The counterintuitive result is that when looking at the acceptance rates of each
department separately, it is difficult to see any significant difference in the admission
rate for males and females. But when we sum up the numbers, we see that overall, the
admission rate among males is significantly higher than among females. This is an
example of Simpson's paradox (Wagner, 1982), an often surprising pattern in the data
that appears in a wide range of cases in data science. Simpson's paradox appears when
a certain relationship exists between two variables in the data as a whole, but disappears
(or is even reversed) when the data is disaggregated into non-overlapping groups.

Table 11.2 Admission rate for the graduate school at Berkeley 1973,
disaggregated by department

Applicants to graduate school at Berkeley for the six largest departments in 1973 admission by department and sex						
	Male candidates			Female candidates		
Department	Applicants	Admissions	Rate	Applicants	Admissions	Rate
A	825	512	62.1%	108	89	82.4%
B	560	353	63.0%	25	17	68.0%
C	325	120	36.9%	593	202	34.1%
D	417	138	33.1%	375	131	23.9%
E	191	53	27.7%	393	94	7.0%
F	373	22	5.9%	341	24	7.0%
Total	2691	1198	44.5%	1835	557	30.4%

What would be a good way of visualizing the reversal of this relationship between variables, so that viewers will not only appreciate the paradox, but will also be able to develop a sensibility and intuition for similar cases they encounter in the future? One answer could be the use of an alluvial diagram, as shown in Figure 11.3. An alluvial diagram is a form of a flow diagram, often used to show a process unfolding over time. The diagram has strata, in our case three: one denoting the department (A, B, C, D, E, and F), a second denoting the sex of the applicant, and a third denoting whether the applicants were admitted or rejected.

The three strata are then linked via colourful fans, each fan denoting a group of applicants. Female applicants are shown in purple (bright purple for those admitted and darker for those rejected) and male applicants in green (bright green for those admitted and darker for those rejected). The horizontal position of the fans shows which department the group has applied to, and the width of the fan shows the share of applicants that have been admitted or rejected. So, for example, the very top horizontal segment of the figure shows the six departments, A, B, C, D, E, and F. The share of applicants accepted relative to those rejected is visualized for each gender, the thickness of the bright coloured bands to the darker coloured bands illustrating that the share of accepted vs. rejected among females vs males is nearly constant between the different departments, and that departments A and B are less selective (wider bright bands and narrower dark bands), whereas departments E and F are much more selective (wider bright bands and narrower dark bands). It may take some practice to get used to these kinds of diagrams and to be able to decipher them quickly, but when one is accustomed to them, they often provide rich visual information that complements tables with numbers.

Some readers may find the information presented in Tables 11.1 and 11.2 easier and more accessible to comprehend, while others may feel more at ease exploring the diagram shown in Figure 11.3. As is often the case with visualizations, an author might want to present the data in a variety of ways to appeal to a variety of expectations among members of their audience.

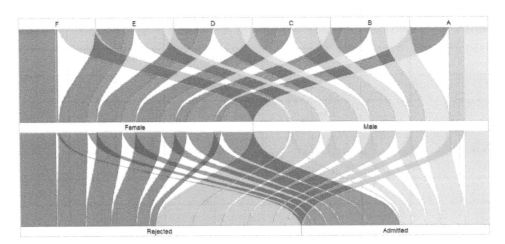

Figure 11.3 Alluvial diagram visualizing graduate admission at UC Berkeley, 1973, for six departments designated by the letters A, B, C, D, E, F. For each department, the fan width represents the share of the female (or male) applicants admitted (or rejected). Females are shown in purple, and males in green. The share of admitted applicants is shown in bright colours, and the share of rejected applicants is shown in darker colours.

11.2.2 Background and history

Despite the relatively recent rise of data visualization in the public media, the practice of visualizing data is not new. The history of data visualization goes back to ancient times when early humans used pictures and symbols to communicate quantities and numerical abstractions such as surfaces, volumes, or masses of grains or other types of goods. The modern era of data visualization began in the eighteenth century when William Playfair, a Scottish engineer and a secret agent, invented the line graph, bar graph, and pie chart. Playfair published *The Commercial and Political Atlas* in 1786 (an extract from which is shown in Figure 11.4), greatly simplifying access to complex data, and influencing the work of statisticians that followed him.

Following Playfair's publications, Charles Minard compiled one of the first flow maps, demonstrating Napoleon's invasion of Russia in 1812 and the retreat that followed (Figure 11.5).

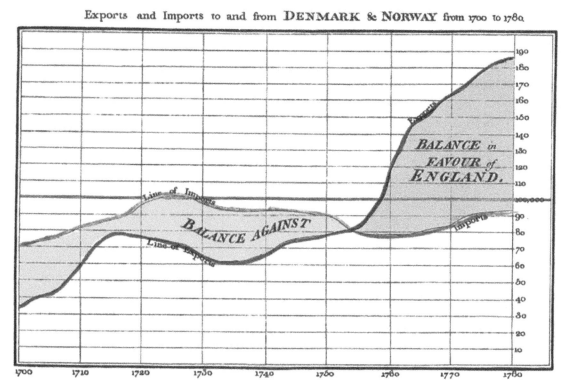

Figure 11.4   Trade balance time-series chart, published by William Playfair in 1786

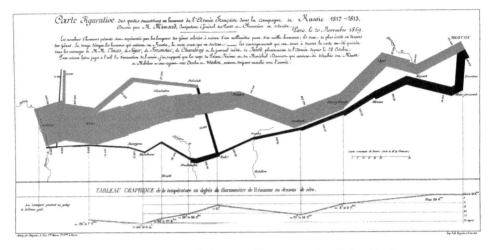

Figure 11.5 Charles Joseph Minard's famous flow map, visualizing the losses over time of Napoleon's troops during the Russian campaign, 1812–13.

From the middle of the nineteenth century, it was epidemiology that provided many of the earliest examples of data visualization. As we saw in Section 11.1, John Snow, a physician and the founder of modern epidemiology, used the map of London to mark the exact location where cholera outbreaks were reported. Identifying patterns on the map allowed him to locate the precise water pump whose infected water claimed hundreds of lives, right in the middle of Soho.

The development of statistical methods led to advancements in data visualization techniques. Florence Nightingale, the founder of modern nursing, used a 'coxcomb' diagram to show the causes of death in the Crimean War in the 1850s (Figure 11.6). Her visualizations

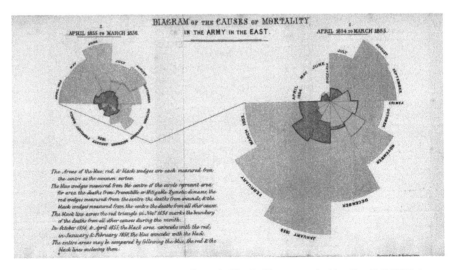

Figure 11.6 'Diagram of the causes of mortality in the army in the East' (1858) by Florence Nightingale, a coloured pie chart to illustrate causes of death in the British Army (in the public domain)

demonstrated the link between mortality rates and sanitation, leading to improved sanitary conditions in hospitals and saving countless lives.

A prominent designer of data visualizations, W. E. B. Du Bois, was an African American sociologist, a scholar, and a civil rights advocate. Towards the turn of the nineteenth century, Du Bois and his team started collecting data to illustrate the discrimination facing African Americans. Inspired by the charts of their predecessors, du Bois experimented with data visualization, setting new standards for those who followed. For example, the chart in Figure 11.7(a) is a development of the pie chart. Here it is used to demonstrate sectors of employment for African Americans and Caucasians.

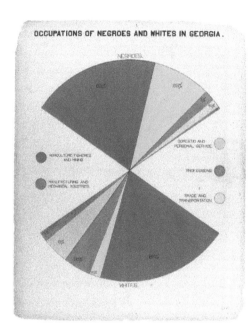 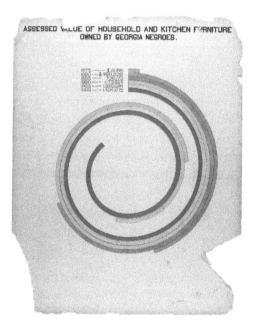

Figure 11.7   From Du Bois's (1887–90) collection of 'data portraits', hand-drawn and painted using ink and watercolours.[1] (a) The circle chart shows radially sliced wedges. Two sets of larger wedges representing African Americans and Caucasians hover opposite one another, around the chart's centre point. (b) Curving bars of colour emanate from a stacked block of text, describing the growth in the value of household furniture owned by African Americans in the state of Georgia.

Please note that this figure contains outmoded language regarding race. The purpose of the figure is to demonstrate early data visualization on discrimination, not to endorse the language or its associations.

Figure 11.7(b) visualizes the dramatic increase in the value of furniture owned by African Americans in the state of Georgia. The chart consists of six concentric spirals, emanating from a stacked block of text. The text lists the value of household furniture owned by black Georgians over a 25-year period. The spirals illustrate the trend of growing wealth over time, where each spiral is longer than the previous one. Conceptually, the spiral diagram combines Playfair's bar chart and pie chart together with Nightingale's rose diagram. Both charts exhibit spatial economy and visual sophistication, creating a composition that is both informative and aesthetically engaging.

In the twentieth century, with the development of computer technology, data visualization became more sophisticated and widespread. In the 1960s, Jacques Bertin, a French author and cartographer, developed a theory of graphical communication that laid the foundation for modern data visualization. In the 1970s, the field of information design emerged, which led to the development of a range of visualization techniques and tools.

11.3 MIND YOUR AUDIENCE

In her influential book *Storytelling with Data*, Cole Nussbaumer Knaflic (2015) highlights the role of context when designing a visualization. When we pay attention to context, we focus not only on the content that is being communicated but also on the medium of communication and how to tailor it to the expected audience. We are putting ourselves in their shoes, concentrating on how end-users may be using, interacting with, or reflecting on the visualization. For an effective experience, designers must empathize with users and consider what would resonate with them most effectively. They need to understand where their viewers are coming from and what are their beliefs, values, and desires. Designers need to be aware of the kind of decisions and challenges facing their users and what the information provided offers them. When designing a visualization, the priority moves away from what we want the user to 'know' or to 'understand', towards what we want the user to 'do' with the information provided, and how it can help them face their decisions.

11.3.1 Background knowledge

Consider the following example of the way these considerations play out in the design of data visualizations. Think of the different audiences that use visualizations that target the wider public and visualizations that target data analysts. The statistician John Tukey (1977) famously compared the work of the exploratory data analyst to that of a 'numerical' or a 'graphical' detective. As a detective, you have a general idea of the kind of thing you are looking for, and although you do not know exactly what you will find, you will know it when you see it, thanks to your experience. The visualizations are often ad hoc, taking for granted domain knowledge, possibly including a variety of acronyms and conventions that would not be necessarily understood by those who lack understanding of the knowledge domain. Others may have great experience and knowledge, but they are not playing the role of the detective and are unwilling to examine the dataset in search of clues. They are interested in the outcomes and the bottom line. These different audiences must be catered for accordingly.

For example, visualization for analysis may take advantage of a variety of encodings and shorthand expressions. These would be understood by the data scientist, but when visualizing data for an audience, you must determine what they already know. Some conventional charts require minimal explanation, such as the scatterplot (see Figure 11.8, for example), the bar chart, and the pie chart. In many cases, designers assume that their audience know how to read such a chart, since they are used frequently enough that the patterns can be deciphered by most adults.

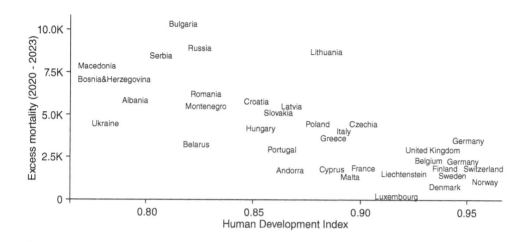

Figure 11.8 A scatterplot showing some European countries and their excess mortality in 2020–23[2]

Other charts, on the other hand, are less typically used. These charts may depict distributions of variables, their central tendency, and measures of variability. Examples of such charts include the density plot, the boxplot, the violin plot, and the spiral plot (see the examples in Figure 11.9).

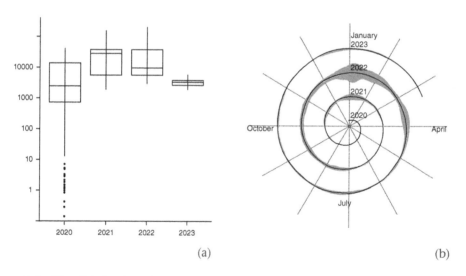

Figure 11.9 The distribution of newly detected Covid-19 cases in the UK: two different representations of the same exact dataset. (a) Boxplots showing the distribution of new cases for each year. (b) A spiral diagram showing the distribution over time.[3]

These visualization methods could be less intuitive to the general public. Viewers may need to be familiar with statistical concepts, and to interpret less intuitive visual encodings.

Histograms are frequently used to display distributions of variables, and boxplots present a distribution of one variable, possibly disaggregated against another non-continuous variable. A distribution is a complicated concept and could be overwhelming for those who are unfamiliar with it. Users may think that the continuous scale denotes time; and the concept of binning could be perceived as abstract and unintuitive. As a result, you must think creatively about how to present the information you want to show, or explain what a distribution density is, and what the bars of a histogram stand for. Visualizing advanced statistical concepts requires either a creative approach or a detailed explanation of the concepts beforehand.

11.3.2 Values and expectations

Your viewers' background knowledge is important, but so also are their expectations, values, and attitudes. When exploring a chart, your viewers come with certain beliefs about what the visualization is about, what it is trying to convey, and how they expect to read it. Some of the expectations are due to certain biases, others are based on aesthetic preferences, and still others are determined by professional norms or organizational culture. To illustrate, at a workshop held a few years ago, one of the authors of this book sought to clarify the distinction between false positives and false negatives. To this end, he presented his audience with a picture of a fishing net and a lake with fish and plastic bags (see Figure 11.10). The fisher's goal was to catch the three fish in the water without fishing out any of the four plastic bags. In terms of data analytics, the fisher's task was an analogy of a classification task, a typical task whose objective is to separate out the 'true positives' (the fish in this example), from the

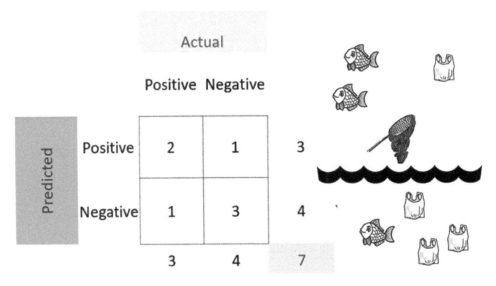

Figure 11.10   An attempted visualization that fell flat, in an effort to explain the concept of false positives and false negatives. The objects captured represent three predicted positives: two true positives (two fish) and one false positive (one plastic bag). The objects remaining under water represent four negatives: three true negatives (plastic bags) and one false negative (fish).

'true negatives' (the plastic bags in this example). The fisher's task is to avoid fishing out plastic bags (which would be considered 'false-positives') and avoid leaving fish in the water ('false negatives'). But this visualization fell flat with the audience, many of whom were vegan, and did not like the suggestion that removing fish from their habitat was desirable while fishing plastic bags from the water needed to be avoided. It was not the idea itself they found disagreeable, but the choice of metaphor that was inconsistent with their values.

When visualizations do not match values and expectations, they can easily fall flat and become ineffective, driving a wedge between the intention of the designers and the understanding of the audience.

Another example appears when distinguishing between the sexes or races in data, especially when this is done using colour. For sex, there is a common distinction using the contrast between blue and pink. Although this colour coding convention is being used in outlets such as Bloomberg, the *New York Times*, the *Wall Street Journal*, *Die Zeit*, and *The Mail*, other outlets are staying away from it, such as *The Economist*, *Morgenpost*, the *Guardian*, the *Financial Times*, and the BBC (Muth, 2018).

11.3.3 Purpose and function

Beyond the user's background knowledge, values, and expectations, a designer might consider the purpose or the function of the visualization. What is the user going to do with the visualization? How would it inform the user's decisions and plan of action? We can distinguish between two possible consumers of data visualization, but the distinction can be extended further.

The data analyst uses the visual in several different ways. One common approach (Knaflic, 2015) is to distinguish between the exploratory function of a chart and its explanatory function. The exploratory function is realized when the user examines the chart to answer a research question or to confirm a hypothesis. Both the designer and the viewer are unsure what they will find in the visualization, and details are important because it is not always clear which details are relevant and which are not. In contrast, the explanatory function is realized when the designer knows what they want to communicate in advance and uses visuals to communicate their idea more effectively. When designing for an explanation, content creation and design derive from understanding the target audience and their expectations.

Users may want to explore the chart in a technical and critical manner, searching for apparent contradictions within the chart or inconsistencies between the chart and other resources. They may search for how to communicate the same insights more effectively, or they may look for evidence as to how the visualization was created. Like a detective, the analyst uses the visualization to search for clues, not only to better understand structures and relationships in the dataset, but also to figure out what are the underlying mechanisms that could have generated the data in its current form. Other readers or viewers may still maintain a critical eye when observing the chart, but they focus more often on the content, the message that is being communicating, and its implications for action.

Multiple languages around the world have an adage that says, 'A picture is worth a thousand words'. Complex ideas can sometimes be communicated more effectively through a visual medium. The same is true for data visualization, which, like language, is a medium of communication. It would be impossible to enumerate all the different ways visualizations might be used to communicate meaning. But as a designer of data visualizations, you would want to reflect on how the choices you make in designing your visual affect your viewers.

11.4 CHOOSING AN EFFECTIVE VISUALIZATION

This chapter has already introduced a range of visualizations, but in most cases a couple of different types of visualizations are enough to convey the desired information. There are plenty of resources about effective visualization of data and about principles that should guide the author of a good visualization. Some of these principles are accepted by most authors, while others are more controversial. Below we summarize some of the important principles, but we also list further resources in the further reading section at the end of this chapter.

- *Allow the data to stand out.* Visualizations can illustrate two main features. They can illustrate the data, which is often messy, and they can illustrate the interpretation, which is often a simplification of the data. To bring the message home more clearly, an author may be tempted to highlight the interpretation and sideline the data or even completely hide it. But viewers may prefer to judge for themselves whether the interpretation has merit. In this case, it is important to show the data and make it stand out. For example, a scatterplot (see Figure 11.11 below) often consists of the data (the points on the chart) and a summarizing feature of the data, such as the average or the best-fitting curve. Where appropriate, make sure that both of these features are included in your chart. When visualizing very large datasets, it will probably not be possible to take this advice at face value, and data reduction techniques will be necessary to avoid overwhelming the graph with data.
- *Maximize the 'data to ink' ratio.* One of the classical ideas is to avoid the temptation to overwhelm the graph with visual clutter. The idea was expressed by Edward Tufte with his call to minimize the 'data to ink ratio' (Tufte and Robins, 1997), thereby telling the story of how one moves from data to interpretation. Taken to an extreme, presentations of data in the popular press are often referred to as 'chartjunk' when adorned with plenty of visual elements that may be related to the content but unrelated to the actual data. This practice distracts the viewer from the main storyline and should therefore be avoided.
- *Always avoid data distortion.* There are choices an author makes when designing a visualization. Some of these choices can mislead viewers by exaggerating features that are virtually random or minimizing real trends to make them appear insignificant. By scaling the axes in certain ways, data patterns can either be exaggerated or remain hidden from view. One of the debates in the literature on

data visualization is whether the *Y*-axis should include the zero point. Whereas some pundits advocate always using zero, others argue against it. We would not want to make a sweeping recommendation on this, merely pointing out that both authors and viewers of visualizations should remain watchful and critical.

The three principles above are generally applicable to any kind of visualization, but specific recommendations are applicable to specific types of graphs. In the following section we will briefly address these.

11.4.1 The most common visualization techniques

The scatterplot is used to depict multiple observations, each observation endowed with (at least) two properties that can be measured along a continuous numeric scale. An example of observations could be vehicles, each endowed with a weight (in kilograms) and a measure of efficiency (in miles per gallon, see Figure 11.11). Each observation (vehicle) is represented by a single dot on the scatterplot and is associated with two properties, one that can be read off the *x*-axis (in this case, the vehicle's weight) and the other that can be read off the *y*-axis (in this case, the vehicle's efficiency).

In the middle of the scatterplot we have added a dot representing a theoretical vehicle whose weight is the average weight of all vehicles observed, and whose efficiency is the

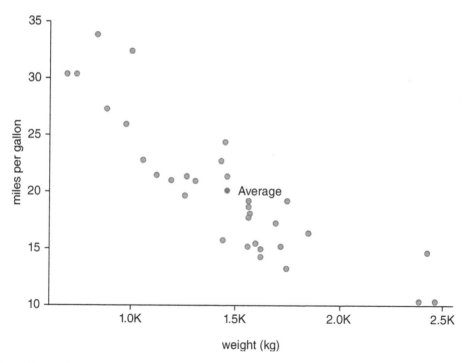

Figure 11.11   An example of a scatterplot. Each of the grey dots represents an observation, in this case a vehicle, and each observation has two properties: weight and miles per gallon.

average efficiency of all vehicles observed. This theoretical observation may be useful if viewers want to quickly focus on the vehicles that are more efficient than average, or those that weigh more than average. Moreover, a pattern emerges in the graph, suggesting that heavier vehicles are less efficient than lighter ones.

A slope graph compares two trends to one another, often showing how different entities develop differently over time. The example in Figure 11.12 illustrates this point. This visual is based on a subset of the NOAA Atlantic hurricane database best track data (National Oceanic and Atmospheric Administration, 2022). The figure summarizes different trends in a large and complex dataset, recording storms between 1975 and 2020.

The chart suggests a slight increase in the average speed of hurricanes, and a slightly greater decrease in the average wind speed of tropical storms. The figure does not tell us whether these diverging trends are the result of a consistent, sustainable, and significant pattern. To judge this, we would need to run a statistical test. But if this is a meaningful pattern, it would mean that the atmospheric mechanisms that determine the storms' average speed is different for hurricanes and tropical storms. It tells us something deep about the mighty natural forces that underpin the data underpinning the graph. And that is precisely what makes a visual effective, when it lays bare that which is hidden from the eye.

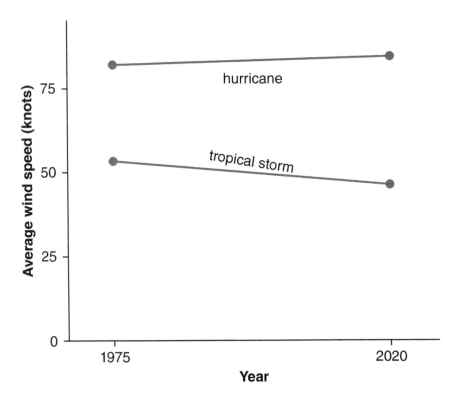

Figure 11.12   Example of a slope graph, comparing hurricanes and tropical storms in terms of change in their average speed

Like the scatterplot, the slope graph shows the relationship between two continuous variables. In this case, the observation refers to each of the storms recorded, and their properties are their wind speed and the year in which they occurred. In contrast to scatterplots, slope graphs have lines linking dots that belong to the same types of observation. In this case, straight lines connect observations belonging to the same type of storm, a hurricane or a tropical storm.

The bar chart is perhaps the easiest visual to read and understand. It depicts counts of some sort, allowing viewers to explore those counts by comparing the extreme ends of the bars. It is easy to identify the category with the largest and the smallest counts. It is also easy to judge how the counts vary from one category to the next.

Bar charts come in all different shapes and sizes and are frequently used in the public media. Figure 11.13 shows an example depicting the titles and durations (in minutes) of some of the lengthiest films on the Internet Movie Database (IMDb), an online source of information related to films, television series, and other videographic and audible content. Bar charts come in all kinds of shapes, colours, and sizes. Figure 11.13 is a horizontal bar chart, which is a good choice when the names of the categories (in this case, the film titles) are lengthy and would not fit if they were placed vertically on the *x*-axis. Stacked bar charts place two bars on top of one another, so for example, each film could be aligned with two bars, one showing the cost of production, and another bar on top showing the profit margin. The length of the two bars, one on top of the other, would then denote the entire revenue of the film.

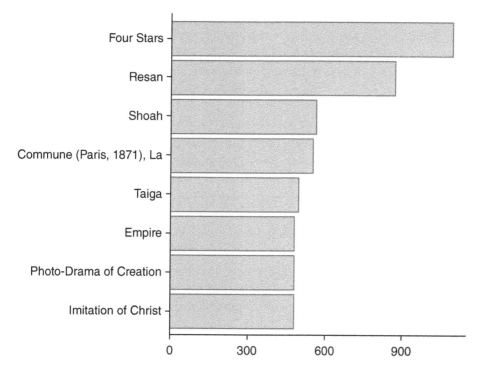

Figure 11.13   An example of a bar chart, depicting the length of some of the longest films on the IMDb

Like the scatterplot, the bar chart summarizes multiple observations, each associating two of its properties. In this example shown above, each observation is a film, whose properties are its title and its length in minutes. But in contrast to the scatterplot where the two properties are quantities on a continuous scale (such as kilograms and miles per gallon), in a bar chart only one of the properties is on the continuous scale (in this case, the length of the film in minutes), and the other property is categorical (in this case, the title of the film).

11.4.2 Visualizations in three dimensions

One of the most controversial ways to visualize big data is to use three dimensions. Many attempts to create three-dimensional visualizations have failed to engage users, partly because the screens on which they are projected are two-dimensional, and this projection makes it often hard to interpret the visualizations in a manner that users find informative. It is for that reason that many authors strongly recommend avoiding the use of three-dimensional charts for the purpose of data visualizations (Knaflic, 2015).

However, some three-dimensional visualizations allow users to interact with the data in a way that is not possible with two-dimensional visualizations. The interaction itself can help users to better understand the data and to identify patterns and trends that would not be visible in two dimensions.

There are several different three-dimensional categories of visualizations that can be used to visualize big data. Some of the most common are as follows:

- Three-dimensional scatterplots are used to visualize the relationship between three variables. Each variable is represented by a different axis, and the data points are plotted as dots in three-dimensional space. By tilting the space and spinning it around, users can view the data from multiple perspectives and identify various patterns.
- Three-dimensional bar charts can be used to visualize the joint distribution of two variables. The density of the data could be represented by the height of the bar. For example, consider the distribution of height and weight in specific communities. Whereas certain combinations of height and weight are common in one community, a different combination of these variables could be common in another community. Comparing the joint distributions of those variables in the two communities can highlight how relationships vary from one community to another. It is important to note that some users find three-dimensional bar charts overwhelming or confusing. In this case, the data could also be visualized using heatmaps or a topographic chart as depicted in Figure 11.14. This shows the association between paper helicopters' flying time and the helicopters' properties. More specifically, different combinations of helicopters' wing length (on the x-axis) and wing width (on the y-axis) are associated with the helicopters' flight time, which exists in a 'third dimension'. Figure 11.14(a) shows a topographic visualization of the data, while Figure 11.14(b) shows a heatmap of the same data. For more details about the context of this study, see Gelman (2020, Chapter 1).

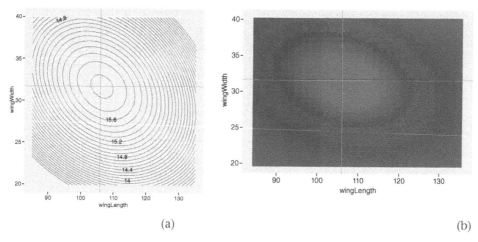

Figure 11.14 Two alternatives to the depiction of three-dimensional data: (a) a topographic chart; (b) a heatmap

- Finally, we mention multilayer network visualization. Modelling relationships between entities in often requires the representation of interdependent subsystems (or layers), in which those entities are embedded. Over the last decade or so the field of complex systems has led to more interest in the notion of multilayer network models (McGee, 2019).
- Multilayer network visualizations are applied to a wide range of real-world datasets in the life and social sciences. This is because there are many systems which have the characteristics of multilayer graphs. The multilevel network depicted in Figure 11.15 is based on data from a study (Zachary, 1977) on conflict among members of a University karate club which split in two after long disputes between two of its factions. The network is thus represented in two levels, with nodes representing club members, ties representing interactions, and levels representing the different factions.

Notwithstanding Knaflic's recommendation to avoid three-dimensional visualizations altogether, there are several notable examples of three-dimensional visualizations that have been used to visualize big data:

- *Google Earth*. Google Earth is a three-dimensional mapping application allows users to view the Earth from a variety of perspectives, illustrating three-dimensional depictions of weather data, traffic data, and population data.
- *The NOAA Climate Data Store*. This is a repository of climate data. It uses three-dimensional visualizations to allow users to explore the data and to identify patterns and trends (McCaslin, 2000).

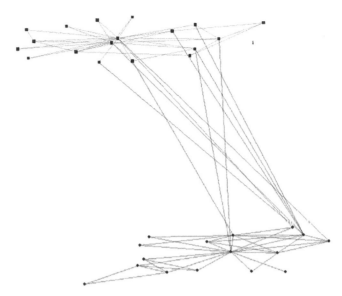

Figure 11.15　A multilayer network visualization of interaction between members of a University karate club (Zachary, 1977)

11.4.3 Other graph types

This chapter has demonstrated the richness and variety of visual possibilities in graphs, and we have not even begun to scratch the surface. But there is a common approach unifying all effective visualizations, and that is that when choosing a graph, you should aim for a visual that will serve the function most relevant to your audience. If the graph is explanatory, find the one that will most clearly get your message across. With graphs that are less common, you will need to take precautions to make sure that they are accessible and understandable, using colour, structure, and form sparsely. Expert designers avoid clutter and unnecessary details, colours, and forms. They show only what is necessary and hide all the rest, avoiding bloated charts that try to show too much and end up showing little. They strip down their visuals to the fewest, most important features of the chart, bearing in mind that end-users may view content on their phones. It may be tempting to try and fit all the details into a small space, but this is often neither possible nor advisable. Consider what is the chart's main takeaway and what makes it engaging and focus on extracting those elements that are the most critical.

11.5 ETHICS BY DESIGN

If the visualization were to convey all the details in the underlying data, it would be overwhelming and ineffective. To be effective, a visualization simplifies the information in a way that is not unlike the way a map is a simplification of the territory. This simplification involves numerous decisions regarding type of graph or image, its format, the colours used, the typesetting, and the relationships between the elements of the graph.

The very same dataset could be represented in a range of different ways, each eliciting a different reaction from the observer. Ethical issues arise when users worry that the choice of form and colour could mislead them, either intentionally or unintentionally. Using the TAFARP data ethics design framework, we might classify the issues into transparency, privacy and responsibility in the following manner:

- *Transparency could manifest as the Misrepresentation or distortion of data.* Data visualization can be manipulated to misrepresent or distort data intentionally or unintentionally, leading to incorrect or misleading conclusions. This can happen when the visualization is designed to emphasize certain aspects of the data or when the data is presented in a way that is not accurate or clear. Transparency could also manifest as *Bias*. Visualization can reinforce existing biases and stereotypes, perpetuating discriminatory practices. This can occur when the data used in the visualization is biased, when it is filtered in some way, or when the visualization itself is designed in a way that reinforces existing prejudices. The transparency of the data and the visualization process is essential to ensure that the audience understands the limitations of the data and how it was analysed and presented. If the data is not transparent, the audience may not be able to evaluate the validity of the visualization, which can lead to incorrect conclusions.
- *Privacy and consent.* Data visualization can raise privacy concerns, particularly when it involves personal or sensitive data. The visualization of such data can lead to the identification of individuals or groups, putting their privacy at risk. Moreover, obtaining informed consent from data subjects is crucial when creating visualizations that involve personal or sensitive data. Without informed consent, individuals may not be aware that their data is being used, which raises ethical concerns.
- *Responsibility* can manifest in terms of Accessibility. Data visualization should be designed in a way that is accessible to everyone, including individuals with disabilities, colour blindness, or those who do not have access to the necessary technology. If the visualization is not accessible, it can exclude certain groups of people from accessing and interpreting the data. Another dimension of responsibility in data visualization is related to the issue of *Intellectual property*. Data visualization can raise intellectual property concerns when the visualization is created using copyrighted data or when the visualization itself is copyrighted. It is important to respect intellectual property rights and ensure that appropriate permissions are obtained before using copyrighted data or creating visualizations.

11.6 INDUSTRY INSIGHTS

Data visualization plays an important role for data-driven businesses and industries, transforming raw data into stories that inform decisions and actions. It enables organizations to communicate complex information effectively, empowering decision-makers to make informed choices and drive their strategies forward. Some examples of how businesses use data visualization to achieve their goals are as follows:

- *Performance tracking.* Data visualization helps businesses track key performance indicators while monitoring the progress they make towards meeting their goals. By representing data in charts, graphs, or dashboards, managers can quickly identify trends, patterns, and areas that require attention. For instance, an e-commerce company may visualize sales data over time to monitor revenue growth, identify peak sales periods, and optimize marketing strategies.
- *Customer insights.* Data visualization helps businesses gain a deeper understanding of their customers. By visualizing customer data, such as demographics, preferences, and behaviour, companies can create detailed customer profiles and identify segments for targeted marketing campaigns. For example, a retail chain can use a heatmap visualization to identify the most popular areas in their stores and optimize product placement and store layout accordingly.
- *Predictive analysis.* Data visualization allows businesses to uncover valuable insights by analysing historical data and anticipating trends about future outcomes. For instance, a logistics company can use visualizations to predict demand patterns, optimize routes, and manage inventory levels more effectively.
- *Operational efficiency.* Businesses use data visualization to identify bottlenecks, inefficiencies, and areas for improvement in their operations. For example, a manufacturing company can use process flow diagrams to identify stages where production delays occur and implement targeted improvements to streamline operations.
- *Risk management.* Data visualization aids businesses in identifying and managing risks effectively. By visualizing data related to market trends, financial indicators, or cybersecurity threats, organizations can proactively identify anomalies in their data, spot risks, and take timely measures to mitigate them. For instance, a financial institution can use real-time visualizations to monitor and analyse market fluctuations, enabling it to make informed investment decisions and manage risk exposure.

In summary, data visualization enables businesses to unlock the true potential of their data by presenting it in a visually appealing and easily understandable manner. By leveraging data visualization techniques, organizations can derive insights, optimize operations, understand their customers, predict future outcomes, and make data-driven decisions to achieve their strategic goals.

SUMMARY

This chapter explored the intimate connections between data visualizations in big data analytics and the art of storytelling. While the history of storytelling is probably as old as civilization itself, data visualization can be traced back to the eighteenth century, when governments and scholars started collecting data (Hacking, 1990), organizing it and using it as the raw material for storytelling. Storytelling is a powerful way to explore the world, shape expectations, influence attitudes, and inform decision-making. The first centuries of data visualizations have seen a large range of creative solutions and ad-hoc approaches. But the past couple of decades have seen a narrowing down of the types of visualizations that are commonly seen in the literature, and the rise of standards and best practices.

The most important suggestion for making visualizations effective is to focus on the target group and audience. Consider their background knowledge, values, and expectations. But it is also important to focus on the purpose and function of the visualization. Some visualizations are constructed to communicate evidence for an argument that the author is making. But other visualizations are constructed for the purpose of exploration and investigation. In this case, the author of the chart does not necessarily know, a priori, what they will find in the diagram they create. The diagram is itself like a model that is used to experiment and to draw conclusions.

Some of the most used visualizations are scatterplots, slope plots, and bar charts, but there are a myriad of other more or less exotic strategies to visualize your data.

ANNOTATED FURTHER READING

One of the first modern books about data visualization that appeared before the onset of big data is Edward Tufte's *Visual Explanations* (Tufte and Robins, 1997). An influential source on the link between storytelling and data visualization is *Storytelling with Data* (Knaflic, 2015). It is well written, very well researched, and informative. More recent resources (Franconeri, 2021; Wilke, 2019) provide best practices for creating effective visualizations, graphics, and images that convey information in an intuitive and efficient manner, guiding the attention of the viewer and taking advantage of their expectations and common conventions. In an articulate and poignant presentation, data scientist and engineer John Rauser describes some of the results from research into the functioning of human visual systems, arguing that this research demonstrates how visualizations can simplify data analysis (Rauser, 2016).

The psychological principles for constructing effective visualizations are surveyed in the book *Graph Design for the Eye and Mind* (Kosslyn, 2006), while the political and economic function of visualization in De Bois's work is beautifully described in the book *WEB De-Bois's Data Portraits: Visualizing Black America* (Witney Battle-Baptiste, 2018).

TEST YOUR KNOWLEDGE

1   Carry out your own research into Simpson's paradox and find some examples in your own profession where such a paradox might occur.

2   Find or design two different data visualizations based on the same dataset. Discuss the advantages and disadvantages of each form of visualization. Think of a third way to visualize the same data to emphasize a finding that is perhaps different or to communicate more effectively. How would your suggestion differ from the visualizations you have identified?

3   Find a visualization of an idea that is abstract or difficult to understand at first sight. What do the authors explain?

4   Find a visualization that you like and answer the following questions (New York Times, n.d.):

   a   What did you notice? After studying the chart and reading the explanation, what details do you see in the graph that are unusual or surprising? Looking at it carefully, paying attention to detail, what can you get out of the graph that is not necessarily obvious at first glance?

   b   What do you wonder? Formulate a question, related to the graph, about something that you would genuinely like to know. What would you need to do in order to answer that question?

   c   How does this relate to you and your community? Think of something that makes this graph relate to you personally or to your community, however defined. Avoid making general statements that relate the chart to nearly everyone, no matter who they are, but concentrate on members of your community.

   d   What's going on in this graph? Write a catchy headline that captures the graph's main idea.

NOTES

1   Note that this figure contains outmoded language regarding race. The purpose of the figure is to demonstrate an early data visualization on discrimination, not to endorse the language or its associations.

2   https://github.com/owid/covid-19-data/tree/master/public/data

3   Though these kinds of visualizations are rarely found in the public domain, a similar chart has been published in the *New York Times*, depicting Covid-19 related incidents in the United States up until 2022 (Shaman, 2022)

REFERENCES

Bickel, P. J. (1975) Sex bias in graduate admissions data from Berkeley: Measuring bias is harder than is usually assumed, and the evidence is sometimes contrary to expectation. *Science, 187*(4175), 398–404.

Engel, O. (2013) The micro-foundations of email communication networks. Doctoral dissertation, London School of Economics and Political Science.

Franconeri, S. L. (2021) The science of visual data communication: What works. *Psychological Science in the Public Interest, 22*(3), 110–61.

Gelman, A. H. (2020) *Regression and Other Stories.* Cambridge University Press.

Hacking, I. (1990) *The Taming of Chance.* Cambridge University Press.

Knaflic, C. N. (2015) *Storytelling with Data: A Data Visualization Guide for Business Professionals.* John Wiley & Sons.

Kosslyn, S. M. (2006) *Graph Design for the Eye and Mind.* Oxford University Press.

McCaslin, P. T. (2000) 3D visualization development at NOAA forecast systems laboratory. *ACM SIGGRAPH Computer Graphics, 34*(1), 41–4.

McGee, F. G. (2019) The state of the art in multilayer network visualization. *Computer Graphics Forum, 38*(6), 125–49.

Muth, L. C. (2018) An alternative to pink & blue: Colors for gender data. Retrieved from https://blog.datawrapper.de/gendercolor/

National Oceanic and Atmospheric Administration. (2022) Atlantic hurricane database (HURDAT2) 1851-2022. Retrieved from NHC Data Archive: https://www.nhc.noaa.gov/data/#hurdat

New York Times (n.d.) What's going on in this graph? Retrieved from https://www.nytimes.com/column/whats-going-on-in-this-graph

Paulos, J. A. (2010) Stories vs. statistics. *New York Times,* Opinionator. Retrieved from https://archive.nytimes.com/opinionator.blogs.nytimes.com/2010/10/24/stories-vs-statistics/

Rauser, J. (2016) How humans see data. Retrieved from YouTube: https://www.youtube.com/watch?v=fSgEeI2Xpdc

Shaman, J. (2022) Here's when we expect omicron to peak. *New York Times,* 6 January. Retrieved from https://www.nytimes.com/2022/01/06/opinion/omicron-covid-us.html

Snow, J. (1854) *On the Mode of Communication of Cholera.* London: C.F. Cheffins.

Tufte, E. R. and Robins, D. (1997) *Visual Explanations.* Cheshire, CT: Graphics Press.

Tukey, J. W. (1977) *Exploratory Data Analysis.* Reading, MA: Addison-Wesley.

Wagner, C. (1982) Simpson's paradox in real life. *The American Statistician, 36*(1), 46–48.

Wilke, C. O. (2019). *Fundamentals of Data Visualization: A Primer on Making Informative and Compelling Figures.* Sebastopol, CA: O'Reilly Media.

Witney Battle-Baptiste, B. R. (2018). *WEB Du Bois's Data Portraits: Visualizing Black America.* Chronicle Books.

Zachary, W. W. (1977). An information flow model for conflict and fission in small groups. *Journal of Anthropological Research, 33*(4), 452–73.

12
GOING FORWARD

CHAPTER CONTENTS

CHAPTER OBJECTIVES

In this chapter:

- You will revisit some of the areas of big data analytics covered so far in the book.
- You will learn about future directions and challenges in big data analytics.
- You will be introduced to some areas to focus on in ethics by design going forward.

12.1 OVERVIEW

Big data analytics continues to be a striving, exciting, growing field full of immense potential. By the end of this chapter, you will understand some of the reasons for this.

Let us start by briefly reviewing some of the aspects of big data analytics that have been covered in this book:

- *Enablers and challenges.* In Chapter 1 we spent some time discussing what data analytics is, its history, and some of the main enablers for the rapid rise of big data analytics in recent times, including reduced storage costs, commodity hardware compatibility, the open-source economy, and increased computational power.
- *Technologies.* In Chapter 2 we examined the big data technology landscape, HDFS and other data storage technologies. We then had a brief overview of big data acquisition and wrangling, followed by an overview of the various types of analytics, such as descriptive, diagnostics, predictive, and prescriptive analytics. We then introduced the big data technologies used in the book for the first time, as well as the TAFARP data ethics by design framework (Figure 2.14, p. 44). In Chapter 3 we introduced Apache Spark in detail.
- *Big data storage.* To effectively process data and harness the potential of big data analytics, adequate storage facilities for the data must be provided. We covered NoSQL databases, the distributed file system, and HDFS.
- *Cloud computing.* In Chapter 5 we covered the origin of cloud computing, its defining characteristics, and their implications for organizations. We also discussed the interaction between cloud computing and big data analytics, as well as the ethical considerations associated with cloud computing.
- *Actionable insights.* Chapter 6 discussed big data analytics and actionable insights, highlighting the main strategic goals of organizations from big data

analytics. The chapter revisited data wrangling in detail, covering the various techniques in hands-on exercises. There were further hands-on exercises on various types of big data analytics to demonstrate how big data analytics results in actionable insights.

- *Graph analytics.* In Chapter 7 you learned about graph analytics and how to use Apache Spark GraphFrames to represent networks and data in graphical form. The chapter also covered hands-on applications on how to draw out insights using graph analytics.

- *Machine learning.* Chapter 8 addressed the extremely important topic of machine learning.

- *Natural language processing.* Chapter 9 covered NLP and how it is used for big data analytics. It discussed methods for cleaning and preparing text in NLP such as tokenization and lemmatization, addressing techniques that fall under NLP such as sentiment analysis.

- *Real-time analytics.* Chapter 10 covered the theoretical and practical aspects of real-time big data analytics and ethical challenges in this space.

- *Visualization.* Chapter 11 discussed the purpose of data visualization, and what makes it effective, and described its history. It also explored various types of visualizations.

12.2 FUTURE DIRECTIONS FOR BIG DATA ANALYTICS

Without big data analytics, which helps to draw out insights that drive actionable insights, big data on its own is not of much use. That is part of the reason why big data analytics continues to grow as a discipline. In whatever sector you consider, it has had some impact and continues to do so: health, retail, the private and public sector, education, and finance, to name but a few. Successes to date have been a force to reckon with, and yet it appears that what has been achieved with big data analytics so far might just be the tip of the iceberg, with so much more to come. In the rest of this section we explore what this 'so much more' could look like.

Big data analytics and the metaverse. The metaverse has in recent times become a topical issue. It is an emerging technology that has the potential to transform our world. Ed Greig, the Chief Disruptor at Deloitte, describes it as 'the internet in 3D'. The metaverse provides persistent, immersive worlds, including virtual reality. This potential transformation could affect how we work, interact, and communicate with each other, our leisure activities, our travel – practically every aspect of life. It is an innovative new approach to life and could have the kind of impact that the emergence of the internet and social media had. As the idea of the metaverse and what it can be used for is increasingly gaining traction, some of the areas where things are beginning to happen or be explored in the metaverse include gaming, marketing and consumer research, retail, tourism, health, and education (Dwivedi et al., 2022). Among the interesting things that have started to take place in the metaverse are virtual concerts, which are said to be making artists millions of dollars (see Forbes, n.d.). Users can buy virtual land and property in the metaverse. The Wall Street Journal (n.d.) discusses this phenomenon and interviews some firms which have bought real estate in the metaverse including Republic Realm, a firm that buys and develops real estate in the metaverse, which bought land in the metaverse for $4.3 million in November 2022, at that time the largest digital property sale that had been made public.

Much like in the real world, the value of virtual land or property depends on its location. Essentially, areas with higher levels of activity and visitor traffic command higher process compared to quieter regions. This example underscroes the crucial role of big data analytics within the metaverse.

Selling price of virtual properties are determined through data-driven insights. Various metrics and indicators are considered such as traffic, the number of visits, clicks, and user interactions within these areas and their surroundings. When a company acquires virtual land or property, they use programming languages and software tools to create various attractions like amusement parks, museums, casinos, or concert halls on their virtual turf. Subsequently, data once again becomes pivotal in maximizing their developments.

These businesses harness big data analytics to collect vast amounts of data generated within the metaverse, encompassing user interactions, behaviors, and preferences. With this data in hand, they can tailor experiences that align with user preferences, ultimately gaining a competitive edge and integrating key economic sectors, including commerce, entertainment, and education, continue to thrive and evolve.

ChatGPT, GPT-4 (and other large language models). In the ethics by design section of Chapter 9, which was about NLP, we focused on ChatGPT. Recall that ChatGPT is powered by AI adept at answering questions, generating responses, and interacting in a conversational way. Large amounts of data from various sources are used to train and develop the model and others like it. One of the sources that has been mentioned for ChatGPT is Common Crawl.[1] This is an open repository of web crawl data – the organization provides a copy of the internet to researchers, companies, and individuals for free. It contains petabytes of data, and raw web pages that have been extracted and made available to anyone who wants access to it since 2008. Using this amount of data to train and develop NLP models provides the model with a lot of information and potentially could increase its accuracy. Big data analytics could be used to analyse large amounts of data, the results of which could then serve as inputs into the models and used as a starting point for generating conversational responses and new insights. Models like this are likely to continue to emerge and play a significant role in how we find and utilize information – big data analytics will be critical to this.

Real-time analytics. As mentioned in Chapter 10, real-time big data analytics is increasingly becoming more important in various sectors and as such its use is constantly increasing. This trend is set to continue. Sectors such as health, retail, finance, and fraud detection rely on real-time (or near real-time) big data analytics to provide immediate insights that they can proactively respond to. As this becomes more prevalent, innovative techniques that keep up with (and perhaps even exceed) these requirements will need to be developed.

Cloud computing. We have already seen that the emergence of cloud computing was one of the enablers of big data analytics, particularly when it came to providing storage and processing power for big data. As cloud computing continues to evolve and innovative technologies and solutions are developed for it, there will be a need for new developments and advancements in big data analytics that continue to keep up with the innovations in cloud computing and provide a means of managing and analysing data to draw out actionable insights in efficient ways. Developments on the horizon for cloud computing include using serverless computing, multi-cloud environments, and edge computing.

Integration with the Internet of Things. In Chapter 1 we discussed the IoT as a source of data. IoT devices all generate vast amounts of data. With the pace at which devices are connected to the internet in one form or the other, there may come a time in the not so distant future when most devices will become part of the IoT (especially in the global North). There are already billions of devices connected to the IoT and it is forecasted that by 2025 the amount of data generated will reach 79.4 ZB (statista, 2020). Big data analytics makes it possible to explore, investigate, and perform descriptive, predictive, and prescriptive analytics on the data to draw out actionable insights from it. As the number of IoT devices increases, the need for novel and innovative big data analytic techniques in this space will also increase.

Visualization and storytelling. When it comes to big data analytics and visualization and storytelling, currently more often what is being referred to are visualizations that are in 2D, such as graphs, charts, and maps. However, visualizations and storytelling that use more of the human senses are beginning to emerge. Examples of these include three-dimensional visualizations, virtual reality, and immersive experiences. If this trajectory continues, innovative solutions will need to continue to be developed in terms of big data analytics that aligns with this. In the health sector virtual reality is being used to enhance patient treatment, an example being the use of the Microsoft Hololens 2 device in healthcare.[2] Such innovative technologies can be used for teaching, training, and collaboration between people in different locations, for better user experiences and better data visualization and utilization. When it comes to immersive experiences (as with the discussion on the metaverse), this can potentially open up novel and innovative opportunities for organizations to interact with data and get more out of it, leading in turn to competitive advantage.

More user-friendly but sophisticated/powerful tools (e.g., low-code and no-code solutions). As technology advances and more powerful tools are developed to support analysis, storytelling, visualization, and drawing out of insights, there has increasingly also been a concerted effort to make these tools available to more and more people. In the early days this was restricted to the few with specialist knowledge. However, we now have no-code development platforms that allow people to develop software applications without writing a single line of code. Examples of no-code machine learning platforms include CreateML[3] (Apple's no-code drag-and-drop platform for iOS development), AutoML[4] (Google's no-code platform which works on the cloud), and RapidMiner[5] (which simplifies data analytics). There are also low-code solutions which, unlike no-code, require minimal coding skills. As the functionalities and capabilities of these platforms continues to increase, big data analytics will also expand to provide innovative ways of working hand in hand with them.

Impact of global smart cities. Smart cities leverage technology and data to maximize productivity and improve citizen's lives. According to the McKinsey Global Institute (2018) report on smart cities: 'Smart cities are being redefined as places where different actors employ technology and data to make better decisions and achieve a better quality of life'. Globally the number of cities becoming smart cities is on the rise, and with this comes the need for innovative new big data analytics techniques and methods. There are already fantastic examples of smart cities which have innovatively used data to create effective and efficient processes. One of these smart cities is London, which was said to be the best smart city in the world by the IESE Cities in Motion Index published in 2021. Data is said to be central to the model that London has put together.[6] See the further reading section for some few articles/reports on what London has done and is doing. As more cities become smart cities, techniques for effectively utilizing big data analytics will need to be put in place to maximize the impact from the adoption.

Quantum computing. Quantum computing represents a groundbreaking frontier in the world of computation, distinguished by its stark departure from the principles of traditional computing. While classical computers, which we use daily, rely on bits as the fundamental unit of information (either 0 or 1), quantum computing harnesses the principles of quantum mechanics to introduce the concept of qubits. These qubits can exist simultaneously in a superposition of states, representing 0 and 1. Moreover, quantum computers exploit entanglement, a phenomenon where one qubit's state can instantaneously affect another's state, regardless of distance. This inherent quantum weirdness empowers quantum computers to perform specific calculations at unparalleled speeds, promising breakthroughs in cryptography, materials science, and artificial intelligence.

12.3 ETHICS BY DESIGN

Throughout the book, there has been an emphasis on ethics by design and its importance in ensuring that the issue of ethics is not treated as an afterthought. We considered a proactive approach to ethics, an approach that helps anticipate and prevent ethical problems, building trust, ensuring compliance with regulations, avoiding harm, and aligning with values. It must balance cost-effectiveness against social responsibilities, prioritizing user well-being. We also introduced a framework, the TAFARP data ethics by design framework, which we have used throughout the book (see Figure 2.14, p. 44). To conclude, we will apply the TAFARP data ethics framework to the various areas discussed in the previous section on the future direction of travel and highlight important areas to be mindful of.

The TAFARP data ethics by design framework identifies six key ethical areas that are extremely important when working with data. Before embarking on any big data analytics project, these six areas need to be explored in the context of each project. Then as progress is made with the project, it is necessary to keep them under review to help ensure that data ethics by design is indeed taking place.

• Big data analytics and the metaverse

1   *Transparency*. In terms of the data that would be collected based on users' engagement, interaction, preferences, and so on, would this be transparent? Would a user know exactly what data is being collected about them? How it is being used? For how long? By whom? And for what purposes? Or would all this be a black box? These are important issues that need to be tackled.
2   *Accountability*. Where does accountability lie?
3   *Autonomy*. How much autonomy would users have? Would they be able to opt out of certain things in the metaverse, or would their data just be collected by default? Would they be 'nudged' to act in a certain way, or to feel in a certain manner to increase traffic? Might they become addicted to a certain reality against their better judgment?
4   *Responsibility*. Similar questions arise to those under accountability. From a legal perspective, for a whole range of things, who is responsible?
5   *Privacy*. Due to the very nature of the metaverse, a lot of personal data might be collected by businesses from users. How would privacy be protected? Who is responsible for ensuring data is secure and personal data is not stolen or data leaked?

• Large language models (such as ChatGPT)

1   *Transparency*. Large language models are not transparent. This is an issue that has been universally raised as a problem (from both the consumer and the regulator perspective). In the future, there's a potential for large language models not only to generate conversational responses but also to include citations and references to the sources of information they rely on. This development could significantly address concerns related to transparency. Notably, certain journals like Nature and all Springer Nature journals have already declared their stance, stating that AI tools, including large language models, will not be recognized as credited authors on research papers. This policy is rooted in the belief that AI tools lack the capability to be held accountable for scholarly work[7].
2   *Accountability*. An example of a tricky position when it comes to ChatGPT (and other LLMs) is potential copyright infringement. The vast amounts of data used to train the model come from various sources; if any of this data pulled from archives,

and/or perhaps web scraping (such as Common Crawl, mentioned in the previous section) then this raises the possibility of legal issues relating to copyright and the like.

3 *Fairness.* One key area of concern is whether there could be unintended bias in the training data used to fit the model?. For a dataset to pass the fairness test, it must not contain bias either intentionally or unintentionally. Large language models may generate content that reflects gender or racial biases, such as biased language or reinforcing stereotypes. For example, generating sentences that assume certain occupations are gender-specific. The model may exhibit bias in favor of or against specific socioeconomic groups, affecting the language it generates about topics related to income, education, or social status, or it may generate offensive, harmful, or inappropriate content, as they may inadvertently combine words or phrases from their training data.

4 *Responsibility.* Who does responsibility lie with? The AI tool cannot be held responsible, so who can? What about instances of misinformation: where (and with whom) does the buck stop? Currently there is a disclaimer on the ChatGPT page about the possibility of the model disseminating the wrong information, which shows that OpenAI (the developers of ChatGPT) have thought about this aspect.

5 *Privacy.* Can it be guaranteed that no private data has been inadvertently picked up from the data sources used to train the model? How can this be handled at the various stages of the process?

• **Real-time analytics**

1 *Transparency and fairness.* When it comes to real-time analytics, as the insights from the data are disseminated in real time (or near real time), extra care needs to be taken with regard to the source of the data. With real-time analytics there is no time to observe the insights and correct any issues. So, it is import to ask questions such as: What is the data source? Is it bias-free? Is it fully representative? Is it transparent?

2 *Accountability and responsibility.* You cannot afford to have accountability and responsibility as an afterthought in the process because once the process kicks off the end-user sees the results from the data processing in real time or near real time. There is no pause button in between that gives you a chance to examine the results and fix any issues. This makes getting the data ethics checks here incredibly important.

3 *Fairness and privacy.* Again, because the end results are disseminated almost immediately, getting issues such as fairness (e.g., no bias) and privacy correct right from the start of the process is important. If you notice that there is a problem after the information has already been disseminated and are at that point trying to correct the issue, it could turn out to be too late and a costly mistake.

● **Cloud computing**

1   *Accountability*. Accountability is key when it comes to cloud computing because the infrastructure the data is being stored and processed on is provided by a third party such as Amazon or Microsoft, so it is important that the lines of accountability and responsibility are very clear.

2   *Responsibility*. Various aspects of responsibility should be explored and clearly defined. For instance, if there is a data breach, who is legally responsible? Is it the cloud vendor? Who ensures legislation is adhered to, for example in terms of geographical storage of data when there is legislation that applies to this?

3   *Privacy*. What needs to be put in place to ensure that employees, for instance, have the correct level of access and cannot access information that their role does not require them to? What needs to be put in place to ensure that customers' privacy is not breached, in terms of security measures such as encryption and security certificates?

● **Integration with the Internet of Things** (Antoniou et al., 2019)

1   *Transparency*. Is the data that is being collected transparent to the user? Or is it a black box that needs to be tackled?

2   *Accountability*. Who is accountable for the data and system that is in place?

3   *Autonomy*. Has the user consented to the use of the collection and use of their data? Are they able to opt out if they wanted to?

4   *Responsibility*. Who is legally responsible? Is this very clear? Are the lines of responsibilities well spelt out to everyone involved?

5   *Privacy*. Given that the IoT will usually involve machine-to-machine communication over a network, issues of privacy and security can be a potential concern. What kind of data is being collected? Is this level of detail really needed? As the process is likely to be automated, there need to be secure processes in place to ensure the security of the system, prevent hacking or data breaches, and protect privacy.

● **Visualization and storytelling**

1   *Transparency*. As mentioned in Chapter 11, it is important that there is transparency in the data and the visualization process to ensure that the audience understands the limitations of the data and how it was analysed and presented. Otherwise, wrong conclusions can be drawn, and this could lead to unfair/bias/ incorrect actions being taken.

2   *Fairness*. Data visualization can be manipulated to misrepresent the data intentionally or unintentionally, so care must be taken to avoid situations such as this as it can lead to consequences that can disadvantage individuals or even whole communities. Visualization can reinforce existing bias in the data, so it is important that the source of the data and the state of the data are well examined to avoid this. Furthermore, in terms of the use of other visualizations such as 3D,

virtual reality, and immersive experiences, it is important that issues that relate to fairness are considered.

• Impact of global smart cities

1   *Transparency*. In smart cities there can be so much going on in terms of data acquisition, processing, and discovery of highlights that if transparency is not prioritized it would be easy for everything that is going on with their data to be a black hole to the public. Ethically this would not be right, so there should be transparency on what is being collected from them, the purpose it is being collected for, and so on.

2   *Accountability*. Who is accountable for the various processes? This needs to be looked into by design, not at the end after all the processes are in place but right at the start before a single process is implemented.

3   *Fairness*. If fairness is compromised, individuals, communities, entire neighbourhoods can be disadvantaged, and if trust is lost it can be extremely hard to regain. So, ideally by applying ethics by design you need to get it right from the start. Also, be mindful that you are not using biased models. For instance, what was the source of the data for the model you are using? If it was based on citizen demographics, was it fully representative or was it biased towards a certain set of citizens to the detriment of others?

4   *Autonomy*. Citizens should have the right to opt in and out of having their data used (and for other related processes). This is important and should be covered as part of the ethics by design process right from the start.

5   *Responsibility*. Who is legally responsible for the various processes and steps? Again, this is extremely important and needs to be worked through and resolved early on.

6   *Privacy*. Extra care needs to be taken to get things right ethically. Privacy should be designed in, so for instance citizens' data should not be used by default because they live in a smart city – there should be informed consent.

• Quantum computing

1   *Transparency*. There are legitimate concerns when it comes to quantum computing because of how potentially powerful it can be, and so as money is being poured into its development, ethical considerations cannot afford to be forgotten. How do you make it transparent, so it is not like a black box?

2   *Accountability*. Who is accountable? How would they be held accountable? These and other relevant questions need to be explored and answered.

3   *Fairness*. It is probably likely that, at least to start off with, only a select few would have access to quantum computers. How do you ensure that they are used in a fair way that does not disadvantage certain countries, communities, or groups?

4   *Autonomy*. Can people opt in or out? Is this clearly laid out? Again, this is an important area that needs to be explored and planned throughout the entire process.

5   *Responsibility*. Who is legally responsible? What are they responsible for? All this needs to be clearly laid out – with great power indeed comes great responsibility.

6   *Privacy*. There is a concern that quantum computing could pose a great risk due to the ease with which it might be able to 'break' modern cryptography and internet security protocols.[8] How would you guard against this happening? Breaches not only can have a negative impact on the individuals whose details are lost but can also cause severe reputational damage to organizations that can be difficult to recover from.

SUMMARY

In this chapter we briefly recapped of the topics covered in the book, discussed the future directions for big data analytics, and concluded with a section on going forward with ethics by design. Remember that each chapter of the book contains a further reading section to point you to additional information on the various topics if you want to go further with them. Big data analytics is truly a fascinating area that continues to grow. For those who choose a career in it there will always be new things to learn and innovative techniques coming up.

TEST YOUR KNOWLEDGE

1   What is big data analytics?
2   List four areas that are likely to be important for big data analytics going forward.
3   What are some of the main ethical issues that might arise in relation to the four areas you listed in task 2?

FURTHER READING (OPTIONAL)

Buchholz, S. and Ammanath, B. (2022) Quantum computing may create ethical risks for businesses. It's time to prepare. Retrieved from https://www2.deloitte.com/uk/en/insights/topics/cyber-risk/quantum-computing-ethics-risks.html

CNET (n.d.) Explaining the metaverse: Everything you need to know about future of the internet. YouTube. Retrieved from https://www.youtube.com/watch?v=7DEVfUk2zCk

Greater London Authority (2018)_ Smarter London Together. https://www.london.gov.uk/sites/default/files/smarter_london_together_v1.66_-_published.pdf

IBM (n.d.) What is quantum computing? Retrieved from https://www.ibm.com/topics/quantum-computing

Lu, D. (n.d.) What is a quantum computer? *New Scientist*. https://www.newscientist.com/question/what-is-a-quantum-computer/

Trahan, R. (n.d.) I spent 100 days in the metaverse. *YouTube*. Retrieved from https://www.youtube.com/watch?v=mufeRQYgqZc

NOTES

1   https://commoncrawl.org/
2   https://www.microsoft.com/en-us/hololens/industry-healthcare
3   https://developer.apple.com/machine-learning/create-ml/
4   https://www.automl.org/automl/
5   https://rapidminer.com/
6   https://www.theagilityeffect.com/en/case/could-london-be-the-best-smart-city
7   https://www.nature.com/articles/d41586-023-00191-1
8   https://www2.deloitte.com/uk/en/insights/topics/cyber-risk/quantum-computing-ethics-risks.html

REFERENCES

Antoniou, J. and Andreou, A. (2019) Case study: The Internet of Things and ethics. *ORBIT Journal*, 2(2). https://doi.org/10.29297/orbit.v2i2.111

Dwivedi, Y. K., Hughes, L., Baabdullah, A, M. et al. (2022) Metaverse beyond the hype: Multidisciplinary perspectives on emerging challenges, opportunities, and agenda for research, practice and policy. *International Journal of Information Management*, 66, 102542. https://doi.org/10.1016/j.ijinfomgt.2022.102542.

Forbes (n.d.) Concerts in the metaverse are making artists millions. Retrieved from https://www.youtube.com/watch?v=p6fr0UFhLjA

McKinsey Global Institute (2018). Smart cities: Digital solutions for a more liveable future. Retrieved from https://www.mckinsey.com/capabilities/operations/our-insights/smart-cities-digital-solutions-for-a-more-livable-future

statista (2020) Data volume of internet of things (IoT) connections worldwide in 2019 and 2025. Retrieved from https://www.statista.com/statistics/1017863/worldwide-iot-connected-devices-data-size/

Wall Street Journal (n.d.) Metaverse real estate boom: Why investors are buying virtual land. Retrieved from https://www.youtube.com/watch?v=uIllSiXVfmI

INDEX